Ecclesiastical Administration in Medieval England

This House I Have Built

A Study of the Legal History of Establishment in England

Is it credible then that God should dwell
with men on the earth? If heaven and
the heaven of heavens do not contain
thee, how much less this house which I
have built!

—2 Chron. 6:18

Ecclesiastical Administration in Medieval England

The Anglo-Saxons To The Reformation

Robert E. Rodes, Jr.

The University of Notre Dame Press

Notre Dame   London

Library of Congress Cataloging in Publication Data

Rodes, Robert E
  Ecclesiastical administration in medieval England.

  Includes bibliographical references and index.
  1. Ecclesiastical law—Great Britain—History.
2. Church of England—Government—History. I. Title.
KD8605.R6 262'.00941   73-22584
ISBN 0-268-00903-1

Manufactured in the United States of America

Sancto
BEDAE VENERABILI
ex Voto

Contents

Introduction

The Church of England as by Law Established gave legal form to the corporate religious experience of the English nation for something like fourteen centuries. In this and two subsequent volumes, I plan to take up the legal history of this peculiar institution, beginning with its inception in Anglo-Saxon times and ending with the relatively contemporary period in which its unique relation to the national life has (perhaps) been put aside.

It is law that gives unity to the subject over this long time span. Whatever the theological significance of the Reformation, by any legal analysis the prelates and officeholders of Elizabeth I's or Henry VIII's establishment were the successors of the men who went by the same titles in Mary's or Henry VII's time. Doing without the pope was an important change, but—I am still speaking legally, not theologically—a less important change than might have been supposed. Papal administration in the Middle Ages was more busy than effective in England, as we shall see.

The juridical continuity of the English church through the Reformation represents, it seems to me, a deliberate choice, and no doubt a popular one, on the part of the English government. The English were more interested in preserving their traditional institutional and social forms than they were in choosing sides in the doctrinal controversies of the day.

This conservative approach to medieval institutions constitutes the great difference between the English Reformation on the one hand, and both the Continental Reformation and the Counter-Reformation on the other. It is clear enough that Calvin set out to establish the ecclesiastical order anew from first principles, and I think it can fairly be maintained that Luther did the same. It is perhaps less clear that the Counter-Reformation was equally revolutionary, but I think this was the case. The typical institutional form of the Counter-Reformation was absolute monarchy, and however reactionary absolute monarchy may be considered today, it represents a good deal of a departure from medieval forms. On the whole, both Catholics and Protestants on the continent sacrificed medieval institutions to theological conformity, whereas the English reformers sacrificed theological conformity to medieval institutions.

xi

To this end, the mainstream of Anglican polity renounced not simply this or that doctrine, but the quest for doctrinal orthodoxy as such. The continual trend in Anglican history was not toward a resolution of disputed questions but toward the development of forms that would enable both sets of disputants to live at peace. The attempt was not always successful; minority groups often found it necessary to part company with the parent body. But the attempt was always made. Much of the history of English nonconformity could be written around a series of Savoy conferences, pamphlets on accommodation, and if you like, South India schemes.

This way of doing things may not be good theology, but it is very good law. It may be that a church should teach a single doctrine and let the chips fall where they may. But a legal order takes the interests in society as it finds them, and if it can do nothing else, tries at least to keep the peace. Striking a balance between conflicting interests is the skill of the jurists par excellence. That it has been also the peculiar genius of Anglicanism is due in great part to the juridical forms in which the English church-state nexus was cast long before the Reformation.

It is these forms and their development that constitute the subject of my three volumes. This first volume is primarily concerned with medieval ecclesiastical administration. It begins with the germinal, and sometimes ambiguous, forms established by the Anglo-Saxons. Then come the ideological and juridical influences that led to the reshaping of these forms after the Conquest. The rest of the volume deals with the actual working out of the resulting system at the various administrative levels of the church.

The second volume will take the secular administration through the Reformation and show how the ecclesiastical administration was subsequently settled. I will begin with what I have been able to find on how and with what justification the medieval secular government intervened in the affairs of the church. This I will follow with a legal analysis of the Reformation—how the lawyers and parliamentarians regarded what they were doing, and how the lawyers' version of the whole affair was made the Church of England's official account of itself, sealed with the brilliantly tendentious antiquarianism of Coke. From there I will take the subsequent administrative developments in church and state through the various vicissitudes of the seventeenth century, up to the Civil War.

The third volume will cover the equilibrium established at the Restoration and the disruption of that equilibrium in the nineteenth century. I will try to show how the characteristic institutions of the earlier settlement were undermined by the parliamentary reforms of the 1830s and by the economic efforts of the lawyers to salvage certain aspects of their system and the frustration of those efforts in the course of the doctrinal and ritual controversies later in the century. Finally, I will resume some of the underlying themes of the whole study and venture a few general conclusions.

I mean all this primarily as a straightforward account of the legal institutions involved. But much of the intelligibility of legal institutions lies in the way they are conceived and what they are intended to accomplish; I will have to give a good deal of attention to these matters. The materials I have studied show two basic approaches at work, which I will try to sort out and identify in the course of the account.

What the Gregorian reformers of the twelfth century, the Laudians of the seventeenth, and the Tractarians of the nineteenth have in common in the juridical forms they envisage and the purposes they expect those forms to serve, I have called High Churchmanship. What, say, Edward I, Coke, and Victoria's Privy Council have in common, I have called Erastianism. The two common themes correspond in general to the political and religious movements I have named them after. But the correspondence is not exact. Lawmen sometimes follow their own traditions with a good deal of disregard for the intellectual currents around them. Sometimes, also, a set of ideological commitments will lie below the threshhold of articulation in the legal forms themselves. In any event, I will not try to follow the respective movements into areas outside the law.

Let me, therefore, define the two approaches in my own way. What I conceive of as High Churchmanship is a tendency to institutionalize the elements of transcendence and withdrawal in Christianity. As no legal institution can really transcend the society that sets it up, the tendency results in institutions with a high symbolic content—hence its affinity for theological movements that stress the importance of sacramental and liturgical forms. When we see a legal form that seems to have no practical purpose, we may suppose that the High Church tendency is at work.

Take sanctuary, for instance. It is difficult to see a practical way in which the ends of criminal justice are served by treating a man who takes refuge in the village church differently from a man who hides in the village pub. The purpose of sanctuary is to give symbolic form to the church's position over against society—to reproach a world where there is violence and arbitrary punishment and to bespeak another world where a man can be free of these things. It is purposes of this kind that characterize the High Church approach to ecclesiastical institutions.

By Erastianism I mean a tendency to integrate the church into the overall institutional structure of society. In this view, the institutions of the church, whether they serve to minister the sacraments, to relieve the poor, to educate children, or to intercede for the dead, are conceived in utilitarian terms and laid alongside secular institutions similarly conceived.

Erastianism is somewhat inclined to subject ecclesiastical institutions to state control simply because it sees the church-state nexus as a single pattern of institutional forms. The whole pattern, it is supposed, should be subject to unified control in the interest of overall functional efficiency. But Erastianism, as I define it, is quite different from other movements that also subject the church to the state. It is different from totalitarianism because it is Christian. It does not subordinate religious to secular ends. It puts religious and secular ends together and seeks a coordinated efficiency in the common pursuit of both. It is different from caesaropapism because it subjects the church not to the monarchy as such, but to the whole machinery of government. In fact, caesaropapism seems in its juridical dimension a High Church form. It attributes a special status to the king becasue he is an anointed representative of God, not because he governs the country well.

In much of the material I have to deal with, there is a kind of dialectical tension between High Churchmanship and Erastianism. If I have drawn a lesson from this study, it is the pervasiveness of this tension, not only in the history of English institutions, but in the continuing ethos of Western Christendom, and, I believe, in the very nature of Christianity itself. I see it as a projection onto the juridical plane of the dialectic between withdrawal and involvement that is central to Christian living, and of the dialectic between transcendence and immanence that is central to the Christian awareness of God.

But I do not want to put too much initial stress on these theoretical insights. They are not a governing thesis that I am setting out to prove. Indeed, I have not undertaken to develop them systematically at all. My intention is simply to present an important body of legal material, pointing out the theoretical patterns as they emerge.

The internal exigencies of the material prevent any simple chronological presentation and impose both gaps and overlaps in the chronological coverage. This volume, for instance, will not add much to anyone's account of how William I and Lanfranc brought the English into the mainstream of continental churchmanship or of the origins and upshot of the Becket affair. It is the major stages in the evolution of the juridical forms that constitute my concern. I envisage a reader who already knows something of the chronological history involved.

The period with which I am mainly concerned in this volume—after the preliminary chapter on the Anglo-Saxons—is one beginning in the thirteenth century, when the church takes on a fairly stable administrative structure and the records become sufficient to show how the structure worked. Chapters 4, 5, and 6 are devoted to this period, dealing respectively with English ecclesiastical administration, parish organization, and papal intervention, as they subsisted with minor variations down to the Reformation. The intervening chapters—Chapter 2 on Gregorian ideology and Chapter 3 on canonical legal theory—do in fact cover an intermediate period, one extending from somewhere around the Conquest to somewhere around the middle of the thirteenth century. But they are intended to supply the theoretical underpinnings rather than the historical origins of the later administrative structure.

The focus on institutional forms requires also a good deal of slighting of the personalities involved. When I speak of the king, the pope, or the archbishop of Canterbury, I realize that Edward I is not Richard II, Innocent III is not John XXII, Winchelsea is not Chichele. It is of course people who make institutions, and I do not mean to discount their importance by concentrating on other things. Here again, I envisage a reader who is not entirely new to the subject, one who has some acquaintance with the major figures in the story and also some sensitivity to the rank and file.

My general intention, then, is by close analysis at selected points to shed new light on historical developments whose main outlines are already familiar. In this close analysis, I have tried not to lose sight of the forest for the trees, but we are in country where it takes a good many trees to make a forest. The life of the law is in its details. We must understand the broad outlines through a careful consideration of the details, or we will not understand them at all.

As this work bears on religious questions not wholly left in the past, I think it is appropriate to state my own position on such questions at the outset, rather than leave the reader to speculate. I am a Roman Catholic, and I was at one time—long before I started this work—an Anglican. I do not, however, find the history of English Christianity as relevant as some people seem to find it to the matters at issue between the two communions. It is possible, I suppose, to relate the theological validity of the concept of a national church to the historical experience of working the concept out. But if there is a polemical moral to be drawn along these lines, I will leave it to someone else to draw. The historical basis of my own conviction derives from a very different period.

Much of the early research for this work was done in a year at Oxford financed by a generous grant from the Ford Foundation. The final revision of the manuscript was done during a year's leave with pay from the University of Notre Dame, which I was able to combine with a year in England on University business. To both the foundation and the university, I am more grateful than I can say for these chances to see the Church of England in its natural habitat. I am also grateful to the university for various forms of supplementary financial assistance, including the subsidy that made publication possible.

The prior and community of Blackfriars, Oxford, lent me a room where I did most of the final revision of the manuscript. It was of course invaluable to have this place to work away from the distractions of a large family in a small house. Collaterally, I profited greatly from their quiet hospitality and their ease in carrying on a venerable tradition.

I have had the benefit of conversations with a number of scholars at Oxford; I could not hope to do justice to all of them. No one I approached there but was most generous with his time and thought. I will mention specifically only Canon (now Dean) Eric W. Kemp, my director of studies, whose faithful and gentle guidance extended to every phase of the research, and the Reverend T. M. Parker, whose kindness to stray scholars is legendary.

Here at Notre Dame, I have inflicted all or part of this manuscript on a number of my colleagues, especially John T. Noonan, Jr. (now at Berkeley) and Thomas L. Shaffer of the Law School, and Father John S. Dunne of the theology department, all of whom have made valuable suggestions.

Finally, my wife has repeatedly gone over these pages in successive drafts, adding immeasurably to such coherence and lucidity as may be found in them.

1. Origins

An institutional study of the English church-state nexus cannot really begin anywhere but at the confrontation between the missionary Augustine and the king Ethelbert in the open air on the Isle of Thanet in 597 A.D. One is tempted to begin it later. The search for institutions among the Anglo-Saxons (particularly the early Anglo-Saxons) is not a very rewarding one. Their institutions were few and ill-defined, and they did not pay a great deal of attention to those they had. Their art, their learning, their piety, their trade, their architecture, and even their wars present a richer fabric to anyone who wants to examine the history of this attractive people.

Research in Anglo-Saxon institutions is difficult also. The proper legal and administrative materials—a handful of laws, charters of varying degrees of authenticity, and finally the vast and enigmatic Domesday Book—raise as many questions as they answer. They must be pieced out with hagiographical accounts, monastic annalists, and all manner of speculation. The work is interesting if you like puzzles, but it is rather like taking a bag of potato chips and trying to put together a potato.

Nevertheless, it must be done. The institutional patterns of the English church-state nexus in the Middle Ages, and even to this day, are in very great part those developed by the Anglo-Saxons. A book written in 1964, treating the means of selecting and compensating parish clergy, grapples with parochial relations adumbrated in the laws of tenth-century kings.[1] The system of electing bishops that appears in the current edition of Halsbury's *Laws of England* (royal nominee rubber-stamped by canonical electors) is fundamentally that used in the reign of Cnut. If we can understand these institutions better by knowing where they came from, we have no choice but to begin at the beginning.

In doing so, I do not mean to adopt, even in a more sophisticated form, the once popular view that the Anglo-Saxons were at one with latter-day Anglicans; that the Reformers of the sixteenth century had only to slough off the continental absolutism imported with the Conquerer to tap once more the primordial roots of their ancestral Christianity. To say that later genera-

1

tions had the institutions the Anglo-Saxons developed is not to say that they thought about them as the Anglo-Saxons did. The Anglo-Saxons gave scope to both royal and papal authority in their ecclesiastical affairs, but they did not manifest any systematic understanding of the relation between the two. It is the ambiguity, not the tenor, of Anglo-Saxon institutions that provides the fuel for latter-day polemic. My purpose in describing them is simply to indicate the foundations on which the more systematic edifices of another day were built.

I. Substrata

The foundations have foundations of their own. Underlying everything else are three different strains of what might be called institutional tradition, each of which made its own contribution to the whole pattern, without being really absorbed into a unified whole. These are:
1. The primordial Germanic traditions, shared by the Anglo-Saxons with related Northern peoples
2. The Celtic tradition of apostolic monasticism, influential in the conversion of certain parts of the country, especially Northumbria
3. The traditional ecclesiastical organization of the Roman Empire, influential on prelates and missionaries sent over from the continent, especially those sent direct from Rome

Let us take these up in order.

A. Germanic Traditions.

1. King, Council, Assembly —The king-council-assembly structure is the common heritage of the Indo-European race; you can see it in Homer. In this structure, the king was the focus of power and authority. Through his descent he linked the people with their gods and with their own heroic past. It was his business to lead them to prosperity in peace and victory in war.

The council, chosen for age (*senate*) or wisdom (*witan*), gave its advice in these undertakings. The composition of this body was loose and depended in great part on the will of the king, except that he had to take the realities of power and authority into account—realities probably based on kinship, personal prowess, or ability to attract a following. Although its composition was loose, its deliberations were generally rather formal. There was no question of counting votes; the members gave their advice in turn until a consensus developed or until the king was satisfied as to whether he had enough support to implement whatever he had in mind.

The assembly consisted of the people in general or at least those among them who bore arms. It met in open air and expressed itself by acclamation. Its function was to give a general consent to the decisions reached by king and council. This consent no doubt provided a further assurance that the decision could be implemented. In fact, the whole structure probably related more to the expediency than to the legitimacy of an exercise of royal power. Our primitive ancestors were not highly committed to law and order and had but little tolerance for governmental action of which they disapproved. It would not take an articulated constitutional theory to convince a king that he had better see who was following him before he leaped into the breach.

The Anglo-Saxons, when they were first evangelized, seem to have had the old structure in pretty much its pristine form. Each of the several Anglo-Saxon peoples had a king, descended from Woden or another of the gods. One of these might become so important on occasion as to be considered *bretwalda*, or "ruler of Britain generally." Others might be so cowed from time to time as to call themselves *subreguli*, or "underkings." But none of these subordinations was permanent. The only enduring power centers were the kings of the different nations.

Each king had his councillors, or wise men, who met to give him advice on important matters. A meeting of these was called a *witenagemot*, or "meeting of the wise." The king had also a body of personal retainers called his *comitatus*, who attended him about the business of government, especially in war. The flexibility of membership in both bodies was such that it is probably profitless to try to determine whether they were formally distinct. What is important is that the king had the advice and assistance of a body of retainers who either attached themselves to his person or were summoned to his side as the occasion served. Inclusion in this body conferred a status, and, conversely, some people probably had a status that gave them the right to be included. Nevertheless, the king had a good deal of discretion (subject always to the realities of power) as to whom he would include and what influence he would accord a given member.

There may have been an assembly of the whole nation, certain laws refer to the participation of the people in their making.[2] More important, though, were popular assemblies drawn from component parts of the nation—originally from tribes, later from hires and hundreds. These did most of the judicial business of the society.

2. Administration and Land Tenure—The king did most of his business under a system that I will call *peripatetic administration*. I mean by it simply that the king and his retainers spent their time riding circuit and performing governmental services for anyone that approached them in their progress. The system was based on the fact that it was easier to move people than to move

food. The people of the different places through which the king and his retainers passed had the duty to put them up for a specified number of nights
with a specified quantity of provisions.

At times, however, the king would assign one of his followers to stand in
for him at a particular locality, and, in return, to collect from the local populace the provisions they had formerly turned over to the king.[3] Such an assignment was both a way of rewarding the follower and a way of decentralizing the administration—the former consideration being probably uppermost
in the king's mind. After the conversion of the country, when legal transactions came to be written down by clerical scribes, grants of this kind were
recorded in charters called *land books* and the land subject to them was called
bookland. The charters read like outright grants, but they were also delegations of public functions. Ultimately, a proliferation of these grants made for
a general change from peripatetic to what may be called *feudal administration*.
But that change was far in the future. Meanwhile, the process of booking
land was of great importance for the church. As a means of giving out royal
revenues, it set the pattern for the church's landed endowments. As a form
of delegated local administration, it set the pattern for the bishop's allocation
of his clergy to parishes.

The character of land tenure developed by this booking process was very
much affected by a peculiarity of Germanic law, which I shall refer to as the
principle of nonaccountability. The principle is that a fiduciary or delegate
need not render an account. If he were given a job to do and a source of
revenue to support him in doing it, he would pocket whatever part of the
revenue he does not use up in doing the job.[4] The principle had a variety
of applications, which we shall have occasion to consider. But it should be
noted here that it enabled the holders of bookland from the king to consider
themselves as in some sense the owners of the land. Instead of having the
revenue that they might do the work of government, they could just as well
think that they were doing the work in order that they might have the revenue—that, in the terminology of later feudalism, they were performing a "service" for their land.

3. Status and Kinship—Criminal justice was done through a system of
status and kinship. The compensation for killing a man, invading his household, or taking his property depended on his rank in society; so did the nature of the oath he would have to take to clear himself of a charge. And it
was the kindred of an accused who would have to help him swear if he were
innocent or help him pay if he were guilty. By the same token, if a man were
to kill another, the kindred of the victim would pursue the slayer and collected the *wergild*, or "blood-price."

The exact composition of the kin-group to which these principles applied
is not clear. The character of the ranks that figured in the system is a little

clearer, but it is too complicated to be gone into. For our purposes, it will suffice to keep in mind three points:

1. The kin-group was probably defined by relation to the particular person involved rather than constituting a permanent clan.
2. The main ranks in society under the king were *thanes*, who could claim by favor or inheritance a position among the retainers of the king, *ceorls*, or "free householders"; and everyone else. The other ranks seem to be elaboration of these.
3. The whole system was greatly complicated by a series of lord-and-follower or master-and-man relations creating analogous rights and duties.

The significance of the whole system for us is that the clergy constituted a new element in the society and had to be brought within the system before they could be protected against others' wrongdoing or held responsible for their own.

4. Religion—It would seem that the Anglo-Saxons regarded their relation with the higher powers as a matter of public concern, but they were not prepared to put the full coercive powers of the community behind a unified approach. Religious change, when proposed, was deliberated in the councils of the several kingdoms, but there was a good deal of tolerance for those who deviated from the consensus, either by being pagan when the kingdom was Christian or by being Christian when the kingdom was pagan.[5]

It is hard to say what, if anything, the old religion contributed to the institutional patterns of the new. The Northumbrians, at the time of their conversion, had a priest, who sat in the witenagemot, and had a place—albeit not a terribly distinguished one—in the comitatus.[6] There may have been similar priests in the other kingdoms, although Teutonic practice generally was quite varied in this regard.[7] The position of such priests may have had some bearing on that accorded their successors the Christian bishops, but as to this we can only conjecture.

Some historians have suggested that the development of private places of Christian worship derived from pagan customs concerning family shrines and ancestral graves. The strictures of the seventh-century archbishop, Theodore, concerning the burial of heathens in churches lend support to this view.[8] Gregory's instructions to Augustine about making churches out of pagan temples[9] may also relate to a transformation of family worship. On the other hand, as Gregory seems to speak to this point on his own initiative rather than in response to an inquiry from Augustine, we cannot be certain that he is reflecting actual English conditions in what he says.

B. The Celtic Tradition.

The Irish ran their church from great monastic centers. Their bishops were hard-bitten ascetics who made little of the dignity of their office; often a bishop was subordinate to the abbot of the house from which he worked. Bishops and clergy alike were tireless in going about the country preaching the Gospel. Even the bishops went on foot, Bede tells how Archbishop Theodore himself had to intervene to put one of them on a horse.[10] The monastic centers for this strenuous apostolate were situated in reasonable proximity to the people to be served, but not as a rule were they in the centers of population or power. Iona, the motherhouse of them all, is on an island off the west coast of Scotland. Lindisfarne, which Aidan, out of Iona, chose as a center for his work in Northumbria, is a similar island in the North Sea. You could see one of the king's houses from it, but you had to walk across a mud flat at low tide to get there.

Their offhand view of the episcopal office seems to have kept the Irish and their English converts from developing much of a territorial organization. The bishop was more committed to the monastery where he was one of the monks than he was to any territorial see. In his apostolic activities, he pretty much went where he was needed and did what had to be done.

Christians organized in the Irish fashion out of Lindisfarne seem to have played the chief part in the conversion of Northumbria, Mercia, and Essex. Their influence was considerably reduced after the Synod of Whitby in 664, when the Northumbrian king adopted the Roman method of computing Easter, and those unwilling to abandon the Celtic tradition on this point retired to Iona. But their tradition of pastoral monasticism, and to some extent their slighting of the administrative aspect of the episcopate, probably affected the mainstream of Anglo-Saxon church life.

C. Roman Traditions.

The influence of the Roman system of church organization spread up from Canterbury as that of the Irish system spread down from Lindisfarne. With the coming of the great ecclesiastical administrator Theodore to the metropolitan see in 669, that influence became uniform over the whole English church.

1. *Territorial Organization*[11] —The church in the Roman Empire was fundamentally urban. The terminology that equates a country dweller (*pagan, heathen*) with a non-Christian has survived to remind us of this fact. The Christians of a given city were united into a single community presided over by their bishop. Priests, deacons, and minor orders of clergy assisted the bishop in his ministry rather than exercising independent ministries of their own.

Indeed, at one time, there was but one mass to a city on any one day—probably concelebrated by the bishop and his priests. The stational churches mentioned in the modern missal tell where the one mass in Rome was celebrated on certain days of the year. Even when the separate churches in a city came to have their own masses (probably in the fourth century), they were by no means independent communities.

But in the fourth and fifth centuries, the city bishops and clergy began evangelizing the countryside in earnest. In doing so, they put up churches in the more important population centers in the civil territory administered from the city. Then in the sixth century such churches came to have permanently assigned clerical staffs. These country churches covered a fairly wide area. The filling out of the local church scene through oratories on the estates of Christian landlords came rather later. Such oratories were known in the sixth century, but they could not be used for baptism nor for mass on the greater feasts.

So the missionary who came to England from Rome conceived of the organization of the church as involving a territory (not yet uniformly called a *diocese*), consisting of a city and the civil district surrounding it, ruled over for ecclesiastical purposes by a bishop. In the city, a body of clergy attached to the bishop's person would assist him in the work of the ministry. In the surrounding district, a set of satellite churches, each with a body of resident clergy, would minister to the local populace. The great obstacle to adopting this system in England would be that there were no cities.

2. The Clerical Familia—In the original conception, all the clergy seem to have belonged to the bishop's household, or familia. He provided them with suitable stipends out of the general revenues of the church. The priests and the clerics in minor orders had liturgical functions; the deacons attended to finances and the like. The chief of the deacons had come by the end of the empire to be called the archdeacon.

With the establishment of country churches, the organization of the city clergy did not change. But a separate organization, duplicating the city one in miniature, was imposed on the clergy assigned to each country church. A priest called an *archpriest* was put at the head of such a church. By the sixth century, these churches had come to have their own revenues as well as their own clergy, and during the course of that century, the administration of these revenues was transferred from the bishop to the local clergy.

While provision was made for giving the clergy separate stipends, they were evidently encouraged to live a common life. Gregory's instructions to Augustine, as reported by Bede, shed some light on this point.[12] Gregory directs Augustine to provide stipends for those of his clergy who are in minor orders and wish to marry, but he indicates that the rest of the clergy should lead a common life. He is a little vague, though, on whether they can be compelled to this if they are unwilling. As for Augustine himself, Gregory says that he must live in common with his clergy because he is a monk; otherwise, he could have had one-fourth of the revenues of his church for himself.

Most of the clergy, then, were in the bishop's familia in the city or in a miniature familia set up in an outlying church. Some, however, must have been in a more independent position. An imperial decree of 398, collected in the Theodosian Code,[13] provides that for village churches or churches on private estates the bishop must ordain clergy from the local inhabitants in order to keep up certain secular responsibilities. Men ordained in this way cannot have been in quite the same dependence on the bishop as clergy in the regularly established churches. Similarly, the Rule of Saint Benedict (first half of the sixth century) provides that an abbot can have one of his monks ordained for the service of the monastery.[14] It is not envisaged that the monk will have anything further to do with the bishop unless the need arises to discipline him. I cannot find anything so early on priests in the service of lay magnates.[15] But Saint Benedict could hardly have provided as he did if there was a hard and fast rule that a priest could not exercise his ministry outside of a familia established by the bishop.

3. *Election of Bishops*[16] —The original manner of choosing men for the episcopate is expressed in the formula "election by the clergy and people of the diocese, subject to confirmation by the neighboring bishops." We may suppose that this meant that the unified clerical familia would choose a man, present him to the populace for acceptance by acclamation, and then present him to the neighboring bishops for consecration. If either the populace or the bishops refused their choice, the clergy would try again.

The formula was amorphous enough to admit of a variety of applications. With the distribution of the clergy into outlying churches (and eventually among the several city churches also), the clerical role came to be restricted to that part of the bishop's familia that eventually developed into the cathedral chapter. The participation of the people of the diocese gave kings and lay magnates scope for intervening. The role of the neighboring bishops gave comparable scope to the metropolitan or the pope. Before the twelfth century, there was no canonical provision for episcopal elections that made at all clear who was to participate and on what terms. Still, it would have been hard to stretch the traditional formula enough to reconcile it with the Irish practice of consecrating bishops in monasteries and sending them forth at need.

4. *Deliberative Bodies*—The ecclesiastical synod of the Roman Empire consisted usually of the bishops of a province, sometimes those of a wider area. It was presided over by a metropolitan or patriarch, who owed his position to the historical preeminence of his see or to the place of his see city as a center of secular administration. It patterned its deliberations on those of

the Roman Senate, and thus had roots in the primordial Indo-European council that was the common ancestor of the Senate and the Anglo-Saxon witenagemot.

As was the case with the witenagemot, there was no formal counting of votes in the synod. Each bishop gave his opinion in turn until a consensus developed. This formal deliberative procedure was supplemented by informal discussion, and probably negotiation, outside the formal sessions. There was no question evidently of carrying a proposal by a bare majority. What was required was a sufficient showing of unanimity to persuade the dissenting bishop to submerge his independent judgment in the common witness of the church.

While there is no convincing evidence that the laity, their representatives, the civil authorities, or indeed anyone other than the bishops had an institutional role in these gatherings, it does appear that a wide variety of persons were encouraged to be present and to make their opinions known. As there was no question of tallying up votes, it may well be that on many occasions no one paid too much attention to the distinction between participation on these terms and the formal participation reserved to the bishops.

5. Canon Law—The bishop of the Roman Empire did a certain amount of his work under the forms of Roman civil administration. These, if they did not get in the way of his pastorate, at least made his pastorate look a little different from that of his Irish colleague. It would be difficult, for instance, to picture Aidan going about with a notary, as Theodore did.[17]

The Roman bishop also articulated his pastoral traditions under the forms of Roman law. Ecclesiastical synods, from general councils on down, expressed their resolutions in the form of "canons." These in substance were pastoral guides, but in form they were legislation. It was their pastoral background, though, that determined their acceptance. What was important was not the jurisdiction of the body that enacted them, but how well they embodied the authentic tradition. Old canons, whatever their provenance, were generally considered better than new ones. Thus, when Theodore held the first synod of the whole English church, he came armed with a book of canons, mostly eastern, from which he culled ten he thought suitable to the occasion. These were duly enacted by the English prelates.[18]

Finally, the Roman bishop was often a judge. In addition to the miscellany of cases that came his way due to the breakdown of civil administration in the late empire, he had a general right to deal with cases involving the discipline of the clergy or the distribution of church property. He also had power to excommunicate the laity for their offenses or put them to penance, and evidently he had some authority to determine their matrimonial status. All of these powers he exercised under the procedural forms of Roman law.[19]

Some of the substantive law came from the Roman also, though much of it came from the canons and pastoral traditions of the church.

When the missionaries landed in England, the canon law as medieval historians know it was still several centuries in the future. But the essence of the system—pastoral traditions structured by Roman law—was discernible even at this early date.

II. Central and Diocesan Institutions

Any description of Anglo-Saxon institutions must be dated with respect to the Danish invasions that set the country by the ears for much of the ninth and tenth centuries and produced a good deal of a hiatus in the records. The story of these invasions can be simply told. From scattered raiding expeditions in the first half of the ninth century, they developed into a systematic occupation of the northern and eastern parts of the country during the second half. Meanwhile, the West Saxon monarchy, which had led a successful resistance in the south and west, gained the initiative by the end of the century, and by the mid-tenth century it had brought the Danish-occupied parts of the country under control. Thus in the late tenth and the eleventh centuries, there was a united Anglo-Saxon kingdom, with certain Danish elements and institutions, under the successors of the West Saxon kings.[20]

Some of the institutions with which we are concerned seem to have passed through all this with remarkably little change. We find a bishop, for instance, in the eleventh century doing just about what his predecessor was doing in the eighth. Other institutions, however, changed radically. The local distribution of eleventh-century churches is very different from the eight-century pattern. We have to deal, then, with two main categories:

1. Institutions developed during the period before the Danish invasions, and appearing thereafter with moderate changes, attributable to the greater complexity of the society and the consolidation of royal power after the invasions. In this category fall the institutions of central and diocesan administration, centering around the monarchy and the episcopate, and the basic forms by which the Christian religion was integrated into the national life. In dealing with these, we can content ourselves with looking at them before and after the invasions, without worrying too much about what went on in between.

2. Institutions that appear so different before and after the invasions that we cannot understand how they developed without determining as best we can what happened to them during the period of the invasions itself. These include the whole local articulation of the church and ministry and some of the accompanying financial arrangements.

Let us turn at this point to the institutions in the first category. In dealing with them, I shall pay more attention to the period before the invasion because the later period has been exhaustively covered in Barlow's recent work. I cannot profitably do much more with it than set forth his conclusions where they are relevant.

A. The Episcopate

1. Dioceses–Augustine set up two proper Roman dioceses in Kent, one at Canterbury, the other at Rochester. Elsewhere, the arrangement was rather fluid in the early days. Bishops tended to attach themselves to rulers rather than territories and to come and go as they or their royal patrons pleased. That, of course, was the Irish tradition. Some bishops in the Roman tradition followed the same pattern either because they had been consecrated with roving commissions or because they had been set wandering by the vicissitudes of the times. It is these men who provide the interesting stories– Wilfrid, who evangelized one province in England and one on the continent during successive exiles from Northumbria; Agilbert, who left the West Saxons in a huff to become bishop of Paris; Colman, who went back to Iona rather than keep the Roman Easter;[21] and a number of others. But it was the archbishop Theodore, sent from Rome in 669, who gave a Roman diocesan structure to the English church.

He had to contend both with the Irish and missionary tradition of freelance bishops and with a nationalistic conception that a bishop's jurisdiction should be coextensive with the kingdom in which he worked. The former gave him but little trouble. One of the canons of his 672 synod provided that no bishop should interfere in another's territory,[22] and, for all that appears, the bishops were content to follow it. But dividing up the kingdoms into more than one diocese each was another matter. It took all the tact and authority Theodore and his successor Bertwald could muster.[23]

Why a king and his people felt threatened by having more than one bishopric among them is hard to see. Perhaps they thought a national bishop would be more closely allied with royal authority than a merely local bishop would be. In any event, the division of kingdoms into separate sees was long resisted and overcome in different kingdoms in different ways. But overcome it was. By the time Bertwald died in 731, all but the smallest kingdoms had more than one bishop.[24] Evidently, the kings and peoples decided the new situation was not so bad after all, for the divisions gave no further trouble once they were accomplished.

2. Election–Theodore seems to have appointed bishops pretty much as he pleased.[25] Except in his time, the main initiative in appointing bishops was royal. The king before choosing a bishop would take counsel with his witenagemot would have enough local clergy and magnates to satisfy the flexible canonical formula of election by the clergy and people of the diocese. There are traces of canonical influence on the early accounts of such occasions.[26]

In the late Anglo-Saxon period, the role of the witenagemot became a little more perfunctory, and its composition changed. You could rely on finding there only the familiars of the king's household and a few notables from the particular part of the country the king was visiting at the moment. Also, in those sees that had monastic cathedral chapters, the tenth-century *Regularis Concordia* provided that the chapter, rather than the clergy generally, was to elect the bishop. Thus, it was a little harder to pay lip service to the canonical formula. Nevertheless, the lip service was paid, and the clerical writers regularly used the canonical formula in describing what happened. Barlow thinks that on some occasions the royal nominee visited the see for some kind of formal acceptance by the chapter and populace, and that on other occasions representatives of the chapter were brought into the witenagemot when the king's nomination was taken up.[27] Sometimes a chapter tried to make an independent choice, but in such cases it probably negotiated with the king rather than standing on its rights under the law.

3. The Work of a Bishop—The Anglo-Saxon bishop had developed his characteristic administrative style by the middle of the eighth century. It combined the peripatetic evangelism of the Irish bishops with the peripatetic government of the Anglo-Saxon kings. The bishop traveled about his diocese, preaching, administering the sacraments, and looking into any other ecclesiastical affairs that were brought to his attention as he passed. In this work, he seems to have been pretty much on his own. In the first decades of the eighth century, children all over the diocese of Winchester died without baptism because the bishop went blind in his declining years.[28] In late Anglo-Saxon times, there were no doubt enough priests about a diocese to prevent a disaster of this kind, but the main role of the bishop could still be described as "supplying the wants left by a remiss and scanty priesthood."[29] The development of a local ministry to assume the bishop's pastoral functions was going on all the time, as we shall see, but even at the Conquest, this local ministry seems not to have adequately covered the ground.

Nor did the bishop have the body of diocesan officials that absorbed so much of his work in the later Middle Ages. By the eleventh century, there was an archdeacon in every diocese—perhaps there always had been—but there is no evidence that he had defined administrative duties to perform. The cathedral chapters were just beginning to come by independent endowments; their coming by independent functions was still in the future.

While his main concern was to exercise his own ministry rather than to supervise that of others, the bishop did have certain supervisory functions to perform. To the extent that his clerical familia did not have an independent organization, he must have been responsible for their work and discipline. He must have had some control also over the growing numbers of priests dependent on local magnates in his diocese. As early as the eighth century, it was his business to ordain these men, to consecrate the places where they were to minister, and perhaps to institute them into their positions as well.[30]

He was probably supposed also, at least in theory, to concern himself with the monasteries in his diocese to the extent of ministering to the spiritual needs of the inmates and seeing that they kept their rule.[31] One of the canons enacted under Theodore in 672, however, seems to afford religious houses some measure of immunity from episcopal intervention. Thus, the exact scope of the bishop's responsibilities in this regard is not clear. It appears that in later Anglo-Saxon times he visited a monastery only when invited, and that nothing like canonical visitation was undertaken until long after the Conquest. We may suspect that in the earlier period also he did not make much use of his rights, whatever they were. He had enough to do without asserting himself where he was not wanted.

In addition to his spiritual functions, the bishop had certain temporal commitments. As a magnate of the kingdom, he had to attend the king in his court and render counsel in the witenagemot. As a holder of bookland, he had to see to the rendering of the governmental services attached to his tenure. Most important, as a landed proprietor, he had to keep his estates intact. Even before the Danish invasions, the church was involved in a good deal of litigation over land. Afterward, the bishop had to recover land the Danes had taken away and to counteract the day-to-day erosion of his estates due to the improvidence of his predecessors, the rapacity of his neighbors, and the intransigence of his tenants.

On the whole, then, the Anglo-Saxon bishop was more of a pastor and less of an administrator than his later medieval counterpart because he had less help with his pastorate and, concomitantly, a good deal less to administer. Still, the faint outlines of the late medieval administrative office are discernible in the eleventh century and perhaps in the eighth century as well.

4. Pope and Metropolitan–The higher echelons of the episcopate, metropolitan and pope, made only a tenuous contribution to the operation of the Anglo-Saxon church. Neither performed any regular day-to-day administrative function. The see of Canterbury had a brief period of real power under Theodore and Bertwald; otherwise, presiding at councils and consecrating suffragan bishops are the only acts of metropolitan jurisdiction we can document, whether in the eighth century or the eleventh.[32] For a time during the ninth century, the suffragans were making professions of obedience to Canterbury, but there are no significant indications of wherein they found it necessary to obey.

Probably much of the importance of Canterbury lay not in its canonical position as metropolitan see, but in its special relation to the monarchy. This relation was adumbrated in the position of the several bishops in the national sees broken up by Theodore. After the breakup, the one-to-one relation of king and bishop was less in evidence until the cataclysms of the ninth and tenth centuries provided England with a united monarchy. When that happened, it was fairly natural that the venerable see of Canterbury should fall into the role of chief advisor to the king in ecclesiastical matters and chief spokesman before him for the church.

As for the pope, he conferred the pallium on English archbishops from the start. At least from Alfred's time, he received the fruits of a royal tax collected for him—the Romescot, or Peter's Pence.[33] Beyond this, he intervened only sporadically in English affairs. His interventions were of the same kind as in later times—only less frequent. He sent legates to sit in on English councils; he tried to protect English monasteries against kings and bishops; he absolved English sinners; he threatened prelates who did not suppress vice vigorously enough; he adjudicated the tenure of English sees.[34] But none of these did he do systematically. We have only a few examples of each for the whole Anglo-Saxon period. What led the pope to act when he did act is hard to say. My guess is that he was fairly passive during most of the period, dealing only with those matters that came by chance to his attention. As he did not act often enough to get people into the habit of going to him, these occasions would no doubt be fairly rare.

Sometimes, the pope got an ambiguous reception when he did move. The great Northumbrian bishop Wilfrid, expelled from the see of York in the late seventh century, was never able to get back more than part of what the pope ordered restored to him.[35] And in the mid-eleventh century, Stigand, whom the pope regarded as intruded into the see of Canterbury, could not be put out till after the Conquest. Papal process in these cases was not simply disregarded. Without it, Wilfrid would not have recovered as much as he did. Similarly, although Stigand kept the see of Canterbury, no English bishop went to him for consecration, nor did Harold go to him to be crowned.

It is idle to argue from evidence of this kind that papal authority was not recognized among the Anglo-Saxons in the way it was in the later Middle Ages. The Anglo-Saxons simply had a different attitude toward authority as such. They treated popes, kings, and bishops all the same. It is one thing to recognize a man's authority, quite another to obey it. There was little to persuade an Anglo-Saxon that he should obey the mandates of any authority when he thought it right to do otherwise. His society was simple enough for the anarchic tendency of his attitude not to be much brought home to him. At any rate, he had more tolerance for anarchy than you and I.

B. Legislation and Legislative Bodies.

Barlow finds eleventh-century English kings legislating on five main topics of ecclesiastical concern:[36]

1. Protection of churches and clergy against violence, financial exactions, and other forms of oppression
2. Clerical morals, including breaches of celibacy, improper exercise of the ministry, and treatment of clerics accused of secular offenses
3. Lay morals, especially marriage, sexual offenses, heathenism, witchcraft, and perjury
4. Enforcement of ecclesiastical taxation
5. Enforcement of Sundays, holidays, and fasts

These are the same topics that can be found in laws enacted by Christian kings before 700.[37] Presumably the royal power was invoked in matters of this kind so that offenders could be subjected to secular penalties.

We may speculate as to whether there was a parallel course of strictly canonical legislation in the English church, in which royal authority played only a subordinate part or none at all. The canons enacted by Theodore in 672 seem to be in this case; so do those enacted under the papal legates George and Theophylact in 785. But there is nothing of this kind in a later period.[35] It is just possible that some of the royal enactments were put in canonical form by the prelates before the king enacted them. There is language in some of the preambles that could support such an interpretation.[39] It seems to me more likely, though, that the bishops drew on existing doctrinal or canonical material and brought it to the king's attention without formally enacting it themselves.[40]

The canonical form of the ecclesiastical synod was known to the Anglo-Saxons, but I suspect it was fused with the witenagemot rather early on. As no vote was taken in either body, and as neither had any inhibitions against hearing outsiders who wished to present their views, you could hardly tell one body from the other by looking at it. In the early times, when the church covered more than one kingdom, we can see gatherings that seem to be of ecclesiastical provenance and gatherings where the king takes a back seat to the bishops in disposing of the matter at hand.[41] But we may suppose that in most cases the meeting of the king with his prelates and magnates passed for either synod or witenagemot as the occasion served.

In the late Anglo-Saxon period, nothing is heard of ecclesiastical synods except for one or two purely theoretical accounts of the canonical form. Rather than suppose such synods met and left no records, it seems reasonable to say that the witenagemot did all the ecclesiastical business that had to be done. Presumably there were enough prelates present to give its deliberations any canonical status they required.

So much for meetings on the national or provincial level. Barlow finds that there may have been diocesan synods—one bishop with his own clergy—from time to time. But here again, when the bishop met his clergy at the shire court, he could do whatever synodal business he had. Barlow's general conclusion is that "in England mixed forms seem general from top to bottom."[42]

As we know, these mixed forms did not long survive the Conquest. I suspect, though, that they left a permanent mark on the institutions of later times in the freedom with which lay and clerical authorities continued to participate in each other's deliberations. The rights claimed by the Angevin kings in episcopal elections and the peculiar position of Convocation in medieval English polity both seem more intelligible in the light of the flexible and ambiguous practices of the early Anglo-Saxons.

Also the ambiguity of the situation had a great deal to do with the character of latter-day polemics. A person seeking historical precedent for a particular allocation of power between church and state can go back to the early Anglo-Saxons and find whatever he is looking for. A number of apologists in many different centuries have availed themselves of the opportunity.

C. Judicial Processes.

In 1072, King William made an ordinance that bishops and archdeacons were no longer to hold ecclesiastical pleas in the hundred court, nor were they to submit spiritual causes to the judgment of temporal men. Rather, the bishop was to hold his own court where he pleased and give judgment according to the canon law.[43] The system abolished here is one of the mixed forms like the witenagemot-synod. It involves a church official doing justice in a popular assembly with the participation of the members of the assembly. The operation of the hundred in this way cannot be documented except through William's ordinance. But an ordinance made by King Edgar between 959 and 963 provides a similar program for the shire court.[44] It orders the bishop and the ealdorman to attend and declare the laws of God and the world—presumably the bishop the one and the ealdorman the other. I suppose that the whole system goes back to the late ninth or early tenth century, when the traditional popular assemblies were first reorganized into instruments of central government.[45]

Barlow supposes that the shire court, with the bishop sitting in it, dealt with contumacious public sinners, with land litigation affecting the church, with wills, and perhaps with matrimony and bastardy. No doubt it exacted the secular penalties imposed by the king for moral and ecclesiastical offenses.

But it is hard to accept the view propounded by a number of historians that the shire and hundred courts thus organized were the only judicial organs *and Kinship.*

ntegration of the church into the secular social structure on which so
the law depended was accomplished very quietly and very early. It is
by a number of legislative enactments (mainly concerning oaths, and
sation for various offenses), but these hardly cover the ground. Rather,
em to manifest a general unwritten custom of assimilating the several
of the clergy to existing ranks in secular society—bishops to kings,
s to the nobility (thanes), and lower clerics to free householders, or
s.[50]

seems also that the clerical *familia* was assimilated to the kin-group.
rt's *Dialogue* has the wergild for a slain cleric collectible by the church,
e does the compensation for violating a nun.[51] Consider also his treat-
t of offenses committed by the clergy:

> For those who are guilty either of grave or of light offenses within the
> church, no penalty [*nihil vindictae*] belongs to those who are without,
> especially as the Apostle says that all causes of the church should be
> judged among the priests. On the other hand, if persons belonging to
> the church should commit some crime among the laity, homicide, for-
> nication or theft, it is decreed that they be followed up in every case
> by those secular persons against whom they have sinned, unless the
> church should be of a mind to make satisfaction for them.[52]

This provision seems more an adaptation of the tribal rule that offenses within the kin-group were of no concern to outsiders than of the canonical rule
that clerics were not to be judged by the laity. It refers ingeniously to the
canonical tradition, but in fact the crucial distinction between offenses within and offenses without has no basis in the canons. It has a firm basis, though,
in tribal custom if the church be regarded as taking the place of the kin-
group.[53]

As to offenses among the laity, it is not clear whether Egbert was claiming for the church a special prerogative or whether the kin-group generally
had the right to read the offender out of kinship rather than make satisfaction for him or abide the blood-feud with him. In any event, Egbert's procedure has affinities both for certain passages in Beowulf as interpreted by
Seebohm and for the latter-day procedure of handing over to the secular
arm.[54]

These matters of status and kinship are simple enough in the telling, but
we should not overlook their importance both as a creative achievement of
early Anglo-Saxon society and as a source of important consequences for the
English church. It is no small matter for a society with complex forms and
rudimentary adaptive mechanisms to digest a major foreign element with no
serious disruption of either the society or the foreign element. But the achievement was not without a price. The establishment of the clergy in different

(not counting the confessional) that the church
William made the bishops set up a system of th
ment of these courts tells against such a view. S
hood of a bishop bringing certain types of cases b
Furthermore, there is direct evidence, albeit sca
hearing cases on their own. The Northumbrian Pries
the eleventh century bishops and archdeacons issued
and exacted their own penalties for noncompliance.[4]
involve appearance in the shire or hundred court, but
the regular processes of those courts. In an earlier peric
as the 690s a law that envisages a bishop hearing cases a
a misbehaving priest to his judgment.

The eighth-century canonical Dialogue of Egbert, archb
66), has more to say on the subject than any other Anglo-
seems to envisage that a cleric or religious accused of an off
clear himself before the bishop, that laymen should not deal
committed within the clerical familia, and that a cleric or reli
a claim to property should pursue it before the ecclesiastical a
(judicantibus aecclesiarum sacerdotibus), rather than resort to s
lay authority (per exteriores potestates vim).[48] I conclude from
the church had from the beginning its own tribunals for dealing
internal problems, so that the shire and hundred courts were limit
in which a lay interest was involved or cases in which secular penal
to be exacted.

Whatever jurisdiction the church had was supported by about the
sanctions as in the later middle ages. A cleric could be put out of the
try and cut off from his share of ecclesiastical revenues; Egbert's Dialo
provides for this.[49] A layman could be excommunicated. These sanctio
almost as old as Christianity, and they appear often enough in the laws,
may be sure they were used in England. The provisions in the laws for se
lar penalties, either in addition to excommunication or instead of it, indic
that, just as in later times, the laity could not be kept in line by spiritual
sanctions alone. In the eleventh century, the effectiveness of excommunication was enhanced by provisions that applied secular coercion to the excommunicate as such rather than imposing a secular penalty as another punishment for the same offense. The excommunicate was assimilated to a secular outlaw, and penalties were imposed on anyone who harbored him. This
practice, which was developed more fully after the Conquest, was no doubt
older than the enactments in which it was embodied, but we cannot tell how
far back it goes.

social ranks was one of many centrifugal forces that affected them in the Anglo-Saxon period, one that their union under a loose and moribund kinship doctrine could hardly counteract. Had they been brought into the social structure in some other way, there might have been a very different church-state nexus in later times.

III. Local Churches and the Origin of the Parish

The medieval parish, with its fixed territorial boundaries, its incumbent with tenure of his position, its patron with a right to choose the incumbent, its fixed sources of revenue, and its generally secure canonical status is in great part a product of the Gregorian reform. Domesday Book, on the eve of the reform, presents a far more confusing picture, the result of the destruction of the Danish invasions, several kinds of haphazard growth, and several more or less abortive systematic programs. There are small local churches, more in some places than others. There are the remains of systems of larger local churches that once served larger districts. There are the monasteries founded by Dunstan and Ethelwold in the mid-tenth century on the ruins of houses broken up by the Danes. There are cathedral churches, secular or monastic. All of these are subject to a variety of arrangements as to landed endowment, tithe and other ecclesiastical dues, cure of souls and the manner of serving it, tenure of clergy and relations with lay patrons or proprietors.

Barlow gives a clear and detailed description of this confusing situation but does not try to tell us how it came about.[55] Other authors describe the situation before the Danish invasion and one aspect or another of the ensuing periods. But I have found no really satisfactory account of the successive stages in the development of the local ministry. Such an account would have a good deal of interest in itself. I think also that the Domesday situation could be made more comprehensible through a dissection of the several chronological layers that made it up. The following account is developed in part from standard source materials but largely from taking one county, Berkshire, parish by parish, and collating the Domesday entries with other material from the Victoria County History.

A. The Eighth Century.

1. Kinds of Churches—As far as I can see, the public ministry in the eighth century consisted of (1) local centers staffed by the bishop's *familia* and (2) monasteries. The establishment of the former was in accord with the Roman system of outlying churches; it was also analogous to the gradual transition of secular administration from peripatetic to feudal forms. We may suppose, though, that the process was a little more haphazard than it would have been in a Roman diocese. It was probably based less on the needs of the faithful than on the fortuitous distribution of the bishop's lands as a result of the generosity of successive kings. As the bishop rode circuit, he would put up with his clergy at one after another of these locations, collecting part of his revenues in the form of food and drink. Then, in due course, the more important of these places would become centers for staffs of resident clergy who would minister to the people between the bishop's visits and perhaps ride smaller circuits of their own. Presumably these priests would have a collegiate organization like that of an outlying church in a Roman diocese.

Monasteries, meanwhile, were being founded in several ways.[56] Some started life as subordinate centers for the Irish monastic episcopate, daughter houses to Lindisfarne or Iona. Others were set up by the piety of kings, bishops, and other magnates. In a number of cases, great ladies embraced the religious life on lands provided by their male relatives. Houses of nuns thus established usually had houses of monks attached to them to do the priestly and some of the manual work.[57]

Many of these houses were substantial, well-endowed affairs, their founders sincere men and women, and often saints—Benedict Biscop of Wearmouth and Jarrow, Hilda of Whitby, Audrey of Ely, and a number of others less famous. We may suppose that such houses as these played an important part in ministering to the surrounding countryside.[58]

These great houses were responsibly founded, adequately endowed, and headed by professed religious. But other houses grew up that were none of these. Some kings were evidently too free in exempting monasteries from the dues exacted of other landed proprietors. It became possible, pursuant to the principle of nonaccountability, for a layman setting up a monastery on his land to secure the benefit of such an exemption while preserving for himself all the revenues of the property beyond what was needed to support the religious. Worse still, he could indulge a desire to run a religious community without subjecting himself to the rigors of the religious life. He could even provide his wife on similar terms with a convent of nuns. Bede, complaining of this practice in 734, said that almost every king's reeve and thane in Northumbria was involved in it.[59]

Houses built on these shaky foundations can hardly have been expected to contribute much to the local ministry. The bishop was supposed to visit them and do what he could for the spiritual welfare of the inmates, but there seems to have been no hope of making them really useful to God or man.[60] Like the great houses, they died out with the Danish invasions; unlike the great houses, they were not revived.

More respectable, but still I think not a part of the regular ministry, were the churches put up by local landholders on their estates. I am inclined to think that the eighth-century bishop regarded the consecration of these churches and what supervision he exercised over the priests who ministered in them more as an accommodation to the landholders than as an adjunct to his own pastorate. It seems to have been in that spirit that Saint John of Beverly, in stories told by Bede, dedicated two such churches at the request of local magnates.

So it was the greater monasteries and the collegiate establishments on the bishop's estates that did the main work of the local ministry in the eighth century. The canon law sharply distinguished the two kinds of establishment, the secular-collegiate from the monastic,[62] but there does not seem to have been much distinction in the popular mind. The Anglo-Saxons, who were perfectly able to coin as many words as they thought they needed, were content to let the one word, *minster* (from the Latin *monasterium*), serve for both. Presumably, then, they both served the same functions, maintaining services for the inhabitants to attend or sending out priests to hold services about the country.

2. *Finance*—These major establishments drew most of their support from their landed endowments. The lands were usually held under some kind of corporate title—the church at such and such place or even the patron saint. The lands that supported the bishop's minsters were evidently all held by the bishop in the name of his cathedral church or his episcopal see.[63] If the revenues were divided by custom among his different collegiate establishments, the division does not appear on paper till after the Conquest. Monastic lands, on the other hand, were generally held in the name of the individual monastery.[64]

All this land was of course bookland. The bishop or the monastery did not "own" it in the modern sense. They drew from it revenues formerly the king's and, in return, stood in for the king in doing justice for the local inhabitants. By virtue of the principle of nonaccountability, they could spend on their ministry and support whatever they did not spend in performing the rudimentary governmental functions they had taken over from the king.

It should be noted in passing that the same device that enabled the Anglo-Saxon king to turn his secular revenues to the support of the church enabled his Norman and Plantagenet successors to draw ecclesiastical revenues to the support of the state. For many centuries, as we shall see, parish priests served in the secular bureaucracy, supporting themselves by whatever of the parish revenues they did not spend in paying a curate to minister in the parish.

I should imagine that not all monasteries held bookland, though all the serious ones did. Some of the more abject of the houses ruled by laymen were probably simply built on land held in the proprietor's own name. Similarly, the church maintained by a lay landholder on his estate would not have had bookland attached to it. The priest might have a share with the peasants in the village fields; otherwise, he would have no land at all.

In addition to bookland, which was fundamentally a share in the king's revenues, the church had certain strictly ecclesiastical sources of revenue. Some of these grew out of the crystallization of customary offerings on the occasion of particular acts of ministry—what came in later centuries to be grouped under the name of *altarage*. One such offering, soul-scot, the ancestor of the latter-day mortuary, probably derived from the pagan custom of burying goods with the deceased.

Other ecclesiastical revenues may have been the result of specific royal grants. It is generally supposed that the pope's Romescot, or Peter's Pence, was in this case. So perhaps was church-scot, which first appears as a compulsory tax in the laws of King Ine of Wessex (688-94).[65] Tithe, which was to become the most important of ecclesiastical dues, came from an ancient canonical practice. It was not enforced with secular sanctions till the tenth century.[66]

We have only snippets of evidence as to what churchmen received any of these payments. It seems, though, that they tended to go to particular local churches rather than to the diocese or to the bishop. Barlow indicates that in the eleventh century the bishop as such had no ecclesiastical revenues except offerings on the occasion of his delivery of chrism or performance of other episcopal functions.[67] Bede refers, however, in 734 to remote hamlets whose inhabitants paid dues to the bishop although he did nothing to minister to them.[68] Perhaps in that early period church-scot or some other comparable payment went to the bishop unless he delegated it to a minster.

As for tithe, it appears that in theory the eighth-century Christian could bestow it on any pious or charitable object he chose.[69] In fact, though, it was a heavy payment in kind and can hardly have gone far from the place where it originated. The later medieval practice was for the churchman to fetch his own tithe out of the field after the harvesters had counted off every tenth sheaf for him. Given the state of their economy, I would be surprised if the Anglo-Saxons did not follow the same practice. So it must at least have been known before the harvest what churchman was going to come for the tithe. In all likelihood, it was customary to divide the tithe between the monastery or minster that served the vicinity and the church, if any, maintained by the tithepayer on his own land. But, there is no indication that the custom had the force of law before King Edgar attempted to revive it in the last half of the tenth century.

3. Distribution—We may suppose that in the eighth century these episcopal minsters and large monasteries were evenly, if sparsely, distributed in most parts of the country. Miss Deanesly describes the situation in the southeast; it would seem that Ethelbert's kingdom and Augustine's diocese were more richly and more quickly supplied than other places.[70] One would have to proceed county by county, if not parish by parish, to see exactly how these establishments came to cover the ground. At any rate, in Berkshire, the county that I have studied in detail, there is evidence for four sites, fairly well spread out.

First, in the northwestern part of the county there was Abingdon Abbey; there is definite evidence for its foundation in the late seventh century.[71] Second, in the east central part of the county, there was an establishment of secular clergy at Sonning. This church, with the manor attached, was held by the bishop of Salisbury at the time of Domesday Book and thereafter until it was made a prebend of Salisbury Cathedral.[72] There is nothing to show when the bishop's tenure originated, but it was probably early, for a document of 909 lists the bishops of the see as "bishops of Sonning."

In the northeastern part of the county, there was a convent of nuns at Cookham, which we know about because it figured in a late eighth-century lawsuit.[73] If this was like other nunneries of the period, it had a house of male religious attached to it, perhaps located at the neighboring church of Bray. The churches of Cookham and Bray, both heavily endowed, appear in Domesday Book among the holdings of a secular minster at Cirencester in Gloucestershire.[74] They may have come together into that position during the confused period of the Danish invasions because they were held together before the Danes came.

There may also have been a monastery at Kintbury, in the southwestern part of the county. There is reference to a secular minster there in a document of 931.[75] and a tenth-century secular minster not otherwise explained is apt to have been an eighth-century monastery. During the time of the Danish invasions, monastic sites were rather systematically taken over by such minsters.

The four sites of Kintbury, Cookham, Sonning, and Abingdon[76] would have afforded a fairly even distribution of clergy about the county, and clergy circulating out of them could have provided the rudiments of a sacramental and liturgical life to the people. It seems likely that in the eighth century, and until the Danish invasions, that is just what they did.

B. The Danish Invasions.

For our purposes, the most important of the institutions wrecked by the Danes was monasticism. Knowles, after examining the evidence, concludes that when the decision to revive Glastonbury Abbey was taken in 943 or 944 there was not a single truly monastic house in England.[77] And it seems likely that this state of affairs had endured for the better part of a century.

Some of the former monastic sites were occupied on a reduced scale by communities of secular clergy. These, I suppose, either drifted in or were introduced when the sites were left vacant by the downfall of monastic

observance.[78] An alternative explanation, that the monks under the pressures
of the times gradually relaxed their observance to the point of becoming secular canons, does not persuade me.[79] In any event, such clergy formed secular minsters on a number of former monastic sites. They were kept in order by rules patterned after that adopted for his familia by the mid-eighth-
century bishop Saint Chrodegang of Metz.[80] Evidently, they were unable or
unwilling to keep up the kind of peripatetic ministry their monastic fore-
runners had done.

The bishops, although they had troubles of their own, may have tried to
take up the slack in some cases by putting up churches in places where they
themselves had no land and where no local magnate was in a position to
maintain a church of his own. Churches that appear in later times in the
hands of the bishop or of the incumbent priest, although neither has land in
the vicinity, may well have been established in this way.[81] So also may some
of the churches that are not mentioned in Domesday Book although they
must have existed at the time. The mention and nonmention of churches in
Domesday Book is a vexed question, but the answer I find most persuasive
is that generally those churches were mentioned that constituted sources of
secular revenue.[82] Thus, if a church was maintained by the bishop in the
exercise of his ordinary jurisdiction, no secular landholder would draw revenue from it, and there would be a reason for its not being mentioned. It is
significant in this regard that the counties where the fewest churches are
mentioned tend to be those where the lands were broken up among a number of small holders who would not have been able to put up churches on
their own estates.[83]

In some parts of England, the establishment of local churches in this way,
supplemented by secular minsters here and there, may have done most of the
work of restoring the local ministry. But in those counties that were longest
under the West Saxon administration, there is evidence of a systematic royal
attack on the problem through providing a church for each of the administrative divisions known as *hundreds*.[84]

While the judicial functions that characterized the medieval hundred cannot be traced back any further than the first half of the tenth century, the
use of comparable subdivisions for other public purposes probably goes gack
much further. It seems likely that each such subdivision originally consisted
of 100 *hides*, or assessment units, and was centered about a king's *tun*, at
which the king's reeves did some of the business of government and collected
payments in kind from the local populace. Providing each of these traditional
units with a church must have been an administrative reform of about the
same order as providing each one with a court. Perhaps both steps were taken
at the same time.

At any rate, someone in the late ninth or early tenth century seems to have attempted to establish on every hundred not otherwise provided for a church, located on a royal manor (the king's *tun* of earlier times), and endowed with half a hide or more of glebe land. The hide is a unit of taxation rather than a unit of measurement, so we cannot exactly determine its size. It seems to have amounted in most parts of the country to 120 acres of arable land, but in some parts as little as 40—in either case, with accompanying rights of pasture and the like in the common lands of the village. The half-hide endowment, therefore, would be a substantial but not a lavish endowment for a local church. In fact most did better than this; in Berkshire, at least, one to one-and-a-half hides appears to have been the most usual size.

The existence of this system of hundred churches is inferred from the data assembled in Domesday Book. Of the twenty-two Domesday hundreds in Berkshire, for instance, all but seven have churches endowed in this fashion, usually on the royal manor from which the hundred derives its name. Accounting for the exceptions is tenuous work and has to be done pretty much one hundred at a time, but for the most part it can be done. I think that the following considerations, taken singly or in combination, pretty well account for all the exceptions in Berkshire:

1. Some churches, like the bishop's establishment at Sonning (Charlton Hundred) did not appear in Domesday Book because they paid no secular services.
2. The glebe endowments of some hundred churches were merged with the secular estates in the same place when both came into ecclesiastical hands. This is probably the case with Marcham church (Marcham Hundred) where we know of the church's endowment from other evidence.[85]
3. If the original hundreds had one hundred hides each, their boundaries must have been altered after the system was set up. In some cases (for example Wantage Hundred), we can reconstruct the situation and hypothesize former hundred-hide hundreds, each with a heavily endowed church.[86]

I am inclined, as I have said, to attribute this system of hundred churches to the late ninth or early tenth century. As its purpose was evidently to fill the gap left by the destruction of the monasteries, it cannot have come in before the monasteries were wiped out in the mid-ninth century nor after they were revived in the mid-tenth. At any rate, the hundred churches covered the ground in some parts of the country when the monasteries were revived, and these churches posed some problems for the revival.

C. The Monastic Revival.

In the middle of the tenth century, a strong movement set in for reviving the monastic life. It was led by the two great monk-bishops Dunstan and Ethelwold and was powerfully supported by the monarchy, especially by

Edgar (959-75), one of the most effective and creative kings since Alfred. Monasteries were revived on ancient sites. Secular canons were turned out and replaced by monks. Lands and offices were put in monastic hands.

Of course, it was impossible to restore the status quo as it had existed before the Danish invasions. I think, though, that the whole movement was characterized by a feeling that the status quo ought to be restored as far as possible. The vigorous, if not brutal, replacement of seculars by monks in so many places can hardly be explained in any other way. Also, there is evidence that the pre-Danish landholdings of the various houses were influential, albeit not decisive, in the building up of their endowments after the restoration.[87]

I suspect this general policy of restoring the status quo was behind a famous enactment of King Edgar purporting to bestow all tithe (except a portion for a church maintained by a thane on his bookland) and church-scot on a class of churches referred to as "old minsters."[88] The law can never have been systematically implemented. Landholders shortly after the Conquest were freely granting out their tithes (or so much of them as were not covered by the exception in favor of the tithepayer's own church) to any religious house they chose.[89] If in doing so they were violating rights established scarcely more than a century before, we should certainly hear of some complaint. So I take it that the "old minsters" were the ones that had existed before the Danes came and that Edgar's law represented a pious wish or an abortive attempt to restore them to the position they had occupied in those days.[90]

Perhaps there was an attempt to restore their ministry as well as their revenues. Edgar's law envisages that each old minister will have a "parish" (*hyrnes*) subject to its claim to tithe. On the basis of the pre-Danish situation, it would have a claim to the cure of souls as well. We might expect that such a claim would be given partial recognition, but not to the point of completely disrupting the system of hundred churches that had been set up in the same territory in the meantime.

In any event, whether to restore their old position or to strengthen their new one, the refounded religious houses were given an extended cure of souls in the surrounding territory—but without undermining the basic system of hundred churches. In some cases, hundred churches as such were turned over to religious houses, complete with the cure of souls in the hundreds involved. Abingdon Abbey seems to have come by the cure in two or three neighboring hundreds in this way.[91]

In other hundreds, as I have said, the boundaries seem to have been altered. In some cases, this may have been done to implement grants of secular jurisdiction. But in others, I suspect it was done to expand the cure of souls of a religious house at the expense of that of a neighboring hundred church. There is, for instance, a hundred called Eagle that shows signs of having been created out of pieces of other hundreds in order to expand the cure of souls of the minster at Kintbury.[92]

The day of the peripatetic ministry was about over by the time the monasteries came by their expanded spiritual responsibilities in this fashion. They had to locate priests about the territory in which they were responsible for the ministry. A number of the peculiarities we find in the period just after the Conquest are attributable to the various possible ways of doing this.

First, a monastery could farm out a hundred church, presumably with all its rights and responsibilities. The monks of Abingdon seem to have done this with the church of Sutton Courtenay, just south of Abingdon. It appears in Domesday Book with a hide of land held of the Abbey by a priest named Alwi. The hide in question was the glebe land of the church.

A monastery could also put a priest into the church with a fixed stipend, or with a fixed source of revenue such as the altarage and a portion of tithe, and keep the rest of the revenues for the general purposes of the monastery. I suppose this is what happened in Marcham hundred, where the monks merged the glebe land into their secular holdings at Marcham instead of giving it to the priest who served the cure for them.[93]

Finally, a monastery could simply take all the revenues arising out of a given church and send one or more of the community to serve the spiritual needs of the local populace. I take this to be the situation at Longworth, one of the Abingdon holdings in Berkshire, where one of the monks was said to be "established in the place of the other brethren" (*illic ceterorum fratrum loco consistens*).[94] However the old minsters provided for the ministry in the territory assigned them, they seem in some cases at least to have made good a claim to exclude others from competing with them. Not long after the Conquest, the monks of Abingdon prevented a local landholder in Marcham Hundred from putting up a church until he had agreed to make them a substantial annual payment.[95] By the same token, in Charlton Hundred, which had always been served by the bishop's establishment at Sonning, the monks had in their turn to submit to a fairly hard bargain in order to put up a church on a holding of theirs.[96]

I am inclined to think this right to exclude competing churches was a peculiar prerogative of the old minsters, one which the generality of hundred churches did not share. Later it became a general right, but just before and just after the Conquest so many new parishes were erected that it is hard to believe that they all had to buy off existing claims.[97]

D. Manorial Churches.

Contemporaneous with the rise and fall of the old minsters and the hundred churches was a continuous increase in the number of churches maintained by local landholders on their own estates. I have indicated that I believe these were regarded at first more as accommodations to the landholders than as adjuncts to the regular ministry. But gradually they came to play a more important part, and ultimately—say, at about the time of the Conquest —they came to dominate the local ecclesiastical scene.

Somewhere in the course of this development, there seems to have come a definite change in the juridical status of some of these churches. For in the late Anglo-Saxon period the maintenance of a church on his bookland was evidently regarded as one of the public duties of a thane.[98] I should suppose he acquired this duty in connection with the restructuring of the ministry on account of the depredations of the Danes.

There is a mysterious benefaction called the Donation of Ethelwulf, made by King Ethelwulf of Wessex, Alfred's father, in 855. It appears that, moved by some kind of religious consideration, he booked the tenth part of his lands to various of his thanes.[99] It would accord with the general tenor of administrative development in the period for him to have imposed on these thanes the duty to maintain churches on the land he gave them.

In any event, it was not every church on a private estate that was integrated into the public ministry in later times, but only that maintained by a thane on his bookland. The distinction is made clear in the passage of Edgar's laws where he reserves a portion for those churches out of his general grant of tithe to the old minsters:

> If, however, there is any thane who has on his bookland a church with which there is a graveyard, he is to pay the third part of his own tithes into his church. If anyone has a church with which there is no graveyard, he is then to pay to his priest from the nine parts what he chooses.[100]

The "nine parts" referred to here are of course what is left after the tenth part, or tithe, has been paid over to the church. The receipt of tithe, the burial of the dead, and a fixed source of income for the priest were all marks of the public ministry. If a church was under lay proprietorship, it could not have these unless the land was bookland and the proprietor a thane.

Edgar's legislation points up a possibility of conflict between the Germanic principle of nonaccountability and the canonical principle that a church could not be part of the public ministry unless there was a fixed source of income for the priest.[101] On the continent, a number of landholders seem to have carried the Germanic principle to the point of pocketing all ecclesiastical revenues beyond what they needed to hire a priest to do the work.[102] But there is no evidence for such a practice in England. The most the lay landholder could do was exact a fixed payment, or *servitium*, from the priest who occupied his church. This payment was sometimes fixed by custom—as is probably the case where the amount is set forth in Domesday Book—sometimes perhaps fixed by negotiation for a particular tenancy; at any rate, it was fixed.[103] Such payments came in as early as the eighth century, and were abolished, over some resistance, in the twelfth.

E. Eigenkirchen.

The foregoing analysis shows the variety of historical elements that went into the local articulation of the church in late Anglo-Saxon times. There were episcopal centers like Sonning that had endured from before the Danish invasions. There were old minsters, refounded under Edgar and provided with expanded cures, exercised in a variety of ways. There were churches established by the bishops in the period of the Danish invasions, with control either reserved or turned over to the incumbent priests. There were the hundred churches with their hide or half-hide endowments. There were the churches maintained by thanes on their bookland, with graveyards and allotments of tithe. There were churches maintained by other landholders, where the priest got anything (except tithe) his patron chose to give him.

In view of this variety, it seems inappropriate to say, as a number of historians have done, that in the period just before the Conquest all English churches were *Eigenkirchen*, that is, were someone's private property. This characterization of the situation, along with the term *Eigenkirche*, appears to have been introduced in Heinrich Boehmer's great essay *"Das Eigenkirchentum in England"*. Since then, it seems to have found general acceptance. It would be hard to find fault with Boehmer's broad and painstaking research, but I do think we can quarrel with the assumptions on which he has proceeded.

The most important of these assumptions is that because the parish church had a relatively consistent institutional character in the later Middle Ages it must have had a consistent development. Boehmer makes this assumption apparent when he brings churches belonging to the king, to the various lords, lay and clerical, to the diocesan bishop, and even to the incumbent priest, under the single head of *Eigenkirchen*. It is also apparent in his attempt to trace the history of the provisions for payment of services by churches to their lords in terms of general rules applicable to all churches at successive periods of time.[104] It seems to me, for reasons developed above, that the evidence does not support Boehmer in this assumption, but rather it indicates that differences of ownership at the time of the Conquest reflect wide variations in institutional history, and that some churches paid services from the eighth century till after the Conquest, whereas other churches never paid services at all.[105]

Further, it seems to me that the very concept of an *Eigenkirche* rests on an understanding of property that if it is not exclusively modern, at least did not come into England till after the Conquest. In view of the principle of nonaccountability, on which Boehmer himself places a good deal of stress, it cannot be meaningfully said that a church was or was not the "property" of the person who absorbed its revenues. All that can be said is that churches were put up by persons—kings, bishops, monasteries, or thanes—who had some official or delegated responsibility for providing the ministrations of religion. If such people went on to pocket all or part of the accompanying revenues, so did anyone who had a public function to perform. The imposition on this state of affairs of a unified pattern based on Roman and canonical conceptions of property was the work of the century after the Conquest, as we shall see in a later chapter.

It should be noted also that Boehmer's subsidiary conclusion that the development of the manorial church was accompanied by a virtual atrophy of diocesan authority[106] seems unwarranted by the evidence. We have nothing on the point from the period immediately preceding the Conquest, but both before and after that period there is evidence that the bishop had and used an effective control over the local exercise of the ministry. There is no reason to suppose that that control was displaced at any time by the rights of the local landholder or of anyone else.

IV. Conclusion

The Anglo-Saxons built their church organization out of the materials they had available. They found ways to absorb the hierarchical orders of the church into their own hierarchical social order. They made their devices for supporting the king's retainers into an effective economic base for a numerous ministry. They adapted their various expedients for local administration as patterns for the local development of the church.

In the resulting system, the traditional canonical structures of the church were overshadowed by a unitary church-state nexus in which, as Barlow says, "mixed forms seem general from top to bottom." King William and his continental churchmen dismantled the mixed juridical forms they found and brought the canonical structure back into the light. But measures like taking the bishops out of the hundred court or convening church councils separate from the witenagemot did nothing to alter the fundamental place of the church in the kingdom. The church never really broke out of the mold in which the Anglo-Saxons had cast it.

To begin with, the bishop never ceased to be one of the king's retainers. His early entree into that amorphous group who rendered the king counsel and received the king's gifts made inevitable his status under the Anglo-Normans as a lord of Parliament and magnate of the kingdom, with all the limitations that status imposed on his canonical powers and his ministry.

Also, the church's economic base was inextricably bound up with the complexities of land tenure. The primordial bookland with which the church was supported was not an outright ownership but a bundle of rights and correlative duties. Under the sophisticated feudalism of the Anglo-Norman state, these rights and duties became more complicated and more rigorously defined. The newly strengthened canonical authority had to operate in a maze of proprietary interests that were only partially under its control.

Nor did the clergy ever escape the economic and social stratification imposed by their early and complete absorption into Anglo-Saxon society. While the Norman landholder did not correct the morals of the local clergy, as Edgar had called on the tenth-century thane to do,[107] the local clergy in the later Middle Ages—and in the nineteenth century for that matter—were still more dependent on the local landholders than on the bishop.

Perhaps more important than any of these patterns is the way in which the patterns were regarded. The Anglo-Saxons left a most ambiguous set of precedents for the precedent-minded generations that followed them. From Henry II to Coke to the Archbishops' Committee on Church and State, English churchmen and historians have addressed themselves to questions like whether the Anglo-Saxons regarded the papal jurisdiction as *jure divino*, whether Anglo-Saxon kings freely appointed their bishops, and whether King William created the ecclesiastical courts. Questions of this kind have no real answers; they represent attempts to impose on the Anglo-Saxons the categories of a more sophisticated structure. The truth is that the nice juridical distinctions of the later Middle Ages were foreign to the Anglo-Saxon situation and probably were foreign to the Anglo-Saxon mind. The Anglo-Saxons had neither the sharp eye for principle of the Gregorian reformers nor the relentless administrative creativity of the Anglo-Norman kings. They left us the flesh and bones of a church state nexus, but the spirit was very different after the Conquest.

2.The Gregorian Reform

The Norman Conquest brought into England a movement for church reform that had been taking shape on the continent during the preceding half-century and more. This movement, called the Gregorian Reform after Pope Gregory VII (1073–85), who first shaped its elements into a common program,[1] envisaged a number of major institutional changes, rooted in ideology, but profound in their practical consequences. Each of these proposals had its own rationale, its own historical antecedents, and its own problems of making its way in the world, but all of them were united by a shaping vision of the church and its place in a Christian society.

The political and ideological history of the Gregorian movement is generally familiar, and most of it need not concern us here. In this chapter, I propose to consider the movement as a legislative program. In this capacity, it had a considerable effect but not quite the one its proponents had in mind. If we are to understand the subsequent operation of the laws and institutions of the church, we must understand what legislative goals the reformers wanted to achieve, what ones they in fact achieved, and why.

The program embraced two main areas of concern—personnel and economics—and a variety of peripheral areas of which I shall consider two. Within each area the reformers had a number of specific rules that they tried to put into force. I will try to show for as many as I can of these rules their origin, their rationale in the Gregorian ideology, and their ultimate fate, especially in England. At the end of the chapter, I will essay a general conclusion as to what the reformers were about.

This chapter is mainly concerned with the twelfth and thirteenth centuries. I find that the chronology of the reform and its effects follows a pattern that is to be discerned in the history of many if not most late medieval institutions: the main ideological foundation are laid down in the twelfth century, the basic institutional forms are established in the thirteenth, and the administrative routines are perfected in the fourteenth. So for the most part we are examining in this chapter a course of legislation that ends with the Fourth Lateran Council of 1215 and a set of institutional adjustments that ends with, say, the withdrawal of *Clericis Laicos* in 1306. We can be pretty sure that by the first date we know what the reformers will attempt to accomplish and by the second we know what they will succeed in accomplishing. Thereafter it is day-to-day administration that concerns us; we will cover it in later chapters.

I have departed from this chronological scheme in just two respects. First, the legatine mission of Cardinal Ottobuono in 1268 brought to England an unusually elaborate statement of the ideological formulations developed in the earlier period. I regard these elements in the cardinal's legislation as a pious reiteration of traditional ideals. Therefore, although they are not a part of the ideological creativity of the period before the 1215 council, I think they can provide evidence of the thought of that creative period.

Second, I have persistently reached into the early fourteenth century and, with greater caution, into the late fourteenth and the fifteenth for evidence of the practical results of the processes of reform. This seems necessary because the chronological distribution of the available records is not uniform, nor are there sufficient records to warrant the exclusion of any available evidence without good reason to discount its probative force. Also, the hypothesis that the institutions of the later medieval period develop along lines laid down in the thirteenth century seem well enough established to warrant a judicious use of the later evidence to evidence to indicate the forces at work in the earlier period.

I. The Clerical Estate

Basic to the reformers' program was a renewal of the freedom and dedication of the clergy. The greatest part of their legislation and propaganda was directed to this end. Underlying their different strictures on the subject, we can discern three main themes, or ways of understanding the place of the clergy in the church. First, there was a theme of *moral superiority*. The cleric was to be a better Christian than the layman. What was merely desirable for the layman would be compulsory for the cleric. Second, there was a theme of *special dedication*. The cleric was God's man, as the layman was the man of his feudal overlord. He was to be free of secular authority, and his time was to be taken up with God's affairs. Finally, there was a theme of *ritual purity*. As mediator of the covenant of salvation, and especially of Christ's bodily presence in the Eucharist, he was to be set apart rather as the priests and Levites of the Old Testament were.

The reformers drew on these three themes indiscriminately rather than separating them into analytically distinct principles. This eclecticism had unfortunate practical consequences. It made it difficult to offer the laity a standard of high Christian virtue free from elements of special dedication or ritual purity appropriate only to the clergy. It prevented any expression of the special dedication of the cleric in terms that distinguished the effectiveness of his ministry from his personal moral qualities.

Most important for our purposes, it prevented the establishment of priorities where the different themes gave conflicting guides to practical measures. Hence, the reformers had to leave important practical questions to be resolved by the pressure of social forces extraneous to their program. These forces, naturally enough, imposed fewer obstacles to ritual purity than to moral superiority or special dedication. Thus, during the period when ideological formulations were being translated into working rules, there was a constant drift toward emphasis on rules dependent on ritual purity at the expense of rules dependent on moral superiority or special dedication. We can see this drift in operation as we consider one by one the particular dispositions of the reform.

A. Rules of Personal Innocence.

The most important of these dispositions were aimed at defining clerical conduct in opposition to lay patterns of sex and violence. Scripture, the monastic tradition, the ascesis of the primitive church, and a miscellany of other elements combined to provide the content of these rules, while their theoretical base was made up of the three themes just discussed. Leaving aside rules directed against robbery, brawling, drunkenness or theft—vices that the reformers touch on from time to time and point out as even less becoming to the clergy than to the laity—we find four rules in this category that merit detailed treatment. The most important of these was celibacy, which the reformers regarded as the cornerstone of their structure.

1. Celibacy—Despite widespread breaches in practice, the principle that priests and deacons are not to marry was a very old one in the church.[2] All the reformers brought to it was a more systematic enforcement[3] and a more copious rhetoric. The three themes of ritual purity, moral superiority, and special dedication all find a place in the polemic they put together from the storehouse of the early church. Thus, Peter Damian, in a series of writings that may be taken as the opening gun of their campaign,[4] sets forth arguments in the category of ritual purity based on the Eucharist as an analogue of the Virgin Birth, reinforced by Old Testament examples of abstention from sex as a condition for participating in divine mysteries. In the category of moral superiority, he argues from the traditional conception (perhaps reinforced by monastic analogies) of virginity as a higher state than marriage. In the category of special dedication, he argues that the responsibilities of a family are inconsistent with a proper attention to the things of God.

While Damian, like all the reformers, interweaves the three themes, rather than distinguishing them, his approach is more unified, less merely eclectic, than we might suppose. He regards ritual purity as in fact inseparable from moral superiority and considers the special dedication incumbent on the priest at all times to be the same as that to which the layman must attain as often as he can. He develops, therefore, an integrated conception of clerical celibacy as a disposition, both affective and eucharistic, of the person toward God, one differing quantitatively, rather than qualitatively, from the disposition required of the ordinary Christian. But Damian does better at achieving an internally coherent doctrine than at giving a practical account of the place of clerical celibacy in the church. The conceptions he falls back on are at root monastic; they impose on the cleric a contemplative vocation that has little to do with his ministry.

The reformers in general do not distinguish between a priest or deacon who marries and one who keeps a mistress.[5] Damian does nothing about ceremonial marriage except to include it in a list of the lame excuses sometimes offered for incontinence. But the doctrine that priests and deacons cannot (rather than should not) marry was not at all as clear as Damian seems to have supposed. Gratian has nothing to offer on the point earlier than Alexander II (1061-73) or Callistus II (1119-24) and nothing fully explicit before the Second Lateran Council (1139). In the late eleventh century, Gregory VII's redoubtable and uxorious opponents, the Milanese clergy, certainly thought they were truly married; and over a century later, Moorman finds examples of married clergy put out of the ministry and told to support their wives rather than being left in the ministry and told to put them away.

At least in England, it was the thirteenth century that saw the final and decisive triumph of the principle of invalidity. As early as the first decade of that century, the secular courts were accepting the fact that a man's father was a priest as sufficient evidence that the man himself was a bastard. At least through the middle of the century there were still a few priests hardy enough to go through ceremonial marriages with the ladies of their choice, but it seems safe to say that there were no further significant attempts of this kind by the end of the century.

That the reformers could not do away with clerical incontinence as they did away with clerical marriage is a commonplace among historians of the subject, as, indeed, it was among medieval authors. Why, in view of this fact, they were unwilling to allow a legitimate outlet to forces they were clearly unable to hold in check has been a matter for considerable speculation. We too will have to consider the question, but it is so bound up with the overall objectives of the reform that we will do better to put it off to the end of the chapter, when we come to take up those overall objectives more at large.

2. *Legitimacy*[6]—The requirement that the candidate for holy orders be of

legitimate birth must have been suggested at an early date, because Gratian gives a number of patristic tests refuting it. It seems to have had some start as a canonical doctrine in France in the ninth century, but it did not make its way into the mainstream of ecclesiastical legislation till the last quarter of the eleventh. At that time it appeared in two forms. One (Poitiers, 1078) applies to sons of priests and others begotten by fornication; the other (Amalfi 1089) applies only to sons of priests. Gratian (ca. 1150) gives only the 1089 version and explains it away by limiting it to those sons of priests who imitate their fathers' vices. But it is the 1078 version that is picked up in the Second Lateran Council (1139) and in the Decretals of Gregory IX (1234). So the rule that finally prevailed was the 1078 one that excluded all illegitimates rather than just the sons of priests. It is in this inclusive form that Saint Thomas Aquinas understood the rule, which he attributed to considerations of ritual purity.

As the rule was directed primarily in one version, and exclusively in the other, at priests' sons, we may suppose it was originally conceived of as ancillary to the campaign for clerical celibacy. This supposition is borne out by the fact that the noncelibate clergy were in the habit of arranging ecclesiastical careers for their offspring and thereby perpetuating the scandal occasioned by their original misbehavior—a practice complained of long before the legislation in question came in. In moving away from this utilitarian base, and turning into a general principle of ritual purity, the rule followed a typical pattern of evolution.

3. Bigamy[7] – The rule excluding "bigami" or twice-married men from the ministry is supported by a firm patristic tradition, resting on tests of Saint Paul's. In the reform period it was generally applied to anyone involved in two or more successive valid marriages, to anyone who had attempted a marriage when bound by another, and to anyone who had married a woman not a virgin. In earlier periods, there had been a tendency to apply it also to a married man who took a mistress or who failed to repudiate an adulterous wife. It had also applied at one time to prevent the remarriage of a priest's widow.

As the relevant Pauline tests apply directly only to plural marriages of the would-be cleric himself, the various extrapolations concerning the purity of his spouse are presumably to be attributed to the corresponding provisions of the Old Testament concerning the marriage of priests. These provisions are relied on from time to time in the patristic texts. Also to be found in the patristic texts is the argument that the Christian priest should symbolize in his person the mystical union between Christ and the church, which is a union of one husband with one wife forever.

But among the fathers these arguments are secondary to those originating in a general mistrust of second marriages. The liberty of remarriage is conceded out of regard to human frailty; not all can contain themselves. But to raise to the clerical estate a man who has thus demonstrated his inability to contain himself is something else again.

When the reformers put this rule into their new synthesis, they kept only one of the three elements in the patristic rationale—the argument based on the priest's duty to show forth in his person the virginal union between Christ and the church. Neither the argument from remarriage as a concession to incontinence nor the argument from Old Testament analogies seems to have any place in their writings. What had become of the first argument is easy to guess: men were being ordained who had demonstrated their inability to contain themselves in less acceptable ways than by marrying twice. Why the Old Testament analogy was abandoned was less clear; perhaps it seemed too dependent on the hereditary character of the priesthood.

The sacramental rationale that monopolized the field among the reformers seems to originate in the same view of marriage as the moral rationale that held first place with the fathers. Both stem from a feeling that the perfect unity envisioned in the Pauline analogy of the union between Christ and the church is blemished in some way by a second marriage. It is this blemish that led the fathers to accord the liberty of remarriage to the laity only reluctantly and to the clergy not at all; and it is the same blemish that led to the view that the twice-married man or the husband of a widow failed to show forth in his person the fulness of the mystery involved.

Despite this common origin, however, the shift in emphasis between the two views is for our purposes significant. The earlier rationale, despite its symbolic origin, is formulated in terms of moral superiority, while the later is formulated in terms of ritual purity. In one case, the clergy are to live up to an ideal, and the laity are to be encouraged to do the same; in the other, the clergy are to embody a mystery in their persons and to be set apart from the laity by the fact.

4. Bloodshed and Blood Judgments—The ancient discipline of the church seems to have visited even justifiable homicide with a substantial penance— evidently lest the passions aroused by the occasion should have got out of hand and turned the mind of the killer from his just and rational purpose.[8] The imposition of this discipline on the laity continued as late as the Norman Conquest of England; the document prescribing the penance of King William's soldiers (who, it must be remembered, had the Pope's blessing for their venture) is preserved. It was evidently the Crusades that furnished the occasion for the abandonment of the ancient discipline as regards the laity.

In the case of the clergy, the rules regarding homicide were always more strict, and they continued after those affecting the laity were given up.[9] In the special treatment of the clergy, the three themes we have discerned in other areas crop up once again. The cleric is to be a better Christian than the layman; the passions involved in killing are even less appropriate to him than to the layman. Similarly, as mercy is a more excellent virtue than justice, it behooves the cleric to be merciful even where the layman may without censure be just. Also, the cleric is a soldier of God; even in a just cause, it is not his business to fight in the armies of men or with the weapons men use. Finally, there is a ritual purity theme: as Thomassin puts it, the Heavenly Lamb will not have his ministers shed any blood but his.

With the progress of medieval administration, this aspect of clerical discipline ceased to be a problem. The differentiation of roles between the soldier and the bureaucrat became fairly well fixed in secular society during the course of the twelfth century. The reformers' new emphasis on the exclusion of clerics from military service coincided with a growing need of the society for their services as a class of men specialized in bureaucratic functions.

The bureaucratic involvement of the clergy brought to the fore another aspect of the traditional discipline regarding homicide—the rule that forbade participation in the rendering or execution of a judicial sentence involving death or mutilation—the *judicium sanguinis*, or judgment of blood. This prohibition, which seems basically derived from the general discipline regarding homicide, relates also to rules excluding the clergy from the exercise of secular offices as such. When most of this latter class of rules succumbed to the pressure of the growing bureaucratic establishments of kings and secular magnates, the blood-judgment rule seems to have been enlisted to do duty for the rest.[10]

The Fourth Lateran Council of 1215 makes no provision at all on the subject of bureaucratic involvement but has the blood-judgment rule elaborately stated in connection with other rules on the subject of bloodshed—military service, duels, and the practice of surgery insofar as it involves procedures where cutting or burning is required.[11] The presence of this rule on surgery, which seems to have no canonical source earlier than the time of Innocent III and which has nothing in common with the other rules except the physical shedding of blood, suggests that the ritual purity theme has come to dominate the discipline on the subject of homicide or bloodshed. Not practicing surgrey would be hard to connect with exalting mercy over justice.

This body of strictures on sex and violence was no doubt intended to give the clergy a basis for a vigorous Christian challenge to the prevailing values of the licentious and violent age in which they lived. The drift toward emphases on ritual purity did a good deal to weaken the force of that challenge. So did the manner in which the reformers understood the alternative themes of moral superiority and special dedication. Their version of moral superiority was based on a primitive ascesis that either through social pressure or through despair, they had long ceased to urge seriously on the laity. Their special dedication in turn, was monastic in inspiration. It belonged to men set apart from the world to sanctify it by intercession, not to men with a special function in the world to sanctify it by exhortation and example.[12] The cleric aspiring to all the virtues the reformers proposed to him might have a powerful effect on the imaginations of his people but he would not have much of either guidance or example to give them in their daily lives.

B. Sumptuary Rules.

Even outside the essential areas of sex and violence, the reformers expected the cleric to show a certain detachment from the world's concerns. Here, though, the rules were of more subtle import and less passionate concern. Once again, the starting place was the ascesis of the primitive church, but the development was rather different. The influence of monastic analogues is less apparent in the early stages, and, in the later stages, ascetic or moral aims seem to give way to considerations of status or esprit de corps rather than to considerations of ritual purity.

1. Secular Employment—Buying things and selling them at a profit (*negotiatio* or *mercatura*) was considered morally marginal by a number of the Fathers, evidently because of the sharp practices it entailed.[13] Even if it could be carried on without sin, it was considered incompatible with the clerical state because it held out the possibility of inordinate wealth, which a cleric should not enjoy, or heavy losses, which he should not worry about. Various canons of the reform period duly forbade the clergy to engage in trade, but their tone does not indicate that the framers were dealing with a serious problem. In fact, there was nothing in medieval society that would have tended to lead the clergy into activities of this kind. The occasional violations that appear in the records were petty and agrarian affairs.

The prohibition of trade applied only to the buying and selling of goods without changing them. The cleric was free to support himself by any kind of productive labor, even if the product was to be sold. In fact, the tradition of the primitive church, following Saint Paul's example, encouraged him to do so.[14] But the practice did not fit in very well with the reformers' overall conception of the clerical state. Except for country clergy working their own lands, clerics seem not to have worked with their hands after the eleventh century. It is perhaps significant that the ability to work at a trade was not considered a sufficient means of support to constitute a title for ordination.

2. Secular Offices—A number of reform canons were aimed at checking the involvement of clergy in secular administration.[15] Many of these have precedents going back to the primitive church, though the blanket prohibition enacted in the Third Lateran Council (1179) of all exercise of secular jurisdiction as such, was new. These canons had only a feeble effect on the burgeoning bureaucratic structures of the time. In England, the obvious in-congruity of bishops serving as sheriffs was successfully opposed, but bishops continued to serve as chancellors and judges, with only perfunctory protest. The employment of lower clerics as chancery and exchequer clerks seems to have raised no official protest at all. Peter of Blois, (ca. 1139–ca. 1204), a writer of some influence though no official standing, did inveigh against the practice at one point, but even he eventually changed his mind. The fathers of the Fourth Lateran Council (1215) were content to let clerics work in secular courts as long as they did not participate in blood judgments. The English legatine synod of 1268 repeated the general prohibition in approxi-mately its 1179 form but added a proviso saving the rights of the king. There is no indication that other secular magnates paid any more attention to this prohibition than the kings had done to earlier ones from which they were not excepted.

The principle adopted to justify this wholesale departure from the rule against taking secular offices was one of charity; the cleric as the superior Christian is the man best fitted to bear rule in secular society, and secular society should not be deprived of his services.[16] In fact, however, as secular administration became more complex, it became apparent that not every superior Christian was qualified to do it. Since the recruitment for any posi-tion tends to be affected by the work the position entails, the ultimate ten-dency of these concessions regarding secular office was not to staff the secular bureaucracy with churchmen but to staff the church with secular bureaucrats.[17]

3. Sports and Amusements—By ancient tradition, the riches of the church were the patrimony of the poor and were not to be used to maintain the clergy on the social level of the rich. This principle worked in combination with more basic conceptions of sobriety and asceticism in producing strictures by which the early church attempted to exclude the clergy, and to some ex-tent the laity as well, from the more extravagent of the current diversions.[18] The broad principles had crystallized by the reform period into general con-demnations of rioting and drunkenness and specific rules against hunting, at-tendance at shows and dances, gambling, and visiting taverns or alehouses.

These four specific prohibitions are duly repeated during the reform period but with a good deal less urgency than is brought to bear on other rules. The only one requiring special mention is that concerning hunting, which touched on a major form of conspicuous consumption and thus met countervailing considerations of social status. It appears that the rule came off second best in the encounter. An important canonical enactment complains of hawks and hounds among the impressive retinues that the prelates found it necessary to carry with them on their visitations, at the expense of those visited.[19] Many who did not take them along seem to have kept them on their estates and sometimes to have enforced by ecclesiastical censures the hunting rights attached to such estates.

4. Clerical Dress—At the beginning of the reform period, the external appearance of the clergy was governed by two principles, each with a long tradition behind it.[20] First, in dress, as in other aspects of his deportment, the cleric was to set an example of modesty and sobriety to all. Second, he was to wear the tonsure, the distinctive cropping and shaving of the head that symbolized the special dedication of his state. During the period when the reform ideology was taking shape, these traditional principles were often reiterated and sometimes made more specific, but they do not appear to have undergone any fundamental change.

It does not appear that the maintenance of a habit whereby the cleric might be distinguished from the layman figured among the objectives of the program at this stage. The tonsure, to be sure, did in fact give the cleric a distinctive appearance, and he was expected not to hide it "as if he were ashamed that the inheritance of Christ had fallen to his lot."[21] Its primary purpose, however, appears to have been a symbolic and liturgical, not an external and visual, setting apart of the the cleric from the layman. As for the clothes of the cleric, it seems to be only by accident that they came to distinguish him from the layman. The canonists continued to demand in the name of sobriety the wearing of a full-length garment (similar to the modern cassock) long after such garments had gone out of style among the laity.[22]

By contrast, when we come to Ottobuono's English legatine canons of 1268, we find the canon on clerical dress so worded as to indicate that its primary purpose—and that an urgent one—is to make the cleric easily distinguishable from the layman. That canon, after comparing the improperly attired cleric to the man in the Gospel parable who was cast out of the feast for not having on a wedding garment, says that in his transgression:

> God seems to be mocked, the honor of the church is obscured, the loftiness of the clerical order is cast down, Christ, by His soldiers' wearing a strange livery, is deserted, and the respect with which the church is adorned is besmirched in that the eye of the observer cannot distinguish the cleric from the layman.[23]

It is obvious that in this language Ottobuono is drawing on typical themes of reform ideology to reach a principle that had not been reached in the formative period. It seems likely that it was a growing administrative necessity rather than a late intellectual development that led him to this principle. By the beginning of the thirteenth century, the growth of bureaucratic government, together with the crystallization of clerical privilege, had brought into existence a kind of semi-clerical riff-raff that was to plague both church and state throughout the Middle Ages, a class of men ready to claim either lay or clerical status as the occasion served.[24] This situation, of course, brought the whole clerical estate into disrepute, as well as being destructive of the esprit de corps that the reformers were trying to develop. Insistence on the continuous wearing of a distinctive habit was an important measure in insuring that the privileges of the clergy were not available to men who were not subject to the discipline of the clergy as well.

The thing to be noted about all these sumptuary rules is that they failed during the reform period to elicit either the intellectual coherence or the moral enthusiasm that the reformers brought to their rules concerning sex and violence. The rules in the present group were carried through the reform period without much change where there was no significant force at work against them; where there was such a force they tended to give way to it. It seems likely that the reasons for this situation are to be found in the administrative history of the time.

Peter Damian had sought to impose on the clergy the monastic ideal of poverty just as he had that of chastity;[25] this ideal, had it made the necessary headway in the reform movement, could have drawn together the scattered elements we have been considering into a vital and unified sumptuary doctrine for the clergy. The keystone, however, of monastic poverty is the common life, and during the vital early stages of the reform a powerful trend toward administrative decentralization was making the goal of a common life for the secular clergy more remote than ever before.[26] Also, the great administrators who held the most lucrative and conspicuous clerical posts were not in a position to implement the ideal of poverty even if they had been inclined to it. The age was one of pageantry, and its image of power was expressed in conspicuous consumption. The man in a position of authority had a "state" to keep up, and the reformers had no practical escape from this necessity to offer him even if he had wanted one.

Indeed, we may suspect that the attitude of the reformers themselves was marked by a certain ambivalence with regard to the sumptuary ideal. If the cleric is the Christian par excellence and the chosen representative of God, and if the aim is to bring all society under the dominion of God, then surely the cleric's access to power and the symbols of power is not all loss. The reformers, even as they called the cleric to a renewal of the Christian virtues of humility and meekness, did not fail to remind him that his vocation was to judge nations and rule over peoples.[27]

C. Rules in Aid of Independence.

To vindicate their conception of clerical dignity, the reformers sought to exclude the clergy from every form of dependence, real or nominal, on the laity. To this end, they marshaled old rules requiring title and free status for orders, excluding lay jurisdiction over the cleric's person, limiting the services a cleric could perform for his benefice, and forbidding him to fill secular offices. To these, they added new rules doing away with services for benefices entirely, forbidding a cleric to do homage to a layman or to receive any office or benefice at a layman's hands. It was the last of these that provided the subject of the familiar "investiture controversy."

Here again, it was where the program was most symbolic that it was most successful. Thus, lay investiture in the strict sense did indeed disappear from the scene not too long after the reformers began their attack on it, while other forms of lay influence over church appointments persisted to modern times. It was much the same with the other rules in this category: the principle was in most cases admitted, but the actual independence the reformers sought continued to elude their grasp.

1. Lay Jurisdiction—The rule that clergy were not to be subject to civil or criminal suit in a lay court was based on typical reform conceptions of their moral superiority and their status as servants of a higher power than the one that purported to judge them.[28] The lay authorities were naturally not much persuaded. The compromise that ultimately developed in England was that clerics were immune from lay persecution for felony but not for treason or for misdemeanors (noncapital offenses) and not from civil proceedings in the lay courts. Even this much was conceded the church more out of respect for the memory of Saint Thomas Becket than on account of the intrinsic logic of the case.

2. Free Status[29]—For obvious reasons, the Romans would not ordain a slave until he had been set free. Slavery in the Roman sense hardly existed in medieval times, but the reformers applied the same rule to the villein status that took its place. By the end of the twelfth century, they had made it impossible for a lord to have his villein ordained and then put him to work in a villein capacity—whether at the altar or in the fields. It was still possible, though, for a cleric who had not the personal status of a villein to hold land by villein services (usually working so many days in the lord's fields) and to perform the services in person.

3. Services—The reformers set out first to control, then to abolish, the imposition of services or feudal dues on ecclesiastical benefices in favor of laymen. Here again, they were formally, rather than substantively, successful. It does not appear that a cleric after the middle of the thirteenth century did service or paid rent for his benefice as such. On the other hand, clerics at every level had to perform services of one kind or another for specific lands with which their benefices were endowed. The familiar controversy over the duties of bishops as feudal tenants of the king was a high-level example of a situation that obtained at all levels. Indeed, where land was given purely for prayers and masses, there was a certain tendency to treat the prayers and masses as feudal dues and to enforce them by secular processes.[30]

So, the only important practical effect of the prohibition of rendering services for benefices was to keep the laity from sharing directly in tithes and offerings attached to the benefices in their gift. For the layman to bestow a benefice on a cleric he could rely on to serve him out of gratitude, blood ties, or the hope of further preferment was of course in no way forbidden by the reform legislation.[31] Indeed, it was the foundation of medieval managerial and bureaucratic establishments and made the right to present a cleric to a benefice a most important and valuable form of lay property.[32]

4. Employment as Layman's Agent—We have already seen that the general prohibition against the acceptance of public offices by the clergy became rather a dead letter. As regards comparable private offices—stewards, bailiffs, and the like—the prelates were still trying as late as the end of the thirteenth century. A set of English synodal statutes of 1295 seem to narrow the prohibition considerably in applying it only to offices carrying the obligation of giving an account to a layman, especially, the canon adds, to a layman apt to seize the goods of the church on this pretext.[33] The actual situation by the fourteenth century was evidently that the clergy did continue to accept such offices, but the goods of the church were protected against seizure.

5. Investiture, Homage, Fealty—It is of course well known that the reformers exerted their full force against any bishop or cleric receiving his ecclesiastical office at the hands of a layman. It is well known also that the ensuing struggle was finally settled by allowing him to receive his temporal holdings from a lay overlord, but requiring that he be invested with the symbols of his spiritual office by his bishop or ecclesiastical superior. Parallel to this struggle was an ancillary one over the rendering of homage or fealty, the formal acceptance of personal dependence that went with early feudalism.[34] It was considered improper for God's servant to be a layman's "man" and equally so for him to place his consecrated hands ceremonially between the unconsecrated hands of a layman, especially, one council adds, as the layman was apt to be an adulterer or a murderer or both.[35] But by the thirteenth century, this ceremony had become little more than a formality of land tenure. The Fourth Lateran Council (1215) contented itself with forbidding a cleric to swear fealty to a layman of whom he held no land.[36]

It should be noted that whatever the reformers accomplished with these rules was merely formal.[37] The abolition of investitures did nothing to diminish the layman's part in choosing the man to be invested, and the limitation of homage did nothing to prevent the real dependence of the cleric on the patron who employed him in his administrative staff and compensated him with benefices in his gift.

It seems, then, that much as the ideal of asceticism was pushed in the direction of an ideal of ritual purity, so the ideal of independence from the laity was pushed in the direction of a symbolic independence. This is not to say that the reform was illusory in this regard or the reformers hypocrites. Man lives by symbols, and a society that submits itself even symbolically to a transcendent ideal of this kind cannot but be profoundly affected. But the effect was a good deal different from what the reformers originally had in mind.

II. Temporal Support

The church's economic base claimed the reformers' attention only a little less urgently than did her personnel. The approach was generally similar. So also were the results. In each case, the reformers assumed a rigorous distinction between the things of this world and the things of God, and an equally rigorous identity between the latter and the things of the institutional church. In each case, they drew on the rules and institutions they found at hand and endeavored to reshape them as principles of sanctification and independence. In each case, the necessities of the times coupled with the molding of thought by contemporary secular analogies presented obstacles not well enough understood to be intelligently met. The results were generally profound in the realm of theory, spotty or equivocal in the realm of practice.

A. Simony.

High on the list of reform goals—perhaps just under the imposition of clerical celibacy—was an all-out attack on simony, a vice denounced by a long tradition firmly rooted in scripture. The strictures on the subject had been expanding in coverage for some time and in the hands of the reformers constituted an instrument for withdrawing the things of the spirit, with all their temporal ancillaries, from the commercial exchange that characterizes the economics of the world.[38]

Simony as such, unlike clerical marriage, seems to have had no voice raised in its defense. Nevertheless, its elimination was a more complex problem than mere reform of morals and correction of offenders. There were, to be sure, practices involving bribery or extortion in the strict sense, against which the reforming authorities were able to move unequivocally and with tolerable success.[39] But cases of this kind, important as they were, did not reach the heart of the problem presented by simony in the medieval church. That problem was basically that the financial structure of the church had developed in such a way as to belie the doctrine that salvation was the free gift of God. Upon this structure the reformers' abstract and perhaps oversimplified definitions of simony impinged with an uncertain effect.

There are two kinds of simony we can talk about. One, which I will call *professional*, occurs when the ministrations of religion are paid for like professional services. The other, which I will call *proprietary*, occurs when sacred things or offices are bought and sold like property.

We may suppose that there was a sort of underworld among the more ignorant elements in the medieval church—clergy and laity alike—in which clearly simoniacal practices in the professional category prevailed throughout the Middle Ages. In the tenth century, it may have been incantations over sick cattle, in the fourteenth, masses for the dead, and in the sixteenth, indulgences.[40] The orthodox doctrine did not condone the sin of simony in these matters, but the uninstructed are not always orthodox.

Supporting this undercurrent of venality and superstition is the perfectly respectable and scriptural doctrine that the priest is entitled to live by his priesthood, the cleric by his clergy. The Anglo-Saxons had given effect to this doctrine by providing their clergy with tithes, lands, and other fixed sources of revenue. But as medieval society developed, these revenues were diverted more and more from the working clergy in the parishes—a process we have already considered and will have occasion to consider again—leaving these clergy more and more in need of additional support.

In meeting this need, there were not many options available. Besides landed endowments, medieval administrative practice offered only two significant ways of compensating personal services. One was household residence, entailing support partly in money, mostly in kind. The other was what might be called *occasional payments—fees* in the modern sense—paid on the occasion of the performance of a given official act. As household residence required physical presence in the household, it was occasional payments that constituted the main supplementary source of income for officials who had to spend much time on their own.

Financing through occasional payments had great advantages for a system with limited fiscal resources. It afforded a rough measure of justice in apportioning the burdens of government to the benefits. It raised no problems of collecting money; an official had only to withhold his services until he was paid. Finally, officials supported by occasional payments, like officials supported by landed endowments, could do the work of a central authority without requiring any central fiscal administration; they had neither salaries to collect nor accounts to render.

It was quite natural, therefore, that the church should avail itself of this system of compensation. Voluntary offerings on the occasion of spiritual ministrations had become customary at least as early as the last days of the Roman Empire. Originally, there was probably no fixed amount, but the general medieval tendency toward the crystallization of customs must have given them a certain fixity and made them something less than voluntary. The ecclesiastical authorities for some centuries preceding the reform period had vacillated between prohibiting and regulating these payments. Finally, at the Fourth Lateran Council (1215), they settled for regulation.[41] The financial distress of the parish clergy, due to the division of landed revenues to non-parochial objects, was such that this source of revenue could hardly have been foregone: probably no prohibition of it would have been enforceable.

Regulation of occasional payments to the clergy took the form of limiting their amount and forbidding the withholding of the services as a means of enforcing the payment. It is the second point that is a direct consequence of the principle denouncing simony; its importance is made clear in the rationale offered by modern authors for the exaction of such payments. The duty to pay and the duty to perform the ministration, according to this rationale, arise independently out of the relation of priest and parishoner. As they are not reciprocal, there is no question of exchange, and therefore no question of simony. How early this modern analysis came in is questionable, but it is clear enough that (except in the rather late development of manual mass stipends, where there was no parochial relation) the priest was not supposed to refuse his ministrations even when the payment he was entitled to was not forthcoming. He was to perform the service, then he was to sue for the payment.

Surprisingly enough, the scant evidence seems to indicate a fairly high level of compliance with this prohibition. The administrative records and the protest literature do touch on the subject but very lightly indeed as compared with other topics of complaint. The canonical legislation in the area, prolific in the period preceding the Fourth Lateran Council, comes to an abrupt end not long after.

But if the rule laid down in the Fourth Lateran Council was by and large obeyed, we should note that it was the most lenient of the rules that had previously been contending for acceptance. We may wonder if the reformers would not have liked to take a firmer line if it had been possible, and we may wonder still more whether the theological subtlety of the medieval peasant was adequate to draw the requisite distinction between the charging of money for the ministrations of the church and the practice actually permitted.[42] In fine, it is doubtful whether the technical victory of the reformers over simony in this area served as a practical vindication of the principle that salvation is a free gift of God.

Turning to the category of cases I have called *proprietary*, we find an area in which the reformers exerted themselves with greater urgency, and, on the whole, with greater success. The most obvious case in this category, the purchase and sale of consecrated vessels, relics, and the like, seems not to have presented enough of a problem to engage the attention of the reformers. But they had a problem in the purchase and sale of ecclesiastical positions.

The opportunity for such purchases and sales inhered in the forms of tenure of ecclesiastical property as they existed at the time of the reform. The ultimate reduction of these forms of tenure to the parochial system of the later Middle Ages will have to be taken up separately, but it should be noted that the attack on simony was one of the weapons used in this reduction. The two matters reached in this way were, the outright purchase of the church by the priest or his relatives on his behalf and the practice of a priest introduced into a church by a patron or other proprietor rendering some kind of consideration out of the fruits of the church. Both of these abuses were the objects of a good deal of legislation during the reform period.[43] What success these particular items of legislation had can scarcely be determined in view of the sweeping changes in ecclesiastical tenure that took place during the period. We may say that they were a part of a generally successful campaign.

A related campaign that proved a good deal less successful was that against the farming of ecclesiastical revenues. This is the old sense of the word *farm*, a practice that became so prevalent in agriculture as to give the word its modern sense of agriculture as such. The farm in the old sense is an agreement whereby an uncertain or fluctuating source of revenue is let out for a fixed periodic payment. It has obvious advantages in that it allows the person to whom the revenues were originally assigned to devote himself to the task with which he was entrusted rather than to the task of collecting his pay. Thus, offerings and occasional payments were probably not farmed, but tithes and landed endowments were farmed regularly. The reform period produced a rash of legislation either forbidding this practice entirely or forbidding revenues to be farmed to laymen.[44] In at least one case simony is given as the reason for the prohibition. This simoniacal character of the practice does not leap to the mind, but two points may be suggested. First, the reformers had as part of their program the investment of tithe with a sacred character, as we shall see. This would call for characterizing as simony the letting out of tithe in exchange for a money payment. The psychological effect of the practice on the person paying the tithe would seem to justify such a view. Second, the early medieval moralists were generally slow to accept the assumption of a risk as something for which compensation might justly be paid, and risk was just the basis for the differential between what the farmer took in and what he paid out.

Be that as it may, the utility of the farming device was such that the efforts to suppress it proved unavailing. Ottobuono in 1268 contented himself with forbidding leases to laymen or leases of more than five years' duration,[45] but even this prohibition was not kept. The Year Books of the later Middle Ages are full of tithe suits by or against lay farmers.[46]

To sum up, it appears that the campaign against simony, like so many other elements in the reformers' program, suffered from a failure to relate effectively to the economic, social, and administrative conditions giving rise to the practices it sought to eliminate. Thus, the reform effort was most successful in the case of out-and-out bribery, where it corresponded with an obvious administrative necessity, and in the case of parish benefices, where it formed a part of a broad program of administrative reconstruction. In the case of farms the reform effort clashed directly with important social and economic interests, and it was by and large unsuccessful.[47] In the case of occasional payments, where the reform objective ran counter to important administrative necessities of the church itself, a compromise was reached—one which favored the reform objective more in theory, the administrative necessity more in practice.

B. *Benefices and Endowments.*

Related to the suppression of simony, and in some cases subsuming it, was an objective far broader in scope, one that the reformers pursued with far greater effect on the economic and social conditions of the time. That was distinguishing property set aside for the support of God's service from property devoted to profane use, bringing the former under ecclesiastical control. This objective was formulated at two levels: first, that of the complex of revenues and endowments attached to a given clerical position and second, that of the particular revenues that went to make up the complex.

On the first level, the principle was that the complex was to belong neither to the owner of the landed estate out of which it arose nor to the cleric who occupied the position, but to the position itself—in the canonist's terminology, the *benefice* was to be attached to the *office*. The rights of the landowner were to be reduced to those of the *patron* in the usage of the early church— mainly the presentation of a suitable cleric to be admitted to the office by the bishop.[48] The rights of the incumbent cleric were to be reduced to a tenure of the office in accordance with the applicable principles of ecclesiastical law.[49]

To this end, the patron was to be excluded from filling the office himself in the case of a priest, from filling it collectively in the case of a religious house or college of priests, from filling it through a hired priest in any case.[50] Nor was he to receive a share of the fruits—subject to some carefully worded exceptions in favor of a religious house or collegiate church.[51] Nor was he to install the incumbent himself; rather, he was to present him to the bishop.

Conversely, the incumbent was to be excluded from treating the office as his own property. He was not to buy it—here the attack on simony came in. He was not to inherit it.[52] He was not to enter it in any way without the approval of the bishop.[53] To make doubly sure he would not inherit it, the son of a cleric, even if legitimate and even if lawfully presented, was not to occupy his father's benefice unless someone else had occupied it in between.[54]

These aims were in general successfully achieved. In the case of monastic or collegiate patrons, the revenues were gradually recovered by the patrons through a process called *appropriation*, but that is another chapter. The hereditary benefice and the benefice listed as a holding of the incumbent in Domesday Book—important elements in the English ecclesiastical picture during the first part of the twelfth century—had disappeared by the thirteenth century. The performance by the incumbent of personal services for the patron persisted, as we have seen, but not in the form of a charge on the benefice or a property right of the patron.

Meanwhile, the particular types of revenue with which the different benefices were endowed provided the reformers with another level of concern. Of these, tithe was the one most effectively subjected to their program. Fortified by a venerable Christian tradition as well as by Old Testament precepts, it naturally assumed a central place in the quest for reform of the sources of revenue.[55] The campaign began with legislation in the late eleventh and early twelfth centuries aimed at recovering tithes from the hands of the laity. At Rome in 1078 it was enacted that the layman who possesses tithes is guilty of sacrilege and must desist on pain of eternal damnation. In other countries, notably King William's Normandy, the reformers contented themselves at first trying to exclude the laity from the one-third portion of tithe that traditionally belonged to the local priest. But after the 1078 Roman canon was repeated in the Second Lateran Council (1139), nothing more was heard of the less ambitious one-third rule. By the end of the thirteenth century, the principle that laymen were not to touch any tithes at all was so well established that the clergy could use it to limit royal custody of vacant abbeys.[56]

Parallel to this process was a fixing of the juridical status of tithe.[57] Its compulsory character was reiterated in an English council of 1127, and enforced in 1175 by excommunication. Such power as the tithepayer retained to choose what church would have his tithes was abolished by the end of the twelfth century. Meanwhile, in the land based economy, it became customary to think of tithe not as a duty of the individual Christian but as a charge on the land itself. As early as 1078, the Spaniards were claiming that it should be collected from lands owned by Jews. A series of decretals culminating in a canon of the Fourth Lateran Council (1215) made the landholder tithe on the gross, rather than the net, proceeds without deducting either his rent or his laborers' wages. The way tithes were collected in most places in England was that every tenth sheaf was counted off at the harvest, regardless of who gathered the harvest or who owned the land.

The first canon making it sacrilege to divert tithes from the church, the 1078-1139 one referred to above, takes a fairly modest theological stand: it simply points to a canonical tradition that these revenues were originally bestowed for religious purposes. A London council of 1127 developed a more ambitious rationale more in keeping with the developing legal form by treating tithe as God's feudal dues (*dominicae*) out of the land. This notion of divine lordship is carried onto a higher theological plane by the Fourth Lateran Council, which prefaces its legislation on the subject by saying: "Neither he who plants is anything nor he who waters, but God who bestows the increase."[58] Tithe, then, is a share of the increase given to God because God has bestowed it, and so it remains throughout the Middle Ages.

In the fourteenth century, this doctrine produced some interesting church-state conflicts in England. The laity, whatever they thought of the theology of the matter, were not willing in practice to pay any more tithe than had been customarily paid in the past. The clergy, following the logic of their doctrine, claimed as God's agents a radical tenth of the gross national product, regardless of any custom of paying less. There was a good deal of legal skirmishing on the point, in which the clergy seem to have had their way more often than not.[59]

As regards landed revenues other than tithe, the doctrine of the reformers was less fully articulated and the results less favorable. There was a long and durable tradition that lands given for religious purposes have God for their owner, which tradition was supplemented by a bid to have the disposition of such lands the exclusive business of the tribunals of the church. By the end of the thirteenth century, however, all this had come to naught, at least in England, and the lay courts were deciding land cases between priest and priest or between monk and bishop as readily as cases between layman and layman.

The developed medieval law recognized this state of affairs by distinguishing between landed interests of this kind, called *temporalities*, and such revenues as tithes, offerings, and occasional payments, called *spiritualties*. Not only were temporalities litigated over like layholdings, in great part they were taxed like layholdings. The policy in the thirteenth century had been to exclude church temporalities from the taxes levied by Parliament on the holdings of the laity (though they were taxed by Convocation), but at the end of the century it was decided that subsequent acquisitions would be included.[60]

In addition, the temporalities attached to bishoprics and religious houses
were considered fair game for royal seizures in the interest of coercing or punishing prelates. They were also taken in charge by the king's escheators during
vacancy of the episcopal or prelatical offices to which they were attached.

The ecclesiastical authorities attempted throughout the Middle Ages to bring
their temporalities far enough into the realm of the sacred to make anyone who
trespassed on them liable to ecclesiastical censures.[61] This attempt was resisted
from time to time as an encroachment on the royal courts of justice, although
there was never any very serious quarrel on the point.

The reformers' efforts in the field of finance, like their efforts in the field
of personnel, were dominated by their understanding of the sacred. They
sought to invest the church's whole economic base with something of the sacred
character of the institution it supported. To this end, they shaped the ancient
strictures against simony into a radical, if largely symbolic, distinction between the means of supporting the church and the means of supporting other
functions in society. They also invoked new conceptions of sacrilege to give
the fixed endowments of the church a sanction other forms of property did
not have. Finally, they claimed for the church through its own administrative
processes full control over the delineation and distribution of its means of
support. This control was intended not only to achieve the administrative independence of the church but also to set a seal on the radical separation of
the church's property from property given over to profane uses.

External opposition and internal attrition prevented this program from
being fully achieved. But it was achieved sufficiently to give commanding
stature in later medieval thought to the idea that somehow God as Lord Para-
mount of creation was entitled to levy a tribute and that this tribute was
properly collected by his chosen servants, the clergy, and dedicated to their
support.

III. The Peace of the Church

The reformers' major bid for a general effect on secular society was directed
at initiating the ruinous petty warfare and marauding characteristic of the early
part of the reform period. This warfare consisted in part of mere lawlessness
that weak central governments were in no position to prevent and in part of more
or less institutionalized practices of private vengeance that made up for the lack
of public prosecution of wrongdoers.[62] The characteristic efforts of secular law
on behalf of a more orderly state of affairs were, first, the system of wergilds

and compensation by which private vengeance might be bought off, and, second, the concepts of the peace of a king or great man, whereby certain persons, places, and times were removed in some measure from the realm of private war.

Into this framework, the church, integrating a number of traditional concerns introduced its own version of the peace. The idea of the peace, as borrowed from secular jurisprudence, lent itself to a tying in of this program with the other objectives of the reform in that it suggested less a making over of society in general than an extrication of certain persons, places, and times from the irremediable corruption of society in general.[63] This conception was reinforced by historical developments that put increased emphasis on the sacramental and liturgical aspects of the program at the expense of the practical.

A. Sanctuary.

The principle that certain holy places are to be places of refuge from violence and even from the ordinary course of criminal justice has both pagan and Old Testament roots. It became attached to the Christian churches from the time Christianity became an official religion in the Roman Empire. The original rationale of the institution is not clear, but we may suggest a combination of a vicarious inviolability derived from the presence of things divine with an idea of an appeal to a higher justice in the person of the deity.

Be that as it may, the basic principle of sanctuary found an obvious position among the institutions of the Germanic invaders of the Empire; it was the peace of God, that attached to his house, just as the king's peace attached to his.[64] Indeed, every free man seems to have been entitled to the peace of his own house, with a compensation for the breach of it according to his rank.[65] Thus, the ancient tradition fitted in nicely with the status of the church as a feudal landholder.

In this context, the church found a practical approach to its goal of mitigating the rigors of private warfare and a vindication of its role as a champion of mercy. The fugitive who took refuge in a church was to be delivered up, if his pursuers would take an oath to subject him to no penalty of life or member—in other words, to accept the wergild, or compensation, by which the blood feud could be bought off.[66] Thus the sanctuary of the church served a twofold purpose of mercy; the unjust marauder was deterred from his wicked purpose by the awe of the Divine Presence, and the seeker of just vengeance was brought to exalt mercy over justice and to make peace with his adversary.

In an age of disorder, then, the church had in the law of sanctuary a practical mitigation consonant with the legal system into which it was introduced and a graphic representation of the tranquility and good order of the things of God, as contrasted with the turbulence of secular society. This harmony between the purposes of church and state was lost when the secular rulers set themselves the serious task of general pacification through the machinery of criminal justice.[67] This event occurred in England during the Conqueror's time; it occurred throughout Christendom in the course of the ensuing century. This put a new cast on the right of sanctuary, as the churches became a refuge not for the victim of private warfare but for the felon fleeing from the increasingly effective processes of royal justice. In some cases, they became ultimately not only a refuge but a center from which he could sally forth for further depredations or a hostel in which he could live in comfort on his ill-gotten gains.[68]

This changed situation deprived the law of sanctuary of its utilitarian basis, and threw on the sacred character of the edifice the full burden of justifying the institution—and of justifying it not as an island of peace in a turbulent society but as an island of turbulence in a peaceful society. The burden was manfully assumed and evidently with a certain success. Procedures were developed and exceptions made, so that the right of sanctuary became only an inconvenience, rather than a stumbling-block, in the administration of criminal justice.[69] In this condition it remained throughout the Middle Ages—a form of reverence for the consecrated church, the Divine Presence, and the relics of the saints its breach a form of sacrilege related on the one hand to acts of criminal violence in the church, on the other to the putting of the church to uses lawful but profane.[70]

B. Protection of Clerics.

In the laws protecting the clergy against physical violence, the same two strands are to be discerned as in the law of sanctuary.[71] In the late Roman Empire, violence to the clergy was specially dealt with because it was a form of sacrilege, comparable to the invasion of the sacred precincts. In the Christian kingdoms of the Germanic invaders, violence to the clergy was specially dealt with because the punishment for every crime depended upon the rank of the victim. These two lines of approach appear in various juxtapositions in subsequent legislation.

The Penitentials reflect this disparity by shifting between treating the killing of a cleric as a form of homicide and treating it as a form of sacrilege, the latter approach predominating after the mid-ninth century. Gratian reflects the same disparity by juxtaposing a set of clerical wergilds evidently enacted by Charlemagne with a series of conciliar enactments on the subject whose central theme is sacrilege.[72]

Thus, while the clergy were always included in the conciliar enactments of the late eleventh and early twelfth centuries establishing the "Peace of God" for the benefit of noncombatants, they soon began to be protected also under canons that denounced violence to their persons as a form of sacrilege. Both types are represented in the canons of the Second Lateran Council of 1139.[73] Canon 11 is a definitive list of those entitled to the Peace of God, including all the clergy;

canon 15, beginning "si quis suadente diabolo hujus sacrilegii reatum incurrit . . .", incriminates those who lay violent hands on the clergy and adds a denunciation of breakers of sanctuary.

The pacification of society by the secular powers resolved the ambiguity between these two types of canonical provision by eliminating any general ecclesiastical enforcement of the peace. In the later Middle Ages, acts of violence to the clergy are treated in the canons only as sacrileges. All the material in the Decretals on the subject takes the form of interpretations of the canon "si quis . . ." .

In England, at least, the church continued to preserve throughout the Middle Ages a jurisdiction to punish this form of sacrilege, concurrent with the royal jurisdiction to punish the same act as a breach of the peace. The royal courts were careful to preserve their own jurisdiction by forbidding the church courts to impose any payment of compensation as part of the penance for the sacrilege.[74]

C. The Peace and Truce of God.

The church's most sweeping mitigation of the practice of private warfare, the peace and truce of God,[75] seems never to have been in effect in England—perhaps because the secular government was never sufficiently ineffective to make it necessary. It deserves some notice, though, as it shows the underlying principles of the pacification program in their fullest elaboration. It consisted of two parts. The truce of God, a kind of hypertrophied Sunday observance, excluded all forms of private warfare from Thursday through Sunday and often in sacred seasons such as Advent, Lent, or Paschaltide. The peace of God extended to certain persons all the time. It came to cover not only the clergy, pilgrims, and other church personnel, but the entire female sex, all the poor and unbefriended, all merchants, travelers, and peaceful tillers of the soil—in short, all those unable to compete on equal terms in the prevailing forms of warfare.

This whole formulation, like that of sanctuary, fitted in very well with the prevailing understanding of the peace in the Germanic law. The king's peace under the Anglo-Saxons was universal at specific times—the week of his coronation and the three times a year when he held court. The extension of the peace to designated persons had also its secular counterpart. It was quite usual for the king's peace to extend to his servants as well as to persons he had taken into it by specific order. This gives the analogous taking of the unbefriended into God's peace a rather attractive theological foundation. Whoever does not belong to anyone else belongs to God; whoever does not have anyone else to protect him has God for his protector.

This whole program of pacification is particularly instructive in that it gives us an important insight into the historical dynamic of the entire reform.

We see here the church faced with an entirely practical problem presented by a serious gap in the institutions of secular society. The clergy moved into the gap with a good deal of reluctance; they were not unaware that the province they occupied was more rightly Caesar's.[76] Having determined to deal with the problem, they drew wisely enough both on their own traditions and on the models presented by secular law. The king's peace extends to persons, places, and times; God's peace shall do the same.

But not as the world gives does God give his peace. Underlying all these institutions of the church we may discern a certain reproach to the world and its ways, a certain sense that the earthly sanctuary, the earthly protection of the poor, are but signs of the true sanctuary, the true refuge, a surer protection against a deadlier wrath to come. It is here that this program relates to the sense of the sacred that permeates the other aspects of the reform. And it is here that the vestiges of the program abide when the practical purpose has come to be better served in other ways.

IV. Ecclesiastical Jurisdiction

Expanding the jurisdiction of the ecclesiastical courts was not, as such, an objective of the reform. But the general reshaping of the church's interests necessarily entailed putting forward jurisdictional claims. Until the time of Innocent III, these claims seem to have been based on a rather simplistic combination of three assumptions. First, it was assumed, reasonably enough, that the jurisdiction of the church was generally delineated by the objects of the church's concern.[77] The second assumption was the general Germanic one that jurisdiction is a form of property and a form of distinction, so that one whose jurisdiction is invaded is both despoiled and dishonored. Thus, when the jurisdiction of the church is invaded, God is despoiled and dishonored. Finally, there was an assumption that the whole church-state complex formed a single judicial system, despite the very different aims of the two authorities. This is why the prelates resisted having a cleric brought to book in both courts for the same offense or having a layman be a bastard in one court and legitimate in the other.[78]

Innocent III, working with the same assumptions, plus one or two additional texts of scripture, produced a more sweeping set of claims for church jurisdiction. His root principle was that the church, through its concern for the poor and unbefriended, through its concern with sin in general, through its concern for justice itself, should stand behind the authority of kings and princes and give a remedy wherever the latter failed.[79] This broad principle as Innocent stated it had more importance for political theory than for practical administration. It was never embraced by anyone in a position to give it effect. But it probably did play some part in supporting the church's assumption of particular government functions—different ones in different countries—that might more logically have gone to the state.

The specific jurisdictional claims made by the reformers on the basis of their general principles can be divided into two categories. In one category fall those claims that were ancillary to the structure of personnel and revenues as the reformers envisaged it; in the other fall those claims that constitute independent manifestations of power in areas of ecclesiastical concern.

The claims in the first category have already been dealt with in passing. They consisted for the most part of claims to exclusive jurisdiction over the persons of the clergy and over the disposition of the property and revenues of the church. As to the persons of the clergy, the exclusive jurisdiction was allowed in England only in cases of felony, although it extended to some civil cases on the continent. As to property and revenues, the claim to ecclesiastical jurisdiction seems to have been accepted by the lay authorities only to the extent that the sacred character of the property and revenues themselves was accepted. Places and things directly set apart for divine service—churches, churchyards, sacred vessels, and the like—were subjected to ecclesiastical jurisdiction without difficulty. Tithe and occasional payments were generally subject to ecclesiastical jurisdiction, but during the fourteenth century the ecclesiastical proceedings were subjected to increasingly jealous review by the temporal courts. In the case of temporalities, the claim to ecclesiastical jurisdiction was asserted but not recognized. The important area of patronage rights—the right to present a cleric to occupy an ecclesiastical benefice—was claimed for the ecclesiastical jurisdiction as something inseparably annexed to a spiritual object. The lay authorities insisted, however, that such rights were a form of secular property with which the ecclesiastical authorities were not to meddle. The exclusion of ecclesiastical jurisdiction from this area was a holdover from an earlier period of proprietary churches, and England was unique in maintaining it.[80]

Turning to the second category of ecclesiastical claims—those that were independent of the structure of personnel and revenues—we find a variety of areas in which the ecclesiastical jurisdiction was actually allowed to operate. The two most important are marriage and testament. These continued to be dealt with by the ecclesiastical courts until 1857, when a secular court was created to take them over.[81] Marriage, by reason of its sacramental status, had long been a subject of ecclesiastical jurisdiction, and the lay authorities made no difficulty about its remaining so, although some of its incidents were held justiciable in the temporal courts. The origin of ecclesiastical jurisdiction over testamentary matters is obscure, but it is generally considered to be related in some way to the distribution of alms for the repose of the soul of the decedent. Only in England did the church succeed in maintaining exclusive jurisdiction in this area.

The general claim of the church to hear the causes of the poor and unbefriended was never recognized in England, nor was the general claim to proceed
in default of secular justice. The general claim to deal with all matters of sin
may have had some effect on actual practice in such areas as defamation, usury,
sexual offenses, and perjury, or breach of faith (*fidei laesio*). In all of these, the
church courts were quite active throughout the Middle Ages. The last of these,
fidei laesio, was used to give the church courts jurisdiction over a wide range
of contractual obligations.[82] In this case, the lay courts had a remedy available
to the plaintiff and did their best to prevent him from proceeding in the church
courts. In the other cases, they recognized the ecclesiastical jurisdiction, but
they attempted to limit the church court to imposing penance on the sinner
rather than giving money judgments in favor of the person wronged.

Where the ecclesiastical and secular jurisdictions impinged on one another,
neither system was prepared in principle to give way to a jurisdictional determination by the other.[83] In practice, the drawing of lines between the two jurisdictions passed more or less by default to the lay courts as having the more
aggressive judges and the more efficacious procedures. In the mid-thirteenth
century, the use by the royal courts of their writ of prohibition to restrict
the ecclesiastical courts was anathemized, but by the end of the century it had
become a matter of course.

The broad jurisdictional claims of the reformers were never abandoned on
paper. They were probably given effect in practice as well unless a writ of prohibition was actually served in a particular case. Presumably the proctors who
represented defendants in the ecclesiastical courts did not consider it their
duty to advise their clients to seek prohibitions. Also, some defendants were
too poor to seek royal writs.[84] Others probably thought they would fare as
well in a church court as in a lay. In any event, some ecclesiastical courts continued to do a brisk business in certain types of cases that would have been
prohibited by the lay courts had prohibition been sought.[85] But all this belongs
to the realm of administrative adjustments and has little to do with the general
objects of the reform.

In the course of the twelfth century, the ecclesiastical jurisdiction began to
be beset by unseemly and debilitating internecine squabbles which culminated
in the patchwork of exemptions and limitations characteristic of the later
Middle Ages. This was in part due to the system of occasional payments that
made jurisdiction a benefit to those exercising it and a burden to those subject to it.[86] It was due in part also, it seems, to a fragmentation of the sacred
character that the reformers sought to impart to all the manifestations of the
church. For the honor of a patron saint or a local church, even prelates relatively immune to the allurements of venality were led to dissipate their energies
in resisting exercises of jurisdiction[87] or in quarrels like that over the claim of
the Archbishop of York to have his cross borne before him in Canterbury

province. Nor, as we shall see, was the central authority of the papacy able to develop techniques for filling effectively the vacuum in local administration caused by these disputes and the resolution of them.

Within this inauspicious framework, some local ecclesiastical courts—notably, the metropolitan court of Canterbury—were able to develop effective techniques for handling certain types of business, but ecclesiastical jurisdiction as a whole did not emerge from the reform period as an effective administrative adjunct to the general purposes of the church. Rather, it took its place at isolated points in the general administrative structure of society. Its development responded to the felt needs of secular government rather than to the policies or aspirations of the reformers.

V. Conclusion—Utility and Vision

If we examine the reformers' work from a utilitarian standpoint—how well it accomplished specific effects on the general working of society—it will obviously not hold up very well. We have seen how many elements in the program were whittled down in practice to something merely formal—from a utilitarian standpoint, to nothing at all. The reformers gave form in their enactments to a structure set apart from all other structures of society—a ritually purified priesthood, consecrated endowment, a sacred jurisdiction. But every bid they made to have that structure permeate the whole of society was tentative, inchoate, beaten back with hardly more than a skirmish, or met with a compromise that left the form of what they sought without the substance.

Some historians, imbued with a utilitarian bias, have saved the reformers from the implied judgment of utter failure by endowing them in retrospect with some object in keeping with the practical results of what they did. But these interpretations are generally inconsistent with the available evidence as to what society was really like or as to what the reformers were really about. Take, for instance, the idea, popular until quite recently with Catholic apologists, that the rule of celibacy served to enable a priest to devote himself full time to his ministry.[88] In fact, as far as one can see, the average medieval priest spent less time on his ministry than the average medieval shoemaker spent making shoes. There were many priests, as we shall see in another chapter, who did not have enough to do to keep them out of mischief. Moreover, this "full-time-job" theory cannot explain the key position of celibacy in the reformers' program. They fought tooth and nail for it, whereas they put up little fight or no fight at all against other practices that interfered with the ministry far more than the care of a family would have done.

A more formidable utilitarian theory, still influential today, is Dean Milman's to the effect that the drive for clerical celibacy was a successful attempt to free the church from the burgeoning structure of hereditary classes and officeholders that was in the process of taking over lay society.[89] It is true that the reformers were opposed to the inheritance of benefices, and it is true that celibacy prevented benefices from being inheritable; but the texts offer no encouragement at all to the idea that the campaign for celibacy was mounted with that in mind. The canons on the two subjects are by and large unconnected, and those on inheritance elicit far less emphasis than those on celibacy.

Moreover, the general administrative history of the time indicates that doing away with inheritances cannot have been a utilitarian goal because all the utilitarian considerations were pointing the other way. Hereditary classes and hereditary offices were developing because they answered important administrative needs in that period of rudimentary government.[90] They afforded a certain continuity of policy without formal institutions for training a new generation of officials. They afforded an undisputed succession when central authority was too weak to resolve disputes. They afforded a succession immune to political influence at a time when political influence was apt to be both violent and corrupt. The church suffered a good deal in this early medieval period from having no alternative ways of achieving these results. The problems of protracted vacancies, simony, ignorance, and the dependence of parish priests on lay patrons would all have been much less severe if church benefices had become hereditary. Indeed, there is evidence that when the campaign for celibacy was strongest the best parish priests in England were married men occupying the places their fathers had before them.[91]

Lea adopts a different utilitarian theory, one that has had a good deal of vogue ever since the Reformation. That is that the whole apparatus of ritual purity, with celibacy at its head, was aimed at enhancing the power and influence of the clerical order in the whole society.[92] The most obvious vice in this theory is that its proponents, Reformation polemicists and nineteenth-century historians alike, greatly exaggerate the amount of power and influence the medieval clergy actually achieved. We now realize that an age when everyone was Catholic was not necessarily one in which everyone thought like Pius IX.

Furthermore, the relative values the reformers put on the different elements in their program, and the character of the compromises they were willing to accept indicate that the achievement of power and influence were secondary considerations for them. They suffered exile rather than allow a king to invest a bishop with his ring and pastoral staff, but they offered only token resistance to his effective control over the choice of the man to be invested. They were ready to die rather than allow a felonious cleric to be tried in a lay court, but they complained only perfunctorily when the lay courts took control of the whole business of the church courts through their writs of prohibition. In case after case we find that it is just in the area of power and influence that they were most ready to give ground in the face of lay opposition. We could deal with other utilitarian interpretations in the same way. We could take, for instance, the theory that the struggle against lay investiture was an attempt to free the clergy from a lay domination that interfered with the reforming of abuses in the church, and show (a) that the doing away with investiture did not do away with lay domination, and (b) that lay domination did not interfere with the reforming of abuses—but there is no need to belabor the point by multiplying examples. There is simply no support for attributing a utilitarian goal to any major aspect of the reformers' program.

Even where practical purposes were stated and achieved—keeping the laity out of tithes, replacing compulsory taxation of the clergy with voluntary offerings to the state,[93] asserting episcopal control over the pastorate, and protecting the parish priest against competition by other clergy[94]—we find fanciful or at least metaphorical purposes stated with the same seriousness as practical ones. A parish priest should not be retained at an annual price because he will have no regard for the eternal reward.[95] Those who enter benefices uncanonically are thieves and robbers because they have not entered the sheepfold by the door.[96] Whenever we start to look at the reform in terms of obvious utilitarian goals like money, power, influence, an effective ministry, or the effective Christianization of society, we are apt to be brought up sharply against evidence that the reformers were at least equally interested in something else.

Nowhere is this more apparent than in the case of clerical marriage. It was as obvious to the reformers as it is to us that forbidding the clergy to marry was driving great numbers of them into fornication. Given the way in which they were recruited, employed, and paid, it could hardly have been otherwise. The relative effectiveness of celibacy in modern times has depended on a social structure in which the Catholic priesthood has no particular attraction for anyone who is not disposed to live up to the obligation it entails. In the Middle Ages, on the other hand, it was the usual means of entry upon a successful academic or civil service career and was required for access to the church preferment with which most academic or government service was compensated. Thus the clerical state held out powerful attractions for men who had no spiritual preparation for the requirement of celibacy and no intention of living up to it. It was not surprising that such men entered into illicit unions when licit ones were denied them.

The reformers, as I say, were quite aware of the problem. But they were unwilling to take either of the possible steps for meeting it—allowing the priest to marry or altering his position in society so as not to attract men who were not willing to make a great sacrifice for a purely spiritual end. Rather, they met the problem by a stress on personal moral responsibility, characterized

by strictures against lust and the insistence that continence is possible for anyone who will earnestly seek the necessary grace.[97] The problem of recruitment,
when it was brought to their attention, they met by comparable strictures
against avarice.[98]

But the nonutilitarian commitment of the reformers goes a good deal deeper
than any tendency to meet practical problems with idealized formulas. One
cannot examine the ethos of the whole program without taking away the impression that, scandalized as they were by clerical incontinence, they considered
clerical marriage a much more serious breach of the principle they had in mind.
Fornication is a sin that can be wiped out by penance, but marriage is a state
with permanent significance in the eyes of God.[99] In the reformers' dominant
vision of ritual purity, the formal, sacramental dedication to sex bulks larger
than any informal substantive indulgence in it. It is this valuing of form as
much as or more than substance that poses in all the areas we have been considering the most basic question of what the reformers were about.

An analysis that offers some promise of a solution is that of Tellenbach,
who sees the dominant conception in the formative stage of the reform ideology as that of the "liberty" of the church—liberty being understood to mean
its proper place in the hierarchical structure of society or perhaps of Creation.[100]
This, it should be noted, is not a utilitarian goal. While it looks to an institutional structuring of power and authority, it does not seek to structure them
in such a way as to achieve an effect on society; it seeks to structure them in
the way that they ought, a priori, to be structured.[101]

Tellenbach's analysis is persuasive in that it accounts for the record of symbolic triumphs and practical defeats that characterized the efforts of the reformers to implement their program. The a priori structural commitment to
the liberty of the church gives no basis for determining in practice where to
compromise and where to draw the line; nor does it give any ground for pre-
ferring practical results to symbolic recognitions.

Such a conception of the liberty of the church gives full scope to the idea
of the sacred that permeated the reformers' program—the idea of things and
persons ritually set apart for the service of God. In the ideology of the reformers,
the high place in society whose occupancy constitutes the liberty of the church
belongs to the church because of the intimacy with which it mirrors in its forms
and structures the ineffable presence of God. This puts at the very heart of
the reform an exaltation of the symbolic over the practical. It is the symbolism
whereby God, whom the heavens of heavens cannot contain, has deigned to
make his dwelling in a tabernacle made by hands.

It is under symbolic forms of this kind that we must look for the underlying
ethos of the reform program. Following the role of Christ as mediator between
God and men, the reformers sought first to commend their world to God
through building His tabernacle in its midst and second to make of the dwelling-

place of God a place to which men, surfeited with the anarchy and violence of the age, could lift up their eyes and hearts.[102]

In the ensuing chapters, I shall apply to the recurring impetus toward structures like those envisioned, and in part achieved, by the reformers the epithet coined for latter-day Anglican examples of the same impetus—High Church.[103] The impetus thus denoted eludes conventional definition because it is a party position rather than a body of doctrine, a direction in which its proponents seek to move rather than an ultimate goal they seek at all times to achieve. I defined High Churchmanship generally in the Introduction as a tendency to institutionalize the elements of transcendence and withdrawal in Christianity. More specifically, we can think of it for present purposes as a stress on the institutional church as a vehicle for honoring God—a tendency to see God's honor as heavily bound up in that of his institutional representatives.

There are elements of historical continuity, I suspect, between this tendency in the period we are now considering and the High Church movements in seventeenth- and nineteenth-century Anglicanism. Even if this were not the case, the different manifestations have sufficient similarities and sufficient roots in the same interpretation of the basic Christian revelation to warrant calling them by the same name.

Among Anglicans, High Churchmanship is generally associated with what is called a "high" doctrine of the sacraments—that is, a stress on their inherent supernatural efficacy. Some development in sacramental doctrine along similar lines seems to have accompanied the movements we have just been considering. It was a favorite polemical device at one time to attribute this correlation to the support given the claims of the clergy by the unique privilege of the priest in offering the Eucharist. There is a certain germ of truth in this view, but actually the matter seems to go a good deal deeper than that. It would seem that the High Church approach to ecclesiastical polity has affinities for sacramental and liturgical—as distinguished from evangelical and personal—piety because it aims basically at a sacramental and liturgical polity. It looks to the institutional church as a *sign* of the presence of God as the sacraments are. It looks to our maintenance of the institutional church as a corporate act of worship offered to God as the liturgy is.

At least in the seventeenth century, Anglican High Churchmanship was also associated with a "high" doctrine of monarchy—an acceptance of the divine right of kings. The Gregorian reformers we have been considering did not, of course, accept such doctrines. Either they assigned the king a safely subordinate place in the divinely ordered hierarchy, or they limited his sway to the things that are Caesar's, excluding him entirely from the things that are God's. The one approach seems as High Church as the other. The seventeenth-century High Churchman, being committed to the Royal Supremacy, naturally sought to relate that supremacy to the sacred character of the king. Similarly, in the period of the Gregorian reform, some effort was made on the continent to make theological kingship into a High Church alternative to Gregorianism. But in England this kind of theological kingship was never much more than an academic doctrine until the Reformation. The practical resistance of the English to Gregorianism was mounted in the name of the king as head of the community, not as vicegerent of God[104]—the approach I characterized in the Introduction as Erastian. High Churchmanship in England was left to the Gregorians.

If in what follows I have occasion to be critical of the High Church tendency, it is not at all by way of condemning it out of hand. That tendency stresses an important aspect of the corporate life of Christians, an aspect which any form of that life must take into account. It must be pointed out, however, that an emphasis on that aspect to the exclusion of others equally important may be dangerous, and in the Middle Ages, it was disastrous.

In any event, let us note that the reformers we have been considering were High Churchmen in that their reform was an enhancement of the status and articulation of the institutional church among the institutions of society. Under their hands, the institutional church, set apart by a vast structure of juridical defenses from the cruel and violent world of men who shed blood and had to do with women, was to stand in that world but not of it, an island of peace, a fountain of mercy, a haven of safety, a towering witness to the sovereignty of God.[105]

We must now consider with what juridical tools these men set out to construct their tabernacle in the wilderness and what they made of it administratively.

3. The Canon Law

The Gregorian ideal was given legal expression through the church's own legal system, the canon law. This system, originating in the primitive church, was completely recast in the twelfth and thirteenth centuries. The scholars and prelates who accomplished the great work of recasting it brought to their task a highly developed set of value commitments—the whole ethos of the Gregorian reform. By contrast, they had only a meager supply of administrative resources. The system they developed out of this combination of materials had a profound effect on the subsequent history of the church.

I will attempt here to give some account of the basic character and typical problem-solving techniques of the medieval canon law as thus developed. To this end, I have tried to construct afresh the appropriate categories of analysis for dealing with the system. Consequently, I have dealt as much as possible with the raw data of legislative and administrative practice in isolation from the analytical framework with which the system was approached by its own proponents. It is possible that a fuller treatment of the subject along similar lines would require assigning a larger role to the work of the commentators who played so large a part in the systematic elaboration of the canons. I have neglected them because my object is in a sense to stand in their shoes and substitute my analysis for theirs.

I. Content

The canon law may be characterized as Christian theology structured by Roman law and brought to bear on the institutional necessities of the Church. The juxtaposition of these three elements—Christian theology, Roman law, and institutional necessity—provides the content of the system, and the tension among them provides the problematic of the system. Let us consider

This chapter was originally published as "The Canon Law as a Legal System —Function, Obligation, and Sanctions," *Natural Law Forum* (now called *American Journal of Jurisprudence*) ix (1964), 45–94.

briefly the contribution of each of these elements to the content, then turn to what seem to me the three most serious problems raised by the tension among them—the problems of function, of obligation, and of sanction.

A. Christian Theology

Theology furnished the root principles of the system[1] —the means of salvation and the corporate and juridical character of the Christian people to whom and through whom the means of salvation were revealed. In addition, it afforded the rudimentary structural elements—the orders of the clergy, the primacy of the Roman pontiff, the claims of the Church to competence over against the state. Much of the substantive content was also theological. The celibacy of the clergy, the indissolubility of marriage, the suppression of simony are examples; all of them, although they are developed in legal enactments, were in origin developments of scriptural or doctrinal themes. Spiritual and pastoral experience added other theological elements to the substantive content, such as the form of electing bishops or the payment of tithes.[2] Much of this material has been taken up in the previous chapter.

In addition to these substantive elements, theology contributed at more than one level to the procedural development of the system. The basic sanction of excommunication was derived from the scriptural attribution of the power of the keys. At another level, the principle that requires a hearing before the sentence of excommunication can be pronounced was formulated with scriptural justifications.[3] At still another level, the late technical development of the *denunciatio evangelica,* whereby a remedy was afforded for private wrongs, was derived directly from the Lord's admonition to "tell the Church" (Matt. 18:15–18).[4]

B. Roman Law.

While the canonists drew freely on the store of rules and terminology afforded by contemporary Roman law scholarship,[5] the major contribution of the Roman law to the canonical system was its structure. It was to the Roman law that the canonists looked for the forms and categories of legal analysis. Their descriptions of how the law operates, their theoretical speculations on the nature of the law, their manner of classifying legal enactments as to subject matter or source were all taken directly or indirectly from the Roman jurists.[6] The great codifications that make up the Corpus Juris Canonici were patterned on those that make up the Corpus Juris Civilis. Perhaps most important of all, the crucial theological principle of the primacy of the pope was given its juridical form of the *plenitudo potestatis* through the analogy of the place of the emperor in the Roman law.[7]

C. The Institutional Necessities of the Church.

The institutional necessities on which this legal system was brought to bear were in great part the simple housekeeping ones of allocating the available personnel and resources to the task at hand. The development of benefices and parishes, the rules against wandering from one diocese to another, and the rules regarding moral and intellectual qualifications for ordination are examples of principles developed to meet these housekeeping needs.

Over and above these, there was the necessity of maintaining both the material resources and the prestige of the institutional church as against the other institutions of society. Much of the legislation we considered in the previous chapter was directed in one way or another to this purpose.

Finally, an institutional necessity at once more subtle and more fundamental than these others imparted to the canonical system a certain subsurface dynamism uniquely its own. That was the necessity, inherent in the nature of the church, of maintaining at once a corporate witness and a personal apostolate. It is to this necessity that we owe, on the one hand, the existence of the canon law in the first place and, on the other hand, its often excruciating failure to live up to one or another of the criteria we set for a secular legal system. There must be a canon law because the church is an institution, the new Israel, gathered by a corporate reception of the Word. An institution must be governed, and a people must have its laws; government cannot be arbitrary, nor can laws be unjust. At the same time, the rule of law as secular jurisprudence conceives it—a government of laws and not of men—cannot be fully implemented in the church because Christ has entrusted his message to men and not to laws. We cannot expect to see clearly defined limits of authority because it is man to man, whole man to whole man, that the word of God must be proclaimed.

The dynamism imparted to the system by this twofold necessity was not articulated by the medieval canonist, nor was it found in the materials on which he drew. But we can see it at work in the air of mutual encouragement and moral exhortation that permeates the legislative work of the councils. We can see it in the attitude of the canonical lawgiver toward his predecessors— the canons of councils held in other times and in other places, the tradition of earlier shepherds of the flock. All of these forms have their counterparts in the Roman law, but there is something in them that harks back to another tradition—that of the chain of epistles that linked together the pastoral wisdom and experience of the primitive church, the words of doctrine and exhortation that passed continually from one shepherd to another that the whole flock of Christ might be nourished with the same spiritual food.

The same dynamism may be discerned in the efforts to insure a single priest for every parish—the very name of parson, *persona ecclesiae,* is suggestive—and to insure that he be instituted by, and in due subordination to, the bishop. This man carries in his person the personal presence of Christ. But he must enter the sheepfold by the door; otherwise he is a thief and robber. His personal presence is the presence of the universal church.

The same dynamism appears in the machinery of visitation and pastoral correction. The involved procedures with which offenses are inquired into, the pastoral solicitude with which offenders are corrected, the public penances with which they are reconciled, seem to involve a delicate, if not always successful, balancing of the personal character of the pastorate with the juridical expression of the interest of the Christian community in its exercise.[8]

II. The Functional Problem

In the working out of a legal system, the problem we may characterize as functional is that of structuring the system in terms of an awareness of what it hopes to accomplish and of what resources are available for the task. In the medieval canon law, this problem became one of establishing practical relations among the three types of elements just discussed. How were the Roman law and theological elements to be related to the institutional necessities of the church in the context of the social and political realities of the time? And how were the institutional necessities themselves to be related to one another according to their relative importance in the light of the limited means available? As they were articulated by the canonists, neither the Roman law nor the theology lent itself to the adequate resolution of such questions as these.

In the first place, the Roman law was developed for a society very different from the one in which it was revived by the jurists of the eleventh and twelfth centuries. Early medieval Roman-law scholarship had, therefore, a strongly academic character. This character was manifested both in an emphasis on internal verbal consistency and in an emphasis on first principles. All of this accorded well enough with the philosophical tendency of the times and contributed to the ethos which the canonists took from the legists.

Another element in the academic approach of the legists was inherent in their material. That was the *plenitudo potestatis* of the Emperor—a power which the canonists took over for the pope, as we have seen. *Plenitudo potestatis*, when attributed to anyone but God, is necessarily an academic concept. A perusal of the Theodosian Code will indicate just how academic it was in the late imperial period, and how much it bemused the emperors and diverted them from measures that might have brought actual resources to bear on the problems of the empire. Here are examples:

A.D. 353   We learn that certain veterans, unworthy of that name, are committing brigandage. We command, therefore, that veterans

of good character shall either till the fields or invest money in
honorable business enterprises and buy and sell goods. But capital punishment shall immediately rise up against [*mox in ipsos
capitaliter exsurgendum*] those veterans who neither till the
land nor spend useful lives in business . . .[9]

A.D. 403   We grant by law to provincials the right to overpower deserters,
and if the deserters should dare to resist, We order that punishment be swift everywhere . . .[10]

A.D. 412   We order that all tribunes who have assumed the duty of searching out vagrants and deserters throughout Africa shall be removed that they may not devastate the province under a pretext of this kind. In the future, moreover, We decree that this
unholy title and office must not exist at all throughout Africa,
and if anyone should attempt to aspire to the forbidden rank
of this office for the sake of plunder, he shall be subjected to
the severity of capital punishment . . .[11]

The desperate spiral of severity and anarchy which these enactments bespeak
is another part of the canonists' inheritance from the Roman law.

The canonists, despite the formidable practical concerns with which their
system was faced, not only absorbed the academic tendencies of the legists,
but added to them through an ill-considered didacticism in their theological
inputs. Let us take as an example the most commonly mentioned instance of
their modification of the Roman law in the interest of a higher conception of
justice. This is the rule concerning the requirement of good faith for prescription.[12] The Roman law required good faith at the beginning of the period of
prescription—a rule which Gratian was content to follow. To the later canonists, however, this seemed to be a condonation of bad faith during the rest of
the period. Accordingly, a decretal of Alexander III adopted the rule that
there must be good faith throughout the period. Finally, at the Fourth Lateran
Council of 1215, an attempt was made to amend the civil law rule as well on
the ground that "every constitution or custom is to be done away with which
cannot be observed without mortal sin." The attempt to modify the civil law
was unsuccessful, but the modification of the canon law was maintained, and
the two systems continue to differ on the point.

Now, the role of prescription in a legal system, as the Roman jurisconsults
evidently knew well enough, is not to render abstract justice between competing claims, but to preserve the generality of legal interests against the un-
certainties of litigation:

> Prescription was brought in for the public good, lest the titles to
> uncertain things be long or well nigh permanently uncertain, whereas the
> time laid down in the law would have been sufficient to allow the owners
> to seek their property.[13]

Whether the requirement of good faith at the outset is consistent with such a value is debatable; rights will still be subject to the vicissitudes of judicial proof involving matters long past. But the inquiry is at least confined to a point of time and will in many cases involve transactions of some notoriety. The canonical rule, expanding the inquiry over a period of many years, must vastly increase the uncertainty of the outcome and, therefore, the insecurity with which rights are enjoyed.

The possibilities of the wrong side winning a lawsuit, particularly a lawsuit that turns on obscure and often forgotten matters of fact, are such that this insecurity must affect the just and the unjust alike. This is the very raison d'être of any principle of prescription, and it is just this that was ignored by the didacticism of the canonists. To put it another way, the abstract pursuit of justice was allowed to overshadow the necessities of the concrete pursuit of justice through the mechanics of a legal system.

The same didacticism affected other aspects of the canonical system, albeit not always in as obvious ways. We see it, for instance, in the area of appellate procedure, where the canon law seems always oriented toward the utopian goal of affording a decision that is abstractly right,[14] whereas both the Roman law and the medieval English law seem content with eliciting the best decision the system is capable of affording.

The combination of this didacticism with the *plenitudo potestatis* put at the apex of the canonical system an image that made it impossible to distribute power effectively between central and local agencies. On the one hand, the acceptance of the *plenitudo potestatis* (which, we must note, is rather an oversimplification of the relation between papal and episcopal authority in Catholic theology)[15] thrust into the background the theological claims of decentralized authority by giving them no satisfactory juridical formulation. On the other hand, the strictly practical claims of decentralization were vitiated by the image of the pope as Peter. Peter was not the head of the largest administrative organization in Europe; he was the Prince of the Apostles, the Shepherd of the Sheep. When a sheep came to Peter hungry, how could Peter not feed him?[16]

It seems to be a principle of this kind that Barraclough has discerned at work in the proliferation of papal provisions to benefices.[17] He insists that this development stemmed from no set purpose of the popes to increase their authority as against the local episcopate, but was rather their response to the importunity of those seeking provisions—a response motivated in great part by the maxim *provisio clericorum opus in se continet pietatis*. Barraclough seems to consider it to the credit of the popes that their undermining of episcopal authority was unintentional. But that so profound a change could be effected without anyone being in control of it does not speak well for the system.

We could multiply examples of the same kind, but let one more suffice. A canon enacted at Amalfi in 1089 and again at Rome in 1099 reads as follows:

> Let no layman presume to offer his tithes, any church, or anything else of ecclesiastical right to monasteries or canons without the consent of the bishop or the permission of the Roman Pontiff. If the bishop refuse his consent through avarice or improbity, let the Roman Pontiff be informed, and let whatever is to be offered be offered with his permission.[18]

As the pope is obviously not able to read the interior dispositions of the bishop, the practical meaning of this provision can only be that the pope stands ready to substitute his judgment for that of the bishop in cases of this kind and invites the laity to bring such cases to his attention so that he may do so. The effect, in short, is to add one more piece to the pattern of centralization without any articulated purpose of doing so.

To sum up what I have said thus far, it seems that the Roman law inputs into the canonical system tended to be academic, and the theological inputs tended to be didactic, so that both militated against an effective allocation of administrative resources for institutional needs. Turning next to the institutional inputs into the system, we find that these were articulated in terms of the High Church ethos described in the last chapter. The upholding of the rights and position of the institutional church was conceived of as an end in itself rather than as a means of disseminating the Gospel and administering the sacraments. This point of view put solid theological props under the diversion of resources from the pastoral ministry to other institutional goals, while the academic and didactic character of the rest of the system militated against giving effective consideration to the competing claims of the ministry.[19]

For an example of this process at work, let us consider the subject of monastic appropriations. The law on this subject as it ultimately developed was that a monastery or other clerical body that held the right of patronage of a parish church could not under the general law serve the parish cure through one of its own number; rather, it would have to present a suitable cleric to be parson, just as a lay patron would have to do. With a license from the bishop or the pope, however, the monastic or collegiate patron could "appropriate" the parish church. When this was done, there would be provided out of the sources of revenue of the parish benefice a sufficient endowment to maintain a *vicar* to serve the cure, and the rest of the revenues would go to appropriating body. The endowment of the vicar was supposed to be sufficient to afford him a *congrua sustentatio*—a minimum amount sufficient for decent, if frugal, living.[20] A license of this kind was not to be given as a matter of course; it required a showing of poverty on the part of the monastery or college seeking to appropriate.

At first blush, these rules look reasonable enough. They fail, however, to focus our attention on the crucial questions of what resources are available and how they can be distributed to do the most good. If we look separately at the requirements of the parish ministry and at the requirements of the monastery, we will find that we have a standard for evaluating each. But we entirely lack a standard for looking at both and deciding between them.

Let us see how the elements we have been considering contribute to this state of the law. In the first place, it was High Church concern for institutional dignity that gave content to the two criteria to be applied: for a monastery to be impoverished was an affront to religion, and the revenues of the church might be appropriately applied to alleviating it; for a parish priest to lack a *congrua sustentatio* was an affront to the clerical order.[21]

Next, it was didacticism that made it a pious work to grant the petition of the monastery if the requisite poverty was shown.[22] It was didacticism also that led to requiring the vicar to content himself with a *congrua sustenatio*. One who has chosen Christ for his portion must partake sparingly of the things of this world.

Finally it was the academic approach that prevented an evaluation of these rules in the light of what they were actually doing in the church—of what kind of man would actually be willing to serve for the sum fixed upon as a *congrua sustenatio*[23] and of whether the poverty of the monastery could be as well alleviated by cutting down its commitments as by increasing its revenues. In fact, as we shall see, low pay had a good deal to do with drawing the best-trained priests out of the parish ministry, and the monasteries were so faithful to Parkinson's second law (expenditure rises to meet income) that by the end of the Middle Ages they had appropriated over one-third of the parishes in England[24] without being significantly better off financially, to say nothing of spiritually, than they were before.

In general, then, the academic and didactic propensities of the canonists led them to consider their system in terms of the articulation of consistent principles, when they would have done better to consider it in terms of choice between conflicting principles in the light of available resources. This approach hampered the functional development of the system at a number of points. It also gave to the High-Church zeal for institutional status more scope than it would have had if it had been squarely faced with the competing claims of the parish ministry. The canon law in its formative period was not without its functional successes—cases in which the available resources and techniques were effectively marshalled for the achievement of the task at hand. But it had its great failures also, and these resulted in no small part from the inadequacies in the canonists' approach to the problem of function.

III. The Problem of Obligation

To raise the question of the nature of the obligation imposed by the law in a given system is ultimately to raise the question of the definition of law or, as some modern authors would have it, the question of what we mean when we assert that such-and-such is the law. The answers given to this age-old question tend to fall into three main categories.[25] The first, the earliest in point of time and perhaps the most prevalent even today, would answer in terms of some moral claim to obedience: the law imposes a moral obligation on the subject because it represents the command of someone whom a relevant principle of morality requires us to obey. The second category of answer, one that gained currency in its present form around the end of the last century and continues to exert a powerful hold on legal scholars in America, would reduce legal principles to empirical predictions. Thus, the statement that such-and-such is the law is a prediction that certain public officials will react in a certain way to the situation envisaged: the statement that the law requires me to do such-and-such is a prediction that certain consequences will be visited upon me if I do not. The third category of answer, articulated for the most part by a school of contemporary English philosophers, would have it that statements about the law are not reducible to statements about anything outside the legal system to which they apply. Thus, although from a statement that such-and-such is the law there may be in some cases deduced a statement about moral obligations or a prediction about the behavior of public officials, the statement itself is not identical with either of these.

The arguments advanced by each of these schools of thought against the others are many and complicated; I shall not attempt to follow them here. But note that the inherent characteristics of a secular legal system are such as to give some measure of support to each. The law does carry with it a certain moral suasion. It is by and large brought home to the subject through predictable actions of public officials. It does have an internally consistent formal structure that may extend to cases where moral suasion or public enforcement are lacking.

To some extent the canonical system lends itself to similar kinds of analysis. It too has elements of moral suasion, official enforcement, and formal structure. Yet the character of the obligation imposed by the canon law is not easily expressed within the framework of these theories developed to define the secular law. With these secular theories in mind, an analysis of obligation in the canonical system may yield some insight into its unique character.[26]

As a vehicle for such an analysis, let us consider the canon *De multa* of the Fourth Lateran Council of 1215. This canon deals with an important subject—the holding of plural benefices—and therefore forms part of a substantial course of legislation and administration addressed to the same sub-

ject.[27] It also gathers in one place an unusually large collection of the typical devices of the canonical legislation of the period; thus, it will give us a
convenient starting point for studying these devices in context. I will begin
by setting forth a translation of the whole canon; then, under certain key
phrases of the canon, I will take up one by one the various devices of which
it makes use, setting each in a context that may shed some light on the nature of the obligation of this canon—and, inferentially, the whole system—
sought to impose. Our concern here, it should be noted, is not with the interpretation of the canon and, therefore, not with the work of those commentators who concerned themselves with delineating the exact scope of
what it commanded and what it forbade. The question before us is the nature of the obligation it imposed on the subject to do what it commanded
or to refrain from what it forbade and the consequences it boded for him
if he did otherwise. For this purpose, it is on the course of legislation
and administration rather than on the course of interpretation and comment
to which the canon gives rise that I have focused.

Here, then, is a translation of the canon *De multa* of the Fourth Lateran
Council of 1215:

> With much foresight [*De multa providentia*] it was forbidden in the
> [Third, 1179] Lateran Council that anyone should receive different
> ecclesiastical dignities and several parish churches, contrary to what
> was laid down in the sacred canons [*Contra sacrorum canonum insti-
> tuta*]. Otherwise the person receiving such dignities and churches was
> to lose them, and the person bestowing them was to lose his right of con-
> ferring them. Since, however, because of the cupidity and presumption
> of certain persons, this statute has thus far borne little or no fruit, we,
> wishing more openly and expressly to oppose this practice, establish
> by the present decree that whoever receives any benefice having cure
> of souls annexed to it, shall be deprived by the law itself of any such
> benefice that he may have obtained earlier. If by chance he should strive
> to retain the earlier benefice, he shall be deprived [*spolietur*] of the sec-
> ond as well.
>
> Furthermore, he to whom the bestowal of the earlier benefice belongs,
> may, as soon as the second is received, freely bestow the first on anyone
> he considers deserving of it. If he puts off bestowing it for longer than six
> months, not only shall the collation of it devolve upon another in accor-
> dance with the statute of the Lateran Council [not the canon referred to
> in the preamble], but he whose benefice it is shall be compelled to as-
> sign for the use of the church so much of the fruits as he is found to have
> received during the time it was vacant.
>
> We order that the same rule be observed in the case of parsonages [*per-
> sonatibus* = prebends?], adding that no one is to have more than one
> prebend or dignity in the same church, even if he does not have the cure
> of souls.

As to sublime and literate persons, however, who ought to be honored with greater benefices, a dispensation can be had from the Apostolic See when reason demands.[28]

A. *"With much foresight it was forbidden in the Lateran Council . . . contrary to what was laid down in the sacred canons."*

Not only do the fathers, in framing this canon, appeal for support to the provision of the 1179 council on the same subject, they also quote directly the words by which the framers of the latter provision appeal in their turn to the authority of those who have gone before. The principle that an old law is better than a new law was traditional and pervasive in the canonical system. It can be seen at work in the first synod of the English Church, assembled by Theodore of Tarsus in 673. In the early medieval canons it takes the form sometimes of lifting canons verbatim from one synod to another, more often of referring to earlier canons for justification or authority.

In context, it seems fairly clear that the purpose of these references to the past is justification; by them the proposed disposition is grounded in the tradition and experience of the Church.

B. *"Because of the cupidity and presumption of certain persons . . ."*

The moral vituperation of those who have acted otherwise in the past is another form of justification that the canons frequently offer for themselves. This vituperation may be simple, as it is here, or fortified by reasons, as in the 1179 canon on the same subject:

Whereas many, not setting a limit to their avarice, attempt to acquire diverse ecclesiastical dignities and several parish churches, contrary to what was laid down in the sacred canons, so that, being scarcely sufficient for one office, they assume the emoluments of several . . . [29]

There may be a reference to scripture:

If anyone goes against this rule (for it is against the doctrine of the Apostle who says that no soldier of God concerns himself with secular things) and behaves in a secular way, let him be put out of the ministry, since, neglecting his clerical office, he immerses himself in the currents of worldly things in order to please the powers of the world.[30]

Sometimes the reasons given are fanciful:

It is good for seed to be multiplied to the sower, but ridiculous to reap where one has not sown, therefore . . .[31]

Usually, as in the instant canon, and in the 1179 one, there is a vice to which the behavior in question is attributed:

> Many . . . have been led to levity, or, what is worse, by cupidity to . . .[32]

Prefatory material of this kind is, of course, part and parcel of the didactic tendency I have already referred to as a major element in the canons of the period. This didacticism is peculiar to the canon law and goes considerably beyond the moral element that is necessarily present in any viable legal system. Consider by way of contrast the preamble to the first secular statute enacted in England on the subject of plural benefices:

> For the more quiet and virtuous increase and maintenance of divine service, the preaching and teaching the word of God, with godly and good example, the better discharge of curates, the maintenance of hospitality, the relief of poor people, the increase of devotion, and good opinion of the lay-fee toward the spiritual persons, be it enacted . . .[33]

This too is an attempt to build a statute on a moral foundation, but here the moral basis is not the sinfulness of the behavior the statute is going to forbid; rather, it is the right ordering of the whole society. This difference between the secular legislator and the canonical legislator in the moral justifications they advance for what they enact is fairly constant. There are exceptions in both cases, but generally the canons look for justification to some immorality or vice involved in what they forbid, whereas the secular laws look for justification to the good social consequences of what they command or the evil social consequences of what they forbid. Specifically, one would have to search the canons at length to find one on plural benefices that took the social evils of the practice more seriously than the avarice of the clergy engaged in it.[34]

C. "Since . . . this statute has thus far borne little or no fruit, we, wishing more openly and expressly to oppose this practice by the present decree . . ."

The interrelation of the different canons that make up a series of provisions on the same subject is probably the most difficult question that faces us in attempting to subject the canon law to any systematic legal analysis.

Let us note in the first place that the crucial considerations for us—the change made in the previous law—appears from the wording of the canon to be of secondary concern to the legislator. Indeed, by omitting a significant portion from his paraphrase of the 1179 canon, he has made it look more like his own than it actually is.[35] This result accords very well with his stated purpose, which is to add his own authority to that of his predecessor because the latter has not received the attention it deserves. He has added a sanction, but that seems to be only by way of pointing up his renewal of the basic prohibition.

This approach explains, if anything can, a puzzling incident recorded in the register of Hugh of Wells, who held the see of Lincoln at the time of the Fourth Lateran Council. Hugh appears to have been particularly zealous in inquiring into the qualifications of persons presented to benefices in his diocese. So it is that we find him inquiring of the papal legate, Gualo, whether a certain pluralist was ineligible. The legate replied that he was not ineligible because he was presented before the council—the implication being that no law that would make him ineligible was enacted until that council.[36] What is curious about this is that our 1215 canon, which must be the one to which the legate refers, does not make a beneficed cleric ineligible to receive a new benefice: it provides that his acceptance of the new benefice will automatically oust him from the old. On the other hand, the 1179 canon, although not perfectly clear on the point, would seem to be rather good authority for not instituting a man into a second benefice.[37] Presumably, then, it was considered unduly harsh to enforce the 1179 canon at this late date, but a person subject to the 1215 canon could not complain if the means adopted for dealing with him was different from that laid down in the canon.

The legate Ottobuono attempted in 1268 to regularize the enforcement device adopted by Hugh, and to integrate it with the 1215 canon. He provided that before a man was instituted into a benefice there should in every case be an inquiry as to whether he held any other benefice with cure of souls. If it appeared that he had such a benefice, he was not to be instituted into the new one unless he showed a valid dispensation. Any institution in violation of these provisions was to be automatically void.

These provisions were integrated with the 1215 canon by means of an exception whereby the cleric could be instituted into the new benefice if he would take an oath not in any way to concern himself with his old benefice or benefices after institution into the new. For breach of this oath, he was to be automatically deprived of both old and new benefices.

Again, from a contemporary standpoint, we would look at this enactment as calculated to plug loopholes by the addition of new sanctions. But this view of the legislation is not what emerges from a reading of the preamble. This preamble is too long to quote in full, but the following may give an idea of what the legate conceived himself to be about. He describes the evils, moral and to some extent social, of the practice condemned, refers to the unremitting efforts of Roman pontiffs and others in authority to combat it, and expresses fear lest it bring down the wrath of God on whole kingdoms; then he says:

Wishing, therefore, to exert our authority diligently against this pestilent and

almost incurable disease, and, as much as it is in our power to cure it, following also in the footsteps of the said legate [Otto in 1237][38] strengthening [adjuvantes] his constitution on this subject, and adding to it, we command . . .[39]

Certainly the new enforcement procedures are for the author of this canon an
important part of what he has accomplished with it. It seems, however, an
oversimplification to say that he has simply added new enforcement procedures
to a canon that previously lacked them. For him, the most important thing
he has done is to add his efforts to those of his predecessors, and so strike one
more blow in the never-ending battle against avarice.

This appears to be the way Archbishop Pecham looks at the work of Ottobuono when he comes to enact his own legislation on the subject at Reading
in 1279.[40] Pecham begins in the usual way by vituperating the practice of
pluralism and by referring to the canons that have addressed themselves to the
subject in the past without success. He then points out that the 1215 and 1268
canons taken together would deprive the pluralist of all his benefices—the 1215
canon reaching all but the last and the 1268 canon reaching that one.[41] He de-
termines, however, to temper justice with mercy and allow those who presently
hold plural benefices to keep the last one taken, although he promises to be
less lenient in the future. He adds also an automatic excommunication for those
who continue to attempt to hold on to their plural benefices.

In 1281, however, we find Pecham temporizing again. In a canon promulgated at Lambeth in that year,[42] he refers to the threats he made at an earlier
time (presumably in 1279) and states that he means by God's help to carry
them out so that by God's help the evil of pluralism will gradually be driven
out of his province. In support of his policy of gradualism, he quotes Deuter-
onomy 7:22:

> He will consume these nations in thy sight by little and little and by de-
> grees. Thou wilt not be able to destroy them altogether; lest perhaps the
> beasts of the earth should increase upon thee.

For the implementation of his policy, he refers to those pluralists who, smit-
ten with terror or remorse by his previous enactment, have turned in their excess benefices, and he orders all others to do the same within six months. If
they fail to do so, he will "proceed canonically" against them. Even if they
do submit, they must make satisfaction for their past violations, "so that
their character may be understood by the churches they have thus defrauded."[43]

Without carrying any further the involved history of the canons against pluralism, we may perhaps find some basis for generalizing about the interrelation
of the canons in the series. The following general principles seem to emerge:

1. The most important role of the canons of earlier times is in constituting
   a tradition on the subject, to which tradition the current legislator can
   appeal.

2. A canon that has been widely disregarded for a period of time requires some kind of renewal before it can properly be put into effect. This principle is not reducible to the rule that a law can be abrogated by contrary custom[44] because the principle obtains even where the contrary custom is grievously sinful and even where it has not been followed for the period prescribed by the rule.

3. This renewal is generally accompanied by some kind of advanced warning, so that those who have violated it with impunity in the past may be given an opportunity to mend their ways. The same principle is presumably responsible for the provision some canons make for being read from time to time to those to whom they apply.[45]

4. The renewal is accomplished through a renewed exercise of personal leadership, of which the promulgation of a new canon or the devising of new enforcement procedures is only evidentiary. This principle seems to represent an irreducible element in the Christian pastorate, breaking through the juridical forms with which it is surrounded; it explains much that is perplexing in the canon law. To it may be attributed not only the attrition of canons in the course of time and the secondary importance of the sanctions adopted from time to time but also such seeming superfluities as a bishop coming home from a general council and enacting its canons in his diocesan synod[46] or a pope issuing a special indult for the application of a general law.[47]

These principles, like so much else in the medieval canon law, relate finally to the characteristic didacticism of the system. They form the basis for the imposition of a moral ideal through the exercise of pastoral solicitude.

D. "Shall be deprived by the law itself . . ."

We have already noticed that the prelates who addressed themselves to the subject of pluralism on the scene in England preferred other sanctions to the automatic one laid down in the 1215 canon.[48] It remains for us to consider the subject of automatic effect a little more at large. It was a favorite, and not usually very felicitous, device of the medieval canonical legislators.[49]

The first thing we must note about this kind of legislative device is its metaphorical quality. In sober fact the law itself deprives no one of anything. There is a particular man drawing down the fruits of a particular benefice, and he will go on doing so until someone persuades or compels him to stop. Whether or not the law purported to have automatic effect, the task of persuasion or compulsion would in the ordinary course of events devolve upon the bishop or the archdeacon or someone exercising authority under them.

This work would sometimes be hampered by lack of zeal—for pluralism was the lifeblood of the clerical bureaucracy of which the bishop and the archdeacon were a part[50]—and would always be hampered by lack of information.

The recordkeeping techniques of the day did not furnish any regular means whereby a pluralist might be expected to come to the attention of the authorities. Generally speaking, a document respecting a man's affairs would be in the possession of the individual concerned. An important technical advance, rather widespread by the time under consideration, was the keeping of a copy of the document in its chronological order in the records of the official who issued it. But, the only person in a position to furnish a dossier of all the documents affecting a particular cleric would be that cleric himself. If he had been instituted into two different benefices, the ecclesiastical authorities would have no record of this fact except that represented by two entries in the registers, completely isolated from one another. The inquest envisioned by Ottobuono's canon on the subject was presumably calculated to make up for this lack of records by the eliciting of live evidence. But the inquest would not have served the purpose unless the inquirer knew where to look for the evidence, and even this much information he had no reliable way of obtaining.[51]

It is against this background of administration that we have to consider the uses of a provision purporting to have automatic effect: what could it add to the ability of the authorities to deal with offenders in general and with pluralists in particular?

In the first place, it might add significantly to the moral suasion of the rule it sought to implement. It seems likely that this was the case with those rules of clerical discipline to which the canons attached the sanction of automatic irregularity for the exercise of the ministry. A priest who became irregular through some momentary lapse added sin to sin as long as he continued to minister; he also jeopardized his tenure of any preferment that might come his way before he was absolved. These were consequences he might well have taken more seriously than he did the rule of conduct to which they were attached.[52]

On the other hand, where the automatic effect in question related not to a man's personal status, but to his tenure of a benefice he ought not in any event to have, it is difficult to see how the automatic effect could rise any higher in moral suasion than the rule it sought to implement. Thus it is that the moral reproaches leveled at pluralists in most of the canons on the subject —they are avaricious, and they assume responsibilities they are unable to discharge—took no additional force from the provision for automatic deprivation.

The one canon that seems to make of the automatic deprivation an independent ground for persuading the pluralist to mend his ways is the 1279 enactment of Archbishop Pecham. The automatic deprivation meant that, in addition to drawing down revenues he ought not to have, the pluralist was purporting to exercise a cure of souls that had not been delegated to him.

> For those who knowingly invade these benefices in this way are putting their sickles into other men's harvests; by the same token, since they do

not enter by the door they are not shepherds but thieves and robbers. Furthermore, they impudently cozen miserable souls, having no power to bind them or to loose them.[53]

This argument seems rather persuasive, but there is no indication that it had any different effect from other forms of rhetoric in other canons. Pecham stated in his 1281 canon that his efforts had indeed led a certain number of pluralists to submit themselves. It does not appear, however, that there were enough of them to make a real dent in the practice. Furthermore, in all probability they were moved by the strictures against pluralism as such rather than by the automatic deprivation, for Pecham says they gave up only their excess benefices, whereas his 1279 legislation purported to deprive them of all.

Besides furnishing an additional source of moral suasion, a provision for automatic effect might furnish an additional set of procedures. This was expressly done in the language of the 1215 canon that refers to the earlier provisions for the filling up of vacant benefices. Since the pluralist is automatically deprived of the earlier benefice, that benefice is automatically vacant. Since it is vacant, it may be filled up in the same way it would have been if the incumbent had died or resigned. Since, however, the machinery set in motion by the canons referred to was developed with a view to filling benefices notoriously vacant and kept so through malice or neglect,[54] it cannot have helped much in the case of the typical pluralist who held onto his multiple benefices by escaping the attention of the authorities.

The provisions invoking the procedures for filling vacant benefices became effective against pluralism, therefore, only when they began to elicit the attention of a class of people more able or more willing than the ordinary administrative authorities to set the procedures in motion. This, the third and most important of the benefits to be hoped for from a provision having automatic effect, came to pass when the automatic deprivation of pluralists began to mesh with the highly developed machinery for bestowing benefices through papal provision.[55]

The exact workings of this system, which by the mid-fourteenth century had probably become the usual avenue of preferment for clerics, need not concern us at the moment. Suffice it to say that after the papal decree *Execrabilis* of 1317, which reserved to the pope the right to fill any benefice made vacant through the pluralism of the holder, it became possible for a cleric who discovered a case of pluralism to file a petition in Rome reciting that such-and-such benefice had become vacant on account of pluralism and requesting that he himself be provided to it.[56] Given the record-keeping techniques to which I have already alluded, it was quite usual for the popes, as well as other persons with large amounts of ecclesiastical patronage, to learn in this way of the vacancy of benefices in their gift, and, if the informant had any claim to their good will, to reward him by bestowing the benefice as requested. Thus, a cleric with any reasonable ground to hope for a papal provision might well expect to succeed to the benefice of any pluralist he brought to light. It is through giving scope to importunities of this kind that *Execrabilis* became—quite by accident, I suspect—the most effective, or the least ineffective, of the measures taken against pluralism in the medieval church. What this boils down to, of course, is administration through the use of paid informers, a device that has never been in very good repute.

The crucial point in this discussion of automatic effect is that no law can achieve an administrative effect beyond the confines of its power to elicit the relevant facts and bring them to the attention of the authorities. When a law purports to apply automatically to a state of facts that has not been authoritatively determined, the result is to introduce a debilitating uncertainty into the structure of the law without any corresponding advantage in effective enforcement. This effect is well illustrated in the passage quoted from Pecham's 1279 canon, in which he accuses the pluralist of cozening "miserable souls, having no power to bind them or to loose them." If we are to take Pecham at his word, the laws against pluralism, developed for the sake of a more effective use of the power of the keys, were in fact leading multitudes of the faithful to seek the exercise of that power from men who did not have it to exercise. Fortunately for the deceived parishioners, Pecham was not altogether correct. There was a principle of "common error," whereby the canons could restore the power of binding and loosing as secretly as they had taken it away.[57]

Where, however, the uncertainty introduced into the law concerned this world rather than the next, the consequences were not so easily escaped. Let us consider, for example, Ottobuono's canon on the subject of bishops who allow monasteries to appropriate the revenues of parish churches. The bishop is forbidden to permit such an appropriation

> unless he to whom he confers it be so manifestly oppressed by poverty, or unless there be some other lawful cause, so that the appropriation may be rather esteemed agreeable to piety than contrary to law.[58]

Otherwise, the appropriation is to be automatically void. Obviously, no religious superior able to do otherwise would allow the revenues of his house to rest on so ephemeral a foundation as this. The result was a regular practice of resorting to Rome for confirmation of appropriations made by local ordinaries. [59]

This is only one example of the uncertainty introduced into the law through the use of dispositions having automatic effect—uncertainty that often found no resolution except by wholesale papal confirmations of transactions tainted or possibly tainted with invalidity. There are a number of confirmations in the papal registers even in cases where no definite ground of invalidity appears.[60]

The possible sources of invalidity that surrounded so many legal transactions introduced into the entire system a climate of nervousness that only an exercise of the *plenitudo potestatis* could allay.

Even the papacy, however, was not a sure refuge against the possible impact of laws having automatic effect. Among the most important of such laws were those dealing with papal rescripts. Much of the business of the papacy—and by the close of the Middle Ages this had come to touch on the distribution of most of the ecclesiastical offices in Europe—was done through these papal rescripts issued at the request of someone involved in the transaction. In the usual case, the pope would have no knowledge of the affair beyond what appeared in the petition. This rescript would therefore be based on the allegations of the petition and would contain a summary of these allegations. The general teaching of the canonists was that if these allegations had been deliberately falsified, the rescript was invalid, and that if false allegations had been made in good faith, the rescript would be invalid if the false allegations were those that actually moved the pope to grant the rescript.[61] This rule meant, of course, that the canonical administration was to be troubled by all manner of documents emanating from the highest source in the system, entirely authentic, but not worth the paper they were written on. Nor was there any way, aside from going into the facts of their original issuance, to tell the valid from the invalid.

This persistent state of uncertainty is attributable, as I have already suggested, to the law's persistent outrunning of its capacity to elicit the relevant facts on which effective administration depends. This in turn seems attributable to the academic and didactic tendencies in the system—tendencies, as we have seen, that had a general effect of diverting the canonical legislator from the functional problem of effectively marshaling his administrative resources for the achievement of a desirable result. Thus it appears to be of set purpose that the legislator attempted by the use of automatic effect to project his activities beyond the reach of his administrative resources. This point is borne out by the language adopted by Gregory X in dealing with underage clerics and clerics who fail to take orders:

> Even though a canon laid down by our predecessor Alexander III of happy memory provided among other things that no one should undertake the governance of a parish unless he had attained the age of twenty-five years, and was to commendable learning and conversation, and that if anyone having undertaken such governance, were not, after warning, ordained to the priesthood within the time prescribed by the canon, he should be removed from it and replaced by another, *since, however, many show themselves negligent in the observance of the canon we refer to, we, wishing to make up for their perilous negligence by the execution of the law, provide by the present decree* that no one shall be

taken into the governance of a parish unless he shall be suitable in
morals learning and age, and we order that any collation hereafter
made to a parish church of anyone who had not attained the age of
twenty-five years shall be entirely without effect. Furthermore, he who
is taken into such governance . . . shall have himself promoted to the
priesthood within a year's time. If he is not promoted within that time,
he shall be deprived of the church committed to him, without any previous warning, by authority of the present constitution.[62]

In other words, the law itself is stepping into the gap created by the neg-
ligence of its ministers. It does not appear with equal clarity that Innocent
III regarded his 1215 canon on pluralism as improving on the 1179 canon
in the same way, but, as we have seen, there is not much basis for saying it
improved on it in any other way. In general, the use of automatic effect
in the canons indicates that it is regarded as a device of especial severity to
be used when other devices have failed. The administrative problem is not
wholly ignored, but no one seems to have taken it very seriously. Here once
more is the legate Ottobuono, speaking this time of clerics who occupy posts
in the secular bureaucracy:

Since indeed with men of ill will prohibitions do not prevent misdeeds
unless they are fortified with punishments, we order that whoever pre-
sumes to violate the foregoing shall be suspended ipso facto from his
office and benefice. Once suspended, should he be so rash as to inject
himself into them, he will not escape canonical punishment.[63]

Why he will not escape canonical punishment is not made to appear. Perhaps
we are not supposed to ask.

E. "As to sublime and literate persons, however, who ought to be honored
with greater benefices, a dispensation can be had from the Apostolic See
when reason demands."

The practice of dispensation, referred to in this passage, seems to be one
of the institutional forms imposed by the early medieval canonists on the
ancient pastoral practice of permitting in a particular case a deviation from
a general rule.[64] This practice dates back to the earliest times and seems responsive to a recognition that the subtle and personal work of saving souls
is not to be fully encompassed in a set of general principles. Attempts have
been made to reduce its primitive manifestations to juridical formulations,
but they are not very convincing. The most that can be said with any confidence is that the bishops felt free on occasion to authorize departures from
the general principles in which the pastoral experience of their colleagues
and predecessors was embodied, but they did so with more confidence when
fortified with the opinions of their fellows and later of the popes.

The canonists who first set themselves the task of imposing a Roman-law structure upon the administrative practices of the Church, found nothing in the Roman system that quite corresponded to the practice in question. While the Roman sources admitted of departing from the letter of the law under certain circumstances, the circumstances were determined by general, equitable principles inherent in the legal system itself and not by an ad hoc exercise of authority.[65] In fact the fourth-century emperors expressly provided that their private rescripts should not be availing against the general law.[66] Thus, the canonists were left to their own devices in developing a terminology and a justification to integrate into their system the prevailing practice in the church.

To give the practice a name, they chose the term *dispensatio*, whose basic meaning was "household management" or something of the kind, and which in more recent times had been used to refer to what we would call "administration." The term corresponds to the Greek "economy," which has some patristic usage in this context, and is still used for the counterpart of dispensation in the Greek church.

For justification, the canonists drew upon the ancient documents themselves, with their talk about necessity, utility, special circumstances and the like, and on the doctrine of the *plenitudo potestatis*, which placed the pope above the canons and, therefore, gave him an unlimited power to depart from them. The two lines of justification could not be fitted together without a certain amount of effort, especially as a number of papal documents expressed the importance of guarding intact the salutary dispositions of the Fathers.[67] Gratian's solution was to hold that the popes adhered to the law not because they were bound by it but in order to set a good example to their subjects, following in this the example of Christ, who allowed Himself to be circumcised and otherwise complied with the Jewish law, although He was not bound by it.[68]

The important articulations of the theory of dispensation subsequent to Gratian were concerned with the grounds on which dispensations might be granted and the nature of the dispensing authority (if any) of prelates subordinate to the pope. The first of these inquiries went not to the power of the pope, which, as we have seen, was considered unlimited, but to the traditional and canonical framework within which that power was exercised. Since by strict logic the power to dispense from the law must be related to the power to make the law in the first place, and since the prevailing doctrine would call for the exercise of that power for the common good, there was some argument for requiring that dispensations be granted only for the common good of the church. Our 1215 canon, by referring to the merits of the petitioner, seems to have clinched the argument that the dispensing power could also be exercised for the private good of the person dispensed. An exercise of this kind was attributed to benevolence, mercy, kindheartedness, or the like and was regarded as a legitimate use of the *plenitudo potestatis*.[69]

As to the power of subordinate prelates to dispense, the strict logic of the position taken would allow them that power only with respect to laws that they themselves had made. We have already seen, however, that they felt free to deviate from papal or conciliar decrees if occasion demanded. The canonists drew on equity, custom, implicit delegation, and whatever other concepts they found at hand to bring their theory into accord with the prevailing practice, but they were never altogether successful.

Against this background, we may suppose the quoted language from the 1215 canon to be serving three purposes: that of justifying the granting of dispensations from this canon in certain cases, that of denying to prelates other than the pope the power to dispense from this canon, and that of setting standards of self-restraint in the exercise of that power by the pope himself. Underlying these uses of a legislative formula, we may discern a certain dialectical tension between formal and personal elements in the canonical system. This dialectical tension was manifested at the local level by a certain informal tolerance of pluralism by local ordinaries in particular cases, never extending to the grant of a formal dispensation and evidently never conferring complete security of tenure in one's plural benefices.[70] On the papal level, the same dialectical tension was found in the relation between the benevolent exercise of the *plenitudo potestatis* and the limitations imposed by canonical practice on the common forms of papal dispensations. Where a given dispensation was frequently granted, the curia would develop a common form, or a standard wording, in which to embody it. Then a whole jurisprudence would grow up establishing what you could and could not do under a dispensation so worded. Then the limitations imposed by this jurisprudence would be themselves dispensed from, the dispensation from them reduced to another common form, the common form subjected to new limits, and the process repeated again.[71]

In sum, despite the efforts of the canonists to impose their forms and categories on dispensation and kindred practices, these practices can be best understood not through those forms and categories, but through two principles we have observed in connection with other parts of our 1215 canon. These principles are that the typical canon embodies a moral judgment upon the practice it forbids and that its enforcement involves an exercise of personal leadership. Under particular circumstances, the one whose personal leadership is required for the execution of the canon may determine in the exercise of his pastoral discretion that there exists a moral and spiritual context in which it is better not to follow what the canon requires. The possibilities for abuse in so broad a discretion as this are obvious, and the canonists attempted to hedge the discretion around in such a way as to limit the possibilities for abuse without limiting the discretion itself. From the dilemma thus created arose the law concerning dispensations.

We began this discussion of obligation with a brief summary of the three approaches to the definition of law that have commended themselves to students of secular jurisprudence—one in terms of moral suasion, one in terms of prediction of physical coercion, and one in terms of pure internal analysis. We saw that all of these had a certain support in the realities of a secular legal system. We should now be able to note by way of contrast that none of them has much support in the realities of the medieval canon law.

(1) The *moral suasion* of the canons lay, as we have seen, not so much in the canons themselves as in the moral principles that led to their enactment. Any just law has a certain basis in morality, but in the secular systems the legal disposition has a moral life of its own, making a bid for the conscience of the subject even in a case not covered by the underlying moral principle. In other words, obedience to the law is regarded as a virtue in its own right, distinct from whatever virtue may lie in the particular conduct enjoined by the law in question. The canons, because of their moralizing preambles, because of the didactic tendencies that affected their content, and, above all, because of the system of dispensations and other elements of pastoral selectivity that limited their enforcement, never quite achieved this independent moral life. Just as it was always considered necessary to appeal to the underlying moral principle to justify the framing or enforcing of a canon, so it was always possible to appeal to the same moral principle to justify not obeying the canon after it was made. Thus, as late as 1366, after all the legislation that had been enacted on the subject of pluralism, a pluralist still found it possible to defend himself by invoking moral principles extrinsic to the law:

> And it is laid down in the sacred canons that a good and industrious and literate person can govern two or even ten churches better than another can govern one; and both he who resides and he who does not reside are understood to serve the altar, so long as they live a good life and expend well the income they derive.[72]

(2) In predicting when some form of *physical coercion* will be applied, the canons seem to have been a good deal less serviceable than we expect secular enactments to be. We have seen that a renewed exercise of personal leadership was considered necessary to the enforcement of a rule however firmly it was embodied in older canons. Every medieval bishop who showed any zeal for the administration of his diocese had the same old problems to contend with. He addressed himself to them, sometimes via the enactment of new canons, sometimes via the enforcement of old ones, with an élan that depended far more on his personality than on the content of the canons. Thus, by consulting the canons, one could predict how his bishop would try to get him to behave but not what, if anything, would be done to him if he did not behave that way.

(3) The same idea of renewal that makes it so difficult to predict the co-

ercive application of the canons makes it all but hopeless to approach them from a standpoint of *internal analysis.*[73] For instance, pluralism was made unlawful for the Universal Church in 1179, yet it was forbidden again in 1215 and treated as having been lawful before. The pluralist was deprived ipso jure of his excess benefices by the 1215 canon, yet in 1247 he was being compelled to resign them. Prelates coming home from a general council would enact some of its canons locally and let others go by the board.[74] In short, there was much important legislation that did not affect the internal analytical content of the law, while much of what any analysis would include in the law was in fact not treated as such. The dynamics of the system are far more remote than are those of any secular system from what can be encompassed within a series of analytical statements that such-and-such is the law.

If, then, the various definitions elicited from the systems of secular jurisprudence will not avail to define the nature of the obligation imposed by the canons, is there a key element in the canons themselves that will open to us the mystery of their obligation? The question bears more investigation, but I would tentatively suggest that this key element is to be found in the teaching office of the church. It is this that unites these two elements of didacticism and personal leadership that have appeared as the common threads in the detailed analysis we have just completed. The canons present themselves to the individual Christian as the corporate witness of the church to the guiding principles governing her interior life. They present themselves to the shepherds of the Christian people as the collected experience of the Fathers in bringing those principles home to their flocks.

The obligation imposed by the canons, then, is less juridical than pedogogical; it is the obligation of a wise man to allow himself to be governed by the counsels and experience of those wiser and more experienced than himself. The peculiarities we discern in the enforcement of the canons are explained by noticing that the obligation is to be guided—neither to follow unthinkingly nor to innovate rashly. "Therefore every scribe instructed in the kingdom of God is like to a householder who brings forth from his treasure new things and old."

The canons as thus conceived have no small appeal as an instrument for ordering the interior life of the church, the corporate existence of the people of God. Yet, for that very reason the canonical system displayed serious defects in meeting the temporal administrative burdens of the medieval church. For even the monumental achievement of the canonists in giving their system a juridical structure could not impose on it that orientation toward external order that is required of a legal system if it is to deal successfully with temporal affairs.

IV. The Problem of Sanction

The most fundamental part of the structure of canonical sanctions is bound up with the same magisterial and pastoral elements we have discerned in the rest of the canon law. Here, the sanction—excommunication was the most usual and the most typical—constitutes an institutionalized and personalized denunciation of a moral failing, calculated to induce in the Christian community a dread of the divine wrath of which this is a foretaste and in the offender himself a change of heart signified by the acceptance of a salutary penance imposed by the pastoral authority. The penance, in turn, was calculated to consummate the repentance of the sinner with an outward sign, both for the edification of the community and for the spiritual well-being of the sinner.

Against the background of this fundamental conception of canonical sanction, let us consider that quintessentially hard-shelled character introduced into legal analysis by Justice Holmes—the bad man:

> You can see very plainly that a bad man has as much reason as a good one for wishing to avoid an encounter with the public force, and therefore you can see the practical importance of the distinction between morality and law. A man who cares nothing for an ethical rule which is believed and practiced by his neighbors is likely nevertheless to care a great deal to avoid being made to pay money, and will want to keep out of jail if he can.[75]

We have, to be sure, already rejected Holmes's attempt to make of this bad man and his affairs a defining criterion of the legal system as far as the canon law is concerned. There remains for him, however, an important subordinate role in the analysis of the system. He appears in the ambit of the medieval church in at least such force that ability to cope with him can be one gauge of the administrative effectiveness of the system.

With the bad man, *suae salutis immemor,* envisaged by Holmes, we will have to include also a rather more frequently occurring type, the good man who is not persuaded in conscience that the behavior denounced by a given canon is actually wrong. We have seen that the didactic tendency of the canons encouraged the belief that violating a canon was morally all of a piece with violating the purported moral principle on which the canon was based, so that the canon would have little moral suasion for one not convinced of the underlying moral principle. By the same token, one who was not convinced of the sinfulness of violating the canon would tend not to think himself affected by the spiritual censures directed against the violator. Such a one, therefore, as regards the efficacy of the canonical sanction, would be in the same case as the bad man.[76]

From the standpoint, then, of the bad man or the convinced nonconformist, let us consider the main sanctions that the canonical system brought to bear on the violator.

A. Excommunication.

Insofar as excommunication was automatic, it may have had some effect in cutting off the culprit from the society of those who knew he had incurred it, but it is doubtful that this had more than minimal effect except on those who were disposed to be his enemies in the first place. Where the excommunication was officially pronounced and applied to a specific person, this effect may have been more pronounced. Here too, however, the culprit would be apt to have partisans of the same mind with himself, who would receive him and insure that the deprivation of the society of faithful Christians did not sit too heavily on him.[77]

The most important effect of excommunication from the standpoint we are considering was provided by the civil processes that could be invoked in support of it. In England, upon proper notice to the secular authorities, a writ *de excommunicato capiendo* would issue, under which the excommunicate would be seized by the sheriff and kept in confinement until absolved or until he gave bond to abide the judgment of the church—that is, to appear before the ecclesiastical court and do whatever was required of him to be absolved.

This made of excommunication a reasonably effective form of mesne process but did not give it any value as a sanction on the substantive law, since anyone who sought absolution and was prepared to abide by the judgment of the court must needs be absolved. Furthermore, its effectiveness even as mesne process depended on the intervention of the secular authorities, which the bishops seem often to have been reluctant to invoke.[78]

B. Irregularity.

The sanction of irregularity was attached as an automatic effect to a number of forms of clerical misbehavior, chiefly those involving bloodshed. It entailed for those not yet in orders a disability to be ordained and for those already ordained a disability to carry out the sacramental function attached to their order. As most of the benefices of the church required the possession and exercise of orders, a person who became irregular stood in danger of losing his benefices if he was found out. This danger must have had some effect in leading offenders to make themselves known and seek absolution rather than face continuing insecurity in the tenure of their positions.

While irregularity of its own nature was a permanent condition of the person affected by it, it was so freely dispensed from that it cannot have had more than a limited effect as a temporal sanction upon the conduct to which it was attached.[79] Rather, its role must have been that of another form of mesne process, leading certain types of offenders to present themselves for the imposition of other kinds of sanctions.[80]

C. Monition.

A monition was a kind of official warning. It might emerge from various judicial or pastoral situations, including an official inquiry into the conduct of a cleric:

> Sir John Marshall, rector of Hamerton, is reported for having absented himself from that church for a long time without cause. On the fourth day of November, 1446 . . . he appeared, and admits that he has absented himself: he alleges fear, however. Therefore he is assigned the following day . . . in the same place to prove in legal form that which he has alleged. On which day . . . he appeared and was deficient in his proof; therefore, he is warned that he reside henceforward and minister in person in his church.[81]

The chief effect of the monition is to pave the way for more severe penalties if the offending conduct is continued or resumed. Thus, it is what might be called a "one-bite" sanction. It can readily be seen, for instance, that if this is the usual way of proceeding against nonresident rectors, a rector may with impunity absent himself until such time as he is caught and proceeded against canonically.[82]

In fact, this one-bite approach seems to have been all but universal in dealing with a number of classes of offense,[83] including, in the case of the clergy, nonresidence, forbidden employments, and even concubinage. Indeed, as we have seen, it was generally considered preferable to give some advance warning before moving even against those offenders whose punishments were supposed to have automatic effect. The object of this use of the monition was evidently to give the offender a chance to reform. Thus understood, it relates to the didactic orientation we have already discerned animating the substantive provisions of the canons.

D. Penance.

For those sins brought to light in the external forum—that is, outside the confessional—a symbolic expiation in the form of a public penance was exacted. The sinner who neglected or refused to accept and perform such a public penance was excommunicated for his contumacy, with the consequences already discussed. Penances of this kind were regularly imposed on those guilty of violence, sexual offenses, and the like.[84]

We have seen a canon of Pecham's that appears to threaten pluralists with the imposition of penances, but in general this sanction seems not to have been used in cases involving the tenure of benefices and the discharge of the duties attached to them. This is perhaps because some action involving the benefice itself was thought to serve better in such cases. While the canons say nothing expressly on the subject, it appears not to have been considered appropriate to visit a single offense with two kinds of punishment, such as penance and deprivation.[85]

The character of the penance imposed when that sanction was resorted to has been perceptively analyzed by Rosalind Hill with examples taken from the register of Oliver Sutton, a late thirteenth-century bishop of Lincoln.[86] The mid–fifteenth-century material appended by Hamilton Thompson to his *The English Clergy* seems to bear out Miss Hill's analysis.[87] Miss Hill points out that each penance was tailor-made to the individual case and sets forth the governing principle as follows:

> In devising a penance the ecclesiastical authority had to bear in mind three points. The penance must be salutary, that is to say that it must be designed to bring the individual to a proper state of grace and to keep him there. It must be deterrent, or sufficiently painful to mind and body to ensure that other people were prevented from committing similar offenses. Finally, in the widest sense of the word, it must be decent, and conducive to public order. It must not expose a person holding a responsible position to such humiliation that it would henceforward be impossible for him to exercise his authority.[88]

The goal of salutariness seems well implemented in the examples. The expressions of contrition and the forms of reparation are ingenious and often moving. One who causes "a great effusion of blood" in the church is required to provide branches and candles for decorations and rushes to cover the floor. Two clerics who quarrel on consecrated ground are to stand at opposite sides of the chancel steps and chant the psalter to one another.

This goal of salutariness was also ingeniously interwoven with that of decency and good order. Thus, where a group of men put a church to military use, they are made to come in procession into the church in question and offer their weapons and armor at the altar. This is salutary. But one among them is a knight, and he may bring his squire with him to carry his weapons and armor for him. This is decent and insures proper respect for the order of knighthood.[89] "The same desire for public decorum," says Miss Hill:

> caused Sutton to take great care to ensure that the penances which he imposed upon members of the clergy were not such as to impair their authority in the eyes of lay persons. Clerks, even those who were young, were rarely beaten in public, and then only by a cleric of senior standing. As a rule, when they received a beating, only members of the clergy were allowed to be present.[90]

This brings us to the subject of deterrence, the second of the goals Miss Hill enumerates and the one of most interest to us from the bad-man standpoint we are considering. In Miss Hill's examples, the deterrent effect was achieved partly by corporal punishment, usually beating, and partly by some form of humiliation, such as appearing barefooted or otherwise incompletely clothed. In the case of the clergy and highly placed laymen, the humiliation was necessarily mitigated by the goal of decorum, as we have already seen.

Beatings and ancillary humiliations, then, done in a form suited to the offender's station in life, constituted the staple of deterrent sanctions in the imposition of penance. We may question whether in the more serious cases they were sufficient to deter.

> A clerk who had joined in a particularly brutal and sacrilegious attack upon the clergy and parish church of Thame was commanded to beg the pardon of every individual whom he had wronged and forbidden to enter his parish church for five months. Every Sunday during this period he was to come as far as the church door, where he was to remain intoning litanies and penitential psalms while the mass was going on.[91]

We may wonder whether anyone who was inclined to make "a particularly brutal and sacrilegious attack" on another would be very much deterred by the prospect of having to perform such a penance as this if caught.[92] We may wonder equally whether the example of John of Heyford, beaten three times in the market place for debauching a nun, would have done much to deter a man minded to the same offense. That deterrents of this kind did not sufficiently deter is borne out by the witness of the clergy themselves in the case of violence to their persons. Their pleas for royal protection against such violence reach the point of desperation by the fifteenth century.[93]

The penances actually imposed, then, seem to have been insufficient to deter or at least insufficient to deter the bad man we are considering. The question that naturally arises is why they were not made more severe. The answer would seem to be that, given the ethos of the system, they could not have been. We have already remarked that the actual practice met the goal of salutariness rather well. The aim of salutary pastoral correction for those who were amenable to such correction could hardly be sacrificed to the deterrence of those who were not so amenable. Many a sinner walking barefoot into church with a candle in his hand must have been led to reflect on the offense he had done to God and neighbor and to resolve to mend his ways, whereas the cruder punishments meted out by the secular authorities would only have hardened him. Thus, the sytem of penance in many cases served the purpose for which it was designed and could not have been radically altered without being false to that most important purpose.[94]

When we turn from the types of offense for which penances were customarily imposed to the myriad administrative violations that sapped the organizational efficiency of the church in so many ways, we come to a still more serious obstacle to the expansion of the system of penance to afford a deterrent. As long as the system was articulated in terms of sin, the severity of the penance had to be proportionate to the moral guilt involved rather than to the need for deterring the offense as determined by its effect on the work and witness of the church. Pluralism, nonresidence, ordination outside the diocese were vices that the church was under an urgent necessity of deterring, but morally they were not to be compared with shedding blood in church or with debauching nuns, and it would have been scandalous to visit them with a comparable penance. Generally, then, as a sanction addressed to the effective administration of the canon law, the system of penance must be considered at best peripheral.

E. Imprisonment.

The ordinary use of a prison in the canonical system, as in the secular systems of the time, was for the custody of an accused person pending the final disposition of his case. A decretal of Boniface VIII, however, allowed an ordinary, if he found it expedient in a particular case, to send one of his own clergy to prison to do penance.[95] Earlier, Gratian had collected a few documents allowing the assignment of a *locus penitentiae;* these texts, however, envisage a monastery rather than a prison.

Whether physical confinement was in a monastery or in a prison, it seems clear from the canonical texts that such confinement was conceived as a form of penance rather than as a distinct kind of punishment. We may suppose that its imposition was affected by the considerations already discussed that limited the severity of penances. In any event, the only persons generally imprisoned under canonical processes in England were clerics who had been previously convicted of felony by the secular courts. The use of this sanction in cases of this kind seems to be the result of a complicated church-state dialectic rather than of an independent determination by the ecclesiastical authorities of the appropriate sanction in such cases.[96] The prelates were under continual pressure from the secular authorities to make the imprisonment of felonious clerics more certain and more burdensome than they customarily did.[97]

F. Money Payments.

There were three ways in which the canonical system provided for the exaction of money. One was as a civil remedy, corresponding to contract or tort damages in our own secular system; one was as a punishment, corresponding to a fine in our system; and one was as an administrative device.

The first, the civil remedy, was available wherever the jurisdiction of the church extended by reason of the sin of one man against another. Thus, one who had pledged his faith to the payment of a sum of money could be admonished to pay it on pain of excommunication, and one who had wronged another could be compelled in connection with the process of penance and absolution to make due restitution in money or in kind.[98] In England the

secular authorities regarded the availability of these remedies in the church
courts as a trespass upon the secular jurisdiction, and they issued writs of
prohibition against proceedings in which such remedies were sought. Nevertheless, these remedies must have been more or less effective, as they continued to be sought and granted throughout the Middle Ages, albeit in cases
pretty much peripheral to the main administrative necessities of the church.[99]
     The second form of financial exaction, that which corresponds to the sec-
ular fine, was used frequently enough as a form of penance, but it seems to
have had less bite than the personal or bodily penances did. The requirement
of public decorum in the imposition of penances, as outlined by Miss Hill,
may well furnish the explanation of this weakness. Financial returns in medieval society were attached to functions of public importance. A man who
had money used it to maintain the prestige necessary to do his job and the
assistants he required in doing it efficiently. Thus, a large sum of money
taken from him would be felt in his public function rather than in his private
comfort.
     Conversely, if, as was often the case, the financial exaction took the form
of a requirement that the sinner establish some concrete memorial of his pen-
itence—an endowed mass, a chapel, or something of the kind—the prestige
gained from the good work might well be so advantageous to the sinner as
to outweigh the financial cost. Under such circumstances, the financial expenditure might be edifying as a tangible pledge of contrition and reform,
but it would not be so burdensome as to afford a deterrent from the sin in
question.
     Even in the realm of edification, the money payment proved infelicitous.
Since it was, or appeared to be, less burdensome to the penitent than personal or bodily penances would have been, it almost inevitably gave the impression of being a kind of bribe by which the rich could avoid the penances
visited upon the poor.[100] This impression was heightened by a fairly common
abuse whereby the pious contribution enjoined as a penance would redound
to the material benefit of the authority imposing the penance. Under the
circumstances, the imposition of money penances fell rather early into a
disrepute from which it never recovered.[101]
     The third use of money payments—as an administrative device—involved
an exercise of control over the money itself or the source of it rather than
over the person of the one possessed of it. Under the name of sequestration,
such an exercise of control was regularly resorted to in order to preserve the
subject matter of a suit *pendente lite*.[102] As a device for the achievement of
substantive administrative results, it has just enough recognition in the canons to raise a tantalizing question as to why it was not put into general use.
It appears in the Decretals in the form of a letter from Gregory IX to the
patriarch of Antioch, ordering him to recall his clergy to residence and, if

they do not return, to use the fruits of their benefices to provide for the service of their cures as long as they remain absent.[103] This would seem a rather practical approach to the problem of nonresidence, as it spared the bishop the necessity of finding the elusive incumbent before proceeding against him. The English ecclesiastical authorities may have used sequestration occasionally in this way.[104] More often, however, it seems to have assumed an ancillary role in a proceeding fundamentally directed at the personal correction of the nonresident.[105]

Another example of controlling revenues for administrative purposes is presented by one of Ottobuono's English canons of 1268, on the subject of dilapidations. It provides that if an incumbent, after a monition is issued, fails for two months to make necessary repairs to a building for which he is responsible, the bishop may himself have the repairs made and pay for them out of the fruits of the benefice.[106] This provision has no counterpart in the general canon law; the only provision in the Decretals envisages personal correction of the incumbent who fails to make repairs, and the canons collected by Gratian say nothing about procedure.[107]

One other use of a comparable device in England is found in the procedure by which a bishop might sequester a benefice to pay the debts of the incumbent. This, however, was in response to a royal writ, and there is no indication the canons authorized it.[108]

Sanctions of this kind, involving the exercise of control over the physical facilities of a diocese rather than over the persons of the clergy, could have given the ecclesiastical authorities a great deal of increased administrative flexibility and made up for many of the gaps in the system of personal correction. It is difficult to fathom, therefore, why such sanctions were not given anything like the scope of which they were capable. There is no real answer to such a question as this, but it is possible to guess. My own guess is that administrative techniques that operated on things rather than persons presented an alien appearance in the canonical structure because the canonical structure was founded on personal moral leadership.[109] We, in our own time, distinguish so readily between the pastoral and the administrative functions of a prelate that it is hard for us to empathize an attitude that would regard them as one. Yet there is much in the canonical materials to warn us that in the mind of a medieval bishop the work of administering his diocese in accordance with the canons is the heart of his pastoral work and ought to be carried out in a manner becoming a shepherd of souls.

G. Suspension and Deprivation.

A number of punishments in the canonical system related to the cleric's tenure of his benefices and his clerical status. They ranged from a short period of suspension from benefice or other source of income[110] to permanent reduction to the lay state. It appears that these should not be regarded as another form of penance but rather as a distinct sanction. Unless the offender failed to appear when summoned, neither excommunication nor absolution formed any part of the procedure leading up to suspension and deprivation: the moral rehabilitation of the offender punished in this way was evidently left to the ordinary process of private confession.

Except in the case of short suspensions inflicted on account of relatively minor infractions, it was not customary to inflict punishment of this kind until the offender had been given a monition and an opportunity to reform.[111] Even where the canons purported to inflict this punishment automatically, as we have seen, the tendency was to give the offender a chance to rehabilitate himself before exposing him to their full rigor. This leniency seems to be another product of the moralizing tendency of the whole system.[112]

The moralizing tendency evidently affected the severity of this class of punishments as it did that of penances. Miss Hill tells us that the cleric who procured ordination outside his diocese without the requisite letters dimissory was "usually punished by a short period of suspension from celebrating mass or from holding a cure of souls."[113] This punishment was probably reasonably proportioned to the moral guilt involved in failing to abide by a technical rule of this kind. From an administrative standpoint, however, the rule was of considerable importance. Wholesale failure to abide by it meant that any bishop who attempted to improve the quality of his ordinands was at the mercy of the least responsible of his colleagues. This was not the kind of consideration likely to occur spontaneously to the mind of a young man aspiring to ordination, thus the moral guilt of the violator could scarcely have been expected to correspond to the importance of the law. In this context, apportioning the punishment to moral guilt overlooked an important educative function of the law: the severity of the punishment plays a significant part in teaching the importance of the law. Punishing one offender lightly because he did not think the violation very important might well lead the next man to think the violation was not very important because it was punished lightly.

Coordinate with the use of suspension and deprivation as a punishment for the moral lapses of the clergy was the failure to use it as an administrative measure. It appears not to have been possible to remove a man from his benefice on the mere ground that he was unable to do effectively the job for which the benefice was provided. Such a one might be assigned a coadjutor to do the work and required to assign him a *congrua sustentatio* out of the fruits of the benefice. This procedure is provided for in the Decretals in the case of a person suffering from some physical disability, and there is a record of its being done in the case of a person unable to speak the language of his parishioners.[114] Under some circumstances, a beneficed cleric might be allowed to resign if he was willing to, although he might instead be accused of proposing a cowardly desertion of his flock—Innocent III dealt with this subject at great length.[115] But in no case could he be deprived of his benefice for mere incompetence or disability. As a canon taken from Gregory the Great, which heads up the title of the Decretals on sick or debilitated clergy, puts it:

> Since, when one is striken in body, we cannot know whether in the judgment of God it was for his punishment or for his purgation we ought not to add to the affliction of those who have been thus scourged . . .[116]

When we speak of the sanctions in a legal system, we refer to the sum total of the measures it takes for imposing upon society the standards it envisages. These measures include motivating desirable behavior, deterring undesirable behavior, and, when undesirable behavior has taken place, reshaping affairs in order to mitigate its consequences as much as possible. The canonical system sought to accomplish all these aims by a powerful and subtle moral witness calculated to instill in the hearts and consciences of men the vision of order on which the system was based. It is because of this concentration on moral witness that the system seems hopelessly ineffective from the standpoint of the determined and incorrigible bad man we have been considering. The sanctions that were regularly imposed were not sufficiently burdensome to deter him, and the sanctions that were sufficiently burdensome were used only as a last resort—deferred for long periods in the hope that the culprit might yet reform. Nor was any effort made while his reform was awaited to mitigate the harm he was doing to the fabric of the Christian society or to the work and witness of the church.

In short, pastoral solicitude was the keynote of the sanction structure of the medieval canon law, as pastoral instruction and exhortation were the keynote of its substantive content. A system of this kind showed a good deal of capacity for governing the Christian community at a time when it was a live option in the society whether to belong to that community or not. But a system that is to order a whole society must check in some way the bad man as well as the good because a whole society will exhibit an important number of such men.

V. Conclusion

What seems to emerge from the foregoing analysis is that the highly developed juridical structure given the canon law by its early medieval theorists did not turn the system from its basic orientation toward the support and guidance of the personal pastorate by the corporate witness of the church. This orientation led the system to its characteristic stresses on formal articulation at the expense of functional application, on pastoral leadership at the expense of legal obligation, and on moral correction at the expense of physical coercion.

This close connection with the pastorate imposed on the canonical system an eschatological understanding of its goals: where secular systems aim at the establishment and maintenance of a concrete and realizable external social order, the canon law aimed at the ultimate establishment of the Kingdom of God over the hearts of men. By the same token, since the goal was eschatological, there could be no question of marshaling available resources for its foreseeable achievement: where secular systems work through the available means of social control, the canon law worked through a personal and corporate witness to the underlying eschatological vision.

The difference between the canon law as animated by these pastoral and eschatological commitments and a secular legal system was obscured by the theoretical elegance and practical unreality of the late Roman secular law— all the more so as that system received renewed theoretical vigor from the medieval legists after it had ceased to be living law in any existing society. But if we look for an example of a secular system not in the Roman law, but in the early medieval secular systems as they painfully shaped their scant resources of social control for the achievement of a rudimentary order in society, the contrast is apparent enough. The churchmen were not unaware of this contrast, but they tended to see it in eschatological rather than practical terms; they found their law superior to the world's law as the Kingdom of God is superior to the kingdoms of the world.

What I am suggesting here is not so much that the canon law was bad as that it was not in the usual sense a legal system. The pastoral and eschatological orientation of the canon law as I have described it arises out of the basic commitment of the church as a religious institution, and it is far more important to the church than a legal system is. But the fact remains that if a legal system is—as most modern jurists would conceive it to be—necessarily oriented toward the imposition and maintenance of a desirable social order through the efficacious application of the available means of social control, the medieval canon law was not essentially a legal system. *Dum colitur Maria, expellitur Martha.* Given the responsibilities assumed by the medieval church together with its great resources in material and personnel, the canon law had necessarily the work of a legal system to do. This work, by and large, it did badly, precisely because its guiding vision was fixed on higher and better things.

4. Provincial and Diocesan Authorities

The three key institutions of the medieval church as it took shape against this legal and ideological background were the papacy, the episcopate, and the parish ministry. Of the three, it was the episcopate, with its ancillary agencies of diocesan and provincial administration, that bore, at least in England, the real burden of running the church. The parish ministry, with its revenues and personnel continually diverted into other activities, was hard put even to maintain minimal standards of pastoral service. As for the papacy, it was active enough in the administration of the English church, but whether its intervention served any useful purpose is more problematical. In this chapter, I will deal with the episcopate and the agencies centered on the episcopate, as the pivotal institutions of ecclesiastical administration in England.

I. Structure

A. Diocesan Officials.

In the church, as in the state, the shift from peripatetic to feudal administration involved the breaking up of central revenues into separate endowments for separate offices and functions.[1] By the end of the twelfth century, when forward-looking administrators were thinking about centralization once again, these functions and endowments had become subject to legal conceptions of property and philosophical conceptions of corporate life that made them sacrosanct. Central authority had to reestablish itself not by abolishing offices and resuming their revenues, but by bestowing the offices intact on central bureaucrats who performed the functions by deputy.

The bishop was in a worse position than other central authorities either to resist the assumption of independent life by his subordinates or to divert their revenues to his own central staff.[2] He had neither the political leverage of the king nor the juridical supremacy of the pope. Further, more often than not he found both king and pope supporting the pretensions of his subordinates in opposition to him. Under the prevailing conceptions of corporate life, it was considered a work of munificence to enrich pious foundations with juridical immunities, and immunity from the bishop came high on the list. On a more practical level, it was more advantageous to both king and pope to detach diocesan offices from the personal authority of the bishop and fill them with royal or papal bureaucrats who would perform the diocesan functions by deputy. As a result of these processes, a fourteenth- or fifteenth-century bishop found himself at the head of a complex variety of officials and institutions, originally dependent on his person, often still acting in his name, but each with an independent juridical life, with which he could tamper only in highly restricted ways.

At the center of the picture was the bishop's cathedral chapter,[3] descendant of the ancient clerical familia that was to the bishop what his comitatus was to the Anglo-Saxon king. The decentralizing movements of the tenth and eleventh centuries had resulted first in separating the landed endowments of the chapter from those of the bishop and then in breaking up most of the capitular endowments into separate "prebends," each supporting one of the canons. This arrangement obtained in something like half of the English dioceses; in the others, there was a community of monks constituting the cathedral chapter, a heritage from the days of monastic dominance in the Anglo-Saxon church. In either case, the chapter had not only financial endowments separate from those of the bishop, but also jurisdictional "peculiars"—enclaves in which it exercised ecclesiastical jurisdiction through its own officers to the almost complete exclusion of the bishop. These were apt to include the cathedral precincts, a large part of the see city, the prebendal or appropriated churches, and many of the secular estates of the chapter.

The bishop was supposed to have a good deal of supervisory authority over his cathedral chapter. If it was monastic, he was its abbot; if it was a secular chapter, he had a general power of visitation. In fact, however, his rights in both cases were severely limited. Often these limitations had been laid down in a series of epic struggles carried on with the usual methods of jurisdictional warfare in the medieval church—a compound of litigation, physical violence, and passive resistance. By and large, these struggles had been given over by the middle of the fourteenth century and replaced by relatively pacific arrangements in which the powers of the bishop were spelled out. Generally, he was left with a primacy of honor, but little power of effective interference.

The administrative functions of the chapter were supposed to involve advising the bishop in all his diocesan affairs.[4] In fact, however, this work was limited to certain official acts such as the alienation of landed estates. In some dioceses, the chapter administered or assisted in administering the diocese during the vacancy of the see; in all of them it had at least a nominal role in the election of a new bishop. Otherwise, the monastic chapter seems to have served no administrative purpose whatever, the secular chapter no administrative purpose beyond providing financial support for high-class clerics and keeping a certain number of these in residence at the cathedral. Even this limited function was as apt to redound to the benefit of the king and the pope as to that of the bishop. While the canonries were generally all in the gift of the bishop, they were the most lucrative positions in the church, and he was often not left to bestow them in peace. The pope claimed a general right to provide to benefices in the gift of ecclesiastical persons, and he exercised it freely. The king, as custodian of the temporalities of the see, claimed the right to nominate an occupant to any benefice in the bishop's gift that fell vacant during the vacancy of the see.

After the peculiars of the chapter, further enclaves of exemption would be found attached to one or more of the great monasteries of the diocese. Some of the Anglo-Saxon foundations (Abingdon, for instance) remained in their primordial submission to the diocesan bishop as long as they existed; but those that were founded under powerful auspices after the Conquest (Battle, for instance) or those that experienced strong administrations in that period (Bury, for instance) were apt to be enriched with far-reaching exemptions, granted or confirmed by papal authority.[5] These would include not only the exclusion of the bishop from any supervisory authority over the monastery itself, but also exclusive jurisdiction for the monastery over a certain number of its appropriated churches or secular estates.

In addition to these monastic and capitular enclaves that appeared in most dioceses, there was apt to be some royal free chapel, in which all ecclesiastical jurisdiction was exercised by the king through his own clerics, or one or more enclaves belonging to the metropolitan or to some other bishop from outside the diocese.[6] Finally, there might be some subordinate diocesan official, such as the archdeacon of Richmond in the archdiocese of York, who enjoyed in his own territory jurisdictional rights more or less beyond the reach of the diocesan bishop.

In that part of the diocese which was not exempt from the authority of the bishop, there were exercised a number of subordinate offices over which he had varying degrees of control. Of these, the most independent, and in many ways the most important, was that of the archdeacon.[7] This ancient office, originally involved serving the bishop as a kind of executive officer and head of the clerical familia. By the end of the twelfth century, it had come to involve the exercise of definite judicial functions over a specific portion of a diocese. In England, there was generally one archdeacon to a county. Having been in existence at the time separate endowments were set up, the archdeaconries were benefices and sometimes cathedral benefices at that. Thus, the bishop could not remove one of his archdeacons without such cumbersome judicial proceedings that it was hardly worthwhile for him to try. In theory, when the archdeaconry fell vacant, the bishop could appoint to it, but his rights in this regard were subject to the same royal and papal encroachments that affected the other benefices in his gift.

The chief duties of the archdeacon were to supervise the clergy in his territory, to institute clerics into parochial benefices, and to hold a visitation in each of the years between the triennial visitations the bishop was supposed to hold. He also had a court, which had had at one time a rather general jurisdiction but was in the process of becoming confined within rather narrow limits. The work of visitation and institution, together with the fact that there was no other permanent judicial officer with less than diocese-wide jurisdiction, made the archdeacon or his court the obvious choice for handling certain matters relating to local benefices and their incumbents when such matters came before the bishop. If the archdeacon was at all reliable or had a reliable official holding his court, a number of such cases would come his way on reference from the bishop; otherwise, the bishop would presumably have had to resort to ad hoc delegations.

In fact, it appears that the archdeacon often could not be relied on for much. The machinery of his court was devoted in large part to collecting the various payments to which he was entitled. The visitations that furnished the reason for the payments in question were often commuted in one way or another so that the clergy might avoid the expense of being visited. Further, the offenses turned up on visitation or otherwise were apt to be punished by pecuniary fines in lieu of corporal penances. In short, most archdeaconries afforded more in the way of financial benefit to their incumbents than they did in the way of administrative benefit to their dioceses.[8] The popes recognized this fact by rather freely bestowing on high-class archdeacons permission to perform their functions by deputy, thus leaving them free to perform in person the bureaucratic services for which they had been given these lucrative benefices. The bishop recognized the same fact by looking to someone other than the archdeacon to assist him in the administration of the diocese.

For this purpose, he had two officials of diocese-wide authority, the vicar general and the official principal.[9] The vicar general's job was basically to do the routine work of the diocese when the bishop was away; at first his powers lapsed when the bishop was in the diocese. But by the end of the fourteenth century it was customary for him to go on doing some of the routine work even when the bishop was present, so the bishop could spend his limited periods of residence on more important matters.

The official principal (in some dioceses he went by a different name, such as commissary general) held the bishop's main court, usually called the *consistory*. This court, with a fixed location, a permanent existence, and a staff of lawyers and officials, went pretty much its own way, although the bishop could sit himself if he chose or (as was more usual) reserve specific cases to deal with in other ways.

The positions of vicar general and official principal were not benefices; the bishop compensated the holders by bestowing on them extraneous benefices in his gift. In theory, he could vary their duties and tenure at will, but in practice the forces of custom and bureaucratic inertia inhibited him from doing so. The historical evolution that combined the two offices after the Reformation into a single freehold office whose functions could not be changed by the bishop seems to have been in process at least as early as the fifteenth century.

There was one official at the local level who figured prominently in the administrative and judicial work of the diocese—the rural dean.[10] Such a dean, set over a group of parishes usually corresponding to a secular hundred, or wapentake, was chosen from the resident clergy of the deanery. Unlike his continental counterpart, the archpriest, he seems not to have had judicial functions. He served the bishop and his courts rather as an ecclesiastical sheriff. He served citations, promulgated excommunications, admonished absent clerics to reside, reported on the performance of public penances, and looked into dilapidations—all at the behest of the bishop or his court, or occasionally the archdeacon. He seems to have done nothing except on specific orders, though it is likely enough that the orders were common forms and the functions they imposed in some way fixed by custom.

In addition to these relatively stable officers, the bishop had various seneschals, bailiffs, and the like to administer his temporal landholdings. He was also apt to have one or more suffragan bishops, occupying benefices in his gift and commissioned to perform on his behalf those functions that required episcopal orders (for example, confirmation, ordination, and consecration of churches). Some of these were bishops consecrated for the purpose and assigned by the pope to titular sees in lands occupied by Moslems; others were Irish bishops set wandering by the vicissitudes of the times or the poverty of their sees.

It would seem that the bishop was apt to be dissatisfied with this pattern of routinization of his business, for the registers show a wide variety of matters withdrawn from routine handling and committed to ad hoc delegations.[11] These delegations also, if they were repeated, tended to crystallize first into common forms and then into offices with some rights of tenure attached. The result was a variety of agencies for routine business, different ones in different dioceses. But the multiplication of such agencies evidently did nothing to abate the number of matters that had to be treated as nonroutine; the volume of ad hoc delegations goes on undiminished up to the time of the Reformation.

It is instructive to contrast episcopal with royal administration in their attitudes toward ad hoc delegation. The royal authorities developed quite early a policy of refusing any request for nonroutine handling of a matter unless there were definite reasons why it could not be handled routinely. The bishops, by contrast, habitually issued special commissions that duplicated the work of routine officials or even of each other.

I suspect that pastoral considerations played some part in this rather fortuitous intrusion of the bishop's person into his administration. He may well have felt that his role as shepherd of souls was not sufficiently discharged by setting up a body of officials and letting them go to work. Also, the bishop, unlike the king, was not in a good position to accomplish his purposes through controlling the operations of his bureaucracy. The canon law was weak on procedural forms for exercising this kind of control. It had nothing corresponding to the royal prerogative writs—prohibition, quo warranto, mandamus, certiorari, error, and the like. Canonical appellate procedure did not make subordinate tribunals correct their mistakes; it did their work over again for them. Further, such control as the bishop might have had through the regular processes of canonical appeal was often denied him by the fact that he could not hear appeals from his own consistory court. The judgments of that court, even if he did not participate in them, were in theory his own, so that they were appealable to the metropolitan rather than to him.[12]

Not only did the bishop lack formal devices for controlling his subordinates; he also did not have nearly as much informal leverage as was available to the king. His subordinates were not always of his own choosing; even if they were, they were not wholly dependent on him for preferment. Also, the bishop was often himself a bureaucrat with a wider field of service than his diocese and with further preferment to look forward to. He was often absent on far-off matters of church or state. If he was capable and his diocese was small, his tenure was apt to be short; he might soon be translated to a more important see. Thus, the all-important knowledge of what to do and whom to see in order to set bureaucratic machinery in prompt and effective motion was not likely to be at his fingertips. It would be easier, when a particular matter came to his attention, to bypass his bureaucratic machinery, as he had undoubted power to do.

B. The Episcopate.[13]

The bishop himself, in whose name the administrative machinery of the diocese was run, need not detain us long. His part in the diocesan administration, his other functions in church and state, his antecedents, and the manner of his appointment have all been exhaustively treated in a series of modern historical works covering intervals of a century or less from the reign of William II through that of Edward VI. I shall do no more than summarize briefly the conclusions that emerge from those works as to the recruitment, appointment, and functions of the bench of bishops.

As regards recruitment, it seems we can classify the bishops in four groups according to their backgrounds before entering on the episcopal office. First come the veterans of the royal bureaucracy. These were men who served the king in one capacity or another, receiving for their support and compensation benefices in his gift, culminating in the episcopate. This class predominated in the late eleventh century, reached a low point in the reign of Henry II, increased thereafter, reaching a peak in the mid-fourteenth century, fell off somewhat later in that century, began increasing again, and became again predominant during the fifteenth.

Next come the ecclesiastical administrators. Sometimes such men enjoyed papal or royal favor, but they were usually the choice of their fellow-clerics. Thus, they were most apt to appear among the bishops when the canonical electors were allowed an untrammeled choice. Except during the relatively anarchic period of Stephen's reign, such untrammeled choice was so rare that this class of bishops was never numerically significant, although in all periods some of them were found in the less important sees.

Third come the scholars and spiritual leaders—monks before the rise of the universities, university teachers thereafter. There were usually one or two of them on the bench. An impetus that seems to have originated with the Fourth Lateran Council of 1215 gave this group something more than minimal representation during the thirteenth century and the first years of the fourteenth, including such men as Grosseteste and Langton. But then the impetus waned. From the middle of the fourteenth century there were only a handful of bishops whose primary work before their elevation was in the field of scholarship, until Henry VIII began bestowing bishoprics on university theologians who supported his claim to a divorce.

Finally, there were the politicians and diplomatists who served the same interests as the bureaucrats but in a broader and more spectacular way. The one who comes most readily to mind is Wolsey at the close of the medieval period, but Gilbert Foliot in the twelfth century seems to have reached the episcopal rank through somewhat similar channels. Men of this kind had, of course, an influence disproportionate to their numbers. The nearest they came to a position of numerical strength was during the reign of Richard II.

The mechanics of the process by which these men came to the bench we will take up when we deal with the papacy, which played the major canonical role. However an appointment came about juridically, the decisive political part in it was usually the king's. By the mid-fourteenth century, cathedral chapters and local magnates had been deprived of what little say they had had in the past, and even the pope was generally content to accept the king's nominees.

As regards the bishop's role after his elevation, there was a good deal of variety. Some bishops had high places in the royal bureaucracy. Others were involved in political and diplomatic activities, serving the king's business abroad or mediating between king and pope. In times of political upheaval, some bishops took advantage of their landed endowments to play a part among the higher nobility. On the other hand, there were always a certain number who confined themselves fairly well to the pastoral and administrative work of their dioceses. Examples are Grosseteste in the thirteenth century, Trillek in the fourteenth, Alnwick in the fifteenth.

But the general trend up to the Reformation was for the number and influence of the full-time bishops to decrease. This is due in part no doubt to a tightening royal control over appointments and a consequent increase in the number of royal servants on the bench. Both outside pressure and personal inclination would presumably have moved such men to continue the careers that had brought about their elevation. Also, it seems likely that the administrative routinizations of the fourteenth century and the compromises effected to settle jurisdictional squabbles had left the function of a bishop in his dioceses insufficiently challenging to command the full-time attention of a first rate man. You could find in the thirteenth century a full-time bishop like Hugh of Wells, who was forceful and sometimes creative in running his diocese, or even one like Grosseteste, who expanded the episcopal function to fit his particular abilities. But the full-time bishop of the fourteenth century, a man like Trillek, impresses us as a decent, competent, middle-rank administrator, nothing more.

C. Provincial Organization.

The functions of the metropolitan bishop in his province were settled fairly early as to fundamentals, though the details varied considerably from province to province, and even between dioceses in the same province. The fundamentals were these:[14]

1. Supervising suffragans through canonical "visitation," a device I will take up in due course. It was too unwieldy and too acrimonious for more than occasional use.
2. A general, ill-defined function of filling in the breach if a suffragan was not doing his job. The general function was given specific content in some cases by legislation (for example, filling a benefice if the suffragan left it vacant too long), sometimes by administrative practice (for example, hearing a case if the suffragan's courts were too slow), sometimes by canonical tradition (for example, appointing a coadjutor for a suffragan too infirm to do his work).
3. Administering a suffragan diocese during a vacancy of the see. This

function was often disputed with the suffragan's cathedral chapter, and
various compromises were made that limited the metropolitan's rights.
In England, his rights were further limited by the successful assertion
of the king's right to hold the temoralities of the vacant see.

4. Supervising the election of a successor to a vacant suffragan see, passing on the fitness of the elect, and consecrating him if he was found
   fit. By the mid-fourteenth century, most of this work was taken over
   by the papacy under its system of provisions.
5. Summoning and presiding at provincial synods.
6. Hearing appeals from the courts of the suffragans.
7. Certain liturgical and ceremonial prerogatives and functions, such as
   the wearing of the pallium and the bearing of a cross within the province.

As regards local variations on these fundamental themes, there were one
or two institutions that seem to have been peculiar to the two English provinces. The most important of these was Convocation,[15] a modification of the
provincial synod on the analogy of the secular parliament. The Convocation
of each province consisted (and still consists) of its bishops, constituting one
house, and its higher clergy together with representatives of some of the lower
clergy, constituting a second house. The two Convocations developed more or
less contemporaneously with Parliament, and, in the later medieval period,
met whenever Parliament met. They were summoned by the archbishops,
who could in theory summon them on their own motion but in practice
came to do so only when ordered by the king. The king so ordered whenever he summoned a Parliament. The function of Convocation, as far as the
king was concerned, was to vote taxes on the clergy, as Parliament did on the
laity. In practice, Convocation, like Parliament, took advantage of the king's
financial necessities to present grievances and sometimes to obtain concessions. It also used the occasion of its meeting to enact such ecclesiastical
legislation as the needs of the church might require.

This institution, while it has roots in conciliar legislation providing for
the voting of clerical subsidies to secular rulers, seems basically homegrown.
Its part in medieval administration may not have been as great as its part in
post Reformation ecclesiology, but it did serve to institutionalize the church-
state dialectic more fully than any continental institution did, and it seems
also to have provided the English church with more opportunity for legislation than the continental churches had.

Of the two provinces making up the English church, one was a good deal
more important and more highly developed than the other.[16] York, with
only three small suffragan sees, had no occasion to develop, as Canterbury
did, a substantial full-time machinery of central administration. Nor was it
large enough or well enough organized to take an independent line in mat-

ters of national concern. This imbalance enabled the Convocation and other provincial institutions of Canterbury to serve in some measure as those of the whole English church.

The same imbalance gave the archbishop of Canterbury a good deal more importance than he would have had as merely one of two metropolitans. As head of the greater part of the English clergy, he was a spokesman for the church vis-à-vis the state and for England in general vis-à-vis the papacy. The importance of this mediating position was enhanced by his status as papal legate. The popes began giving legatine powers to the archbishops at a rather early date because they found it difficult to get the secular authorities to admit legates *a latere* into the country. By the mid-fourteenth century, the custom had become so firm that the archbishop's legatine powers were said to inhere in his see: he was characterized as *legatus natus*. As the records seldom specify in what capacity a given action is taken, it is not clear what specific things, if any, the archbishop did as legate. We can only say that his combined sources of power and influence made him easily the first prelate, and perhaps the first magnate, in the kingdom.

Canterbury profited by its special position to develop a court system capable of holding its own in the jurisdictional quarrels of the day and of expanding its functions not only at the expense of the suffragan sees, but even at that of the papacy. This court system as it existed at the close of the Middle Ages included, in addition to the archbishop's Audience, where more or less routine handling was given to matters reserved for the personal disposition of the archbishop, two courts separated from the archbishop's personal jurisdiction, specialized in provincial, as distinguished from diocesan, business. One of these, the Prerogative Court, exercised the jurisdiction of the metropolitan to administer the estates of those who died leaving goods of significant value (*bona notabilia*) in more than one diocese. This court did not play as important a part as it was to do after the Reformation. Aspects of its jurisdiction were debatable as late as the fourteenth century, perhaps later; and it was not fully evolved as a court till the fifteenth.

The court that played the largest part in Canterbury's expanded metropolitan jurisdiction was the Court of Canterbury, commonly called the Court of Arches, after the building where it sat (the church of one of the archbishop's jurisdictional enclaves in London). This court had a general appellate jurisdiction over the province and original jurisdiction in cases presenting grounds for bypassing the suffragan. Its development was relatively early. It was sitting in a fixed place by the middle of the thirteenth century. By the end of the century, it had moved from Canterbury to the capital and had gained a staff of full-time specialized judges and administrative personnel. Practice before it was regulated by a series of archiepiscopal statutes, beginning with one of Archbishop Kilwardby (1272–78).[17]

The advantage enjoyed by so stable and well-organized a court as this in the competition for business was obvious. Other English ecclesiastical courts, although they too were moving in the direction of routinizing their business and stabilizing their personnel, had nothing nearly so elaborate to offer.[18] The papal judges-delegate, in addition to being usually the nominees of one of the parties, were part-time judges, having neither special experience in particular types of litigation nor a staff with developed routines for expediting their business. As early as the late thirteenth century, the archbishops of Canterbury were boasting that their court was something very special among the ecclesiastical courts of the world.

Accompanying these superior advantages to litigants, the Canterbury Court developed a number of devices for making its jurisdiction available in the first instance, bypassing the courts of the various suffragans.[19] The broadest of the powers that could be relied on for this purpose was that of acting in the case of a failure of the suffragan to render justice to one who invoked his jurisdiction. A procedure developed rather early whereby a process would issue out of the Arches commanding a suffragan bishop to hear a given case within a specified number of days or else cite the defendant to come into the Arches and answer the plaintiff there. The use of this device to encroach on the jurisdiction of the suffragan by giving him an unreasonably short time to hear the case was one of the abuses dealt with by Archbishop Winchelsea in 1295.

Another device for bypassing an inferior jurisdiction was the *provocacio*, a document in which a defendant cited into a lower court, asserting some kind of vague fear that he would not get justice there. This device invoked the appellate jurisdiction in advance of any determination in the court where the proceeding was originally brought. It was of course quite destructive of any system for the orderly devolution of cases, and an attempt was made in the Fourth Lateran Council to curb it. In fact, however, it continued to be used, and continued to draw cases from the lower courts, into the Arches.

In other cases the jurisdiction of a lower court may have been bypassed through "letters of request," which would issue if the lower court could be persuaded that a case was so difficult that the appellate court should be asked to handle it. I have found no direct evidence of the use of this device before the Reformation, but it was expressly permitted in the Statue of Citations of 1532, and it is unlikely that the framers of that statute invented it.

A final device enabled the Arches to draw cases not only from the lower diocesan courts, but from the Roman see itself. This was the "tuitorial appeal."[20] By this procedure a party appealing to Rome appealed at the same time "for protection to the Court of Canterbury." The Arches would then intervene to protect the status quo while the appellant was prosecuting his appeal either in Rome or before papal judges-delegate. It might also deal with ancillary aspects of the case itself, such as costs. At some point, it began going further and disposing of a number of these cases on the merits. By what right it did this is not clear. Perhaps the parties consented, or perhaps a disposition on the merits grew out of the inquiries necessary to the extension of the protection requested. In cases of this kind, the Canterbury Court always insisted that it was acting as ancillary to the Roman see, and, indeed, the whole proceeding may well have come out of the archbishop's powers as *legatus natus*. Be that as it may, the Canterbury Court did in fact deal with these cases through its own machinery, excluding *pro tanto* that of the Roman see.

The metropolitan authority of Canterbury, as we have been considering it, seems to be the only element in English ecclesiastical administration that showed real possibilities for creative development in the direction of more effective techniques. We may wonder why those possibilities were not more fully realized. The question is especially troublesome in that the defects in other parts of the system do not seem to be of a kind that a vigorous and creative central administration could not have overcome. Could another Theodore, or even another Lanfranc, not have made something of the late medieval organization of the English Church?

The short answer is that another Theodore or another Lanfranc would not have gotten the job. Still less, if he had gotten the job, would he have been able to hold it and do as he pleased in it. Much of the weakness of the English church administration lay not in its internal organization but in the limitations imposed on it from without.

D. External Limitations: Royal and Papal Government.

The crown and the papacy were the two millstones that ground the English church administration. Both had wide scope for intervening in local affairs, and both had policies rather different from those the local authorities were supposed to implement. I will consider them specifically in other chapters, but I must note in passing here how they diverted the resources and limited the options available to local administration.

It was in the area of personnel that the outside influence was most forcefully felt. Both king and pope had large and growing bureaucratic establishments, which they had to find parish or diocesan benefices to support. To place his clerics, the king had many benefices permanently in his gift and others that came his way from time to time. Still others, by custom or political leverage, he could get the regular patrons to fill with his men. The pope, for his part, claimed in theory a right to "provide" a man of his choosing to any benefice in Christendom and in practice an increasingly unrestricted right to provide to any such benefice in the gift of a churchman. Between the two of them, king and pope accounted for the pick of the benefices a bishop might otherwise have used to support his own staff. They contributed also to the general uselessness of archdeaconries and cathedral chapters in diocesan administration by filling many of them with men who were not of the bishop's choosing and not available for his work.

More problematical was their effect on the parish ministry. The canonical standards for an incumbent—that he be of full age, take the necessary orders, hold only one benefice, and reside on that—were inconsistent with any significant bureaucratic service on his part. They were scarcely formulated in the Third and Fourth Lateran Councils before the popes were dispensing from them, and the kings insisting that clerics in the royal service should be exempt. For most of the Middle Ages, the bishops acquiesced and indeed participated in this diversion of beneficed clergy from the ministry; they too had staffs to support. In the thirteenth century, however, there were some bishops who made a real effort to enforce the canonical requirements across the board. It might have made a difference to the church if these had not found king and pope making common cause against them for their pains.[21]

Another interest shared by royal and papal government was in the levying of taxes on the local clergy.[22] The king sought grants from Convocation; in theory these were voluntary, but he often applied a good deal of pressure (along with some redress of grievances) to get them. The pope, although he sometimes sought such grants and even offered concessions in exchange for them, generally set more store by his rich and varied sources of revenue that needed no consent from the local prelates and clergy. Each authority tried on occasion to stop the local hierarchy from complying with the demands of the other. In these efforts, neither had much long-term success. The royal government in a pinch could resort to coercion, as Edward I did to prevent the enforcement of *Clericis Laicos*. While the pope had no such direct power and indeed could not keep a number of his collectors from being spectacularly ejected from the country, he made up in persistence and ingenuity for what he lacked in brute force. It would be rash to say he came off second best in the battle to siphon off the revenues of the English church.

Whether these exactions were a serious financial drain is hard to say. We cannot point to an English prelate who made a bid to put the money to better use or to any important activity of the English church that was curtailed for lack of funds, though we cannot discount the possibility that creative prelates and new activities might have arisen had the funds been there. In any event, the exactions were a burden in other ways. A good deal of local administrative energy was dissipated in the thankless task of collecting them. And when king and pope quarreled over them, a good deal of local political and diplomatic energy was dissipated in trying to keep on the right side of both parties at once.

Besides these sources of joint royal and papal interference, there were certain concerns peculiar to the crown. Royal writs, especially that of prohibition, confined the prelates' jurisdiction within narrower bounds perhaps than they needed, certainly than they desired. Royal courts, enforcing the right of patronage as temporal property, interfered with the bishops' discretion in letting men into benefices, and the incumbents' security in staying there once let in. Finally, the king supported his ancestors' (and to some extent his subjects') pious benefactions in some disregard for the authority of the prelates and even, on occasion, for the needs of the ministry.

The papacy, meanwhile, besides pursuing its own interests at the expense of local ecclesiastical administration, followed a cautious political and diplomatic policy that often led it to prefer the king's interests to those of the English church. Not only did popes fail to back the hierarchy in its disputes with the royal power, they filled English bishoprics with royal nominees, dispensed royal clerics from ecclesiastical duties, immunized the pious foundations of kings and their favorites against the exercise of episcopal jurisdiction, and for a while even supported royal financial exactions.

But it was through general inefficiency and misgovernment as much as through the implementation of any particular policy that the papacy hampered the effectiveness of local administration. Almost any stage of a local process was in danger of interference through cumbersome, expensive, and often misguided proceedings initiated in far-off Avignon or Rome. Censures inflicted by the local authorities were set aside or even disregarded by the curia. Bishops had to keep full-time agents, and even use bribes, to filter their business through the array of auditors, notaries, and functionaries who surrounded the pope without any adequate division of authority or business among them. A newly appointed bishop would often have to mortgage the revenues of his see to the Italian bankers who advanced him the expenses of being confirmed and who enjoyed incidentally by papal delegation the right to excommunicate their defaulting debtors.[23] In addition, the papacy was aggressively jealous of its prerogatives of interference and exercised them regularly to no particular end.

The effect on English church administration of all these different forms of royal and papal interference was inhibiting rather than disrupting. However loudly the bishops complained, they did have funds and benefices to keep up their staffs and were able in general to do the work they were expected to do. They found few occasions for serious confrontations. On the other hand, they found few occasions for innovation either.

Crown and papacy used up the bishops' maneuvering room and left them little financial, jurisdictional, or political scope for creative action. In short, they were among the powerful forces that contributed to holding local ecclesiastical administration in well-worn grooves.

II. Functions

Thus structured, the English ecclesiastical administration set itself a series of tasks that was formidable enough, though rather narrower in scope than an overall supervision of the work and witness of the church would have demanded. The most pervasive concern of the authorities was with the clergy— their recruitment and placement, their deportment, and sometimes their protection. Next came the revenue-producing property by which the church was supported—maintaining and managing it, collecting and distributing the revenues. As to the church's life of faith and worship, they endeavored to keep up minimum standards of reverence in the use of sacred places and objects, of propriety in the observance of sacred times, of regularity in the performance of the liturgy and the administration of the sacraments, of diligence and orthodoxy in preaching and teaching. Finally, they gave what attention they could to the moral life and discipline of the faithful and their conduct as members of the Christian civil community.

A. Clergy.

*1. Recruitment—*A diocesan bishop, or someone in bishop's orders deputed by him, would hold ordinations at varying intervals, sometimes in the cathedral, more often in the chapel of an episcopal manor. He would give about a month's notice so the candidates could be on hand, and would ordain anyone with the requisite qualifications who came.[24] The authorities made no attempt to control recruitment except through routine checks on those who presented themselves.

The first of these checks was evidently up to the archdeacon of the place where the candidate lived. A local man was supposed to be presented by his archdeacon to the ordaining bishop. A man from outside the diocese, unless he had a papal indult, was supposed to present "letters dimissory" from his own bishop. These a careful bishop would not issue until he had had the archdeacon summon an inquest of lay and clerical neighbors to report on the man.[25] Presumably a careful archdeacon would summon the same kind of inquest before presenting an ordinand to the local bishop.

In addition to general bad character, the archdeacon's inquest would presumably have brought into the open any canonical irregularity or disqualification arising from age, illegitimacy, marital status, or notorious acts of violence. Some irregularities of bodily defect might be apparent on observing the ordinand. Otherwise, he was left to his own conscience to report any irregularities and procure dispensations. If he failed to do so, he was barred in conscience from ministering in the order received and could be put out of all his preferment if he was eventually found out. A number of ordinands took on this burden at first but came forward to be dispensed and rehabilitated later on. For most irregularities, dispensations were not hard to come by at any stage.

Orders had to be conferred in a sequence, the four minor orders, the subdiaconate, the diaconate, and then the priesthood. Presumably, therefore— though I find no direct evidence on the point—a man had to show he had received one order before he could be admitted to the next. For this purpose, he probably showed "letters of orders" from the prelate who had previously ordained him. Every ordained cleric was given such letters and had to show them for a number of other purposes.

Every ordinand was supposed to show a "title" or means of supporting himself in the ministry.[26] These titles were carefully recorded, as the bishop was personally responsible for the support of anyone he ordained without one. How a title was established is harder to say. Where a man had a benefice or a presentment to one (a certain number of fledgling bureaucrats were in this case) he must have had documents in his possession to show for it. In other cases, the evidence of neighbors was received or even the unsupported oath of the ordinand himself.

However titles were established on paper, the bulk of them seem in fact to have been fictitious. From half to four-fifths or more of the orders conferred were either on a title of the ordinand's patrimony or on a title conferred by some religious house, most often a poor one (the former being the more usual device in the early fourteenth century, the latter from the late fourteenth century). Nothing like these numbers can have had either the five marks a year of personal resources that they were supposed to have for a patrimonial title, or any genuine work to do for the religious houses that sponsored them. These titles can hardly have been more than formalities to protect the ordaining bishop against liability for support. To this end, they were often fortified with assertions that the respective ordinands were content with them.

The reason for this phenomenon, I suspect, is that the prospect of employment at a salary, which was the genuine source of support for most ordinands, did not become a canonical title till after the Reformation. The medieval practice would allow only a benefice, a patrimony, a pension (not a personal obligation, but a fixed charge on specific revenues), or a place in a monastery (only after the Council of Trent was profession required).[27] So, if you were planning to be a chaplain or a parish curate, you would have to claim a nominal patrimony (a shilling in your pocket would no doubt save you from perjury if the oath was carefully worded) or get some monastery to promise to put you up if you fell on bad times.

The intellectual qualification of the ordinand was looked into when he presented himself to be ordained.[28] The bishop sometimes performed the examination himself; more usually, he deputed examining chaplains. It is not clear what form the examination took, but it seems often to have been perfunctory. Even at its best, it was not directed to the matters most required for an intelligent exercise of the ministry. It evidently sought, first of all, a reading knowledge of Latin, and thereafter some skill in the university trivium of logic, grammar, and rhetoric. Theology, belonging to the more advanced part of the curriculum, seems not to have been required. The rather amorphous standards for the examination, together with the fact that it was postponed to the last minute, must have made it easy for the examiner to be lenient and hard for him to be strict.

If a bishop had been disposed to improve on this rudimentary screening, or even enforce it rigorously as it stood, he would not have been adequately protected against men who left his diocese to be ordained by less exacting colleagues. He could have checked on the moral qualifications of such men before letting them have letters dimissory, but their intellectual qualifications would have to be left to the ordaining bishop. Furthermore, a sufficiently resourceful candidate could get a papal indult to be ordained without letters dimissory. These were given out so freely that the Council of Trent had to legislate against their unrestricted use. The candidate perhaps could find a bishop willing to ordain him with neither indult nor letters.[29] In the latter case, he received his orders illicitly and could be forbidden their exercise. It was customary, though, to restore him after a short suspension without checking on his original qualification for the orders he had illicitly received.

On the whole, we can probably say of the screening process that it kept out men notoriously debauched, irregular, or illiterate. But it certainly did not maintain the close-knit and dedicated clerical body the church envisaged. While theologians and canonists alike taught that the cleric had a special vocation manifested interiorly by God and confirmed by the church, tonsure and orders were in fact conferred upon anyone seeking them unless he fell into some well-defined category of disqualification. (Not until the Council of Trent did a bishop have the power to refuse ordination without giving a reason.)[30] This situation, involving as it did an abdication of the responsibility of bishops and clergy for the spiritual formation of those aspiring to their state, must have been an important contributing factor in the careerism of many of the higher clergy and the abjection of many of the lower.

2. Placement—The ecclesiastical authorities exercised no systematic control over the employment of the many members of the clerical proletariat who ministered for wages.[31] Legislation was enacted to keep them from moving from one diocese to another without appropriate evidence of their orders and their good standing where they came from. Fairly effective steps were taken to keep them from drawing worshipers and their offerings away from regular parish services. After the Black Death, provision was made for forcing them to take on parish cures when they were needed, and efforts were made to keep their high wages from drawing men out of the parish ministry. But there was no general administrative control over their hiring and firing as such.

As regards the beneficed clergy, the situation was different. However a man was nominated to a benefice, only the bishop could actually put him in. And once he was in, his tenure was fully protected: he could not be put out except for specific misconduct established in full judicial proceedings. To be sure, the bishop's authority in these matters was exercised in the shadow of the jurisdiction of the lay courts, whose judges were both zealous and imaginative in protecting the rights of the patron. A bishop might have to answer before them for whatever he did. Subject to the possibility of this happening, the bishop endeavored routinely to satisfy himself whenever a man was presented to a benefice as to the availability of the benefice, the right of the patron making the presentment, and the suitability of the presentee.[32]

As in the case of candidates for orders, the requisite inquiries were made through a jury of mixed clergy and laity summoned by the archdeacon's official. If the presentee was not from the immediate vicinity of the benefice, an ancillary inquiry was perhaps required in the place where he came from. A set of entries in the register of Archbishop Chichele (1414–43) indicates the scope of the inquiries made. In addition to the particulars of the benefice and its patronage, they covered the age and orders of the presentee, whether he had another benefice, his life and conversation, and in one or two cases his learning and his legitimacy.

It is not surprising that pluralism and lack of learning, the two matters on the list that a man's neighbors would be least apt to know about, were the ones that gave the authorities the most trouble. The inquiry about pluralism was no doubt put in obedience to Ottobuono's canon. The measures taken to exclude the unlearned were less systematic. The inquests in Chichele's register show, as I say, a few cases where learning is inquired into, more where it is not. Other registers show bishops (Hugh of Wells and Grosseteste in the thirteenth century, Bekynton in the fifteenth) who examined presentees and made some of them pursue further studies as a condition of holding their benefices.[33] On the other hand, some registers show no evidence at all of such a practice. Also, by the end of the fourteenth century some bishops at least were allowing presentees to take possession of benefices through their proctors without coming forward in person at all.[34]

To be sure, a cleric who employed a proctor to take care of his benefice was probably a responsible bureaucrat and, therefore, can hardly have been illiterate.

The filling of benefices presented the ecclesiastical authorities with additional problems in the form of financial irregularities in the surrounding transactions. Where such irregularities involved no more than isolated instances (usually a presentee who had given some consideration to the patron for presenting him or to his predecessor for resigning), the authorities were content to rely on the ordinary processes for the detection and punishment of offenses, reinforced by an oath required of the presentee to the effect that he had given no such consideration.[35] The one legitimate excuse for a transaction of this kind, where an incumbent wished to retire because of age or ill health, reserving a pension for himself, was taken care of by the development of other arrangements under the control of the ordinary.

The authorities were more seriously taxed by a number of less straightforward devices favoring either simony or improper tenure of benefices.[36] These included:

1. The holding of benefices through nominal incumbents who bound themselves to pay over the proceeds to someone else;
2. The exaction of resignation bonds, whereby the incumbent bound himself to resign at the request of someone else or upon the happening of a specified contingency;
3. The purchase of next presentments, entitling the purchaser to present to a given benefice on its next vacancy; and
4. The negotiation of exchanges of benefices.

The nominal incumbent was particularly useful as a means of circumventing the rules against pluralism. The resignation bond was especially favored as a means of holding a benefice until some other person, such as a younger relative of the patron, became eligible for it. It was more prominent after the Reformation then at this time. The purchase of next presentations presented no ground for objection in theory; the right to present was a piece of real property, and the possession of it could be transferred for any specified period the owner chose. Such a transaction, however, by increasing the liquidity of the patronal right, tended at least to facilitate simony. Exchanges of benefices also were unobjectionable in theory; as they did not involve a temporal consideration for a spiritual thing, the canons, albeit without much enthusiasm, permitted them. But they too, in bypassing many of the formalities involved in the filling up of the benefices, contributed to the liquidity of ecclesiastical livings.

It was this potential liquidity that made room for the development in the fourteenth century of the profession of the *chop-church*, or broker of ecclesiastical preferment. How such a man operated is not very clear, but he probably gathered an inventory of benefices through buying resignation bonds and next presentments and listing incumbents who wanted to make exchanges. These he would then bestow on his customers through present-ment or, more often, through exchange. The exchange was apt to be more or less fictitious: instead of another customer taking possession of the first one's old benefice, the chop-church himself or a strawman would hold it until it was wanted for another transaction. If these matters were handled routinely and through proctors, the fictitious character of the exchange might never be noticed.

Thompson finds that the chop-church's profession grew rapidly in the latter part of the fourteenth century and continued vigorous but rather more circumspect thereafter. The increased circumspection was no doubt due to Archbishop Courtney's 1392 constitution on the subject. In addition to ful-minating ecclesiastical censures against the chop-church as such, Courtney made three important new rules. First, the presentee to a benefice had to swear that he had given nothing to the patron *or anyone else* for the present-ment; the earlier legislation had mentioned only the patron. Second, all con-tracts, bonds, and the like that reduced an incumbent's full tenure and enjoy-ment of his benefices were made invalid. As the secular law, which had only recently arrived at the possibility of not enforcing a sealed instrument ac-cording to its tenor, would not recognize this canonical invalidity. Courtney provided further that anyone bound by such an obligation was to make the situation known to his bishop, who would impose a suitable penance on him and try to extricate him. Finally, Courtney provided for a searching examination by the bishop before permitting an exchange. The parties were to appear in person, not by proctors, and show evidence that they had been properly instituted into the benefices they proposed to exchange. The bishop was to make sure the benefices were of equal value. Any exchange consum-mated in violation of these requirements was to be void, and the parties and their intermediaries were to be subject to ecclesiastical censures.

While all this good legislation was evidently not given immediate effect (in 1399, the clergy were still complaining about improper exchanges), it did re-sult in a tightening of the screws. But the chop-church's profession was a long time dying out. The term appears in Lambarde's *Eirenarcha* (1581) as the designation of a mystery or craft. The trade (though not the name) was involved in a lawsuit as late as 1869.

While the ecclesiastical authorities were cracking down on chop-churches, the secular authorities were suppressing another major source of preferment for unbefriended clergy, namely, papal provisions. The universities, which had been sending lists of eligible graduates to Rome, were suffering by the 1390s from increasingly effective enforcement of the Statute of Provisors, and both clergy and commons were taking their part in Parliament.[37] No list of graduates appears after 1404. Various efforts were made to take up the slack. Henry IV tried a committee to recommend graduates to patrons, but nothing came of it. Measures enacted by the bishops in 1417 and 1421, giving preference to graduates in the filling of certain benefices, failed because they did not provide any means by which the patrons of these benefices could have their attention called to deserving graduates. The situation was further complicated by negotiations between the universities and the religious houses that had a great deal of the available preferment in their gift. The religious wanted to trade their cooperation in the placement of graduates for more favorable treatment of religious students. The universities were not willing to make concessions of this kind because they hoped the Statute of Provisors might be repealed in exchange for the pope's assistance in the war with France. The upshot of all this was that the placement of graduates continued a problem till the nineteenth century.

3. *Supervision*—In an age when the cleric's primary dependence was on his patron or employer, the bishop's primordial personal supervision over him survived only in attenuated forms. The chief concern, correction of morals and deportment, was generally modest in scope.[38] Bishops and archdeacons on their parish visitations dealt fairly regularly with drinking, rowdiness, and, of course, incontinence. Some of them evidently tried to keep track of any cleric who had a woman living in his house, even if age, relationship, or other circumstances made her "not suspect." Illicit forms of trade were taken up from time to time. While a visitation questionnaire, drawn up perhaps by Grosseteste, invited informants to report more at large on the life and conversation of the local clergy there is no indication that they in fact did so.

The idleness of many clerics without cures called for other kinds of supervision. Sometimes, these men were analogous to "masterless" layman, and the problem was to punish their offenses or make them go to work.[39] More often, with the proliferation of endowed masses beginning early in the fourteenth century, they earned their living by saying mass in the morning, and the problem was to keep them out of mischief for the rest of the day. From time to time, a bishop would have to appoint someone to look into the affairs of the stipendiary chaplains in a given parish and compel them to participate in the parish liturgy or assist the parish priest with his pastoral work.

The royal government stretched the bishop's supervisory powers by looking to him for the enforcement of royal process on the clergy.[40] While the bishops succeeded in establishing that they could not bring a cleric physically into court, they did use ecclesiastical citations to compel attendance, and they sequestered benefices to pay off judgments.

4. *Protection*[41]—The clergy, as a pervasive, wealthy, and sometimes deservedly unpopular element in society, came in for a good deal of physical violence, sometimes for the sake of robbery or extortion, sometimes to

avenge real or imagined injuries. To protect them, the authorities kept the 1139 canon *Si quis suadente diabolo* vigorously in force. The excommunication it imposed on all who laid violent hands on clerics or monks was regularly brought to the attention of the faithful from the pulpit, and offenders were regularly brought into the church courts and put to penance.

The penances imposed consisted, as we have seen, of varying combinations of fasts, beatings, and public expressions of repentance. The judges were evidently prepared to mitigate the penance exacted if some kind of provocation appeared. As we saw in the last chapter, the pastoral function of these penances required a leniency that interfered with their use for maximum deterrent effect so that the clergy found it necessary to seek supplementary protection from the secular authorities.

The abuse of lay process was a form of violence to the clergy that the ecclesiastical authorities were particularly unable to cope with. In the fifteenth century especially, it was a favorite trick to accuse a cleric of rape in order to extort money from him. The secular authorities were vigorous, and on the whole successful, in resisting the imposition of ecclesiastical censures on persons who resorted to lay process for this or any other purpose. The king was prepared, however, to provide some relief in exchange for financial subsidies. In this way, Henry VI in 1448 was persuaded to issue a blanket pardon to all clergy accused of rape.

The institutional patterns we are considering here evolved out of the ambivalent status of the medieval clergy. In the historical organization of the church, the cleric's place was in the bishop's familia. In Gregorian ideology, he belonged to a cohesive spiritual elite with a special mission from God. But in everyday life, he belonged to a professional class performing vital and specialized services at every level of society, and his place was in the establishment where his services were required.

This ambivalence was perhaps inherent in the religious synthesis to which medieval society aspired. At any rate, a case can be made for not condemning it out of hand. We noted in an earlier chapter the similarity between the clerical familia of Roman times and the Germanic institution of the comitatus. The similarity should make us wary of attributing divine origin to the clerical familia. And the obvious administrative necessities that effected the evolution of the comitatus into the institutions of late medieval government should make us wary of condemning the rather similar evolution of the clerical familia. By the same token, we have enough grounds for doubting the soundness of the Gregorian conception of the clergy so that we should be reluctant to condemn late medieval society for adhering to the letter of the Gregorian reforms without the spirit.

But granting all these cautions, there seems still to be room for objection in terms of the bishop's basic responsibility for a creative development of the work and witness of the church. His rule was limited to the imposition of objective standards, and those less rigorous than he would have liked to impose or than by tradition he should have imposed. The real initiative, the real scope for creativity, rested with the general forces of social development, forces shaped in many ways by Christianity, but outside the control of the institutional church. The pattern is both characteristic and portentous.

B. Property and Revenues.

1. Protection of Property—The processes and censures of the church were regularly engaged in protecting the physical plant, and the temporal endowments as well, from all manner of usurpations, trespasses, and other invasions.[42] Some such invasions were sacrilegious, as when the church building was robbed or when its sturdy construction was taken advantage of in some bit of petty warfare. Some invasions were merely financial, albeit with hints of of coercion in the background: we may suspect such a situation when a monastery grants a pension to a cleric whose brother is the sheriff or where a local magnate collects a periodic sum for protecting a religious house.

Some invasions were directly and seriously violent, involving dramatic confrontations between the spiritual anathemas of a local prelate and the temporal might of a powerful neighbor's retainers. Such confrontations might be produced by a dispute over secular estates, by the desire of some powerful person to make a benefice available for a friend, relative, or retainer, or by one of the perennial jurisdictional disputes between the clergy of a given place and the local civil magistrates.

By contrast, some invasions were no more than petty harassment—taking tolls of ecclesiastical tenants who claimed immunity by royal charter, infringing the local monopoly of the bishop's fair, cutting down trees or hunting in a bishop's forest, or stealing a prior's swans.

In all these cases, secular remedies were available as well as ecclesiastical,[43] and the victims sought whatever combination they felt would best serve in a given case. The lay authorities maintained in principle that temporal property rights should not be protected by church proceedings. It is probable, however, that they only invoked their principle when there was a genuine justiciable issue as to what the rights were. In many cases the cooperative efforts of church and state were no doubt required to cope with obvious lawlessness.

2. Collection of Revenues—To collect his secular revenues, a churchman had the same feudal and manorial courts as any other landholder. He did not hesitate, however, to supplement their processes with ecclesiastical censures when it seemed necessary.[44] In the margin of a record of the Feudal

Court of Canterbury, for instance, there is a drawing of a sad-faced peasant doing penance for neglecting his feudal services to the archbishop.

Specifically ecclesiastical revenues, gifts, occasional payments, and tithes were of course collectible only in ecclesiastical proceedings. They could be sued for in church courts, and people who did not pay could be reported on parish visitations. At least in the case of tithe, the parish priest could also excommunicate defaulters without any process.[45] The prelates attempted to enforce through these processes any gifts that had been left or donated but not paid over, any occasional payments that appeared to be customary, and a full canonical tithe, whether customary or not.

Tithe was the main source of controversy in all this. The prelates insisted, as we have seen, that it was a mathematical tenth by divine right. Neither law nor custom could make it anything less, though a commutation might be accepted if it represented a fair equivalent in something easier to measure. In making good their claims, the prelates had to contend with peasants who insisted on making the parish priest finance a harvest festival out of the proceeds, with landowners who tried to deduct the wages of their harvesters and tithe on the net instead of the gross produce of their fields, and with the lay courts who tried to enforce customary exemptions or commutations at less than full value.[46] Judging by the complaints of the laity over the years, the prelates won despite these obstacles more often than not.

Another class of revenue to be collected were the subsidies imposed on the clergy by Convocation. As we have seen, the king got these regularly, the pope occasionally. The archbishop of Canterbury also got them from time to time; his collections were on a much smaller scale, but they were becoming increasingly burdensome by the late fifteenth century.[47]

Whoever was to receive the subsidy, the job of collecting it was carried out under the archbishop's supervision by collectors appointed in each diocese by the bishop.[48] When the king was the beneficiary of the subsidy, he intervened actively in the collection process. Perhaps the pope did the same when he was the beneficiary, but he was more inclined to displace or supplement the whole process by using collectors of his own. It appears that subsidies for the archbishop himself were not collected very efficiently.

The job of collector was generally assigned by the bishop to a religious community, since the community would have a staff to collect the money and a safe place to keep it. The job was a thankless one, and everyone was reluctant to take it on; by the same token, the bishops sometimes showed vindictiveness in assigning it. In the first half of the fifteenth century, a number of communities persuaded the king to grant them immunity from the burden of collecting subsidies for him; the bishops attempted to disregard these immunities, and a complex and inconclusive set of legal maneuvers resulted.

It is not clear how the collectors went about getting the money from one who neglected or refused to pay. They seem to have had some power to excommunicate such persons; also, where the subsidy was for the king, the royal authorities were prepared to issue a writ of assistance to the sheriff for them.[49]

3. Control of Mismanagement—The main financial irregularities with which the ecclesiastical authorities were concerned were poor management, invasion of capital, and farms. There may have been cases of outright dishonesty as well, but as every officeholder was expected to meet his personal living expenses out of the revenues of his office, the line between carelessness and embezzlement would have been hard to draw.

Cases of mismanagement usually involved religious houses. The authorities coped with them by imposing controls on the discretion of the superior.[50] He might have to account for the money in his hands or take counsel with someone before spending it. He might have to appoint bailiffs or seneschals to look after his temporalities. He might have to curtail the financial commitments of his house so that there would be more money for paying debts.

Invasion of capital was not recognized as such, because medieval accountants did not distinguish between capital and income accounts.[51] Still, it was perceived that in some way the incumbent of a benefice or other endowed position harmed his successors if he borrowed money to be paid back out of annual revenues over a long period, if he granted corrodies (room and board for life) in exchange for lump sum payments, if he spent on current expenses the sums received from his predecessor for dilapidations, or if he sold land or standing timber for cash. All these practices were legislated against or dealt with on visitations, though it does not appear that they were significantly curtailed.

Farms I took up in an earlier chapter in connection with the taint of simony that seems to have furnished the main contemporary objection to them. Other objections were that if the farmer was a layman it would be unseemly for him to collect sacred revenue such as tithe, that the farm could be used to circumvent the laws against pluralism, and that if it ran for a long time it would impair the future value of the benefice.[52] Bishops tried to check up on farms on their visitations, and some even required them to be licensed in advance. Even so, as we saw, the applicable legislation, limiting farms to five years and forbidding them to laymen, was not effectively enforced.

4. Distribution of Revenues—Since the end of the twelfth century, there had been a general canonical rule that tithes should be paid to the parish priest of the parish in which they arose. In many cases, however, tithes had been granted to other churches or religious houses before that time. In other cases parish revenues themselves had been divided between rectors and vicars. As a result, tithe rights in many places were a good deal of a patchwork. The ecclesiastical authorities had to sort out conflicting claims, sometimes through administrative action, more often in court proceedings. In most cases, the lay courts deferred to them in this work, even when (as often happened) the disputants resorted to physical violence.

Another financial task of the authorities was coping with minor gifts and collections for parish liturgical and charitable purposes.[53] These funds were administered by parish representatives—either the churchwardens or comparable officials chosen ad hoc. Such officials had access to the regular church courts to collect the sums due them. In addition, the bishop or archdeacon on his parish visitations would hear their complaints, examine their accounts, and sometimes inquire on his own initiative as to whether their funds were being properly applied. This aspect of the administrative task, perhaps because it effectively tapped the resources of local self-government, seems to have been rather successfully accomplished.

The ecclesiastical authorities had another task in protecting the parish priest against a depletion of his revenues by competing candidates for the bounty of the faithful. The English prelates tried to be very careful who collected alms in their territory; they even imposed severe restrictions on the distribution of papal indulgences.[54] They did not satisfy the parish clergy, who still complained of the competition of the friars, or the moralists, who still complained of the deceptions of the pardoners; but they did a good deal better than their colleagues on the continent.

It was also the protection of parish revenues that made the authorities strict about licensing chapels, oratories, or other competing liturgical services.[55] If they did not require the permission of the parish priest, they at least imposed safeguards to maintain his offerings. Typically, these safeguards included a fixing of the times for alternative services, a requirement that everyone attend the parish services on specified occasions, and a reservation of certain functions, such as burial, to the parish priest.

An unfortunate result of this zeal for parish revenues was that the parish structure could not be modified to meet changes in population or need.[56] Whatever power a bishop had in theory to create new parishes was in fact not exercised after the mid-twelfth century. The best anyone was able to do who wanted services in a new place was to have a chapelry erected, dependent on the original parish both as to finances and as to personnel. Even the uniting of two moribund parishes into a single viable one could be done only with the consent of the patrons and incumbents of both.

Of these functions performed by the ecclesiastical administration with respect to the property and revenues of the church, those that appear to have been vigorous and reasonably effective were the same ones a secular government might be expected to perform in aid of the prevailing system of private property. First and foremost was the maintenance of peaceful enjoyment against violent invasions. Then came summary procedures for collecting the financial returns, and orderly procedures for adjudicating rights of ownership. Somewhat less effective were the procedures for maintaining the permanent sources of revenue against waste by persons entitled only to the income. Least effective of all, and in some cases entirely atrophied, were the procedures for subjecting property rights and other rights of the same kind to the overriding necessities of the church.

C. Faith and Worship.

Fabric, worship, and ministry provided the three main heads of specifically religious, as distinguished from financial or moral, concern for the church authorities. The objectives they set themselves under these heads were respectively:

1. to see that church and churchyard were kept in repair, were properly furnished, and were treated with due reverence;
2. to insure the proper performance of mass and liturgy, attendance by the people at the proper times, and the due observance of Sundays, Holy Days, and sacred times; and
3. to maintain rudimentary standards of pastoral and catechetical work on the part of the clergy, rudimentary standards of instruction and orthodoxy on that of the faithful.

The repair and furnishing of the church fell by the general canon law on those who received the tithes, especially the rector.[57] By a custom that had grown up in England, however, the parishioners were responsible for fencing the churchyard, maintaining the nave of the church, and furnishing the sacred vessels. The main responsibilities left to the rector or vicar were the chancel of the church and the house in which he or his curate lived.

The responsibilities of the parishioners were discharged through an expansion of the primordial machinery of local self-government. Sometime in the fourteenth century, it became possible to prod this machinery into operation by ecclesiastical censures. The incumbent could also be compelled by censures to do his part; or else, by a disposition peculiar to England, the bishop could sequester his living and make repairs out of the proceeds. The incumbent, if the deficiency came about before his time, could recover the cost of repairs from his predecessor or the latter's estate. But it was not always possible to see that he then applied the money to the repairs in question.

As regards misuse of the sacred premises, the authorities imposed penances on people who robbed them or committed breaches of the peace in them.[58] In cases of bloodshed, they also held the church polluted and unfit for divine service till reconciled by a bishop. They maintained a right of sanctuary for criminal defendants and tried unsuccessfully to extend it to civil defendants and goods left for safekeeping.

A more pervasive, if less serious, problem with churches and churchyards was the use of them for activities innocuous but secular.[59] Lay people kept holding fairs, markets, or games in the churchyard, or secular courts in the building. Clerics kept pasturing their sheep or cattle in the churchyard; one rector even made two tombstones into a watering trough. Given the central place of church and churchyard in the life of the village, a certain amount of this kind of thing was probably inevitable. Inquiries on the subject formed a standard part of parish visitations, but there is no indication of how seriously offenses were taken when found.

As with the buildings and grounds, the authorities tried to see to the furnishings and equipment of the church. Everything necessary for the liturgical observances was to be on hand, to be kept in good repair, and to be put to no profane use.[60]

The authorities tried of course to make sure the mass and other prescribed services were performed and that the parishioners attended them.[61] They had to deal with a few cases where services were omitted or conducted so negligently the parishioners complained. Many complaints concerned the burial of the dead; clergy failed to meet the funeral procession till it came to the churchyard, or they omitted or slighted the interment office or funeral mass. A few cases of nonattendance were dealt with. The records distinguish between negligent and heterodox absentees; presumably the latter were punished more severely.

Besides enforcing church attendance, the authorities occasionally punished people for working on Sundays and holy days or for eating on fast days.[62] The evidence suggests sporadic rather than systematic enforcement. The possibility of punishment was real enough, however, to enable a late fourteenth century parson to use it for blackmail.

The only pastoral activity that regularly engaged the attention of the authorities was visiting the sick—taking them the sacraments, not passing the time of day with them.[63] This obligation was expressed in several canons and provided a standard item of inquiry on visitations. In at least one diocese, a parish priest was required to leave a substitute for this purpose whenever he spent the night away from the parish and was subject to suspension if a parishioner died without the sacraments through his neglect.

In the way of instruction, a parish priest was supposed to set forth the main tenets of the Christian religion to his people and to read them periodically the list of misdeeds which the provincial councils had visited with automatic excommunication.[64] He was also encouraged to bring in outsiders to preach to them, though after 1408 such preachers had to be licensed.

There are not many complaints of failure to live up to these modest requirements.

There was one priest complained of in 1519 for refusing to instruct children. It is reasonable to suppose that this duty, so important after the Reformation, had some basis in medieval canons or practice, but in fact, I can find none except for this lone complaint.

Beyond imposing these rather elementary requirements, the administration did very little to elevate the standards of the parish ministry. The authorities contented themselves, in short, with regular liturgical observances and a few other externals without trying to reach with their administrative operations below the surface of the Christian life.[65]

D. Moral and Social Concerns.

Of the sins of the laity that related neither to the worship of God nor to the support of the institutional church the only ones that the ecclesiastical authorities seem to have made systematic efforts to ferret out and correct were those of the flesh. The effort seems to have been less to bring hidden offenses to light than to deal in a salutary way with offenses that were sources of open scandal in the parish community.

It was probably the same criterion of scandal that governed the reporting by parish representatives of a variety of other sins that involved neither religion nor finance. The only example that occurs with any frequency is that of defamation. In the majority of cases, it was a *communis diffamator* (or more frequently, *diffamatrix*) that was reported rather than a person who defamed a given individual on a given occasion. I am inclined to think, therefore, that there was no general practice of reporting such offenses, much less of inquiring for them, but that the processes of ecclesiastical correction constituted the last resort of long-suffering neighbors in cases of especial flagrancy.

Where the sin in question was against a particular person rather than the community in general, it was generally left to the victim to complain through a private litigation in the courts. The most important matter dealt with in this way was, again, defamation. This subject gave the church courts a major part of their business until long after the Reformation.[66] In all but a few cases of defamation, the lay courts did not afford a remedy. They made no difficulty about the assumption of jurisdiction by the church except in cases where the defamatory matter complained of was testimony given in a secular court.

Of other private civil wrongs dealt with in the ecclesiastical courts, the most frequent was breach of contract. We have already discussed how these cases came to the ecclesiastical courts under the theory of *fidei laesio* and how the secular courts took steps to stop them. Here as in other matters, the secular courts made no objection to the correction of the sinner but they treated as a serious invasion of their own rights any attempt to give financial redress to the person injured.

Where a civil wrong was committed by unknown persons, and thus could not be made the subject of secular proceedings, a bishop might be asked to use the powers of his office to give such redress as was possible. Thus Oliver Sutton, the late thirteenth-century bishop of Lincoln, issued a general excommunication of the unknown persons who killed two oxen belonging to a man and wife who had "tearfully set forth" their plight to him.[67]

Turning from private sins the wrongs to those involving the body politic in a more general way, we find that three classes of offenders in this regard were included (along with violators of the liberties of the church) in the general excommunications established in provincial councils and read from time to time in church.[68] These were, first, common criminals and breakers of the peace; second, perjurers and other abusers of legal process, lay and ecclesiastical; and, third, violators of the basic political settlements of the kingdom, especially the Magna Carta. Sometimes these general excommunications were so drawn as to bear upon those who took the lay side in some current church-state dispute, in which case the king would have them withdrawn. Generally, though, the secular government seems to have welcomed the church's support in its police functions. These general pronouncements, and whatever was done by individual bishops to apply them to specific offenders, may have made a certain contribution to the maintenance of political stability and the suppression of lawlessness.

The ecclesiastical administration lent similar support from time to time to other policies initiated by the secular government.[69] The most important was the Statute of Laborers, a comprehensive regulation of wages and employment in response to the labor shortage brought on by the Black Death. Not only did the bishops cause this statute to be read in churches and fortified with ecclesiastical censures they also enacted one of their own to regulate clerical employment along parallel lines. The ecclesiastical legislation was in part motivated by the same economic necessities as the secular, but the need to set the laity an example was among the reasons adduced for it.

Another secular objective which the ecclesiastical administration furthered (albeit somewhat less wholeheartedly) with the spiritual resources at their command was the prosecution of the war with France. Indulgences were offered to encourage the faithful to pray for the success of the national arms, and services were held in thanksgiving for victories won.[70]

In addition to these policies shared with the secular government, the church implemented certain social policies peculiarly its own, which the secular authorities either did not fully favor or did not consider it their responsibility to implement.[71] For instance, except for certain local customs, what little was done against prostitution seems to have been done by the bishops. In the early thirteenth century, the bishops attempted to assert their authority against tournaments. In later times it seems likely that they took the initiative in licensing physicians, surgeons, and midwives, as they did in reminding mothers to take good care of their children. The church also provided the only generally available remedy against usury, although the ecclesiastical authorities do not seem to have taken active steps to suppress this vice.

In three areas that we would be inclined to consider civil, the church not only provided a spiritual foundation for the work of government, it actually undertook the entire administrative responsibility for carrying out the work through its own agencies. These three areas were marriage, decedent estates, and poor relief. All of these remained in ecclesiastical hands until after the Reformation. The administration of poor relief was gradually secularized in the reigns of Elizabeth I and James I, while probate and matrimonial jurisdiction continued to be exercised by the church courts until 1857.

In the case of marriage, the sacramental character of the relation gave a ground for ecclesiastical jurisdiction. Even in our own time we are used to the exercise of a certain amount of judicial authority by the church in the area. On the other hand, there is in modern times a distinction between civil and ecclesiastical marriage: anyone whose conscience will allow him to escape the judgment of the church may do so and still live up to the civil requirements for maintaining a family. The medieval church, by contrast, not only controlled access to sacramental marriage, it controlled the opportunity to live in sin with impunity. Thus, spurious impediments presented the same problem for the medieval ecclesiastical courts as collusive divorces present for the modern secular courts.[72]

In addition to controlling entrance into the married state and adjudicating the status at the behest of the parties, the ecclesiastical authorities determined questions of marital status or legitimacy on reference from the lay courts. There was also some attempt to exercise pastoral supervision over the marriage relation. Failure of husband and wife to live together was evidently reported with some regularity in parish visitations, and one set of returns shows the visitor actually reconciling two couples.[73]

In the area of decedent estates, the ecclesiastical courts appointed executors and administrators and arranged for the distribution of goods in rather the same way as our probate courts do today. This work was supplemented by that of parish visitors, who received reports of legacies diverted or withheld and of executors who failed to account. The ecclesiastical authorities also attempted, mostly through general excommunications, to prevent interference by husbands, masters, and other superiors with the right to make a will or with the assumption of possession by the executors.[74]

Poor relief was a function that had long been assumed by the church because of the traditional doctrine that the surplus property collected through the generosity of the faithful was to be devoted to that purpose.[75] Generally, it was a function that required no large-scale administrative effort. In an agrarian society with a stable population and a soceity in which it was well understood that charity covers a multitude of sins, the funds available for poor relief were probably quite sufficient for the demands upon them. The distribution at the parish level was not always perfect, however, and we find parish clergy—especially nonresidents and their underpaid substitutes—complained of on visitation for failure to keep hospitality. The hospitality in question evidently involved the feeding and lodging of travelers and persons otherwise unable to fend for themselves. If the parish clergy were remiss in devoting their ecclesiastical revenues to purposes of this kind, it seems likely that the failure was made up out of funds in the hands of the parish churchwardens, disbursed under the supervision of the diocesan authorities.

The abuse opposite to the failure to provide for the poor was the diversion of the available means of relief to persons not truly in need of it. In this area, the ecclesiastical authorities attempted to suppress the solicitation of alms under false pretenses, punishing those found guilty of this offense, and in some cases requiring a license from the bishop in order to solicit at all.[76] On the other hand, the vagabond laborers or "sturdy beggars" that posed such a problem after the Black Death were generally left to the secular authorities to cope with, albeit with some support from the bishops.

In this pattern of moral and civil concern, there seems to have lurked a certain unresolved tension between the moral and the civil. The system of ecclesiastical intervention in this area was no doubt intended in its inception as a genuine moral support both for the lives of individual Christians and for the institutions of society. The limited scope of its practical capacities made it in fact a good deal less than that. The fact that at the Reformation those who were most interested in a moral refurbishing of the church were the ones who most particularly wanted no part of this system gives eloquent testimony of its failures.

III. Resources and Techniques

The administrative style of the medieval English church authorities was compounded of technical and cultural elements. The technical elements were supplied in part by the general experience of the Western church, in part by the developing techniques of English secular administration. The cultural elements consisted of the patterns of Gregorian and canonical thought as we considered them earlier. The formal and didactic character of those patterns did not influence the choice of administrative techniques as much as it did the choice of goals, but it did make the authorities more chary of some devices (for example, sequestration) and more impressed with others (for example, automatic excommunication) than strict practicality warranted.

A. Legislation and Dissemination.

The Fourth Lateran Council (1215) inaugurated a spate of provincial and diocesan legislation in England that took most of the thirteenth century to run its course. Thereafter, we find only a few bits of creative legislation (Courtney's constitution against chop-churches, Chichele's on the licensing of preachers, and others developed for similar specific needs).[77]

The canonical legislator, as we have seen, always tended to think of himself as giving new force to old principles rather than as making new rules. It was no great step for him, therefore, as the springs of legislative creativity began drying up, to give more and more of his attention to devices for bringing existing rules to the attention of those subject to them. The most favored device for this purpose was having a given rule read in churches at specified times. There are in the records numerous orders from bishops or councils to set forth one thing or another in this way. The subject might be anything from Magna Carta or the Statute of Laborers to interfering with the execution of wills or chopping down the bishop of Hereford's trees.

Foremost among the matters thus dealt with was a great general excommunication, a more or less exhaustive list of those classes of offenders who were automatically excommunicated. It was set forth in a number of councils, with slight modifications from one occasion to the next.[78] The lay powers intervened if the strictures became too political or too hard on the king's officials. The parish priests, for their part, in reading the list, tended to stress the duties of parishioners toward the clergy and to leave out items of broader religious or social concern.

Specific misdeeds, especially by unknown persons, could be treated in the same way as those general classes of wrong. I have already mentioned Bishop Sutton's excommunication of the unknown persons who killed two oxen. Other bishops did the same with those who beat a certain rector, detained a certain testator's goods, plundered a certain galley.[79] Sentences of this kind were not read in all churches as the general ones were, but only in the parishes where the offenders were presumed to live.

There was a ceremony available for promulgating the sentence of excommunication, whether particular or general. It involved ringing bells and dashing lighted candles to the ground to symbolize the extinction of the spiritual life of the offender.[80] Perhaps it was not used for every excommunication, as it was explicitly ordered in some cases but not in others. The psychological effect of this ceremony on the wrongdoer or his neighbors may have been one of the reasons why some parishioners forcibly prevented the reading of sentences of excommunication in their churches. As far as I can see, they had nothing to gain juridically, though they may have supposed they had.

Next to promulgation in church, the most frequently used means of dissemination of rules was circularizing the clergy.[81] This was usually done by having the archdeacon or rural dean read a document at some local meeting, though one set of injunctions, issued in 1287, was sent to all parish priests in writing to be bound in their missals. Most of the matters put before the clergy in this way involved their own conduct, although on one occasion they were ordered to cite lay offenders into court. The canons on celibacy for instance were supposed to be "carefully and openly recited" to the clergy four times a year. It is hard to believe that forgetfulness was a problem in enforcing these canons, but the authorities professed to be worried about it.

B. Supervisory Techniques.

One of the few ways in which the churchmen were ahead of their secular colleagues was in the development of devices for personal supervision, that is, for regulating the future conduct of particular individuals as distinguished from "adjudication," which deals with the past conduct of particular individuals, and "legislation," which deals with the future conduct of people in general. Their pastoral tradition, which hindered them in so many ways, may have helped them here. Unfortunately, however, they lacked the sophistication to exploit fully the potentiality for pastoral flexibility in the devices they were using.

The most important of these devices was (as it is in modern administration) the requirement of a license, that is, of prior approval by someone in authority before a given act may be validly or licitly done. There is little evidence of licensing for supervisory purposes either in the Roman law or in medieval secular law.[82] It probably came into the canons as a corollary to the traditional control of the bishop over the spiritual life and ministry in his diocese. The rule that a priest could not be put in charge of a parish without the bishop's license appeared in connection with the investiture controversy. As the law developed, a bishop's license was also required to have a private oratory, to appropriate a church to a religious community, to solicit alms in the diocese, to hear confessions (and later to preach) outside one's own parish, and, in some places, to let a benefice to farm. The cases of pluralism, nonresidence, matrimonial impediments, and the like, in which dispensations were regularly granted, should be added to the list. A dispensation is simply a license not to comply with a general rule. The power to license or dispense gave the bishop a certain amount of control over all these matters,[83] though the standards were often so definite or so lenient as to leave him little room for discretion in its exercise.

Akin to the requirement of licensing was that of confirmation, whereby the act of one authority could not be taken advantage of without review by another. The confirmation of elections and the inspection of sealed documents were the main examples of this device.[84] It appears that procedural regularity was the primary concern in reviewing elections, although the fitness of the person elected was open to consideration. The inspection of sealed documents, by the same token, was primarily a device for insuring authenticity. For this purpose, documents affording or recognizing rights could be examined not only by authorities superior to those who gave them but also by inferior or collateral authorities or by the same authorities at another time.

I am in some doubt as to the extent to which it was possible to consider on such a scrutiny of a document the question of whether it was prudently granted or properly used. On at least one occasion, the pope revoked a whole class of privileges on the ground that they were being misused.[85] But I find no record of a pope or bishop doing as the royal authorities did with their writ of quo warranto and examining particular privileges one by one to see which should be allowed to continue.

The same examination that served to control authenticity of documents served also to control the exercise of rights without the necessary dispensations or documents. Thus, attempts were made from time to time to call in all the pluralists and nonresidents in a diocese and compel them to show their dispensations or give up their claims.[86] How successful such attempts were is another question; there would have been serious obstacles to bringing to book anyone who failed to come in when called. More successful perhaps was the requirement sometimes imposed on parish visitations that any priest ministering in the territory visited bring in for inspection the proofs of his ordination.

These devices all aim in one way or another at controlling future behavior or conditions through controlling present rights. Supplementary to these were a certain number of devices for controlling future behavior directly.[87] There were in the first place varying degrees of authoritative exhortation that may be supposed to have moved with varying degrees of urgency the consciences of those to whom they were addressed. Then there were monitions, whereby the authoritative exhortation was fortified with the threat of a definite censure if the prescribed act or omission was not forthcoming.

Finally, there was the promissory oath, a device of which the ecclesiastical authorities made a good deal of use for a variety of purposes. Persons instituted into benefices were made to swear that they would not pay money to their patrons. Persons found guilty of sexual offenses were made to swear that they would cease from their illicit relations and avoid the company of their former paramours. Persons entering into offices or benefices were made to swear that they would faithfully discharge the duties attached, would obey their superiors, or otherwise conduct themselves in desired ways. Sometimes these oaths were fortified with pecuniary penalties for breach in case the spiritual consequences of perjury were insufficient to deter the hardened sinner. Thus fortified, they seem a close relative of our modern penalty bond, which can also be put to a wide variety of uses.

C. Visitation.

Much of the routine work of correcting offenses and solving specific problems was done through the process of visitation. This process has a long pastoral tradition: Saint Paul may have used something like it to supervise the Christian communities he set up.[88] As it operated in England, though, it had less affinity for traditional canonical forms than for secular counterparts like the General Sessions or the Eyre. The common elements seem to have come into both church and state by way of the Frankish monarchy; it is not clear whether it was church or state that first introduced them into England. At any rate, the medieval English visitation, despite its pastoral origins, was in many ways just what its secular counterpart was—a set of formal inquiries put to the local populace by an itinerant official for the purpose of enforcing the law.

The two basic forms of visitation were parochial and monastic, the latter having, naturally, less affinity for secular analogues.[89] The monastic visitation began with a procession, a sermon, and a reading of the documents establishing the visitor's authority. The visitor would then proceed to his actual inquiries, examining the community collectively in chapter and the individual members or a representative sampling of them privately. He probably used for this purpose a questionnaire he had drawn up in advance. There is little evidence that he inspected the physical premises or the documentary records, but he seems to have found out in some way most of what such an inspection would have revealed. He coped as best he could with the difficulties of sifting the truth out of the statements he heard, affected as they often were by fear or favor in one direction, by pettiness or spite in the other.

Whatever he decided was worthy of further proceedings would then be taken up in a full chapter of the community. Persons accused of misconduct with sufficient frequency or earnestness would be confronted with the accusations and required either to clear themselves under oath, sometimes with compurgators, or to do penance. Matters concerning the corporate discipline of the house rather than the lives of individual religious would be embodied either in formal exhortations or else in formal injunctions, binding as a matter of obedience and, if need be, fortified with excommunications. The visitor could evidently modify both the rules and the organization of the house by such injunctions. If things were bad enough, he could also depose the superior. This, however, he was reluctant to do, as the person deposed could resort to appeals and other dilatory proceedings that could set the whole house by the ears for years.

To accomplish its original purpose of renewing the zeal and spirituality of the community visited, the visitation would have had to elicit the willing cooperation of religious and superiors basically committed to the pursuit of perfection and willing to receive correction for that purpose. In fact, cooperation of this kind was not often forthcoming, perhaps because of a misplaced solicitude for the honor of the house. The device came finally to be used, therefore, not for spiritual renewal and redirection along the paths of perfection, but as a corrective to major financial and moral failings. Used in this way, it suffered from the leniency carried over from the underlying pastoral tradition, from the almost complete lack of systematic provisions for follow-up between one visitation and the next, and, most of all, from the simple magnitude of the job that was to be done and of the economic and social forces militating in the opposite direction.

The parish visitation was carried out in somewhat the same way as the monastic. The basic unit of visitation was usually the deanery. The visitor would ensconce himself in the head church of the deanery, and the dean would assemble the clergy, together with lay representatives of each parish, to meet with the visitor and respond under oath to a detailed series of interrogatories, adding any other matters they thought deserving of attention.[90] At first, there was evidently no fixed number or status for the lay representatives. Gradually, however, the function of attending attached itself to the developing office of the churchwarden—two or more men chosen annually in each parish to act for the community of the parish in its ecclesiastical affairs.[91]

We have already considered the subject matter of the inquiries put and the matters turned up on these occasions. As with the monastic visitations, it is not clear how far the visitor filled out his secondhand information with a physical inspection of the various churches of the deanery he was visiting.[92] There must have been some such inspection, however, for we find reference to a practice of lending equipment about from one parish to another to fool the visitors.

Matters turned up on a parish visitation might sometimes be disposed of by the visitor, but the more usual procedure was to leave them to be dealt with at a later date, usually by an official delegated ad hoc for the purpose.[93] Persons accused of offenses would be cited to come before this official and either purge themselves or submit to penance. Beneficed clergy found nonresident would be cited to come before him and show their licenses. Those responsible for the fabric or equipment of the church would be admonished to make good any deficiencies, and this official would have the duty of checking up on them.

The parish visitation, then, had better follow-up procedures than did the monastic visitation. It also showed less ambiguity between legal and pastoral aspirations, it was quite firmly legal. Thus, it was probably reasonably effective, or would have been if systematically carried out, at achieving the limited purposes at which it aimed.

The work of visitation was primarily that of the bishop and the archdeacon. Every parish in the diocese was supposed to be visited by the bishop at intervals of three years and by the archdeacon in the intervening years.[94] Religious houses were visited by the bishop if they were not exempt and usually also by some official of the order or congregation to which they belonged. None of these different kinds of visitation was ever carried out as often as it was supposed to be.

In addition to these visitations at the diocesan level, the law gave the metropolitan the right to visit his suffragans, and he did so from time to time.[95] His visitation would begin with a personal examination of the bishop and would then be extended to the cathedral chapter and finally to the parishes and nonexempt religious houses. His rights in the parishes were not as complete as those of the local ordinary, and some archbishops made more of parish visiting than others did.

There was hostility and often resistance to the visitation process at every level. In the case of the metropolitan, the main objections were to the financial exactions involved and the interference with local jurisdiction. A great deal of litigation resulted, generally groundless, but quite effective to delay or discourage visitations. The archbishops had to make important concessions to their suffragans before they were finally permitted to visit them in peace. At the monastic level, hostility was more often motivated by considerations of the honor and autonomy of the house. It resulted in reticence on the part of the inmates and in zeal for procuring and enforcing exemptions from Rome.[96] In the case of parish visitations, the objections were almost entirely financial. They resulted mainly in attempts to commute the visits for cash.[97]

The financial exactions that caused all the trouble in the parishes and much of it elsewhere were called *procurations.*[98] They were based on the right of the visitor to be fed and lodged with his retinue at the expense of those he was visiting. This right, the cornerstone of all forms of peripatetic administration, could be abused either by taking too large or too hungry a retinue or by collecting more cash than the food and lodging cost. The Third Lateran

Council (1179) attempted to counter the first of these abuses by limiting the number of retainers the visitor could take with him. The rule seems to have been violated regularly and with impunity, though it continued in force. The second abuse could in theory be countered if those visited insisted on furnishing food and lodging rather than cash. But in practice the visitors, who needed the money for other work, were usually successful in getting it.

Some archdeacons even succeeded in establishing that they were entitled to cash procurations of so much a year whether they visited or not. For the parishioners, this arrangement was cheaper and less troublesome than a visitation, and for the archdeacon it provided a fixed source of income with no duties. Where the archdeacon's office was functionally moribund and his visitations little more than formalities anyway, it must have been easy to see the practical advantages of such a cash cummutation as outweighing the canonical strictures against it.

D. Apparitors.[99]

The great bulk of petty moral offenses were dealt with not in the visitation process but in regular courts—sometimes the bishop's, more often the archdeacon's—to which they were reported by officials called apparitors, or summoners. Historians have characterized these people as policeman, or even members of a gestapo, but I can find no canonical basis for their being anything but process servers. The courts they served evidently turned them into policemen either by allowing them to cite verbally or by arming them with blank citations to be filled in at need; either way they could then circulate in the community and cite anyone they thought needed citing.

The abuses of their office, described by several provincial councils as well as by Chaucer, included blackmailing the innocent, taking bribes from the guilty, and boarding too sumptuously off the populace, especially the clergy. Various canonical documents attempted to limit the numbers of these people as well as their exactions, but it was not until after the Reformation that the more helpful expedient was tried of not allowing the apparitor to cite people until proceedings had been initiated by someone else. In fact, even this did not work very well; as long as the church courts concerned themselves seriously with the correction of petty moral offenses, the apparitor had a prominent and disreputable part in the work.

E. Clerical Felons from the Lay Courts.[100]

When a cleric was accused of felony, he had to be handed over to the ordinary; he could not be sentenced in the lay court. But before handing him over, the lay court (over the theoretical objections of the prelates) gave a verdict on whether he was guilty or not. If he was convicted on this verdict, the ordinary had to imprison him pending further proceedings. Clerics in this case provided a special class of disciplinary business for the ecclesiastical authorities.

Canonically, the secular conviction was *coram non judice*; it could not by itself be the basis for a punishment. It was accorded, however, the status of an accusation or, more accurately, of a common suspicion. A man could be held under it until he had made a canonical purgation by swearing to his innocence with a specified number of compurgators. Release in this way was sometimes blocked by an order of the lay court forbidding purgation either permanently or for a time. It is not clear under what circumstances such an order would issue.

Even without such an order, the canon law would not allow purgation if there was clear evidence of guilt. Accordingly, the imprisoned cleric was not allowed purgation until an inquest of worthy and knowledgeable persons had reported favorably as to his life and conversation generally and as to his innocence of the crime of which he stood accused. It was also possible for individual objectors to come forward and make their case at the time and place fixed for purgation.

If the cleric confessed his crime, if he was not cleared by the inquest, if the objectors made out their case against him, or if (as almost never happened) he failed to obtain the necessary compurgators, he was degraded and imprisoned for life. This form of punishment, unusual in the canon law, seems to depend on a 1261 constitution of Archbishop Boniface, who justified it by pointing out that laymen for the same offenses suffered death. Perhaps its use was part of the general church-state settlement on the matter of clerical offenders. The lay authorities tried to make sure these clerical prisoners were not too well treated, and the bishop was fined if any of them escaped.

It has been argued that this canonical process was rather a whitewash. No one underwent it unless he had already been convicted by a lay jury; yet great numbers underwent it successfully, made their purgation, and were released. It is easy to see why the purgation itself was no great obstacle. The compurgators had only to swear to a general belief in the credibility of the accused. They did not have to be closely acquainted with him: sometimes one set of them would serve a whole group of accused. It is easy to see how individual objectors could be kept from making their case. They were often bribed or intimidated by friends of the accused. Other times, they were discouraged by repeated postponements or other procedural obstacles. On the other hand, it is hard to see why the inquest, which was composed in about the same way as a secular jury, should go wrong more often than the secular jury did. So it is possible that a good number of those cleared by inquests were in fact innocent.

F. Nonroutine Administration.

Much of the administrative business of the church was originated or handled outside the routine channels we have been considering. A conscientious bishop took his information where he found it and deputed others to do the same. He also initiated some business (though not nearly as much as the pope did) on the petition of those concerned in it, as when two parishes were united on the petition of clergy, parishioners, and patrons.[101] Finally, some business was undertaken on orders from the king. Such orders might concern the correction of moral abuses in a church of royal foundation, the protection of royal rights and jurisdictions, the searching of ecclesiastical records for information pertinent to lay proceedings, or the implementation of some national policy like the exclusion of aliens from English benefices.[102]

Many of these matters, as well as some brought out on visitations or other routine procedures, were not suitable for simple reference to the regular courts or the regular administrative process. They might be disturbing the general peace and harmony of a parish and require a certain amount of tact in the handling. They might involve field work that could not be routinely done until the next visitation. They might involve some complex legal and administrative problem unsuitable for the courts to handle. They might have come first to the bishop's attention when some routine matter developed such complexities that the routine processes could not cope with it.[103] In any of these cases, a bishop would displace his routine agencies with an ad hoc commission. In one register, we find these commissions issuing for such diverse purposes as to check whether a church has been polluted in a recent brawl; to look into the scandalous behavior of the stipendiary priests celebrating at a neighboring church and start canonical proceedings against those in need of correction; to look into dilapidations in a church whose vicar has just died and make them good out of the estate; to impose penance on an adulterer too important to be dealt with by the regular courts; to admonish a nonresident rector to reside.[104]

The freedom with which the system subjected matters to nonroutine rather than routine handling was both a virtue and a vice. It gave the problem-solving devices of the system a flexibility consonant at once with the pastoral origin of all ecclesiastical administration and with modern conceptions of what an administrative system should be. On the other hand, it inhibited the development of effective routines for handling matters that would have lent themselves to routine handling; to that extent, it may have limited the capacity of the system to grow.

Also, there seems to be in medieval English history a certain connection, not easy to define, between the crystalization of administrative routine and the development of what we call the rule of law. We might put it that the earliest check on power was the routinization of its exercise. The power of the church, then, to the extent it was not routinized, was not effectively checked. Thus it is that the kind of crystallized custom that operated so banefully on the internal organization of the church seems to have done little for the protection of the individual citizen. The potentialities for arbitrary treatment that disturbed the laity as early as Clarendon were still disturbing them in the time of Charles I.

G. Judicial Process.

The church maintained a series of courts for routine handling of adversary proceedings under requisite rules of formality. The busiest of these courts were well organized, staffed by a responsible and knowledgeable bench and bar, and prepared to handle with reasonable dispatch whatever business was brought before them.

We have already given some attention to the organization of these courts and, in passing, to some of their business. The cases that the system channeled into judicial rather than administrative processes fall into rather definite categories, some of which were better handled than others:

1. *Criminal business,*[105] or, more properly, the correction of sinners, was generally handled, even when it came before the regular courts, in a summary, nonadversary fashion that should be considered administrative rather than judicial. A certain number of cases, however, were handled in a more plenary fashion, with specific charges being made, answered, and if necessary put to judicial proof. The few cases involving a formal canonical accusation—as the canonists put it, cases in which the office of the judge was promoted by a private person—seem to have been dealt with in that way, as well as some of the cases in which the judge acted on his own, (*ex officio mero*). Whether the accused had a right to this formal treatment whenever he controverted the facts or whether such treatment depended on the judge's estimate of the complexity of the factual issues is not clear.

2. The courts seem to have handled *matrimonial* and *testamentary cases* in a routine and workmanlike way; the only complaint commonly registered was with exorbitant fees for probate of estates. Attempts were made to deal with this abuse through provincial legislation, but the complaints continued to come in.[106] The archdeacons' courts and a number of other small local courts enjoyed probate jurisdiction of one kind or another, and I suspect that it was these, difficult as they were to supervise, that caused much of the trouble.

3. In the *vindication of private wrongs*—what would be called the law of obligations in the civil law, or what we would call the areas of tort and

contract—the ecclesiastical courts seem to have granted effective remedies insofar as the canon law gave them jurisdiction and the secular
courts allowed them to use it. We have already considered what those
areas were. In practice, most of the cases of this kind seem to have involved either defamation or breach of faith.[107] As we have seen, the
theoretical availability of writs of prohibition from the lay courts did
not prevent the church courts from doing a flourishing business in
cases of the latter class.

4. In the *collection of ecclesiastical dues,* the church courts were if anything too effective. The main complaint of the laity was that they had
to pay such dues even in cases where the secular law forbade them to
be collected.

5. In the *distribution of church property and revenues*—such cases as a
vicar's claim to augmentation of his endowment, a dispute over whether
a pension is owing out of a certain church, a dispute between rival
claimants to burial rights in a given place—the courts were in theory
available to those wishing to litigate, but there was a certain pressure
on the parties to submit them to administrative handling and to treat
them as involving problems to be solved rather than rights to be vindicated. The records show ad hoc commissions to investigate and memo-
randa of supervised compromise as often as they show straightforward
adjudication.[108]

In conducting these different kinds of business, the church courts seem
to have had no special difficulties in making their process effective.[109] The
usual device for bringing persons under the control of the court was the citation supported by threat of excommunication. Woodcock, author of the
most extensive study of the work of a group of medieval ecclesiastical courts,
finds that this device was as effective as its secular counterpart of outlawry.
Default judgments were sometimes used, however, and sometimes the court
took physical possession of the property or income of person to be brought
in or of the subject-matter of the suit.

In the court system as a whole, two major defects can be discerned. First,
the flexibility of the jurisdictional delegations and the proliferation of tribunals with claims to independence made it difficult to maintain central control over the allocation of business or the housekeeping arrangements of the
different courts. As a result, the possibility of exorbitant fees and abuses of
process was always open. Second, the aspiration to do full justice between
the parties led to an appellate process in which all questions were open that
had been open in the proceeding appealed from. This failure to set limits to
the appellate process made it possible to draw out a litigation more than
could be done in the secular courts, where someone appealing a judgment
had to point out a definite error in the proceedings appealed from.

How serious these defects were in practical effect is difficult to say. The complaints about abuse of process and exorbitant fees were frequent, but one may suspect a certain amount of exaggeration for rhetorical or polemical effect. Where abuse of process was involved, the lay courts stood ready to punish offenders, as did at least some of the ecclesiastical courts. Occasion for such punishment seems to have been neither remarkably rare nor so frequent as to suggest a serious problem.

As for appeals, the damage was not limited to the handful of spectacularly frustrating cases that went on interminably through one appeal after another. More significant were the important cases that were never brought for fear they should suffer the same fate. I have already pointed out, for instance, that such fears made bishops reluctant to depose abbots under their jurisdiction. This reluctance to take certain classes of cases to court, and the concomitant tendency to reserve important matters of internal ecclesiastical administration for nonroutine administrative handling, had as their most serious consequence a certain estrangement of the courts from the primary function of the whole system in carrying on the work and witness of the church. The full significance of this estrangement was not felt till long after the Reformation.

H. Fact-finding.

For the work we would call fact-finding whether in court or in administrative procedures, the English ecclesiastical authorities used three methods:
1. purgation through a ritual oath with compurgators,
2. evidence in the modern sense of witnesses and documents, and
3. inquests comparable to the secular institution of the same period that was the forerunner of the modern jury.

As a rough, not wholly accurate, generalization, we may say that purgation was used in matters primarily between the individual and God, evidence was used in disputes between parties, and inquests were used in matters of public administrative concern.

Purgation was an import into the system from the customs of the Germanic invaders of the Roman Empire. It was, however, assimilated early and thoroughly and belonged to the common law of the Western church.[110] It had in common with the less respectable Germanic import of the ordeal that it was fundamentally an appeal to the judgment of God in a matter where He alone knew the truth. It was available to clear an accused whose offense was the subject of a general rumor ("common fame") or of an informal denunciation. Where there was a formal canonical accuser in court ready to give evidence against him, he was not allowed a purgation unless the case against him failed on the evidence.

Trial by evidence seems to have been an inheritance from the Roman law. It involved the examination of relevant documents and the propounding to witnesses of interrogatories set by the parties or the court.[111] The tendency of modern trial procedure to allow the judge to listen to almost anything and decide afterward what probative force, if any, to accord it did not prevail in canonical trials. Witnesses and their testimony were excludible on grounds we would regard as impairing but by no means destroying the probative value of what they had to say.

In gathering the testimony of witnesses, there was no trial in the modern sense. The interrogatories were composed in advance and put to the witnesses at whatever time might prove suitable—either in court or elsewhere if there was some good reason. The answers were reduced to writing as quickly as possible and thereafter formed part of the documentary record on which the case was decided. It was not necessarily the judge who was to decide the case who presided over the taking of testimony; sometimes a commissary or examiner was deputed for that purpose. Even when the case was decided by the one who heard the testimony, the procedure did not lend itself to a conception of the evaluation of testimony as inseparable from the hearing of it. Rather, what was envisaged was the making up of a documentary record that the judge could pore over at leisure and that a series of appellate tribunals could pore over after him.[112]

The inquest seems to have been a Frankish institution which the Normans inherited from the Carolingian Empire and brought to England with them.[113] In essence it consisted of representatives of the local populace who met with a representative of central authority to answer under oath such questions as he may put concerning local affairs. It would seem that the English church did not copy it from the English state but that both took it from Normandy, where it represented a parallel development in church and state. We need not pursue its subsequent fate on the continent except to point out that it seems to have been no part of the general canon law or of French canonical practice in the later Middle Ages. The *inquisitio* of the general canon law contemplates a hearing of witnesses in the modern sense rather than an inquest such as we are here considering.[114]

The order for an inquest of this kind would generally refer to inquiring *per viros fidedignos et juratos*. Generally, a mixture of clergy and laity would be summoned to respond. The total number added up to twelve—not invariably but often enough to indicate that we are on the right track in assuming a connection with the secular institution.[115] Perhaps the crucial difference between men as summoned for an inquest and the same men as canonical witnesses was that on the inquest they answered collectively rather than individually the questions put to them. Thus, their answers raised no problem of conflicting evidence but established what were to be considered the true facts for purposes of the matter at hand. Presumably they answered at one time, at least in theory, on the basis of their own knowledge, as did their secular counterparts. We know that by the fifteenth century secular jurors had begun taking steps to inform themselves—first by making informal inquiries, later by making formal examination of documentary evidence, and finally by hearing live testimony. Some entries in the fifteenth-century register of Archbishop Chichele indicate that the ecclesiastical inquest was pursuing a parallel development at about the same time.

The ecclesiastical inquest was put to a variety of uses, most of which we have already had occasion to consider. Examples are the determination whether criminals from the lay courts were to be allowed purgation, the fixing of responsibility for dilapidations, the determination of the various questions that arose when a cleric was presented to a benefice, the decision on a petition to unite two parishes, and sometimes the disposition of a dispute over ecclesiastical dues.[116] Among the constitutions of Clarendon is one that seems to look to a more widespread use of inquests in the rendering of criminal accusations in the ecclesiastical courts, but it does not appear that anything came of it.

The fact-finding devices of a legal or administrative system may be conceived of under two aspects: they may be regarded as calculated to get at the truth of the matter in issue so that official intervention may be justly ordered, or they may be regarded as simply intended to dispose of the business at hand after official intervention has proceeded as far as it can go. The two views are not incompatible, but insofar as the second is emphasized the system will stress order and expedition in its fact-finding, and insofar as the first is emphasized it will stress accuracy.

Of the three fact-finding devices we are presently considering, that of purgation is the least concerned with accuracy; it simply disposes of the case when nothing more can be done. It does not seem to have been supposed, as a modern rationale might suggest, that the prevailing piety of the time made perjury unlikely; rather, it seems to have been supposed that one who cleared himself by a false oath would not escape punishment because God would punish him for his false oath.[117] The procedure thus understood was not a bad way of handling a question of the private spiritual state of a Christian. The oath vindicated the church's public witness to the values it upheld; the rest was between the accused and God. But in a proceeding to determine whether a man was fit to hold a cure of souls, such an approach was incongruous.

In contrast to the process of purgation, the process of assembling written testimony and documentary evidence seems to sacrifice expedition entirely to accuracy. Tracing a few major cases through their convoluted sets of appeals will indicate how great the sacrifice sometimes was. Worse, it seems quite likely that the sacrifice was made in vain. Once the written record was made up, it is hard to see how one man's determination of the truth it indicated was any better than another's. Thus, there is no reason to suppose that the appellate process made any general contribution to the accuracy with which the system determined facts.

It is only the inquest, then, that made a determination of fact having reasonable potentialities both for accuracy and for final effect. It is unfortunate therefore that the uses made of this device were more or less peripheral to the major administrative and legal decisions that came before the system. This limited use is perhaps attributable to the lack of authority for the device in the general canon law. Or perhaps the device suffered from the idealism that led the canonists generally to value theoretical perfection above practical effectiveness.

I. Sanctions.

We considered at some length in the last chapter the system of canonical sanctions and the English experience in using it. As we saw, the English had one or two variations on the general law, the most important being in the use of sequestration to control the actions of the beneficed clergy and to collect money from them. The English church was also fortunate in the effectiveness of the processes used by the secular government in aid of ecclesiastical sanctions. The most important of these were the writ *de excommunicato capiendo*, whereby an excommunicate could be jailed until he submitted to the church, and the writ *de vi laica amovenda*, whereby the sheriff could be called in to suppress forceful interference with the exercise of ecclesiastical authority. But despite these useful local contributions, it is generally true that the sanctions available to the medieval English ecclesiastical administration were those of the general canon law, and their weaknesses were those discussed in the last chapter. We need do no more at this point than summarize the effect of these weaknesses on the ability of the local authorities to do their work.

Let us first consider what the available sanctions did effectively accomplish:

1. With reasonable regularity, they got people into court who were personally summoned to come. The spiritual effects of excommunication, coupled with the possibility of physical restraint by the secular authorities, served this purpose as well as did comparable sanctions in the secular law.
2. They brought known sinners, in direct confrontation, to submit and do penance. The consequences of failure to submit to penance were precisely the same as the consequences of failure to come into court

when summoned; these were more severe than the penance was apt to be.

3. They were reasonably effective in compelling the payment of money, either through the sequestration of the ecclesiastical benefice of the debtor or through the threat of excommunication if a given payment was not made, or through making payment a condition for absolution from a given offense.

4. They secured relative immunity from illegal interference in the ordinary processes of ecclesiastical administration—visitation, reading of proclamations, serving of citations, and the like. The intervention of the secular authorities on behalf of the churchmen was of some importance here, but the ordinary ecclesiastical sanctions—cutting off divine service in a place where the exercise of ecclesiastical jurisdiction was impeded and excommunicating specific malefactors—were evidently effective enough against an average lot of irate parishioners.

What was it, then, that the available sanctions did not effectively accomplish?

1. For the reasons set forth in the last chapter, they did not provide an effective deterrent to serious or prevalent sins or against violence not related to the exercise of jurisdiction. Persons guilty of such things did penance when brought to book, but the possibility of such penance did not loom large enough to deter others from the same offenses.

2. They did not effectively control pluralism, nonresidence, and other vices involving physical absence. The potentialities of sequestration for controlling this kind of misconduct were never fully realized, while devices requiring that the offender be caught up with were difficult to carry into effect. Furthermore, as we have seen, the offender, when caught was usually given a chance to amend before being punished.

3. They did not effectively maintain the character of the parish ministry. We have seen that the cleric could be removed from his post only for moral failings, not for inability to do his job. And even forms of correction less drastic than removal had to be addressed to specific overt acts rather than to a general tendency to inactivity or incompetence. It is difficult, for instance, to see how the authorities could have processed through the canonical steps of purgation or penance the complaint of one set of parish representatives on visitation that their priest "did no good in the parish."[118]

These specific defects suggest a more general consideration, which is that the available sanctions, taken as a whole, may have borne less heavily on the clergy than on the laity. Clerical esprit de corps, in the context inherited from the Gregorian reform, made the authorities reluctant to impose upon the cleric any punishment that would reduce him to financial destitution or otherwise impair his public image.[119]

It was, then, just at the point where the institutional necessities of the church called most urgently for the effective exercise of administrative control that the available sanctions proved weakest. The medieval ecclesiastical administration was better able to serve as an adjunct to secular administration and better able to exact the externals of Christian discipline than to set its own house in order.

IV. Conclusion

We may conceive the system I have been describing in three ways. First, it was an *administrative system*, charged with the exercise of discretion in allocating and coordinating the available resources of personnel and material to carry out as well as possible the mission of the church. Second, it was a *legal system*, charged with applying the available means of social control to enforce certain specific rights and duties and to redress or punish their violation. Finally, it was a *pastoral system*, charged with confronting the individual with the demands of the Christian religion in such a way as to move him to live up to them. The three conceptions are of course not mutually exclusive; nor were they in fact distinguished in practice. It is by distinguishing them for analytical purposes, however, and turning our attention to them one by one that we can discern the basic defects of the system.

A. As an Administrative System.

Considered as an administrative system, it lacked freedom of action. The intellectual ascendency of the jurists had put every aspect of it into a structure of legal rights and duties, protected by legal forms and therefore immune to the processes of administrative intervention. Not only had many delegated functions hardened into property rights early in the development of the system, but there was a continuing tendency for new developments to go the same way as fast as they were effectively routinized.

This tendency, a part of the crystallizing tendency we see in all medieval institutions, was complemented in the English ecclesiastical administration by a tendency to confine the effective work of the system within a few well-defined categories of administrative concern. We see this latter tendency at work in the prevailing conception of the duties of a bishop, in the screening of candidates for ordination or preferment, in the supervision of the clergy, in the promotion of the Christian life in the parishes, and in the delineation of the business of the courts.

The tendency in question is attributable to a number of forces themselves,

probably due in the long run to the prevailing legalism. The most important
of these were the following:

1. The operation of so much of the system by part-time personnel whose
   primary concern was with something else. Such men tended in the exercise of their ecclesiastical offices to do no more than was required of
   them by an objective standard. Often, too, they deputed their fund-
   tions to others who were of no more than minimal competency.
2. The propensity of royal and papal authority for interfering with any
   aspect of the system that was not protected by cast-iron precedent.
3. In many areas, a general hostility to administrative intervention on the
   part of those affected by it. Only firm precedent could keep this hostility in check. Whatever was new in the way of administrative action
   would be resisted.
4. Perhaps most important of all, the continuing necessity of every administrator's justifying all his actions to some higher authority in church
   or state. Because of a general effect in medieval administrative concepts
   the higher authority could not be satisfied by a showing that the lower
   authority acted within the limits of the discretion entrusted to him, but
   only by a showing that he did "right." In the nature of things such a
   showing could not be assured unless there was a definite precedent to
   support it.

These forces combined to transform the whole administrative system into
a system for the enforcement of specific duties, while the crystallization of
delegated functions tended to create a series of specific rights. The result of
the whole process, then, was to enhance the conception of the system as a
legal system at the expense of the conception of it as an administrative system.

B. As a Legal System.

Considered as a legal system, it had all the defects of the general canon law
as I described them in the last chapter. Its aspirations were too high for a practical choice of goals or an expeditious handling of business. The rights and
duties to which it was addressed were selected by the force of circumstances
rather than by a functional choice. The character of the obligation it imposed
was equivocal. And its sanctions were too lenient to accomplish many of the
tasks it imposed on itself.

In addition to these general defects intrinsic to the canon law, the system
was affected by a tendency to take business out of the channels of routine
handling either by assigning ad hoc delegates to dispose of it or by pushing
it to a negotiated settlement rather than a legal decision. Treatment of this

kind detracted from the system's orientation toward the rule of law; it was an administrative technique, as baneful for the system-qua-legal-system as the various forces of legalism were for the system-qua-administrative-system.

I suggested in the last chapter that these defects, including the basic failure to answer to our conception of the rule of law, were attributable to the pastoral tradition behind the canon law. This suggestion is borne out in the English experience in that the areas in which the system functioned most successfully as a legal system—the administration of decedent estates, the determination of marital status, the collection of money—were precisely the areas in which it operated at the farthest remove from pastoral concerns. Conversely, in those areas most intimately involved with the primary witness of the church, the capacity of the system to function effectively as a legal system was most flawed by its necessity to function also as a pastoral system.

C. As a Pastoral System.

Considered as a pastoral system, it suffered from the legalism that surrounded all its organizations and procedures, making the exercise of pastoral solicitude subject to legal rights and duties of the kind we have seen surrounding the visitation process. Furthermore, the financial support of the pastorate, which might have looked like hospitality and alms in a truly pastoral context, looked in the legal context superimposed on the situation very like financial exactions and even venality.[120] This impression was enhanced by endemic tendencies to financial overcommitment which led most medieval officials to be rather strict in exploiting their sources of revenue. Thus, the juridical barriers to pastoral communication were reinforced by economic barriers even more formidable.

The most serious effect of these barriers was on the receptivity of those to whom the pastoral efforts of the system were addressed. I have pointed out the almost universal hostility aroused by the visitation process; I suspect that similar hostility was to be observed at every level of the pastorate. It takes an extraordinary gift of humility to undergo a real change of heart at the behest of a man who has come to take a large sum of money away from you and perhaps have you beaten into the bargain.

But even without such barriers to pastoral communication, the system could not, qua pastoral system, have done the work of governing the church. The quantities of property, the heterogeneous personnel, and the variegated interests that fell under the control of the medieval ecclesiastical authorities could not have been kept in line by the exercise of pastoral diligence. The legal and administrative work unquestionably needed doing.

The problem in the system was not that it was administrative, pastoral, and legal at once; it had to be. The problem was that it failed to assign the respective aspects their proper places in a harmonious whole. The pastorate is necessarily personal and necessarily incapable of being specified legally. As the duties inherent in the pastorate cannot be specified, it requires a certain exercise of discretion to control, supervise, or enforce the performance of them. It is at this level that the administrative aspects of the system belong. What can be specified legally is who can act administratively and with what procedures. This kind of determination—together with certain peripheral matters involving definite rights and duties, such as marital status, the application of pious gifts to the purposes specified by the donors, or determining who is responsible for dilapidations—is what is proper to the legal aspects of the system.[121]

5.The Parish Ministry

The ideological, legal and administrative forces we have been considering had an uncertain and often haphazard effect on the parish ministry. In turning my attention to the parish ministry as such, I shall be bringing together a number of things we have already touched upon in passing. It is essential that I focus on the parish ministry directly, for it is here that we see what was most crucial in the failure of the medieval church to achieve that Christian civilization to which it aspired. In dealing with the subject, I shall deal, first, with the parochial structure envisaged, and in part achieved, by the Gregorian reformers; second, with the changes wrought the structure by the financial and institutional pressures that followed on the reform period; and, third, with the actual conduct of the ministry within the framework thus developed.

I. The Institutional Transformation

It is not clear whether the imposition of a stable personal character on the local ministry figured among the objectives of the Gregorian reform or whether the measures that had that effect were adopted with a view simply to strengthening the cohesiveness of the church organization and its control over the clergy and their revenues.[1] In any event, the canons of the reform period did in fact set up a program for a stable personal ministry to replace the fortuitous arrangements that had grown up in the past.[2]

Every church was to have its own particular priest, responsible to the bishop for the "cure of souls" in the locality. The priest was to be personally present, was to be attached to no more than one such church, and was not to move off to another. By the same token, he was not to be dismissed on whim by those who had put him there, but was to remain where he was unless the bishop found him unworthy and removed him. Along with this security of tenure, he was to be given a certain measure of financial security. He was not to be given an annual stipend but was to have fixed sources of income among those parish revenues—tithes, offerings and the like—that the reformers were in the process of recovering from profane uses.

The complex structure that this program was to reshape in England was that developed by the vicissitudes and expedients of late Anglo-Saxon times as we considered them in the first chapter. This structure presented a number of different forms of church tenure, which were affected in different ways by the Gregorian legislation, though they came in the end looking pretty much alike.

A. Churches Belonging to Local Landholders.

Churches belonging to local landholders became the model for all the others—some were hundred churches on royal or formerly royal manors; others were in one of the two classes mentioned in Edgar's law about the thane and his bookland. If they were once hundred churches, they had both glebe and tithe; if they were on bookland, they were entitled to tithe by Edgar's law; if they were neither, they were paid for as the proprietor chose. In any case, if the church had fixed sources of revenue, the proprietor could not (as a continental proprietor or an English monastery might do) absorb the revenues and hire a priest to serve the cure. He could, however, let the church to a priest for an agreed-on *servitium*. Also, unless he agreed otherwise, he could evidently change from one priest to another as often as he chose.

Accordingly, what the Gregorian legislation required was the abolition of the *servitium* and the establishment of fixed rights of tenure for the priest. The abolition of the *servitium* met with some resistance but surprisingly little, all things considered.[3] Parish priests continued from time to time to make payments to their patrons, but these were clandestine, recognized as simony, and prosecuted as such.[4] They were not made under color of legality after the twelfth century. As for giving the priest rights of tenure, I can find no evidence of any resistance at all. It was, of course, the general tendency of the the times to establish life tenure in every kind of manorial status, and there was nothing to make the parish ministry an exception.

It was without much difficulty, then, that the lay proprietor of an earlier period was reduced in the course of the twelfth century to a canonical patron, whose right in the church was limited to that of presenting to the ordinary a suitable cleric to occupy the position when it fell vacant. The change was reflected in the documentary style, which shifted from grants of churches with their appurtenances to grants of the advowsons of churches, and in the legal process, which developed a special set of writs to deal with suits over advowsons instead of treating churches in the same way as other landed property.[5]

While the rights of the proprietor in existing churches were being thus reduced, the freedom to set up new proprietary churches was reduced still further. Before the middle of the twelfth century, it had become impossible for a landholder, without buying off existing parochial rights, to endow a church on his own land (whether out of secular revenues or out of tithes that he was free to bestow on any ecclesiastical object he chose), or even to admit his tenants into his private chapel to hear mass.[6] Those whose consent was required tended to drive a hard bargain in these cases. Often they left the new foundation with less than the rights of a full-fledged parish and the founder with less than the rights of a canonical patron.[7] In any event, no layman had any *more* rights than a canonical patron except over a household chaplain, who ministered only to those of the household and received only secular wages.

B. Churches Belonging to a Body of Clergy.

Churches belonging to a body of clergy were in a special case because the proprietors were not limited to a *servitium*. They could absorb all the revenues and serve the cure through one of their own number or through a hired priest. Many churches, as we have seen, were held in this way as a result of the monastic revival under Edgar. Others had been given to monasteries or collegiate establishments by lay proprietors. By the late twelfth century, it became the rule that a religious house acquiring a church from a layman could not exercise any further rights in it than the layman had possessed.[9] Thus, a house could not without further permission absorb any of the revenues of a church it was given after that time. But churches it had received earlier—say, up to the first century after the Conquest—it could treat in the same way as churches it had always possessed.

The most important change made by the reform legislation in the treatment of churches of this kind was the requirement that the community designate a particular priest to be responsible to the bishop for the exercise of the ministry in each such church. Some canons went further and required that the priest so designated not be changed without the bishop's permission.[10]

During the course of the twelfth century, further refinements were adopted in the interest of providing a certain measure of financial security for the priest in question.[11] The religious or collegiate proprietor was of course subject to the general legislation against hiring a *conductitius*, or stipendiary priest. Other legislation required that the priest be left a sufficient portion of the revenues of the church to maintain himself in a suitable style. Finally, toward the end of the twelfth century, it became customary to provide fixed sources of revenue for his maintenance—a practice that was made compulsory by the Fourth Lateran Council in 1215.

This meant that the religious house, like the lay proprietor, was basically limited to presenting to the bishop a fit person who would exercise the cure of souls and avail himself of the fixed sources of revenue provided for his support. If these sources of revenue were all the church afforded, the person so presented was called a parson or a rector like the person presented by the lay patron.[12] If they were only part of the revenues of the church, the person presented was called a vicar, pursuant to a canonical fiction that the community itself was the parson. There could also be an intermediate stage where the priest received all the revenues, (and thus was a parson, not a vicar) but made a fixed annual payment, called a pension, to the religious house. Some of these pensions had been set up in the settlement of various conflicting claims; others had existed from the time when it was legal for all patrons to exact them.

These changes in the tenure of the church did not expressly affect the right of the religious house to serve the cure with one of its own members. If there was a tendency to do so, however, it died out as the changes progressed.[13] In the first place, it was considered improper for monks to serve parochial cures, and some of the reform legislation forbade it. This legislation did not apply to canons regular, and even the monks sometimes ignored it. Still, the temper of the times favored keeping religious in the cloister, and the independence envisaged for the man who served the parish cure accorded ill with the discipline of a religious house. Also, the financial independence required by the canons made it of no advantage to the house to install one of its own members. Finally, the person serving the cure was required to reside on it, and there were rules against religious living alone.

Where the proprietor of the church was a college of secular canons rather than a religious house, the division of the collegiate endowments into separate *prebends* for the several canons had the effect—more or less independently of the Gregorian legislation on the subject—of making a single priest responsible for the cure of souls in each such church. In later times, the canon who occupied the prebend to whose endowments the church belonged would be regarded as the rector of the church. Like other absentee rectors, in most cases he was eventually made to endow a vicarage.[14]

C. The Church in which a Community was Physically Located.[15]

The church was evidently not strictly subject to the canons requiring the community to appoint one man to answer to the bishop for the cure. Some of these churches were monastic (described in Domesday Book as "the church of _____" and in contemporary grants as "the church of _____ and the monks there serving God"). Others were collegiate, either new foundations or survivals from the days before Edgar's monastic revival. Still others were heavily endowed churches belonging to the old hundred system or churches on episcopal manors that had escaped the tendency to centralization of diocesan administration. In any event, they harked back to the ancient pattern of serving the cure of souls through a body of resident clergy, and the Gregorian ideal of every church having its own priest did not directly affect them.

So the cure of those who sought the ministrations of religion in a monastic or collegiate church often remained a corporate responsibility down to relatively late times. On the other hand, there were forces at work that resulted in a good many cases in reducing such churches to the general pattern. First, in the monasteries (including a number of collegiate establishments that became monastic through the introduction of canons regular in the twelfth century)[16] there was a good deal of pressure to keep seculars out of the enclosure. Many monasteries, therefore, set up extern churches outside their gates to serve the needs of the local inhabitants. These, since they were basically parish churches like any other, tended to come under the jurisdiction of the local ordinary, and, ultimately, under the vicarage system.[17]

Some collegiate churches of secular canons also shed their parochial functions through building ancillary parish churches in this way, even though they had no comparable reason for doing so. Meanwhile, where the parochial function was retained in the collegiate church, there was a certain tendency to delegate it to a specific person, usually with a specific endowment, as was being done with all the other functions in these churches.[18] In that case, of course, the person to whom the function was delegated would be in about the same position as a canonical incumbent in some other parish.

There were a few ancient corporate cures that were not turned over to religious in the twelfth century and were not sufficiently prosperous to have successful careers as colleges of secular canons with prebends, endowments, choir services, and the like. These appeared in later times simply as split rectories—parishes in which the cure of souls was divided among two or more persons. This state of affairs was denounced by the canons and continued to be denounced through the thirteenth century. A number of split rectories were united under the pressure of such disapproval, but others continued down to modern times.[19]

D. Churches Belonging to the Incumbent Himself.

In some cases, the incumbent or his ancestor had no doubt been placed in the church by the ordinary; in others, he was put in by a king, a secular magnate, or even a monastery. In any event, the amorphous character of land tenure in the time just before and just after the Conquest had made it easy to to assimilate the position of the priest in his church to that of a secular tenant in his freehold; and the tendency of all tenures to become hereditary at the time had been at work on ecclesiastical tenures as well as lay.

The enforcement of the reform legislation imposing celibacy on the clergy and forbidding hereditary benefices meant that a priest holding his church in this way as a feudal tenant might well have no son to succeed him, and even if he did, the son might not be allowed to occupy the father's church. In either case, the church, on the death of the incumbent, would fall back into the hands of the one who gave it out.

This state of affairs is reflected in a number of twelfth-century grants turning over to some cathedral or religious house a church with the appurtenances that such-and-such priest had formerly held of the grantor.[20] In other cases, such grants are given out while the priest is actually in possession and are so worded as to preserve his rights and sometimes even those of a son:

> Know that I have conceded to Saint Mary of Lincoln the church of Brand the priest of Corringham, and his (its?) land, to wit two carucates and a half by way of prebend, in such a way nevertheless that Brand himself and his son after the father's death shall hold the said church and land by way of prebend of Saint Mary as long as they live.[21]

In other cases, rights of this kind are expressly recognized by the ecclesiastical overlord, often in exchange for a pension to be paid by the incumbent priest.[22]

Generally, documents of this kind appear in the records only where the church changed hands in the course of the twelfth century; we may assume that other churches went through a similar transformation without changing hands. In any event, the trend to hereditary incumbencies was effectively checked, and churches that began the twelfth century as the feudal holdings of their priests ended the century as canonical rectories in the same or different hands. The feudal tenant had been made into a canonical rector and his overlord into a canonical patron or proprietor.[23]

E. Churches Belonging to the Ordinary.

Some of these stood on ancient episcopal manors, centers of the peripatetic diocesan administration of Anglo-Saxon times. Others had been founded by local worshippers who lacked either the inclination or the bargaining power to reserve proprietary controls over them. The more important of these churches were among the episcopal properties distributed in the eleventh or twelfth centuries for the endowment of the cathedral chapters. They fell under the same rules that governed other capitular churches and eventually had vicarages established.[24]

Meanwhile, those churches that the bishop kept for himself tended to serve the same purposes for him that other churches served for their proprietors—they were sources of economic return and sources of compensation for his bureaucratic personnel. This being so, the bishop's relation to them came to be regarded as similar to that of other patrons to churches in their gift. Bishops did impose pensions on their churches, even while resisting the efforts of other ecclesiastical proprietors to do the same.[25] But they did not make their churches any general exception to the canonical pattern.

The canonical pattern, then, was pretty well imposed on the entire English parochial system by the end of the twelfth century. Pursuant to this pattern, every church had a distinct set of revenues constituting its permanent endowment, had an incumbent priest responsible to the ordinary for the spiritual needs of the inhabitants of the locality it served, and had a patron entitled to present to the bishop a qualified priest to fill the incumbency when it fell vacant. If the patron was a layman, he could have no further right than this. An ecclesiastical patron might have in addition a fixed pension payable out of the revenues of the church or might even "appropriate" the revenues to its own use, leaving only a minimum endowment to support a vicar to serve the cure. Rights of this kind as they existed at the close of the twelfth century were generally survivals from a period in which there had been fuller proprietary rights.[26] It was possible for ecclesiastical patrons to acquire such rights over churches where they had not had them in the past, but only with the consent of the ordinary.

So much for the canonical pattern. Two elements in the pattern, however, were not canonical. One was carrying the respect for vested rights to such a point as to interfere with the erection of new parishes where they were needed. This particular barrier to effective ecclesiastical administration appeared early in the twelfth century, and was still giving trouble in the eighteenth. The other noncanonical element was the jurisdiction of the lay courts over cases involving patronage rights. This jurisdiction evidently survived from the days when churches were owned as other land was owned. It prevailed, as we have seen, over the church's claim that the right to present to her benefices was properly her business.

In this developed parochial structure of patrons and incumbents, a certain number of exceptions must be recognized. These were sometimes of considerable local importance, though there were not enough of them to have a serious general effect on the English church. I have already referred to the split rectories in this connection. There were also ancient corporate cures like those in the peculiar jurisdiction of Dorchester Abbey, Oxfordshire, that escaped both the twelfth-century pressure to put in rectors and the subsequent pressure to put in vicars.[27] Then there were the royal free chapels.[28] Some of these were ancient collegiate churches like Saint Peter's, Wolverhampton; others were hypertrophied household chaplaincies like Saint

George's in Windsor Castle. Typically, in either case they would contain a group of canons endowed with prebends out of lands and churches in the gift of the king and would be totally exempt from ecclesiastical jurisdiction. In some cases the churches with which the prebends were endowed participated in all or some of this exemption.

Finally, there were parochial chapels, or chapels of ease. These were village churches that, because of late foundation, were unable to secure full parochial status but remained in partial dependence on some other church. Aside from terminology, the marks of dependency might include the collection of payments, the obligation of the villagers to seek certain religious ministrations at the mother church instead of the local chapel, the right of the rector of the mother church to appoint the chaplain of the chapel, or any combination of these.[29]

This, then, was the parochial system as it existed in England on the eve of the great administrative and financial transformation to which I have so often alluded, the change from feudal to central-bureaucratic administration. This arrangement had three main elements in common with the other administrative arrangements subjected to the same transformation. First, it had been fully articulated locally. Second, its local units were separately and irrevocably endowed. Third, the endowment of them had fairly well accounted for all the financial resources available to the system as a whole so that no large-scale centralization would be economically feasible without tapping these decentralized resources anew.

We have seen how in this context the revenues of the parishes were put to work to finance central-bureaucratic expansion at every level of church and state. We have also seen something of how the available sources of revenue were fought over by the various agencies of central administration. Finally, we have seen what the ecclesiastical authorities did and did not do to support the parish ministry in the face of these demands on its financial resources. At this point, we shall have to see how these financial operations affected the parish ministry itself.

II. The Economic Transformation

A. Nonresidence.

Ancillary to the parochial system I have been describing was a canonical rule that the priest who enjoyed the parish revenues should live and minister in the parish. Dispensations and violations of this rule became endemic in the church as the twelfth century renaissance opened up wider fields of personal usefulness to the clergy, while the bulk of the available funds remained in the endowments of the parish ministry. In considering how parish funds were diverted to other objects, therefore, we must begin with nonresidence and see how a priest assigned the cure of souls in a particular parish, with the attendant revenues, might be able to serve other needs in other places. The following reasons for nonresidence seem to have been the main ones.

1. *Pluralism*—A man with two benefices must necessarily be nonresident on at least one of them. If you were properly licensed for pluralism, residence on one benefice was evidently accepted as an excuse for not residing on the others.[30] Of course if you resided on none of them, you would need some other excuse. There were two entirely different classes of pluralists: poor ones in parishes where it took the revenues of two or more benefices to make up a decent living, and rich ones who constituted the sublime and literate persons of *De Multa*—men whose services to the bureaucratic establishment or to the cause of higher learning were more than a single benefice could adequately reward. Needless to say, men in the former class tended to reside on one or another of their plural benefices,[31] whereas men in the latter class tended not to.

2. *Commends*[32] —Where a benefice was vacant and there was no suitable person available to fill it, it was possible to turn it over to someone *in commendam*, or in custody. The person thus put in charge would be entitled to collect the revenues and would have to see to the service of the cure, but he would not be required to reside. This device was originally used to enable a neighboring parson to provide for services in a place where there was no suitable incumbent available or to afford a period of probation to a would-be incumbent who lacked some needful qualification. The use of the same device as a convenient way of turning the revenues over to a nonresident for reasons unrelated to the service of the cure was regarded as an abuse. For this, the Second Council of Lyons in 1274 sought to provide a remedy by limiting the duration of any such arrangement to six months. It appears, however, that this limitation was sometimes either dispensed from or disregarded.

3. *Study*—Bishops often permitted—and no doubt on occasion encouraged—their beneficed clergy to absent themselves for a time for purposes of study, a practice that was regularized by Boniface VIII in his constitution *Quum ex eo* of 1299.[33] Boniface put a seven year limit on such absences. But whatever this practice might have done to raise the intellectual quality of the parish clergy was vitiated by the lack of an administrative machinery to see that the person licensed in fact spent his time in study, by an extremely liberal interpretation of *Quum ex eo* that brought both chaplaincies and bureaucratic services under the head of study, and, I suspect, by failure to see that the student returned to his parish when the seven years were up.

4. *Bureaucratic Service*[34] —An important prelate or secular magnate would

carry enough weight in Rome to get a suitable number of clerics of his bureaucratic establishment exempted from the requirement of residence on their benefices. Also, a promising bureaucrat might himself make enough of an impression in Rome to be granted a dispensation for nonresidence while in the service of his patron. The king, meanwhile, as to his own clerics, succeeded in enforcing an ancient custom that even without a dispensation they could not be made to reside. Finally, in the ranks of the clerical bureaucrats we must include a certain number beneficed in and around London who were able to keep technical residence without neglecting their administrative tasks. These, we may suppose, did not do much more for the parish ministry than they would have done as nonresidents.

5. *Business in Rome*[35] –The service of the Holy See was, of course, a special case of bureaucratic service, and one particularly apt to commend itself to the dispensing power. I suspect it constituted in itself a license for nonresidence, though there may have been a formal dispensation in every case. Dispensations were also given on occasion to men pursuing their own affairs at the curia, while a man pursuing the business of the church in which he was supposed to be residing was said not to be nonresident at all.

6. *Gratuitous Dispensation*–In the matter of residence, as in other matters, the popes often dispensed on the basis of inadequate information or insufficient grounds. Boniface VIII, in his decretal *Quia per Ambitiosam,*[36] complained of the improvident dispensations for indefinite nonresidence extracted from him and his predecessors through the ambitious importunity of petitioners and revoked all such dispensations then outstanding.

7. *Violators not Caught*–As we have seen, the authorities had no very good way of reaching a man who was physically out of their control. They had a hard time bringing nonresidents to book, and they must have been discouraged at the outset by the fact that their man, when they finally ran him down, might turn out to have a perfectly good dispensation.[37] Moreover, the occasional successful proceeding generally resulted in nothing more serious than an order to reside in the future. So it seems fair to say that an unlicensed nonresident had little to fear from the authorities and reasonable to assume that not all these who stayed away with impunity were licensed.

It should be noted that this whole pattern of nonresidence grew up around situations in which it was felt that the needs of the parish ministry itself would be served by a temporary absence. The tacit shift to a situation in which other purposes were served at the expense of the parish ministry was characteristic of the development of medieval ecclesiastical administration. Nor was it without justification. A number of modern commentators have argued very persuasively that both the traditions of the church and the claims of universal Christianity warranted the diversion to other objects of revenues raised in the parishes.[38] Unfortunately, however, in this as in so many other areas, the change took place without any formulation of either its nature or its purposes and, therefore, under no rational control. Neither the consequences of nonresidence for the parish ministry nor the justification for risking those consequences was ever sufficiently weighed by the authorities.

There is no adequate evidence on the extent to which parish incumbents were nonresident at any given period during the Middle Ages. The records, such as they are, support estimates of from 10 to 30 percent in most places and times, though the figures from a poor diocese such as Hereford could be much lower.[39] Vicars were significantly less apt to be absent than rectors. I suspect that the really important consideration in all this was the size of the parish revenues: if these were sufficiently above the going rate for a curate, they would be given fairly often to a man who had better things to do than to serve the cure.

It was the duty of the nonresident to see that someone carried on the ministry in his absence.[40] There is some evidence of a canonical rule that he should endow a vicar, as a corporate rector did, but in practice it was a stipendiary chaplain he left in his place. He was supposed to make himself responsible for the character of his chaplain and to supervise his conduct and service of the cure. Saint Thomas Cantilupe, according to the Bollandists, was careful to keep up the buildings in his parishes, maintain hospitality and almsgiving, and even see that his curates were able to preach.[41] But this is in the realm of hagiography. The ordinary nonresident evidently contented himself with leaving a priest in the parish who was able to go through the motions of administrating the sacraments and conducting the liturgy.

The most persistent complaint from the parishes about nonresidence involved the failure to keep hospitality or otherwise provide for the poor. It was probably not that the poor were not being provided for, but that the parishioners had to provide for them out of their own pockets. As regards other grounds of complaint, the curate for a nonresident incumbent was slightly (but only slightly) more apt to be incontinent or illiterate than was a resident incumbent or his assistant.[42] But he was not significantly more remiss in serving the cure, nor was his parish significantly more apt to report dilapidations.

On the whole, it seems that the effect of nonresidence is not to be determined by comparing parish A, served by a stipendiary curate for a nonresident incumbent, with parish B, served by a resident rector or vicar. The incumbency was probably a little wealthier and more secure than the curacy, but not a great deal. They were about the same kind of positions and would have attracted about the same kind of men. If the incumbency had been worth a great deal more than the curacy, it would have been given to an academic or bureaucrat who would not have resided. The economics of nonresidence, in short, skimmed off whatever parish revenues exceeded a certain amount, leaving the man who served the cure, whatever his title or canonical status, with a certain minimum earning capacity and a corresponding minimum capability.

The real vice in this situation, it seems to me, was that it prevented the development of any professional leadership among the parish clergy. There was no upper-rank parish priest whom a colleague could hope to emulate at the beginning of his career and succeed at the close. This lack must have affected the quality of the ministry in all the parishes, not only those that were in the hands of nonresidents.

B. Appropriation.

The assumption of parish revenues by religious houses or other corporate bodies operated, like nonresidence, to skim off excess funds from the parish ministry and apply them to other purposes in the society. The beneficiaries of the practice included cathedral chapters, religious houses, collegiate churches hospitals, chantries, and Oxford or Cambridge colleges[43]—the institutional embodiments of all the learning, most of the piety, and much of the social service of medieval England. By the Reformation, they had appropriated well over one-third of the parishes in the country.[44]

From the end of the twelfth century, as we have seen, no new appropriation was permitted without a license. But the growth of institutions financed through the practice made such licenses increasingly sought after and increasingly easy to get.[45] Thanks to the perpetual overcommitment of these institutions, the canonical showing of need was never a problem. I have pointed out that the need was not weighed against the possibility of cutting expenses or the desirability of keeping funds in the parish. If a house did not eventually appropriate all the parishes in its gift, the forebearance was probably due to the need of providing for secular clergy of its bureaucratic establishment rather than to any inability to get a license.

Many appropriations, especially after the mid-fourteenth century, were granted to new foundations, colleges and chantries, that could hardly be regarded as already in need. It appears simply that the foundation was regarded as a work of piety and the appropriation as a way of encouraging it.[46] Everyone whose license was required for the appropriation was included in the prayers and masses offered by the members of the foundation.

An act of Parliament, the Mortmain Act of 1279, required the appropriator to get a license from the king as well as from the ecclesiastical authorities.[47] This act applied in terms to transfers of lands to corporate bodies, but it was interpreted to apply to appropriations, no doubt because they had the same effect of depriving the kings and secular magnates of various opportunities for financial benefits when one tenant succeeded another. Royal licenses were no harder to get than ecclesiastical, but they involved a fairly complex procedure along with substantial cash payments to the royal treasury.

The requirement that a vicarage be endowed in a parish where the rectory was appropriated was enforced with considerable vigor, especially after the Fourth Lateran Council. Those appropriations that had come down from the full proprietary rights of an earlier time were systematically inqiured into and provided with vicarages, while parishes newly appropriated were generally provided with vicarages at the time the appropriation was licensed.[48] A few appropriated parishes escaped this movement in one way or another, and in a few cases beginning late in the fourteenth century, the pope dispensed from the requirement of a vicarage or allowed the vicarage itself to be appropriated.[49] In most cases, however, the appropriated parish had a vicar holding a perpetually endowed benefice in the gift of the corporate rector.

The canons required that the vicar's endowment be sufficient to afford him a *congrua sustentatio*. Provincial councils attempted in 1222 and again in 1439 to set this amount at so many marks, but in practice little uniformity was achieved.[50] The ordination of a vicarage would usually specify that the vicar was to have the offerings of the parishioners on specified occasions and the tithes of certain specified products (the so-called small tithes, as distinguished from the "great tithes" of staple grains and the like, which belonged to the rector). The vicar might have in addition a patch of glebe land on which to grow a crop or at least a garden to raise vegetables for his table. In some places the vicar might live with the religious who appropriated the rectory. How he fared under such an arrangement differed greatly from one place to another.

A vicarage set up by a bishop might be insufficient for the vicar to live on or might become so in a variety of ways. The monks who were supposed to feed him at their table might move out of the parish and leave their holdings to a bailiff.[51] The course of agriculture in the parish might be altered, increasing the rector's great tithes at the expense of the vicar's small tithes. Or the patterns of piety in the parish might change, reducing the income from the offerings allocated to the vicar. When any of these proved to be the case, the vicar's share of the parish revenues was supposed to be augmented by the bishop, either on his own motion or at the suit of the vicar. In theory, the canonical rule of *congrua sustentatio* was absolute, so that a showing that the vicar had not enough to live on was sufficient to require the augmentation of the vicarage. The needs of the appropriator were not weighed against those of the vicar in an augmentation proceedings any more than the needs of the parish were weighed against those of the appropriator in granting a license for appropriation.[52]

The appropriator had two weapons available for resisting augmentations. First, the vicarage was in its gift, and it could bestow it on a man who could be relied on not to seek augmentation; sometimes it would even exact an oath to that effect.[53] Second, the appropriator could make use of the procedural devices available to medieval defendants for stalling canonical proceedings and making them expensive.[54] The vicar, whose problem was poverty in the first place, would be apt not to have the resources to counter these devices effectively. A canon of Archbishop Chichele in 1439 attempted to remedy this situation by giving him a summary *in forma pauperis* proceeding;[55] what effect this had on augmentations does not appear.

To be sure, if the ordinaries had made a habit of augmenting vicarages on their own motion, as they had the power to do, these devices for resisting the vicar's claims would not have assisted the appropriator. In fact, however, although augmentation procedures were sometimes carried out more or less summarily on the basis of information elicited in parish visitations,[56] it does not appear that the ordinaries could be counted on to act in augmentation cases unless the vicar complained, and, even then, they sometimes took some prodding. The register of the mid-fourteenth-century bishop Trillek of Hereford, a more than average conscientious administrator, shows three cases where the Court of Arches had to intervene to have an augmentation suit heard in his court.[57] What with one thing and another, then, vicarages were by no means augmented as often as they ought to have been: successful augmentation proceedings were never unknown, but they were of infrequent occurrence.

In this financial and legal context, did the vicar in fact have enough to live on? The consensus of those who have addressed themselves to the question recently seems to be that he did.[58] That is, by the modest standards of the villagers among whom he served, he was in no want. On the other hand, he was probably not in a very good position to keep up with his obligations in the way of hospitality, almsgiving, or repairs to the fabric of the church.

On the whole, it seems fair to say that the system of appropriations and vicarages had the same effect on the parishes to which it applied that the system of nonresidence had on other parishes: it skimmed off and applied to purposes outside the parish such of the parish revenues as were not required to maintain in circumstances of decent frugality a priest to perform the work of the parish ministry. Thus, the question of how many rectories were appropriated, like the question of how many were in the hands of nonresidents, is not exactly to the point in determining the effect of the system on the parish ministry. It may be supposed, since both the means and the motivation were present, that where the parish revenues afforded an excess it was skimmed off in one way or the other.[59]

Some of the money diverted from the parishes through nonresidence and appropriation simply made up for inefficiency in the management of other sources of revenue, but most of it went to support socially useful work. Public and private administrators lived off cathedral prebends with appropriated churches or off parish rectories on which they did not reside. They traveled about the country with their retinues, putting up at monasteries that drew on the revenues of appropriated churches to defray the cost of entertaining them.[60] The intellectual life of the community was supported by monks studying in the cloister or living in the universities on monastic funds, by parish priests (Wyclif for one) living in universities instead of parishes, and by colleges enjoying appropriated churches. Monasteries and hospitals with appropriated churches contributed substantially (if rather less than their apologists have supposed) to social service and poor relief.[61] Much of the religious energy of the community went into the enrichment of monasteries, the enhancement of their worship and intercession, the beautification of their churches, or into the foundation of chantries supported by appropriations, or (witness Langland) by the ministrations of nonresident parish priests. All these were important functions of medieval society, and some of them contributed to the positive achievements which that society has handed down. But none of them contributed to the work of ministering in the parishes.

III. Performance

The actual position of the priest who did most of the work in the typical parish must have been somewhere in the yeoman class.[62] He had not the wherewithal to keep up a higher state and the period was not one in which economic and social status were sharply distinguished. In some parishes, the priest may have been reduced to a more abject state, or hard put to keep out of such a state, but these were probably rare. Unbeneficed chaplains may have been in a more penurious position than were resident parsons or vicars, but such of them as had fairly stable relations with nonresident incumbents were probably not too much worse off than their beneficed colleagues. The nonresident did not customarily concern himself greatly with conditions on his benefice, and if he had a chaplain in charge who gave him no trouble, we may suppose he did not generally interfere with him.

This economic and social position, it may be supposed, did not attract men who were in the ranks of the elite in medieval English society; still less did it elevate its occupant to those ranks. Especially was this the case in that the society offered a number of far more attractive, as well as more remunerative positions to members of the secular clergy who could make the grade. For a young man suitably befriended, or whose talents gained him attention, there were unlimited opportunities for fame, fortune, and honorable public service in the bureaucracy. For one more studiously inclined, a career at

Oxford or Cambridge offered both comfort and distinction. And for men who lacked the ambition or the talent to scale these heights of administration or learning there were well-paid and undemanding posts as stipendiary chaplains serving chantries, teaching grammar schools, or dispensing the ministrations of religion in the households of great men. Such men were probably a little better paid than the run of parish incumbents—in the last half of the fourteenth century and the first half of the fifteenth, it was evidently as hard to limit them to nine marks a year as it was to raise vicars to twelve—and they had much less exacting work as well as more congenial living conditions in many cases.[63]

While such men as Grosseteste in his time and Wyclif and Langland in theirs protested the diversion of the clergy from the cure of souls, the piety of the time seems to have regarded these alternatives as entirely acceptable manifestations of the priestly vocation. Pantin quotes eloquent apologies for royal and papal bureaucrats, Thompson yet more glowing ones for the chantry priest, while those who pursued learning could call the very Decretals to witness that they were to "shine in the Church of God like the splendor of the firmament."[64] Added to the verbal testimonials in favor of these different ways of serving God was the silent witness of the pay scale together with accompanying gradations of social status. Even one who did not seek out the most lucrative career from crassly materialistic motives could hardly be blamed for supposing that the church gave the richest recognition to the services she valued the most.

There were of course men, sometimes men of great talent, who read in the teachings of Christianity an injunction to spurn riches and honors alike. But these men did not enter the parish ministry either. They were naturally drawn to the religious life, especially that of the friars. The friars did do a good deal of preaching and hearing confessions in the parishes, but whether they strengthened or undermined the ordinary parish clergy by doing so is a moot point. In any event, the friars were heavily committed to the academic life and much in demand as the confessors of great men. So we may doubt if they put their best men to this parish apostolate.

The day-to-day work of Christian ministry in the parishes, then, fell to the lot of clerics with the pay and status of the higher peasantry—men who lacked the ambition or the talent for better paid or more highly valued work. It remains to be considered what kind of ministry and witness these men provided at the grass-roots level.

Most of them probably possessed rudimentary moral and intellectual qualifications. The screening process we considered in the last chapter, while not exacting, was sufficient to exclude men of open scandal or obvious illiteracy, and it was not the candidates for the parish ministry that had the resourcefulness or the influence to escape undergoing this process. So a parish priest had probably undergone it before being ordained and, if he was a parson or vicar rather than a curate, had undergone it again before being admitted to his benefice.

Once established in a parish, the priest had to live up to the modest standards imposed by the visitation process. Generally, he would not be turned in unless he did something to shock or annoy his usually tolerant parishioners. Even if the authorities did find him out in an offense, they were more apt, at least the first time or so, to put him to penance and leave him in his post than to remove him. We may suppose that this process did something to limit the number of incorrigibly scandalous priests in the parishes but not that of men who fell into serious vices from time to time or men who were habitually subject to less serious ones.

Specifically, it appears that a parish priest could with relative impunity—and probably without seriously imparing his position in his parish community—frequent the local alehouse with his parishioners, drink, gamble, play games with them, make merry with them, and even on occasion brawl with them, unless he was significantly more rowdy or more violent than his neighbors. Similarly, he might hunt, fish, and even poach as his neighbors did, despite the canons on the point. Finally, he might fall into occasional sexual irregularities, or he might maintain a stable if unhallowed relation with some woman and even raise a family, although he could not make a prolonged practice of open promiscuity.

As to the actual work of the ministry, it would seem that a priest, to keep out of trouble, would have to carry the Sacrament to the sick, bury the dead, keep up the prescribed liturgical observances, show some reverence toward the church and churchyard, and, if he was charged with the repair of the chancel, make some effort to meet his obligation in that regard. Men who failed in any of these respects seem to have been a fairly frequent exception rather than the rule. In addition to these obligations, the parish priest, if he himself did not preach (and he probably did not) was probably expected to provide a preacher from time to time. Manning says that a goal of three or four sermons a year was set in the thirteenth century but that by the mid-fourteenth weekly sermons were aimed at.[65] Even in the later period, however, I should suppose that a parish priest could have kept out of trouble with the authorities by providing no more than two or three sermons a year.

Turning from these minimum standards enforced by the authorities to the higher standards lived up to by the more conscientious clergy in the parishes, we find in the literature a model parish priest, who cannot have been wholly hypothetical. Chaucer's portrait of the model parson shows some evidence of being drawn from life, and Myrc and the other authors of instructions for parish priests cannot have been writing entirely without an audience.[66]

It must be supposed, then, that there were a certain number of parish priests who were reasonably competent and faithful in instructing their flocks in the rudiments of the Christian religion, both in the confessional and in the pulpit; who shared the troubles of those who were in trouble; who valued good relations with their parishioners enough to be circumspect if not forbearing in collecting their lawful revenues; and who were abstemious or indeed puritanical in their personal lives. Some indeed evidently came to know their individual parishioners well enough to give effective guidance to each one with his own particular problems; the interference with this close relationship was a regular basis of complaint against the hearing of confessions by the friars.

The friars, whatever may have been their impact on a parish with a conscientious priest in charge, must have been of some help in making up for the deficiencies of the more perfunctory parish priests. Also, those parishes in the hands of a hired substitute for a nonresident seem to have enjoyed on occasion at least the sublime and literate presence of their rector. Thompson gives examples of such men seeking a country holiday or a prudent absence from a sticky quarrel by a period of personal ministration to their parishioners.[67] Such men no doubt contributed a certain amount of learning and polish to the rustic Christianity of the villages.

The actual impact of this pastoral organization on the practice of Christianity by the people is most difficult to gauge.[68] The essential message of Christianity was presented to the laity through vernacular treatises, through rhymed passages to commit to memory, and through pictures on the walls and in the windows of the churches. The normal Christian probably learned the Pater, the Ave, and the Creed somewhere in the course of his education and in most cases probably understood something of the basic economy of salvation and of the sacramental and liturgical life. Whether he responded to all these stimuli with genuine piety or religious emotion, or with an external and superstitious reverence, they were so pervasive that he can hardly have ignored them.

In addition, he probably was aware of an ascetic—sometimes a little dreary and puritanical—manner of living as something he should admire but could hardly hope to achieve. He may have tended to associate the avoidance of fornication with this higher level of Christian morality rather than with the simpler set of observances that could be expected of him. Whether from habit or from conviction, he attended mass regularly and participated in other liturgical or paraliturgical observances. He probably conceived of the efficacy of these observances in ways that a modern sophisticated Catholic would consider less than orthodox.

What final judgment can we offer on the institutional pattern that sup-

ported this level of Christian awareness in the population? My own feeling
is that its great flaw lay in a certain alienation that it produced between the
individual Christian and the witness of the Universal Church. We can see
three kinds of priests in the parishes—those who fell short of the minimum
standards set by the authorities, those who met those standards, and those
who met a higher standard. Each contributed in his own way to the alienation
I have in mind.

First, the priest who fell short of the minimum standards was not sufficiently repudiated. His vices were apt to be treated as examples of human
frailty, to be countered with measures of pastoral correction. It would have
been more to the point to treat such vices as a failure to proclaim the full
witness of the church, and to counter them by a decisive reaffirmation of
that witness.

At the other extreme, the model priest, like the patron saint, must have
seemed more a person to be admired than a person to be emulated. Even
though he was not outrageous in his ascetic practices, as some of the saints
were, one feels that a certain measure of gloom was to be expected of him.
One feels also that he was readier to edify and comfort his brethren and
absolve them when they fell than he was to show them how they could
live in a manner consistent with their profession as Christians without unduly
taxing their spiritual resources.[69]

Finally, the minimum priest—making up the bulk of the parish clergy, we
may suppose—was too well integrated into the social life of his community.
His manners and morals were those prevailing among his people. He mixed
freely into their social life, and often into their economic life as well. Pro-
pitiating the higher powers and calling down their blessing on the main events
of life, death, and agriculture, he performed a useful function in the village,
one which the villagers well understood, and one which the authorities reinforced through their mechanical standards of performance, and their technique of using the parishioners to report on the performance of the priest.
This is a far cry, of course, from the office of the priest as a personal proc-
lamation of the Word of God, a personal witness to the personal commitment Christ demands of His followers. Here was a man unshakably rooted
in the village folkways but not quite firmly planted in the church of God.

Between the priest who set an example that they could not follow, then,
and the priest who performed a service independent of his personal character
or theirs, the villagers cannot have found much of a guide in the slippery
paths of their own lives. Rather, the witness of the church as it was presented to them must have taken the form of a tension between undue severity
in theory and undue leniency in practice.

This tension is comparable to that set up at the other levels of the ecclesiastical structure where Gregorian High-Church ideals clashed with prevailing
economic and social pressures. As in other cases, the authorities tended to

resolve the tension by emphasizing liturgical or ritualistic aspects of their program at the expense of practical or moral aspects. These liturgical aspects, being the ones that clashed least with the prevailing economic and social forces, were the ones the ecclesiastical authorities were best able to implement. At the same time, in the High Church value system they were quite as important as the more practical aspects that had to be let go. Just as the authorities found it more possible, and no less important, to keep a cleric from marrying than to keep him from fornication or to keep him from writing a blood judgment than to keep him from serving in the secular courts, so they found it more possible and no less important to see that he kept up the prescribed observances in the parish than to see that he was a practical and creative spiritual leader.

The alternative, that of hiring better or more practical or more creative or more learned men to serve in the parishes, would have required a drastic alteration of the pay scale to make parish positions competitive with other positions open to the clergy. This alternative would have involved either making more lucrative benefices resident—thus depriving someone else of the services of the incumbent—or finding some other source of revenue for parish priests. The first approach would have involved a severe disruption of existing institutional patterns in which the ecclesiastical authorities themselves were heavily involved and for which they had not failed to find ideological justifications.

The second approach would have involved a recognition that priests could be drawn from one job into another by the prospect of higher pay. Within the ideological framework inherited from the Gregorian reform, no such recognition was possible.[70] A priest, who had chosen Christ for his portion, was supposed to be above these considerations of temporal reward. If he failed to reach the heights of virtue proposed to him, the Gregorian ideology admitted of preaching at him, bearing witness against him, even giving up hope of reforming him. But it was against the whole tradition to come up with the necessary funds to let him have his way.

6. The Papacy

The Roman curia through which the *plenitudo potestatis* of the papacy was exercised tended, like any bureaucratic organization, to follow the line of least resistance. In the peculiar circumstances of the papacy, the line of least resistance meant first of all granting petitions instead of denying them. The petitioner was usually the only person interested in a matter who was actually present in Rome or Avignon.[1] To grant what he asked was to send him away happy and dispose of the case; to refuse him was to risk discontent and further importunity. Financial considerations militated in the same direction. As the system of occasional payments operated, you paid an official not for expending time and effort about your affairs but for exercising his jurisdiction in your behalf. So the curia supported itself by granting requests. No one was any the richer for a day spent investigating requests and turning them down.

Venality and convenience at the lower echelons were reinforced by a sense of noblesse oblige at the top. Whether the pope thought of himself as Peter feeding the sheep or as a medieval prince acting with due munificence, graciousness, not administrative efficiency, was his concern.

Besides obliging the petitioners, the line of least resistance meant disposing of a case with the materials at hand rather than canvassing the far-flung church to find what was necessary to dispose of it right. It was easier to dispose of a case *ex parte* than to find what adverse interests there were and give them a chance to be heard. It was easier to deal with a case in the posture it presented at the moment than to find out what was really involved. It was easier to dispose of a case in hypothetical terms (by a rescript that would be automatically void if the facts were not as recited therein) than to make a responsible determination of the facts. It was easier to solve a problem at the curia than to see that it was properly dealt with by some other agency. It was easier to take care of it with a new exercise of the *plenitudo potestatis* than to untangle its current legal status.

If a matter was disposed of conveniently, it did not matter much whether it was disposed of well or badly. The curial officials were a long way from the field where the consequences of their decisions would be felt. A matter once acted upon, whatever was done with it, could be expected not to come back to the curia for years, if at all. Even if it did come back, it would not be likely to come in such a form as to cast blame on the officials who had dealt with it the first time. Typically, the second presentation of the affair would allege some error or contumacy in the local handling of the first— something for which the local authorities were to blame—or it would present a different version of the facts, the blame attaching to whoever was not telling the truth. Also, it seems that nothing came from the curia that was not at least perfunctorily cleared with the pope himself: he would have had trouble fixing responsibility on anyone else.[2]

If the papacy had been more like other bureaucracies, the tendency to follow the line of least resistance would have been checked by the necessity of accomplishing the work that had to be accomplished. However poor the feedback techniques, a sales department that does not sell, a production department that does not produce, a procurement agency that does not procure will eventually be found out. But the papacy, as we have seen, set its goals in terms of canonical didacticism and Gregorian ideology. It had no clear practical goals against which administrative performance could be measured.

With the papal bureaucracy operating along these lines, the problem for a person with business at the curia was not so much getting it handled favorably as getting it handled at all. Even at best, the numbers and industry of the staff would probably have been insufficient to cope with the volume of business that presented itself. The insufficiency was made worse by the way the staff was organized. There were routines established for handling business, but they were so convoluted and so inefficient that it was not hard to slow them through malice or inertia or to bypass them for lucre.[3] A matter could languish about the curia for any length of time before it came routinely to the attention of someone with the power to dispose of it. Conversely, those who had influence could and would use that influence on behalf of their friends (including sometimes those who became their friends by dint of substantial payments)[4] to get a particular matter dealt with out of the ordinary course. This practice, of course, made the time lag for the unbefriended matter even longer than it would otherwise have been and made suitable friendships (and expensive friendships too) a virtual necessity for anyone with business at the curia.

I. Functions

This combination of benign insouciance, vagueness of purpose, and *plenitudo potestatis* led the papacy into a variety of functions. Generally, it was a matter of drift. Only in one or two cases, and these not very important ones, is there any indication of an actual decision that something could be more effectively done at the papal level.

A. Appointment of Bishops.[5]

From the close of the investiture controversy to, say, the end of the reign of Innocent III (1216), the popes' main concern with episcopal appointments was to substitute election by cathedral chapters, subject to confirmation by the metropolitan, for the amorphous tradition formula of election by the clergy and people of the diocese. The idea was evidently to eliminate the occasions for coercion and improper influence that inhered in a procedure not clearly articulated. A series of enactments, culminating in those of the Fourth Lateran Council (1215), spelled out just how the chapter was to proceed and on what grounds the metropolitan could reject their choice.[6]

Papal intervention in this period was generally limited to supporting and clarifying the electoral process or hearing appeals by those dissatisfied with the outcome. Appeals usually concerned the regularity of the election process or the fitness of the person chosen. They were given added scope by the adoption of the old canonical formula of election by the *major et sanior pars* of the electors; the supporters of a defeated candidate could always claim that they were the *sanior pars*.[7]

Innocent III, if he annulled an election or failed to confirm it, would generally allow the chapter to try again.[8] If he felt that the chapter could not be trusted to make a free and informed decision at home, he would send for representatives to hold the election in Rome. If political considerations required for example, after the lifting of the interdict in King John's reign), he might even order the chapter whom to elect or not to elect. But only if all else failed would he bypass the election process and provide directly to the see.

But Innocent's successors were less abstemious. In the course of a little over a century, they used their powers of provision first to supplement, then to displace, the election process. This development began early in the second quarter of the thirteenth century with the use of papal provisions to deal more summarily with certain problems arising from disputed elections. In the first place, where the candidate was suitable or suitably befriended but some canonical irregularity had vitiated the election process (and the law on the subject was so complicated that it took considerable care to avoid such an irregularity), the pope, instead of sending the matter back to the chapter as Innocent III would have done, simply provided the candidate.[9]

Second, where an election was disputed, the popes began, instead of deciding the dispute, to provide to the see against the claims of both disputants. The latter might be given substantial benefices on resigning their claims to the disputed see—partly to console them for their loss, partly to recoup their expenses in the curia.[10]

Finally, where the chapter's candidate was rejected, the popes began providing another man rather than giving the chapter another chance.[11]

In addition to those cases where provision was used after the electoral process had gone wrong, there had always been a certain number of cases where a bishopric happened to fall within some special class of benefice reserved for papal provision. Some of these classes had been so reserved from relatively early times. The most familiar example is that of benefices falling vacant by the death or resignation of the incumbent at the curia; it seems likely that England owed her great seventh-century metropolitan Theodore of Tarsus to some forerunner of this custom. The custom was given express recognition in Clement IV's decretal *Licet Ecclesiarum* of 1265, and the class of reserved benefices was gradually added to over the next half-century or so.[12]

Meanwhile, beginning no later than the first few years of the fourteenth century, the popes began supplementing these general reservations with specific reservations—reserving such and such a benefice for papal provision and forbidding the regular collators or electors to meddle with it. Such a reservation might be made when the benefice fell vacant (though it could then be circumvented by the ordinary collator or electors acting before they received official notice)[13] or the benefice could be reserved in advance, before it fell vacant. During the reign of Edward II (1307–27), dealt with in Smith's monograph, English bishoprics came increasingly under such special reservations.

By the middle of the fourteenth century, the method of filling episcopal offices by reservation and by provision had completely displaced that of capitular election.[14] It appears that John Trillek, elected to Hereford in 1344, was the last pre-Reformation English bishop to hold his see through election by his chapter. A few men were elected in the old way during the troubles occasioned by the Council of Constance, when it was not clear who, if anyone, was pope, but Martin V, on coming into undisputed possession of the apostolic see, seems to have treated these men as improperly elected.

The main reason for the displacement of the system of capitular elections seems to have been its inability to operate without continual papal intervention. Guillemain, in a well thought-out study of the situation in the crucial period of Benedict XII (1334–42), describes the functioning of the elective system thus:

. . . vices of the system of elections to bishoprics and abbacies had provoked continual and increasing resort to superior authority—under the circumstances, to the papacy. The confirmation of bishops who were not immediately dependent on the Holy See had belonged to the metropolitans ever since the Council of Nicea, and the confirmation of non-exempt abbots had belonged to their ordinaries; the ill will of metropolitans and ordinaries inclined those interested to seek pontifical approval for their elections—one would be consecrated by the one who granted the confirmation. The workings of the electoral system gave rise to incessant conflict: the minority of the electors and their candidate could claim that the majority was not the sounder part [*sanior pars*] of the electing body. If neither side gave way, there would be an appeal to the Holy See. Such appeals were heard ever since the twelfth century, and made compulsory by a decretal of Alexander IV (1254–61). Thus, the pope came to be in control of the electoral process, whether he confirmed one of the candidates or whether he simply provided someone else. The first popes of the fourteenth century, then, had done nothing more than to systematize an existing practice—a course to which they were the more inclined in that the number of their interventions served to increase the financial resources of a monarchy at its height, as well as checking the interference of laymen who, not content with being the patrons of minor benefices were striving to place their men in elective benefices as well.[15]

While the papacy may not have been responsible for the actual undermining of the electoral system, it was responsible for the conditions that made the electoral system inoperable. Both the readiness of the popes to overturn a decision of the confirming authority and their willingness to tolerate a utopian legal formulation like *sanior pars* made it impossible to treat any election case as finally decided until the pope had decided it. If this was to be the attitude toward the local authorities, it is small wonder that the papacy came to regard their involvement in the process as superfluous.

Whoever appointed bishops, it was important to the English kings to have a major say in who they were to be. Up to the time of Edward II, the kings generally did better in bringing pressure on the cathedral chapters than in getting the popes to provide royal nominees. It was probably for this reason that Edward at the beginning of his reign made some effort to firm up the English chapters against papal provisions. His firmness, however, proved unequal to that of John XXII, and he found himself gradually compelled to get bishoprics for people by sending to Rome and asking for them. In this, he was no more successful than he was in the other aspects of being a king.

His successors did better. By the mid-fourteenth century, when the system of papal provisions to bishoprics was fully consolidated, it became somewhat unusual for the pope to turn down the nominee of a king. Later kings, even when armed with acts of Parliament on the subject, showed little interest in going back to trying their luck with the chapters.[16]

The popes, for their part, had no particular reason for resisting the royal demands. Aside from a desire to slip in a few of their own bureaucrats among those to be rewarded with English bishoprics, they had no articulated policy that would make the king's servants unsuitable occupants of episcopal office. Their main concern seems to have been with the principles involved. As Smith puts it, John XXII, through his policies, "established securely the principle that a bishop, even though a royal servant, owed his post not to the king but to the pope."[17]

B. General Administration.

In handling the church's multiplex affairs, the papacy reserved only a few functions to itself, more or less excluding the operation of local ecclesiastical authority. In other areas, papal intervention served sometimes to supervise the work of local authorities, more often to duplicate or to frustrate it. On the whole, the supervision fell off, and the duplication increased with the passing of time so that in the end it was competition rather than policy that determined most of the functions the papacy performed.

1. Reserved Functions—Of the reserved functions, the most important were political and diplomatic. In the thirteenth century, the popes intervened on several occasions to head off confrontations between English prelates and kings—after Innocent III's Pyrrhic victory over King John, they were generally anxious to avoid such confrontations.[18] Up to the time of the *Clericis Laicos* fiasco, they tried to do the negotiating over clerical subsidies to the crown. In the fourteenth and early fifteenth centuries, they negotiated directly with the kings over papal provisions. Sometimes they went over the heads of the English hierarchy; sometimes they tried to involve the hierarchy in their resistance to royal demands.

The withdrawal of *Clericis Laicos* preserved the system of subsidies voted by Convocation and thus gave the local hierarchy a certain scope for bargaining with the crown without much possibility of papal interference. Sometimes they made good use of their bargaining power, but they did not offer after Clarendon to give formal assent to a negotiated local settlement not sanctioned by the general canon law. Rather, they picked their way between the conflicting demands of the two systems, departing from the one on grounds of conscience or from the other on grounds of *force majeure* as the occasion served.[19]

In addition to attempting diplomatic solutions to church-state problems, the popes sometimes found English affairs within the ambit of their secular diplomacy.[20] Thus, they attempted from time to time to effectuate settlements between England and France and to assume the power to judge England's claim to suzerainty over Scotland. They also attempted to intervene in various domestic difficulties in the reigns of John and Henry III.

On the administrative and judicial level, the popes took pretty well exclusive control over disputes involving the internal organization of the hierarchy—suffragan versus metropolitan, bishop versus chapter, ordinary versus ordinary, abbey versus cell.[21] They also explicitly reserved the power to canonize saints and authenticate their relics—a power that had a good deal more importance in those days than it has now, considering how much money changed hands at the shrines of saints and how the apotheosis of a dead factionalist could be fitted into the political maneuvering of the time.

A less felicitous subject for reservation to the papacy was that of dispensations. Since the logic of the canonists required that only the author of a law could dispense from it, it was usually considered by the end of the twelfth century that only the pope could dispense from the general laws of the church. This power, limited in scope, was sometimes delegated to a local ordinary as a favor, but generally an illegitimate who wanted to take orders, a layman who wished to marry a distant cousin or a priest who wanted to hold two benefices, would have to get permission from Rome.

The principle behind this rule, though scarcely of compelling logic, seems innocuous enough. The vice was in the subjects to which the principle applied. If a dispensing power has any appropriate place in a legal system, it is to deal with cases that cannot be adequately foreseen in framing the general law. If a class of cases develops in which a dispensation is habitually granted, it should be built into the general law as an exception and administered accordingly. It was the failure to do this that swelled the volume of petitions to Rome with cases where dispensations were issued almost as a matter of course. It was probably the didacticism of the canonical system that prevented amendment of the general law as soon as the need for wholesale dispensations became apparent. Of course, once the dispensation machinery was in full operation, financial considerations made it almost impossible to stop.

2. *Supervision*—Much of the popes' supervision over the local hierarchy was carried out through a voluminous correspondence, flexible in form and content, containing advice on the general law and exhortations, commands, or even permissions to carry it out. Sometimes permission was given to go beyond the general law in the exercise of pastoral authority or to enforce the general law in the face of indults to particular persons to be exempt from its operation. Sometimes these letters recite that they are granted as a special favor to the person to whom they are addressed; sometimes they recite that they are issued in response to a report the pope has heard concerning conditions in the recipient's diocese.[22] Though many of these documents found their way into the Corpus Juris Canonici, they can be called legal only with the qualifications suggested in our chapter on canon law. They were intended, as I suggested there, to support and guide the personal pastorate by the corporate witness of the church.

In the way of more formal supervision of the local authorities, the popes

admitted formal appellate procedures from local decisions, deputed papal mandatories to do over what local authorities had neglected or done amiss, and, in
rare cases, imposed sanctions on local authorities who had done wrong.[23]

The greatest part of this supervisory activity—including almost all the really
creative uses of the available techniques—belongs to the reign of Innocent III
(1198-1216). I suspect that Innocent was more concerned than his successors
with the creative supervision of local authorities because he appreciated better
than his successors did the importance of local authorities in a viable organization.[24]

3. Duplication—I know of no case in which relief could be had or a favor
obtained from local ecclesiastical authorities that the papacy could not or
would not grant. Nor do I find a case in which the pope refused to entertain
a suit or petition on the ground it could be better handled by local authorities.
Occasionally, the pope would refer a matter to the proper ordinary of the
place from which it arose[25]—whose status in handling it, whether as ordinary
or as judge delegate, would then be ambiguous—but in general a matter that
was not to be dealt with at the curia would be referred to some prelate who
had no claim to deal with it as ordinary.

So the typical petitioner or litigant had a choice to make whether to take
his business to the local ecclesiastical authorities or to the Holy See. The Roman
alternative had several important advantages. In the case of a lawsuit, if you expected the loser to appeal to Rome, you might save a step and perhaps gain a
tactical advantage by anticipating him.[26] The standards of appellate review
were such that a decision of the local court would not make much difference
one way or the other once the case got to Rome.

In the case of a petition, you would probably find the papacy more willing,
as it was obviously more able, to grant it.[27] If you went to the local ordinary
and he turned you down, you could still go to Rome with a good chance of
getting what you wanted. If, on the other hand, the ordinary did what you
asked, you might find you had overlooked some limitation on his power; there
were many such limits and it was hard to keep track of them all. Then you would
have to go to Rome for a confirmation of what he had done. Worse, a rival
might get to Rome before you and have your grant from the ordinary set aside.
Either way, it was better to go direct to the final authority than to take chances
on the powers of the local ordinary. The clergy were not slow to learn the lesson.
They resorted regularly to Rome not only in cases where the ordinary was competent to act but in cases where he had already acted, and acted favorably at
that.

When it came to formal judicial business, the courts established by the local
hierarchy, as we have seen, competed with the papacy by giving better service.
It was obviously cheaper to go to a local court than to petition the Holy See to
appoint delegates. Also, the local court was staffed by full-time judges, full-

time clerical staffs, and full-time advocates; it could probably elicit a better-informed decision faster than the pope's ad hoc delegates could. It appears that as the thirteenth century progressed these advantages began to make themselves felt so that the incidence of papal proceedings in ordinary cases fell off dramatically.

The situation as it developed, then, was that you were more apt to get a favorable decision *ex parte* or a decision immune to collateral attack if you took your business to Rome; whereas you were more apt to get a quick or an informed decision if you stayed home. In later years, it seems to have been chiefly men who wanted a firm title to their benefices, men who wanted permanent dispositions of property and similar rights, and persons disputing with more powerful adversaries who resorted to the Apostolic See.[28]

Toward the end of the fourteenth century, the papacy adopted a policy that gave new scope to its judicial business—a policy of providing informers to benefices made available through the information brought forth. We have already seen that this course was adopted with benefices automatically vacant and reserved to the pope under the 1317 antipluralism canon *Execrabilis*. The same thing was done in cases involving disciplinary deprivation rather than automatic voidance—a papal mandate would issue instructing the mandatories to examine whether the vicar of such-and-such had committed fornication and, if he had, to deprive him and collate so-and-so (presumably an informer) to the vicarage.[29] These informer proceedings have not received much attention from the historians, but they seem to have become quite common by the end of the fourteenth century. They no doubt gave the popes a wide range of cases of clerical discipline to deal with, as well as cases of pluralism and other irregularities in the tenure of benefices.

Cases dealt with in this way no doubt were free from the defect of excessive leniency that plagued local disciplinary proceedings. Since the offender was not present as a repentant sinner, he did not elicit the pastoral solicitude that might give him another chance in his benefice. On the other hand, as a means of filling a benefice with a worthy incumbent, the *ex parte* informer proceeding does not seem much better than the local disciplinary proceeding. Indeed, the informer may have had disqualifications of his own. He, however, would be present at the mercy seat and could have a dispensation included in the package.[30] He could then go home to remove the mote from his brother's eye with the beam safely removed from his own.

C. Distribution of the Clerical Bureaucracy.

A function that was in some ways rather successfully centralized—although there is no indication that it was intentionally so[31]—was the distribution of the bureaucratic personnel that the clergy supplied to every level of church and state. Papal control over this function was established through the control of the most important dispensations required by the clerical bureaucrat and through the control of a substantial portion of the benefices available for his support.

Of the dispensations, the most important were those permitting pluralism and nonresidence.[32] The power to dispense for pluralism had been reserved to the pope at least since the 1215 canon *De Multa Providentia* discussed in Chapter 3. A series of enactments in the course of the fourteenth century made it increasingly difficult to hold plural benefices without the necessary dispensation.

The power to grant licenses for nonresidence, on the other hand, was shared by the local ordinary. There were advantages, however, in seeking such a license from the pope rather than the ordinary. The pope could give a blanket dispensation, applicable to any or all benefices, whereas the ordinary could give it only for specific ones. The ordinary's power under the constitution *Quum ex eo* was limited both as to the purposes and as to the time for which a man could stay away, whereas the pope could and sometimes did give broader licenses.[33] Especially, he gave express permission to be nonresident while in the service of one or more specified magnates. There seems to have been a current interpretation of *Quum ex eo* which included such service under the head of study, but the pope could put the permission in black and white. Also, the pope could, and often did, allow a nonresident to let his benefice to farm, thus making it easier for him to realize on his income.[34] Sometimes, also, the pope would allow a nonresident canon of a cathedral to participate in revenues that the cathedral statutes reserved expressly for residents. Finally, from time to time a particularly zealous bishop would come along who made an issue of limiting nonresidence. With the papacy, this was seldom a problem.

Papal provisions, either to a specified benefice or to the next benefice of specified character that became available, must have become by the middle of the fourteenth century the most usual way of filling the benefices in the gift of ecclesiastics. These provisions were subject to the same pitfalls—and the same safeguards, such as they were—as other papal rescripts, but even so they seem to have presented the aspiring cleric with a better chance of getting a benefice than he would have had among the local prelates. This situation had a kind of snowball effect. The more papal provisions there were, the fewer benefices were available for filling by the local prelates and the more clerics had to go to Rome or Avignon for their preferment.[35]

The system of papal provisions was further supported by the system of dispensations. A man who had to go to the papal court to get his dispensation for pluralism might just as well get his additional benefice at the same time. Thus, of the ninety-three provisions issued in 1348, one of the peak years, thirty-eight were to pluralists or to men who would become pluralists by virtue of the provision in question, whereas only sixteen dispensations for pluralism were issued independly of provisions. The tie-in between provision and pluralism not only tended to attract would-be pluralists to the system of provisions; it also served to reconcile the local prelates to the system, since they needed pluralities for their higher subordinates and sometimes for themselves.

After the mid-fourteenth century, the impact of papal provisions in England was restricted by the authority of the secular government, with increasing severity as the century progressed.[36] But the vigorous suppression of provisions seems to have been left to the Lancastrians. In 1398, after almost a half century of statutory prohibitions, there were still fifty provisions, while in 1448 there were only seven. I doubt whether the volume ever fell much below this figure. The fifteenth-century kings had permission from Parliament to license the acceptance of papal provisions, and they in fact used their power to do so. We may suppose that the papacy in this period ceased to be a Mecca for unbefriended clerics—we see the universities complaining in Archbishop Chichele's time—but it continued to be a place to which kings, prelates, and great men could resort for preferment for their high subordinates, or where a royal servant on his master's business might pick up something special to take home. Also, even when the grants of provisions fell off, the pluralism dispensations went on unabated.[37]

This great complex of ecclesiastical patronage was drawn on not only by clerics desirous of advancement but also by the universities, for which it was a kind of placement service and by all manner of great men who wished to compensate their bureaucratic staffs beyond their personal resources. For the prelates, resort to the papacy was, at least while the system of provisions was at its height, an absolute necessity. The benefices in the gift of the local ecclesiastical authorities were so burdened with the holders of provisions that the local authorities had not sufficient preferment at their own disposal to keep up their own staffs.[38] Indeed, in 1348 an abbot found it necessary to seek a papal provision in order to put his own nephew into a benefice in the gift of his own house.

The lay magnates did not have the same problem of having their own sources of patronage pulled from under them by papal provisions, for the system was generally scrupulously limited to benefices in ecclesiastical patronage. On the other hand, the benefices in their gift were apt to be less numerous and less lucrative than would be the case with kings or bishops. Their patronage would presumably be limited to the parish churches on their landed estates and would not include the cathedral prebends that were the staple support of the higher clergy. It is not surprising, therefore, to find some of the most important dukes and earls among the best customers of the papal patronage machinery.

The kings, through their landed estates, through their royal free chapels, through wardships and escheats, and through the custody of bishoprics and abbeys during vacancy, were able to dispose of a good deal of preferment in their own right. Using their own courts and agencies, they maintained their rights in this patronage with great vigor, and I should say with 50 to 75 percent success, against competing claims of papal provisions (the conflict came in cases where the king had temporary custody of ecclesiastical temporalities, among which he included advowsons). Also, the king made good a claim that his servants could not be required to take orders or to reside, so he had no need for papal dispensations on these matters. But the kings did have to seek papal dispensations for pluralities. And, at least in the fourteenth century, they found it appropriate to supplement their own patronage, extensive as it was, with a substantial number of papal provisions.

In general, then, it seems that only the king was in a position to maintain an adequate bureaucratic establishment without resorting to the pope and that even the king found it desirable to do so rather often.[40] Thus, the papacy had the major say in the general allocation of the clergy to bureaucratic work. This great power was not used, however, in any way inconsistent with the general policies of the prelates and magnates in the field, nor, realistically, could it have been. Rather, it served the common advantage of the higher clergy and of the whole body of those having occasion to employ their services.

Perhaps the most important contribution of the papacy was the maintenance of certain standards of fairness in the distribution of bureaucrats. By controlling pluralism, the popes insured that there were enough benefices to go around.[41] By bestowing the largest favors on the persons most influentially supported, they insured that the largest and best-paid staffs would serve the most important people and, consequently, the ones with the most for them to do. The other great contribution of the papacy was in finding places for unbefriended clerics, especially university graduates, and thereby maintaining a central means of access to the bureaucracy for men qualified to fill places in it. These were men who could probably have made their own way if they had come to the attention of suitable patrons; but the papacy afforded a more efficient way of placing them than leaving them to cast about for someone who could use them.

Despite the polemics of the time, it is not true that the popes filled great numbers of English benefices with Italians.[42] They did skim off a few places for their own staffs but not at all in any outrageous proportion. Generally those who enjoyed benefices through papal provisions and dispensations were the same kind of men who would have had them anyway. In fact, much of the opposition to papal intervention in these matters was really opposition to the system of clerical bureaucracy as such—opposition either from people who wanted a resident clergy or from people who wanted their incompetent relatives put into benefices instead of competent civil servants. Such opposition, to the extent it was well taken, was utopian.[43]

We hear from time to time of the desirability of a permanent civil service with a cohesiveness and esprit de corps that cuts across departmental lines and with enough security in their means of livelihood to have a certain independence in their actions. Out of a number of disparate purposes—to befriend the unbefriended, to secure the good will of the influential, to distribute the benefices of the church so that there were enough to go around —the popes created something that looks very much like this kind of permanent civil service. It is ironic that one of the few solid achievements of the medieval papacy should be in a matter so remote from the central concerns of the Christian religion.

D. Favors.

In addition to the dispensations that kept the bureaucracy going, the papacy had a number of other privileges available that served the Christian community and its members in one way or another. It was papal dispensations for instance that permitted the involved matrimonial structure through which the hereditary aristocracy maintained itself.[44] From the Fourth Lateran Council of 1215 down to the 1918 Code, persons with one set of great-great-great-grandparents in common needed a dispensation to marry, as did in-laws, cosponsors at a baptism, and persons one of whom had committed fornication with a relative of the other. Such dispensations were sought by landed families (or by their feudal overlords on their behalf) in order to settle family strife, to provide for daughters who had not sufficient dowries to attract husbands outside the circle of their relations, or to rectify unions that had been contracted knowingly or unknowingly within the prohibited degrees. It is perhaps because of the dilatoriness of the curial processes or perhaps because of the difficulty of keeping track of the impediments that the bulk of these matrimonial dispensations seem to be granted after the event. In such cases, the offending parties were sometimes required to remain apart for a time and sometimes also to atone for their misdeed by some pious work if their means served. In one case, it was provided that neither of the parties was to be allowed to remarry on the death of the other.

The papacy's dispensing power in the matrimonial field was not entirely at the service of family arrangements. On occasion, we find the papacy smoothing the path of true love by dispensing from the publication of banns on account of anticipated family objections to the match.

The papacy also served the cause of the upper-class English family by giving permission to enter religious houses or place others in them, either as inmates or as boarders, and by protecting the right to dispose of property by will. It was no doubt in many cases these families also that benefitted from papal permission to place underage clerics in benefices (although Italian curial families were major beneficiaries here) and from papal absolution from irregularities incurred by young clerics sowing wild oats at Oxford or Cambridge. In the fifteenth century, they also appeared alongside the bureaucrats as beneficiaries of pluralities and provisions.[45]

Finally, the papacy contributed to the spiritual life of the upper-class family by providing opportunities to receive the ministrations of the church outside the normal channels. For those who could afford to build collegiate churches or chantries, there were papal confirmations of licenses granted by others as well as special privileges that only the pope could bestow.[46] For those who could not afford such foundations or as further spiritual enrichment for those who could, there was the household chaplain. From the papacy, the pious layman could have permission to have a chaplain—or even several of them—follow him around, say mass on a portable altar, say mass before daybreak, provide him with the consolations of religion during times of interdict, and bestow on him a plenary indulgence at the hour of his death. A layman might also receive from the papacy permission to entertain religious at his table and feed them dishes forbidden by their rule. If his health required, he could also be dispensed himself from keeping the fasts required of other laymen.[47]

Turning from the layman to the priest, we find that he had important favors available from the papacy in addition to better and more numerous benefices and the permission not to reside on them. He received absolution from his irregularities. He could receive the portable altar and mass-before-daybreak privileges without waiting for a patron to seek them for him.[48] He could receive permission to collect alms for some such good cause as the repair of his church and to reward the contributors with indulgences.[49] Finally, he could be appointed to the nebulous but probably significant privileges of an honorary papal notary or chaplain—the equivalent of the modern monsignor.[50]

Some religious used this status of papal chaplain to escape their rules. Others received more specific indults permitting them to have their own rooms, eat meat, absent themselves from choir, or even take secular benefices for themselves.[51] Whole houses also sometimes resorted to the papacy for relaxation of their observance in one way or another, as by eating meat, or by covering their heads in choir.[52] In most cases, however, comparable relaxations were evidently undertaken without any special permission.

Religious houses, collegiate churches, and even bishops found it desirable, as we have seen, to resort to the papacy to make new appropriations of parish churches or confirm those already made. Often, too, the papacy was ready to give them more than the general law permitted in the way of exploiting their ecclesiastical endowments or avoiding the corresponding burdens. Permissions were thus given to refrain from putting in vicarages, to suppress vicarages already put in, and to let churches to farm to clerics or laymen for a fixed annual return.[53]

Various foundations and individual prelates sometimes also received from the papacy a grant of complete or partial exemption from the jurisdiction of ordinaries or other superiors. No great jurisdictional enclave was set up after the early part of the twelfth century, but collegiate foundations were still honored with exemptions from ordinary jurisdiction within their own precincts.[54] Also, individual prelates were occasionally given for their own lifetimes exemptions that would evidently not have been available on a permanent basis. John de Pontissara, bishop of Winchester, for instance, was given in 1297 an exemption from the metropolitan jurisdiction of Canterbury to last as long as he held the see.[55] At the other end of the social scale, a certain prior in 1448, reciting that he was afraid bad monks would have his abbot remove him, obtained an indult that he could not be removed from his position without a great and reasonable cause.[56] Two contemporary priories fared better still: they got papal bulls erecting them into independent abbeys.[57]

The papacy was also willing sometimes to serve the general religious observances of the community at the expense of the vested interests of parish incumbents. We have examples of indults to hold mass in a hospital even before the parish mass (albeit saving the parish priest a share of the offerings) to expand the ministrations offered at an outlying chapel and even to make a chapel into an independent parish church.[58]

Another class of men who made frequent resort to the Holy See were ordinaries and religious superiors, who found it possible in this way to counter the favors procured by their subordinates.[59] Thus we find bishops procuring papal indults to be free of papal provisions or to make their clergy reside despite papal permission not to. We find one religious superior procuring an annulment of the exemptions his surordinate houses have obtained from his jurisdiction and another procuring the cancellation of a papal permission to one of his subjects to take a secular benefice. We find a bishop receiving permission to visit the exempt religious houses in his diocese and even a bishop receiving an indult against being excommunicated by papal delegates. None of these indults was foolproof, however; as we have seen, a petitioner might get a dispensation or a provision reciting that it was to take effect notwithstanding indults to the contrary.

Considering the whole range of papal favors, I cannot see any general policy behind them beyond a simple desire of the papacy to be accommodating. The papacy did most of its business *ex parte*, and if a man put in an appearance with a plausible request, there was no one to suggest that the pope should be mean and say no rather than be nice and say yes. To be sure, as the volume of requests elicited by the favorable responses increased, there grew up a considerable bureaucratic establishment with a vested interest in keeping the volume up, and there came to be a substantial financial interest in doing so as well.

It was no doubt these financial and bureaucratic considerations that militated against a more effective handling of the situation presented by these requests. Clearly enough, what should have been done is that favors routinely given out should have been built into the general law for administration at the local level, while nonroutine favors should have been limited to cases in which considerations were present that could not be dealt with under a general law. Not only was such a course not attempted; as far as I know, it was never suggested. Rather, those who opposed the prevailing pattern of papal favors rested their opposition on the desirability of adhering to the existing law.[60]

II. Institutional Resources

Perhaps the most effective resource of the papacy was the canon law. Everything the popes uttered, whether as a general rule or as a rescript in a particular case, was eligible for compilation by the canonists and for use as a rule of decision in subsequent cases. Except for a few documents of earlier provenance, the parts of the Corpus Juris Canonici after the mid-twelfth century *Decretum* of Gratian are all papal whether enacted in general councils or handed down as decretals or rescripts. The consequences at the administrative level of introducing something into the canon law were, as we have seen, not altogether predictable. But, such as they were, they were firmly under papal control.

Another resource of sorts was the curial staff that processed the vast flow of *ex parte* petitions. Unfortunately it was the only organized staff the papacy had. With all its detailed intervention in local affairs, the papacy had virtually no field organization at all. For matters of major concern in the field, the pope sent a legate or a nuncio. Such a man might have very broad powers, but their duration was limited. The legate Gualo, who figures in the register of Hugh of Wells in the early thirteenth century, seems to have concerned himself with the day-to-day operation of the English church in much the same way the pope himself did with his correspondence. The cardinals Otto and Ottobuono in 1237 and 1268 respectively held synods. But thereafter the papal envoys seem to have limited themselves to political and financial—to the exclusion of pastoral or administrative—concerns and to have worn out very quickly such welcome as they received.[61] The papal collectors who supplemented the financial work of the legates may have been more or

less permanently resident to the number of three or four. But the bulk of
the pope's work in England was done through ad hoc delegations to different
English prelates, and through what might be called documents launched at a
venture.

A. Ad Hoc Delegations.

The usual way for a papal proceeding—either an original proceeding or an
appeal from a decision of the ordinary—to begin was for an interested party
to procure a papal rescript directing certain named persons to hear the matter and act on it. While some rescripts purported to be *motu proprio*, I doubt
if the pope had sufficient sources of information to act at the administrative
level without someone's putting him up to it. So we may take it as the general rule that the papal machinery was set in motion by an interested party.
It appears that until the middle of the thirteenth century anyone with the
resources to conduct a serious litigation would resort to this process rather
than to the local tribunals; later, the papal proceedings came to be fairly
rare. The form of the proceeding, however, did not change; this perhaps accounts in part for the increasing rarity of its use.

Almost any local prelate could be chosen to hear one of these cases. Unless he had a good excuse, he would have to serve, although he could subdelegate all or part of his duties. The pope could, of course, choose anyone
he pleased for such a delegation, but, in the absence of some obvious source
of bias like kinship, he would be apt to choose the persons requested by the
petitioner.

When the rescript of appointment was delivered to the delegates, the opposite party would be cited in. He would have various objections to make
to the form of the rescript, the persons of the judges, or whatever. From an
adverse decision in any of these matters, either side could prosecute an inter-
locutory appeal. Under some circumstances, a party could appeal by way of
provocacio in anticipation of an adverse decision on a matter yet to be heard.
From a judgment against him on the merits he could appeal once again. Some,
but not all, of these grounds of appeal could be avoided if the original rescript
was fortified with the clause *appellatione remota*, but the remaining grounds,
including disqualification in the judges and manifest unfairness in the decision, were sufficient to give color to appeals in most cases. Also, even where
there could be no appeal, there could be a *supplicatio* or administrative recourse, which constituted a new proceeding to set aside the results of the
old. This process could also be undertaken where the original matter was not
strictly judicial—an election, for instance.

An appeal in the strict sense stayed the proceedings appealed from, although a *supplicatio* did not. But even an appeal did not work a stay if the

judges appealed from regarded it as frivolous. Thus, the losing party coming back with his rescript for appellate proceedings might find himself excommunicated by the original judges and the excommunication alleged as a basis for not hearing the new proceeding.

In any event, the appellate proceeding would be committed to a new set of judges-delegate, this time one chosen by the party who sought the rescript initiating the appeal. They would be presented with objections to the form of the appeal as well as with the merits of the case to decide over again. The formal objections could then be made the subject of further appeals, resulting in further delegations, and so *ad infinitum*. There being no full-time courts in the system, the appellate tribunal had neither more prestige nor more power nor more official standing than the tribunal appealed from, so there was nothing to keep a disgruntled litigant from seeking another chance as often as he wished.

Nor could a litigant escape this tangle by going physically to Rome. There evidently came to be a class of prelates resident at the curia who habitually heard cases, but these too worked only on ad hoc delegations.[64] Before this group arose, and perhaps afterwards to some extent, we may suppose that a case would be given to any prelate who happened to be passing through.[65] Furthermore, the litigant who succeeded before a judge at Rome would have to come back to England with his judgment. Once there, he might find his adversary objecting to its authenticity or its validity or both and procuring a set of judges delegate in England to hear his objections.

Indeed, the death of one or all of the parties was not always sufficient to bring one of these litigations to a close. Where the case involved the right to a benefice, the pope might favor a benefice seeker with a "surrogation" to the rights of one of the litigants when those rights were vacated by death or resignation. The beneficiary of the surrogation would then proceed with the case.[66]

Brentano, describing the epic litigation in the late thirteenth century between the archbishop of York and the chapter of Durham over the former's metropolitan rights, shows the system of papal judges-delegate in all its complexity and futility. I can add a few examples of less prominent suits, culled from my sampling of the papal registers.

1. A case between the prioress and convent of Campsey (plaintiff) and the prior and convent of Butley (defendant), last rescript in 1229.[67] The case involved the right to certain tithes and other revenues and was begun by the plaintiff before certain judges-delegate, who decided in favor of defendant. Plaintiff then appealed and had a second set of delegates appointed to hear the appeal. Meanwhile, the first set of delegates had excommunicated the plaintiff—presumably, they had regarded the appeal as frivolous, had therefore refused to stay their proceedings

and so had excommunicated plaintiff for not obeying their sentence. Defendant then urged before the second set of delegates that plaintiff could not be heard because she was excommunicated. The second set of delegates refused to admit this exception to their jurisdiction, so defendant appealed from their refusal and had a third set of delegates appointed to hear this appeal. Before this third set of delegates, plaintiff argued that as her excommunication by the first set was in disregard of her appeal to the second set, she had a right to urge them to set it aside. The third set of delegates, however, refused to accept plaintiff's argument, and she appealed from their decision. The 1229 rescript I came upon was on this appeal, appointing a fourth set of delegates to hear it.

2. A case running from before 1245 until 1253 between the rector of Paxton and the warden of a certain chantry in Lincoln cathedral.[68] It seems that the bishop had imposed a twenty-mark pension on the rectory in favor of the chantry and had fortified his charter with a sentence of excommunication. The rector, however, rashly braving (as the warden's rescript puts it) the excommunication, got a rescript to certain delegates in common form for the recovery of improperly alienated revenues. He planned to use this rescript to have the warden silenced in respect to his claim to the pension. The warden, however, "running to the Apostolic See for succor," recited that the rector had enough to live on and asked that he be compelled to pay the pension. This petition was evidently a *supplicatio* rather than an appeal. It simply ignored the earlier delegation. A set of delegates was duly appointed to hear it, although not the ones the warden asked for. The case was settled in 1253 before a third set of delegates.

3. A case, 1398–1400, between a rector and a neighboring priory concerning tithes.[69] The rector, fearing the local influence of the priory, got a papal delegation to the dean of Lincoln to hear the case. The dean subdelegated to one R.E., who decided in the rector's favor. The priory, following the proper procedure in a case of subdelegation, appealed to the dean, who appointed another subdelegate to hear the appeal. Once again the decision was in the rector's favor. The priory then appealed directly to Rome. Although, according to the rescript, the case had not properly devolved upon the apostolic see—presumably because the priory should have tried the dean again—the pope appointed a certain Polish bishop to hear the case, evidently in Rome. But the prior's proctor proved contumacious, and the bishop treated the appeal as abandoned, giving sentence for the rector. Two years later a papal mandate issued to summon the prior and convent, who had been excommunicated for disregarding this sentence. Presumably the end of the case had not yet arrived.

This account of the papal judge-delegate procedure may indicate not only why the development of efficient full-time local ecclesiastical courts led to a decrease in resort to the papacy, but also why the Court of Arches with its tuitorial appeal was able to exclude papal jurisdiction over particular matters. The tuitorial appeal, it will be recalled, was ostensibly to preserve the status quo while the papal authorities were disposing of the case. But in the not unlikely event that the papal authorities never did succeed in disposing of it, the position taken by the Arches *pendente lite* might well turn out to be decisive.[70]

In any event, a drastic falling-off in the incidence of papal proceedings occurred at just about the same time as the effective development of the Arches Court in the late thirteenth century. To illustrate how drastic this falling-off was, consider the case of Osney Abbey, which was involved in fifty-eight cases before judges-delegate, all but eight of which came between 1170 and 1240 and none of which came after 1279.[71]

B. Documents Launched at a Venture.

The pope, just as he had no full-time courts, had no full-time machinery for the execution of his processes. Just as he might call on someone to decide a particular case for him, so he might call on someone to execute a particular mandate, either with or without an investigation of the relevant facts.[72] Or he might leave it with the beneficiary of the document to use it in whatever way best served his purposes. Even if the document was addressed to an executor, the executor had no special status beyond what the document itself bestowed on him. Papal process, in short, was not fed into a subsisting administrative machinery, as royal process was, but was launched into the local scene to make its way in the world as best it could.

But the way of a lone and unbefriended document in the medieval world was beset with pitfalls against which high provenance alone was not sufficient to preserve it. Let us consider what might befall such a document after it left the papal curia in the hands of its gratified beneficiary or his proctor and before it achieved its intended purpose.

1. Indult of Exemption[73] —In the first place, someone might be armed with a papal indult protecting him against rescripts of that kind. We have seen, for instance, that certain bishops were given indults against papal provisions, and others were given indults to make beneficed clergy reside despite papal licenses of nonresidence. A careful seeker of papal favors might protect himself against such indults as this by having his own rescript armed with a *non obstante* clause reciting that it was to take effect despite anyone's indult to the contrary. On the other hand, the holder of the indult might have protected himself by having his indult exempt him in terms even from rescripts containing such a clause or by having it recite that it could not be overriden by any document that did not make special mention of it.

2. General Annulment[74] —Every so often, the popes expressed remorse over one class or another of their favors and annulled them wholesale, or at least such of them as had not yet taken effect. Licenses for nonresidence were thus dealt with in the early fourteenth century, as we have seen; appropriations were dealt with in the same way in the late fourteenth to mid-fifteenth. And in 1448, the head of the Hospitallers in England had all papal exemptions of houses of his order from his jurisdiction annulled—evidently, without having to offer a reason.

3. Prior Rescript—Since, as we have seen, the pope did most of his business *ex parte* and was concerned to be accommodating to those who sought his help, it is not surprising that his rescripts were sometimes inconsistent with each other. The most frequent case was that of two men being provided to the same benefice,[75] but there are other examples, such as curing at the request of A, a canonical defect that formed the basis of a lawsuit committed to judges-delegate at the request of B.[76]

The canonical rule intended to bring some order out of the situation presented by inconsistent rescripts was that the first of two such rescripts would prevail unless it was mentioned in the second or unless the holder of the first had been too dilatory about putting it into execution.[77] Thus, the holder of the second rescript might well find himself barred.

The consequent importance of being first at the curia is well illustrated by two cases in the papal registers involving benefices whose incumbents were deprived by the local ordinary for prolonged failure to take orders.[78] In each case, the ordinary, after depriving the incumbent, collated his own man to the benefice, and in each case he did so improperly because the ipso facto vacancy created by the failure to take orders had lasted so long that the right to fill the benefice had devolved upon the pope. In one case, the deprived incumbent was the one who got his petition to the curia. The pope ordered him absolved and collated to the benefice by papal authority, the bishop's man being dispossessed. In the other case, it was the bishop's man who was the first to be heard. He alleged that he was afraid his collation by the bishop would not stand up against the deprived incumbent's appeal to the apostolic see. The pope ordered him collated again, this time by papal authority.

4. Questions of Authenticity[79] —Since there was no one whose specific business it was to give effect to papal documents, there was also no one whose specific business it was to pass on their authenticity. Thus, it was possible at any stage in a canonical proceeding for one party to call into question the authenticity of the documents on which his adversary's case depended. It was even possible for a religious house to have its whole cartulary called up for wholesale reexamination at the behest of the ordinary whose jurisdiction was restricted by the documents in question. Also, any official called upon to give effect to a document might question it on his own initiative.

When a document was called into question, the pope evidently preferred to have it examined in his own chancery, although he often committed the examination to judges-delegate. In either case, the examination was directed not so much to the physical appearance of the document as to its use of good Latin and the style in use at the curia. The presence of a record in the registers was not always decisive in favor of a document, and presumably the absence of such a record would not have been decisive against it. In some cases the pope sent his judges-delegate examples of authentic letters to compare with the suspected forgeries. In other cases he determined by examining a copy of the suspected document that it was not genuine.

Actually, the availability of these objections to authenticity seems not to have troubled the holders of genuine documents as much as one might have supposed. In a fairly substantial number of forgery cases I have come across, there is only one clear example of proceedings being delayed on the alleged forgery of a document that was ultimately upheld as genuine.[80] Perhaps those who dealt with documents developed a sixth sense for matters of that kind. Be that as it may, the claim of forgery was always available, at least in theory, to stop the execution of a papal document.

One case in the Decretals suggests a further problem: that the document might, unbeknownst to the holder, be in fact forged.[81] The case involves almost a classic confidence trick. The victim, a cleric who had come to Rome for letters to initiate a lawsuit on behalf of his church, fell in with a countryman resident in Rome, who promised to get him the letters, then prepared the letters himself, and no doubt pocketed the expenses. It was not until the unsuspecting victim got back home with the letters and tried to use them that he found out they were forged. He had to go back to Rome to get his benefices returned to him, to say nothing of starting his lawsuit again.

5. *Questions of Fact*—Where a rescript called on the executor to decide whether the facts were as alleged, he had, of course, to make appropriate inquiries before executing the rescript.[82] But whether or not this procedure was called for, it was always possible to object to a rescript on the ground that it was rendered invalid by false or misleading statements leading to its issue. This ground of invalidity, like forgery, could evidently be raised at any stage of a proceeding based on the rescript. Even after the rescript was fully executed, rights based on it could evidently still be impugned on this ground. Neither the passage of time (not even the forty year prescription if bad faith could be alleged) nor a favorable determination by someone who investigated the facts before putting the rescript into effect could prevent a person adversely affected by a rescript from alleging that the facts were mis-

stated and attempting to have it disregarded or set aside. When the papacy began rewarding informers with the benefices of those informed on, it was no longer necessary even to be adversely affected.

It must not be supposed that the kind of misstatement required to invalidate a rescript was necessarily a serious one, or even one that the petitioner could have avoided making if he had been more careful. Consider this case:

> A became archdeacon of a certain archdeaconry on the death of B and held it until his death. Thereupon C. alleging that the archdeaconry was vacant by the death of A, procured a papal provision to it. Later it turned out that A was an intruder and held the archdeaconry without a sufficient canonical title. C's provision is void, since the archdeaconry is vacant by the death of B rather than by the death of A as stated in the petition.[83]

*6. Revocation or Annulment—*In addition to directly opposing the execution of a rescript, a person who wished to avoid its effects could, by setting forth the grounds of his objection, procure a new rescript annulling the old.[84] His ground for doing this might be some kind of misstatement or other basis of invalidity, or it might be simply an allegation that the prior rescript was being misused. Thus, a religious superior procured an annulment of an indult permitting one of his subjects to take a secular benefice by alleging that the subject was now contemning his, the superior's, authority. An annulling rescript of this kind might require an investigation (by delegates chosen by the objector, presumably) of the grounds of invalidity or abuse alleged against the rescript to be annulled; on the other hand, it might not. In the latter event, the holder of the earlier rescript could presumably claim the new one was invalid as based on misstatements of fact (as, for instance, if the subject were to claim he was not contemning the authority of his superior). Thus, in either event a lawsuit would ensue.

*7. Problems of Scope—*Papal rescripts were subject to various limitations of scope that were not immediately apparent on the face of the documents.[85] Such limitations might prevent an unwary petitioner from having the benefit he expected. For instance, a dispensation authorizing a cleric to take a benefice although he was illegitimate would not, without an additional clause, permit him to resign the benefice he first took under that dispensation and accept another in its stead. Similarly, a dispensation from the matrimonial impediment of consanguinity in, say, the fourth degree (four generations away from the common ancestor) would not permit a marriage if the parties were related by multiple consanguinity in that degree (more than one set of common ancestors or more than one line of descent from a single set). Similarly again, a dispensation from the effects of illegitimacy would not be effective in the case of a man born of an adulterous, incestuous, or sacriligious (one of the parties in orders or under solemn vows) relationship.

All these rules, and many others like them, depended on the elaboration by the papal chancery of its common forms, a process intended no doubt to impose some measure of routinization on the distribution of papal favors. It is possible that rescripts in common form were more easily come by than others. Certainly, the chancery, in order to get its business done, would have had to put its documents in common forms whenever the situation admitted of doing so. On the other hand, it is quite clear that papal largesse was not to be limited by either the scruples or the convenience of the chancery. Thus, the common forms must often have assumed the character of a trap for the unwary petitioner. A more knowledgeable seeker of favors would take care to have included in his rescript a series of clauses negating the usual restrictions on the common forms. Here is a description from the Calendar of Papal Registers of a suitably broad rescript:

> Extension of dispensation as the son of a priest . . .—to be ordained priest and hold a benefice even with cure—so that he may hold three other mutually compatible benefices with and without cure, even if canonries and prebends in cathedral, and principle elective dignities with cure, *personatus* or offices in collegiate churches, and to exchange them as often as he pleases for mutually compatible benefices. His illegitimacy need not be mentioned in future graces.[86]

In addition to built-in restrictions, a number of common forms seem to have had built-in procedures. The failure of the executors to follow the procedures would then void action taken under the rescript.[87]

8. Resistance—The local hierarchy were not immune to the temptation to use direct and illicit means from time to time against the enforcement of the mandates of their distant superior.[88] A bishop might slip a man into a benefice before a papal provisor had a chance to make good his claim. Or a local ecclesiastical court might continue to conduct a litigation after a papal judge delegate issued an inhibition. A powerful prelate might even use force to prevent the execution of a papal judgment.

The problem, of course, was again the lack of a distinctively papal enforcement machinery. The papal mandatories were required to carry out their duties with such forces as they had at their disposal by reason of whatever position they held on the local scene. In the prestige-conscious and somewhat unruly society in which they operated, it might take more than a papal mandate to make a powerful and important prelate subservient to the orders of a less powerful or less important one.

Occasionally, a papal mandatory was ordered to call on the secular arm for assistance if necessary.[89] But it is not at all clear that the secular arm would have responded. The two standard writs available in the royal chancery for the enforcement of ecclesiastical processes were the writ *de excommunicato capiendo,* by which a person excommunicated by the ecclesiastical courts could be imprisoned until he submitted, and the writ *de vi laica amovenda*, by which direct physical violence could be eliminated from among the moves and countermoves in an ecclesiastical controversy.[90] The first of these would not work against a corporate malefactor, who could not be imprisoned, or against a great prelate, whom the king would not allow to be excommunicated. The second would not work against inaction, locked doors, or passive resistance. Also, the term *vi laica* leads me to question whether the writ was available when the force was exerted by clergy or monks.

Finally, it does not seem that either writ was available to the executor of a papal mandate as such. Fitzherbert is fairly clear that the writ *de excommunicato capiendo* lay only on a signification from a bishop or some exempt ordinary (such as the chancellor of Oxford) who had been given this privilege by special grant of the king. It did not lie on the signification of an ordinary not a bishop or of the pope himself. On the other hand, the fact that a bishop was acting on a papal mandate would presumably not of itself have kept the writ from issuing on his signification. As for the writ *de vi laica amovenda*, Fitzherbert is less clear, but it appears to have lain only for a bishop as to a church in his diocese or for the incumbent or would-be incumbent himself. Also, it probably lay only for the possession of a church or benefice as such and not for other rights.

In fact, the secular arm was raised more often to harass the holder of a papal rescript than to protect him. A series of statutes beginning in 1350, preceded by other parliamentary documents of less than statutory force, imposed serious penalties on those bringing papal provisions into England or taking cases to Rome that belonged in the king's courts.[91] Also, the king claimed a general right, independent of any statute, to punish summarily for contempt anyone who brought in papal process prejudicial to his crown and dignity. A person who ran afoul of any of these rules could be stopped at one of the ports and his papal documents confiscated. His temporal goods could be declared forfeit, and his bishop could be ordered to sequester his ecclesiastical livings. He could be imprisoned at the pleasure of the king and not let out until he had paid a heavy fine.[92] Even so, the holder of the papal document might, by patience, persistence, and judicious use of the potentialities of papal litigation for wearing out an adversary, eventually prevail over the best the royal processes could do. But it might be a costly victory and one long coming. A 1398 case, over a parish church in Ireland, marks the success of a papal provisor after an imprisonment of six years and more.[93]

To be sure, all these dire consequences could befall the holder of papal process only in special cases. Except for the laws against provisions and two others of minor importance,[94] there was no law forbidding the use of papal process as such; indeed, in many cases it was expressly recognized by the secular law.[95] Even in the case of provisions, it does not appear that the penalties laid down in the statutes were customarily invoked until the matter had been litigated in a common advowson proceeding and a decision rendered against the provisor.[96] On the other hand, the cases in which the king might regard his crown and dignity as impugned by a papal document were various and not always predictable.[97] Many persons thought it prudent to get royal permission before seeking or using papal favors.[98]

The only real solution to the problems presented by this paper deluge, as well as to the evils of the judge-delegate system, would have been for the pope either to maintain a permanent court in England, with its own full-time apparitors and judges, or else to refer all matters to the local ordinary of metropolitan, who could act on them through his own full-time personnel and agencies. That neither of these measures was arrived at seems to bespeak once more the persistent failure of the popes to understand what they were about. The great machinery of the curia simply ground out the appropriate response to each situation presented as if it were a unique favor and as if the *plenitudo potestatis* existed in fact as well as in law.

III. Finance

Aside from the imposition of papal bureaucrats on local benefices, a practice probably more prevalent in the thirteenth century than later, the operations of the papacy were financed by a variety of measures that, I suspect, brought the papacy more blame than money. The particulars have been dealt with in detail, especially by Lunt, so that we need do no more than summarize here. The different forms of papal revenue arising from England were basically the following.

A. Peter's Pence.

Peter's Pence was an annual sum paid the papacy since Anglo-Saxon times. It seems originally to have derived from a royal grant, but by the early thirteenth century it was collectible in the ecclesiastical courts and was regarded as a spiritual matter. The work of collecting it had devolved on the English hierarchy by the end of the twelfth century. Its measure was supposed to be a penny on every hearth in the country, but its exact incidence is not clear. At any rate, the local ecclesiastical authorities forwarded a fixed amount of 299 marks to Rome, keeping the excess for themselves. Lunt's statistics indicate that the excess was about three-fifths of the total amount collected.[99] Early in the fourteenth century, the popes attempted to get the whole amount for themselves but were strenuously rebuffed. For two-fifths of the collection, the pope evidently took the entirety of the blame.

B. Royal Tribute.

Part of the agreement between King John and Innocent III whereby England was made a feudal dependency of the Holy See was the payment of an annual tribute of one thousand marks. The payment was made from time to time, with decreasing regularity, through the reign of Edward II. The Edwards tended to use it to buy favors from the popes, and the popes from time to time authorized the kings to tax the clergy in order to collect it. Edward III made one payment in 1333 in return for unspecified favors. That payment was the last. In 1366 Parliament officially repudiated the tribute on the ground that John had no power to grant it.

C. Subsidies and Direct Taxes.

The popes attempted to make use of the machinery of Convocation to collect from the English clergy subsidies comparable to those collected by the kings. The English clergy tried some negotiating for concessions in exchange for such grants, but there is not much indication that they were successful. By the same token, the popes had a good deal less success than the kings did in eliciting funds in this way. They had less to offer and far less pressure to apply.

The popes had some success up to the mid-fourteenth century in imposing comparable income taxes on the English clergy by papal fiat without going through Convocation at all. The kings made gestures of opposition to such taxes but were eventually reconciled to them by being given substantial cuts of the proceeds. Sometimes also the kings took over collecting machinery for taxes of this kind—on what pretext does not appear. Here again, we seem to have a situation in which the pope got all of the blame for a tax and only a fraction of the money.

The Crusades, both while the last of them were going on and long after, furnished a pretext for the collection of papal revenues and for royal participation in them. The king would receive a tax on ecclesiastical revenues to finance his going on Crusade, would collect the money, and would not go. The same pattern seems to have been followed by prelates and lay magnates alike all over Europe.

For a variety of reasons, none of these exactions by royal and papal cooperation was successfully negotiated after 1336. Subsidies by Convocation, however, continued to be asked for and sometimes granted.[100]

D. First Fruits.

The pope by the close of the Middle Ages was collecting the first year's revenues of every incumbency of every benefice filled by his provision. This papal right seems to have evolved out of the right of the local ordinary to collect revenues during vacancy. Its assumption by the papacy was protested in the early fourteenth century along with other papal revenues, but it was firmly established by the time of the Reformation,[101] although its volume fell with the enforcement of the Statute of Provisors.

E. Fund Drives and Indulgences.

The Holy See, like all pious objects, came in for a share in the gifts and legacies of the faithful. Often, special drives were conducted to increase the flow of these benefactions, and the contributors were rewarded by substantial indulgences. Often through the early years of the fourteenth century it was some crusading project or other that furnished the occasion for such a drive, although the resulting funds were not always used for such purposes. The popes evidently felt no moral scruples against diverting special funds to the general purposes of the Apostolic See.[102]

As the Crusades began to drop out of the picture, the system of fund raising began to look more and more like the organized sale of indulgences that figured so prominently in the German Reformation. That the system did not produce such scandal in England as it did in Germany was, I suspect, due to the restrained enthusiasm with which the English hierarchy responded to the indulgences.

F. Procurations of Legates.

When the pope sent legates into England, he imposed a tax on ecclesiastical livings to pay their expenses. Like all procurations, they amounted to considerably more than the expenses they were meant to pay, so the legates all took considerable sums home to Rome with them. These procurations did not arouse very great opposition among the English, or, more accurately, they did not figure prominently among the grounds of opposition to papal legates in England. The English attempted on one occasion, however, to draw the line at paying procurations for papal legates in France. It was supposed, with good reason no doubt, that such legates were engaged in negotiations prejudicial to English interests in that country. Even so, the legates were ultimately allowed to collect.

G. Fees and Occasional Payments.

Needless to say, the dispensations, favors, rescripts, provisions and the like that we have been considering were not to be had without substantial payments both in the form of official fees and in the form of gratuities to the various persons involved in the transactions. These sums could be substantial. There is a case of a canon borrowing £100 to meet unspecified expenses in the curia, one of a priest offering a 200-mark donation to be surrogated to a right in a prebend, and cases of newly confirmed bishops being permitted to borrow from 100 to 1000 marks to pay expenses in the curia.[103]

The popes also found occasion to impose special taxes on the recipients of their favors and on other special groups. Such taxes included one ounce of gold annually from every exempt religious house, a special payment by bishops making *ad limina* visits to Rome, the "spoils" of clerics dying intestate, and, on one occasion, a special tax of one-fourth to one-half of the annual income of every benefice held by an Italian in England. Some indication of the impact of these various taxes may be had from the abbey of Bury, which, as I have already mentioned, set about methodically to extinguish or compound for all jurisdictional or financial rights exercised over it. In about 1398, it compounded for all papal dues with an annual payment of twenty marks. This should be compared with the £40 with which it compounded for certain royal dues at the same time.[104]

I have said that the popes got more blame from these arrangements than they did money. I might add that they got more money than they gave service. While the point would be hard to document, it appears that England, being among the more prosperous as well as the more docile of the outlying countries, paid more than its share of the papal revenues. To be sure, it probably also accounted for more than its share of the business of the curia. But given the capacity of the curia to handle business without actually disposing of it, we may suppose that the English got very little for their money in the way of business effectively disposed of. This state of affairs was recognized in contemporary literature from the thirteenth century on. It had a great deal to do with the popular acceptance of the Reformation.

IV. Conclusion

To sum up in a word what was wrong with the papal administration as we have been considering it, it was overextended. A romantic conception of pastoral solicitude, a utopian conception of the *plenitudo potestatis*, and an epic bureaucratic inertia had combined to embark the papacy on administrative functions it lacked (a) the power, (b) the money, and (c) the information to carry out effectively.

The lack of sufficient power and money meant that administrative functions had continually to be exercised in such a way as to maintain the shaky political and economic position of the organization. This pattern was foreshadowed in the settlement of the investiture controversy at the beginning of the twelfth century. The lay authorities, as we have seen, were persuaded to abandon in principle the claim to invest prelates with their spiritual jurisdiction. On the other hand, they were very little disturbed in their actual power to determine what prelates were to be invested. The popes, in other words, held onto this particular portion of their power by exercising it in such a way as to eliminate political opposition to it.

This was not simply a pattern for the working out of major confrontations of lay and ecclesiastical power; it was a pattern of day-to-day administration. Over and over again, disputes over episcopal elections were settled by a papal provision of the person elected; objections to the system of provisions were anticipated by making provisions at the request of potential objectors.[105] It sometimes seems as if the whole machinery of papal government operated only to preserve the theoretical recognition of the *plenitudo potestatis* by conforming its exercise to the faits accomplis of potential opponents.

Even where the papacy took an independent line, it did so with a good deal of diffidence, in isolated instances, and took care to placate those damaged by a liberal bestowal of other favors. For instance, when the pope decided not to confirm the election of Edward I's chancellor to the See of Ely, he consoled him with an archdeaconry and a dispensation to hold £1000 worth of benefices in plurality.[106]

The papal reluctance to bring on confrontations of secular and ecclesiastical power was shown also, as we have seen, in the supervision of local prelates. The failure to back Winchelsea on nonresidence of royal bureaucrats and the failure to back Pecham on opposition to royal writs of prohibition are prime examples. If there were no comparable examples in a later period, it was because the local prelates had already learned their lesson.

There was a certain wisdom in this kind of temporizing, as the papacy had no very effective weapon to use in an actual power confrontation. The interdict with which Innocent III enforced the claim of Stephen Langton to the see of Canterbury against King John was successful but only at the cost of depriving the English people of the ministrations of their religion for some seven years. No one, least of all the popes, seemed interested in trying the same thing again; nor did anyone seem interested in a repetition of the Becket affair.

Even where there was no potential power conflict, the general force of papal administration seems to have been exerted for its own sake rather than for the accomplishment of results in the real world. Where, for instance, a man holds a benefice to which he is not entitled and the pope confers it on an accuser who is not entitled to hold it either, dispensing the accuser from whatever disability he is under, it seems that nothing has been accomplished except a vindication of the power of the papacy to dispense from canonical disabilities.

The financial activities of the papacy were carried out in a similar way and produced a similar diversion of administrative functions from administrative objects. We have seen how the acquiescence of English kings in papal taxation was frequently purchased with large shares of the resulting funds. But economic necessity brought on more serious administrative diversions than these. For one thing, the papal legates, whose task seems originally to have been to provide the local hierarchy with a spiritual and disciplinary shot in the arm, came to be wholly involved in the collection of money. After Ottobuono's mission in 1268, I cannot find that a papal legate concerned himself with anything else.

Also, the system of favors and dispensations came to be almost entirely subordinated to the financial necessities of the papacy. Here, of course, economic overextension went hand in hand with the unrealistic administrative practices that prevailed in the granting of favors. Every favor granted meant more petitions for such favors with a concomitant increase in the number of persons required to process the petitions and hence an increased need for the money to be had from granting such petitions. Either a drastic letup on the granting of favors or a substantial modification of the general law to cover a situation previously dealt with by dispensations would have brought on an economic strangulation of the curia.

Unfortunately, the papacy had no practical political and economic goals sufficient to produce any meaningful results from the sacrifices it made in the interest of political and economic expediency. Even when the creative impulses of the Gregorian reform and the new canon law were still powerful —before they petered out in the course of the thirteenth century—the ideological formulations were not effectively translated into criteria for the use of available power for attainable ends. Still more was this the case in the later Middle Ages. Aside from a few futile gestures toward the Holy Land and a more successful campaign against the heretics in Bohemia, the political and economic resources the papacy was able to muster seem to have been used for no higher end than their own preservation.

Here, the High Church vision of a liturgically structured society coincided with the inherent tendency of bureaucratic establishments to perpetuate themselves. While the bureaucratic instincts of the curia were satisfied with a maintenance of functions and prerogatives, the loftier aspirations of High

Churchmanship were satisfied with a symbolic recognition of the place of the Apostolic See among the institutions of Christendom—with the vision of the People of God united under its divinely appointed head.[107]

It would be unhistorical to deny the power of this symbolic pattern over the hearts and minds of medieval Christians, and it would be ungenerous to deny that it was in some way deserving of that power. But in the end the gulf between symbol and reality, the remoteness of the symbolic leadership from an effective presentation of the work and witness of the church in the real world, must have been felt in the very foundation of the symbolism.[108]

The unreality imposed on papal administration by lack of real political and economic goals beyond symbolic and institutional survival must have been greatly enhanced by the expedients imposed from lack of information. The curia, with its rescripts issued on *ex parte* recitals and void if the recitals were false, with its legislation of automatic effect, with its canons that everyone wrote glosses on and no one carried out, must have lived in a hypothetical world, a world of models—may we not say a dream world?

> Once out of nature, I shall never take
> My bodily form from any natural thing,
> But such a form as Grecian goldsmiths make
> Of hammered gold and gold enameling
> To keep a drowsy emperor awake
> Or set upon a golden bough to sing
> To lords and ladies of Byzantium
> Of what is past, and passing, and to come.[109]

The final judgment on the medieval High Churchmen as ecclesiastical administrators must be not that they were corrupt—all men are corrupt—but that they were dreamers. Poets and visionaries to the last, they built a system that gave no quarter to human frailty. In the long run, human frailty gave no quarter to their system.

Citations

Acts of Parliament and post-medieval cases are cited in accordance with the forms generally used in legal writing. The Corpus Juris Canonici is cited in accordance with the method used by the compilers of the source notes to the 1918 Code of Canon Law. A complete description can be found in Bouscaren and Ellis, *Canon Law* (Milwaukee, 1948), 11–13. Examples of the most usual forms are:

c. 7, D. I = First part of the *Decretum* of Gratian, canon 7 of Distinction I.

c. 116, C. I, q. 1 = Second part of the *Decretum*, canon 116 of question 1 of Cause I.

c. 13, X, I, 2 = canon 13 of title 2 of Book I of the Decretals of Gregory IX. The abbreviation "X" attaches to the Decretals because they were originally conceived of as "extravagantes," i.e., supplementary to Gratian.

c. 5, I, 3, in VI° = canon 5 of title 3 of Book I in the *Liber Sextus* of Boniface VIII.

Conciliar material I have cited by canon, place, and date (c. 6, Clermont 1130), followed by the source from which I took the material. Most of my research was done too early to take advantage of the definitive compilation of the English material from 1205 to 1313 by Powicke and Cheney, but I have added citations to their work and made a number of corrections in the light of it.

The other abbreviated citations (omitting a few for which there is a full reference in the half dozen or so footnotes immediately preceding) are:

Acta Langton	*Acta Stephani Langton, Cantuariensis archiepiscopi, A.D. 1207–1228* (C.Y.S. 1, ed. K. Major, 1950).
Ames	*Year Books of Richard II*, ed. Deiser, Plucknett, and Thornley (Ames Foundation, Cambridge, Mass., 1914–).
A.S.C.	= *Anglo-Saxon Chronicle* (cited by year).
Attenborough	F. L. Attenborough, ed., *The Laws of the Earliest English Kings* (1922).

Barlow	F. Barlow, *The English Church, 1000–1066* (London, 1963).
Barraclough	G. Barraclough, *Papal Provisions* (Oxford, 1935).
Bede, H.E.	Bede, *Ecclesiastical History of England* (cited by book and chapter).
Bodl.	= Material in the Bodleian Library, cited by call numbers.
Boehmer	H. Boehmer, "Das Eigenkirchentum in England" in *Festgabe für Felix Liebermann* (Halle, 1921), 301–53.
Bloch	M. Bloch, *Feudal Society* (Chicago, 1961).
Bowker	M. Bowker, *The Secular Clergy in the Diocese of Lincoln, 1495–1520* (Cambridge, 1968).
Brentano	R. Brentano, *York Metropolitan Jurisdiction and Papal Judges Delegate, 1279–96* (Berkeley, 1959).
Burn	R. Burn, *Ecclesiastical Law* (4 vols., London, 1775).
c.	= canon or, in statutory material, chapter.
Cal. Close Rolls	*Calendar of the Close Rolls* (H.M.S.O.).
Cal. Papal Reg.	*Calendar of Entries in the Papal Registers relating to Great Britain and Ireland* (H.M.S.O.)
Cal. Papal Reg. Pet.	*Calendar of Entries in the Papal Registers relating to Great Britain and Ireland—Petitions.* (H.M.S.O.).
Cal. Pat. Rolls	*Calendar of the Patent Rolls* (H.M.S.O.).
Cheney	C. R. Cheney, *From Becket to Langton* (Manchester, 1956).
Cheney, *Episcopal Visitation*	C. R. Cheney, *Episcopal Visitation of Monasteries in the Thirteenth Century* (Manchester, 1931).
Churchill	I. S. Churchill, *Canterbury Administration* (2 vols., London, 1933).
C.J.C.	Codex Juris Canonici, the Code of Canon Law in force in the Roman Catholic Church since 1918.
Co. Inst.	Coke's *Institutes*, cited by number and original pagination.
Cox	J. C. Cox, *The Sanctuaries and Sanctuary Seekers of Medieval England* (London, 1911).
C.Y.S.	= Canterbury and York Society
D.D.C.	*Dictionnaire de Droit Canonique* (7 vols., Paris, 1935–62).
Deanesly	M. Deanesly, *The Pre-Conquest Church in England* (New York, 1961).
Dispensation Report	*Dispensation in Practice and Theory, Being the Report*

	of a Commission appointed by the Archbishop of Canterbury in 1935 (London, 1944).
D.N.B.	*Dictionary of National Biography*, cited by person.
Doc.	*Councils and Ecclesiastical Documents relating to Great Britain and Ireland*, ed. Haddan and Stubbs (3 vols., Oxford, 1869-78, vol. iii).
Drew	C. Drew, *Early Parochial Organization in England: The Origins of the Office of Churchwarden* (St. Anthony's Hall Pub. no. 7, York, 1954).
Dugdale	W. Dugdale, *Monasticon Anglicanum*, ed. Caley, Ellis, and Bandinel (6 vols. in 8, London, 1817-30).
Edwards	K. Edwards, *English Secular Cathedrals in the Middle Ages* (Manchester, 1949).
E.H.R.	*English Historical Review.*
Ferry	W. A. Ferry, *Stole Fees* (Washington, 1930).
F.G.A.	A. Fitzherbert, *La Graunde Abridgement*, various sixteenth-century editions, cited by title and number.
Fitzh. N.B.	A. Fitzherbert, *New Nature Brevium* (9th ed., Dublin, 1793).
Fliche	A. Fliche, *La Réforme grégorienne* (3 vols., London, 1924-37).
Gabel	L. C. Gabel, *Benefit of Clergy in England in the Later Middle Ages* (Northampton, Mass., 1928).
Ganter	B. J. Ganter, *Clerical Attire* (Washington, 1955).
Gee and Hardy	H. Gee and W. J. Hardy, *Documents Illustrative of English Church History* (1896).
Gibbs and Lang	M. Gibbs and J. Lang, *Bishops and Reform, 1215-1272* (Oxford, 1934).
Godfrey	C. J. Godfrey, *The Church in Anglo-Saxon England* (Cambridge, 1930).
Hartridge	R. A. R. Hartridge, *A History of Vicarages in the Middle Ages* (Cambridge, 1930).
Heath	P. Heath, *The English Parish Clergy on the Eve of the Reformation* (London, 1969).
"Hereford Visitations"	See *E.H.R.*, xliv, 279, 444; xlv, 92, 444.
Hill, "Public Penance"	R. M. T. Hill, "Some Problems of a Thirteenth-Century Bishop," *History* (N.S.) (1951), 213.
Holdsworth	W. S. Holdsworth, *A History of English Law* (various editions).
Johnson	J. Johnson, ed., *A Collection of the Laws and Canons*

of the Church of England, (new ed., London 1850-51, vol. 2).

Kemp

E. W. Kemp, *Counsel and Consent* (London, 1961).

"Kent Visitations"

"Some Early Visitation Rolls Preserved at Canterbury," *Archaeologia Cantiana*, xxxii (1917), 143; xxxiii (1918), 71, ed. Woodruff.

Knowles, M.O.

M. D. Knowles, *The Monastic Order in England* (Cambridge, 1940).

Knowles, R.O.

M. D. Knowles, *Religious Orders in England* (3 vols., Cambridge 1950-59).

Lea

H. C. Lea, *An Historical Sketch of Sacerdotal Celibacy in the Christian Church* (Philadelphia, 1867).

Lincoln Visitations

Visitations in the Diocese of Lincoln, 1517-31, (3 vols., L.R.S. xxxiii, xxxv, xxxvii, 1940-47).

L.R.S.

= Lincoln Record Society.

Lunt

W. E. Lunt, *Financial Relations of the Papacy with England to 1327* and *Financial . . . , 1327-1534* (cited as i and ii) (Cambridge, Mass., 1939 and 1962).

Manning

B. L. Manning, *The People's Faith in the Time of Wyclif* (Cambridge, 1919).

Mansi

G. D. Mansi, et al., ed., *Sacrorum Concilium Nova et Amplissima Collectio* (facsimile edition, Paris, 1903).

McGrath

J. McGrath, *The Privilege of the Canon* (Washington, 1946).

Moorman

J. R. H. Moorman, *Church Life in England in the Thirteenth Century* (Cambridge, 1946).

M.P.L.

J. P. Migne, ed., *Patrologia Latina . . .* , (Paris, 1844-68).

Pantin

W. A. Pantin, *The English Church in the Fourteenth Century* (Cambridge, 1955).

Pollock and
   Maitland

F. Pollock and F. W. Maitland, *The History of English Law before the Time of Edward I* (2d ed. 2 vols., Cambridge, 1898).

Powicke and Cheney

F. M. Powicke and C. R. Cheney, *Councils and Synods* (ii, 2 parts, Oxford, 1964).

Reg. Antiq.

The Registrum Antiquissimum of the Cathedral Church of Lincoln, ed. Foster and Major (8 vols., L.R.S. xxvii-xxix, xxxii, xxiv, xli-xlii, xlvi, li, 1931-58).

Reg. Bekynton

The Register of Thomas Bekynton, Bishop of Bath and Wells, 1443-1465, ed. Lyte and Dawes (2 parts, Somerset Record Soc. xlix, 1, 1934-35).

Reg. Chichele	The Register of Henry Chichele, Archbishop of Canterbury, 1414–1443, ed. Jacob (4 vols., C.Y.S. xlv, xlii, xlvi, xlvii, 1937–47).
Reg. Grandisson	Register of J. Grandisson, ed. Hingeston and Randolph (3 vols. 1894–99).
Reg. Gravesend	Rotuli Ricardi Gravesend, ed. Davis and others (C.Y.S. xxxi, 1925).
Reg. Greenfield	The Register of William Greenfield, Lord Archbishop of York, 1306–1315, ed. Brown and Thompson (5 parts, Surtees Soc. cxlv, cxlix, cli–cliii, 1931–40).
Reg. Lacy	The Register of Edmund Lacy, Bishop of Exeter, 1420–1455, ed. Dunstan (3 vols. + Devon and Cornwall Record Soc., new ser. vii, x, xiii, etc., 1963–).
Reg. Langley	The Register of Thomas Langley, Bishop of Durham, 1406–1437, ed. Storey (Surtees Soc. clxiv, 1956).
Reg. Parker	Registrum Matthei Parker, diocesis Cantuariensis, A.D. 1559–1575, ed. Thompson and Frere (3 vols., C.Y.S. xxxv, xxxvi, xxxix, 1928–33).
Reg. Pontissara	Registrum Johannis de Pontissara, episcopi Wyntonensis, A.D. MCCLXXXI-MCCCIV, ed. Deedes (2 vols., C.Y.S. xix, xxx, 1915–24).
Reg. Sudbury, London	Registrum Simonis de Sudbiria, diocesis Londoniensis, A.D. 1362–1375, ed. Fowler (2 vols., C.Y.S. xxxiv, xxxviii, 1927–38).
Reg. Sutton	The Rolls and Register of Bishop Oliver Sutton, 1280–1299, ed. Hill (4 vols., L.R.S. xxxix, xlii, xliii, xlviii, 1948–54).
Reg. Swinfield	Registrum Ricardi de Swinfield, episcopi Herefordensis, A.D. MCCLXXXIII-MCCCXVII, ed. Capes (C.Y.S. vi, 1909).
Reg. T. Cantilupe	Registrum Thome de Cantilupo, episcopi Herefordensis, A.D. MCCLXXV-MCCLXXXII, ed. Griffiths and Capes (C.Y.S. ii, 1907).
Reg. T. Corbridge	The Register of Thomas of Corbridge, Lord Archbishop of York, 1300–1304, ed. Brown and Thompson (2 parts, Surtees Soc. cxxxviii, cxli, 1925–28).
Reg. Trillek	Registrum Johannis de Trillek, episcopi Herefordensis, A.D. MCCCXLIV-MCCCLXI, ed. Parry (C.Y.S. viii, 1912).
Reg. W. Giffard	The Register of Walter Giffard, Lord Archbishop of York, 1266–1279, ed. Brown (Surtees Soc. cix, 1904).
Reg. Winchelsea	Registrum Roberti Winchelsey, Cantuariensis arch-

	iepiscopi, A.D. 1294-1313, ed. Graham (2 vols., (C.Y.S. li–lii, 1952-56).
Richardson	J. W. Richardson, *The Just Title in Canon 730* (Rome, 1936).
Robertson	A. J. Robertson, ed., *Laws of the Kings of England From Edmund to Henry I* (Cambridge, 1925).
Rot. Grosseteste	*Rotuli Roberti Grosseteste, episcopi Lincolnensis, A.D. MCCXXXV–MCCLIII*, ed. Davis (C.Y.S. x, 1913).
Rot. Hugh of Wells	*Rotuli Hugonis de Welles, episcopi Lincolnensis, MCCIX–MCCXXXV*, ed. Phillimore, Davis, and Salter (3 vols., C.Y.S. i, iii, iv, 1907-9).
Rot. Parl.	*Rotuli Parliamentorum* . . . (6 vols., London, 1783).
R.S.	= Rolls Series
Ryder	R. A. Ryder, *Simony* (Washington, 1931).
Selected Letters of Innocent III	*Selected Letters of Pope Innocent III concerning England (1198-1216)*, ed. Cheney and Semple (Nelson's Medieval Texts, London 1953).
Sheehan	M. Sheehan, *The Will in Medieval England* (Toronto, 1963).
Smith, *Episcopal Appointments*	W. E. L. Smith, *Episcopal Appointments in the Reign of Edward II* (Chicago, 1938).
S.S.	= Selden Society
Stenton	F. M. Stenton, *Anglo-Saxon England* (Oxford, 1943).
Stenton, *Abingdon*	F. M. Stenton, *The Early History of Abingdon Abbey* (Reading, 1913).
Tellenbach	G. Tellenbach, *Church, State and Christian Society at the Time of the Investiture Contest* (Oxford, 1940).
Th. Pen.	= Theodore's *Penitential.*
Th. Code	*The Theodosian Code*, ed. and tr. Pharr (Princeton, 1952).
Thom.	L. Thomassin, *Ancienne et nouvelle discipline de l'église*, ed. André (Paris, 1867).
Thompson	A. H. Thompson, *The English Clergy and Their Organization in the Later Middle Ages* (Oxford, 1947).
Thompson, "Pluralism"	A. H. Thompson, "Pluralism in the Medieval Church," *Associated Architectural Soc. Rep. and Papers*, xxxiii (1915), 35.

Tierney   B. Tierney, *Medieval Poor Law* (Berkeley, 1959).

T.R.H.S.   = *Transactions of the Royal Historical Society.*

1233 Questionnaire   See Mansi, xxiii, 328 ff.

V.C.H.   = Victoria County History (followed by abbreviation of county).

Visitations of Lincoln Religious Houses   *Visitations of Religious Houses in the Diocese of Lincoln,* ed. Thompson (3 vols., C.Y.S. xviii, xxiv, xxxiii, L.R.S. vii, xiv, xxi, 1914-33).

Wakefield Rolls   *Court Rolls of the Manor of Wakefield,* ed. Baildon, Lister, and Walker (5 vols., Yorks. Archaeol. Soc. xxix xxxvi, lvii, lxxvii, cix, 1901-45).

Whitelock   *English Historical Documents c. 500-1042* (Eng. Hist. Doc. i) ed. Whitelock (London, 1955).

Wilkins   D. Wilkins, ed., *Concilia Magnae Britanniae* (4 vols., 1737).

Winchester Synodal Statutes   "1262 x 1265, Synodal Statutes of Bishop John Gervais for the Diocese of Winchester," Powicke and Cheney, 700-723; *Reg. Pontissara,* 207-39.

Woodcock   B. Woodcock, *Medieval Ecclesiastical Courts in the Diocese of Canterbury* (Oxford, 1952).

Y.B.   Year Books, ed. Maynard (11 parts, 1678-79). Cited by regnal date and page.

Notes

1: Origins

Note: In annotating this chapter, I have not attempted to give precise references for all the places I have relied on Stenton, Barlow, Deanesly, or Godfrey.

1. Paul, *The Deployment and Payment of the Clergy* (Westminster, 1964).
2. See, for instance, the preamble to the laws of King Wihtred of Kent (695). Attenborough 24, Whitelock 361.
3. Maitland, *Domesday Book and Beyond* (1897), 226–44.
4. Boehmer, "Das Eigenkirchentum in England," in *Festgabe für Felix Liebermann* (Halle, 1921), 300, 335, 341.
5. The prohibition of the old religion under Ethelbert's grandson Earconbert (640–64), Bede, H. E., iii, 8, was probably addressed to lapses by Christians; the conversion of Kent must have been pretty well complete at the time.
6. See Coifi, "primus pontificum," complaining in the Northumbrian witenagemot of how little his service of the gods has advanced him in the royal favor. Id., ii, 13.
7. Godfrey 65–66 refers to a couple of other incidents involving pagan Anglo-Saxon priests. Schütte, *Our Forefathers,* i (Cambridge, 1929), 230–38, describes the state of the priesthood among the various Teutonic peoples.
8. *Th. Pen.* II, I, 4.
9. Bede, H. E., i, 30. Gregory made a similar suggestion to Ethelbert, id., I, 32.
10. Bede, H. E., iv, 3. See also id., iii, 14, describing how Aidan gave away a horse that the king had given him for his travels.
11. This and the following section are based primarily on Addleshaw, *The Beginnings of the Parochial System,* 2d ed. (1959).
12. Bede, H. E., i, 27.
13. *Th. Code* 16:2:23, ed. Pharr (1952).
14. Holy Rule, c. 62.
15. The canon of the Council of Chalcedon (451), collected by Gratian as c. 26 D. 87, deals with clergy serving laymen in their secular affairs, not with clergy acting as private or household chaplains.
16. This and the following section are based on *Thom.* iv, 199–242; Claeys-Bouuaert, *Evêques, D.D.C.,* v, 569, 575; Van Hove, "Bishops," *Cath. Ency.* ii, 581; Zeiller, *Histoire de l'église,* eds. Fliche and Martin (Paris, 1936), i, 341–42; 381; ii, 398–402, translated in Lebreton and Zeiller, *History of the Primitive*

Church, i, 486–87; ii, 116–21; Palanque, *Histoire de l'église,* iii, eds. Fliche and Martin (Paris, 1936), 438; Gratian, D. 62–65; Kemp 12–17.

17. Deanesly 107. A number of historians, e.g., Deanesly 58–59, attribute the fiasco of Augustine's Oak, Bede, H.E., ii, 2, to Augustine's Roman administrative style.

18. Bede, H.E., iv, 5. *Doc.,* 118-21, gives source notes for all the canons adopted at this synod. Whitelock 650 n says that the book from which Theodore took them was probably that compiled by Dionysius Exiguus. Canons 7 and 9 show how these canons were treated when they had to be modified to meet local conditions. Instead of being reworded to embody the change, they were stated in original form followed by a statement of how they were to be implemented.

19. *Th. Code* 16:2:23. Id., 16:2:41.

20. Cnut, who invaded England in 1015, made himself king and reigned until 1035; although he was a Dane, he seems to have regarded himself, and to have been regarded, as a successor to the West Saxon house. His reign involved a displacement of dynasties, whereas the earlier invasions had involved a displacement of peoples. Stenton 403.

21. Deanesly 91–103, Bede, H. E., iii, 7, and id., iii, 25–26, respectively.

22. Bede, H.E., iv, 5, canon 2.

23. Stenton 134–37 describes some of the early stages of the division. The division of the Northumbrian diocese is bound up with Wilfrid's story. For a quarrel between Bertwald and the West Saxons over the division of their see, see *Doc.,* 267, 275; Whitelock 279.

24. Bede, H.E., v, 23, lists the bishoprics existing at that time.

25. Id., iv, 2, 3, 6.

26. E.g., *Doc.,* 268.

27. Barlow 108–110.

28. Stenton 147. The third canon of the council of the southern province in 747, *Doc.,* 363, and the third canon of the legatine synods of 787, *Doc.,* 449, both required the bishop to make an annual circuit of his diocese.

29. Barlow 92–93.

30. See the sixth canon of the 747 council, *Doc.,* 364, on ordination; Bede, H.E., v, 4–5, and *Th. Pen.* II, I, 4–5, on consecration of churches and control of ministrations in them; the ninth canon of the 747 council, *Doc.,* 365, on institution. I have reservations, though, about whether Stenton 150 is right in applying the last of these to village churches.

31. See the fourth and fifth canons of the 747 council, *Doc.,* 364. As regards keeping the rule, these in terms call on the bishop to exhort the superior, not to correct the religious directly. The 672 Canon on immunity is c. 3, Bede, H.E., iii, 5.

32. Kemp 28–29.

33. Lunt, i, c. 1.

34. Examples include: legates: in 787: A.S.C., an. 786 D, 785 E, *Doc.,* 447–48, Whitelock 770–71; and in 1062: Barlow 106–7; protection of monasteries: *Doc.,* 123–24, 276–77, 394–95; absolution: Barlow 300; threatening prelates: Whitelock 820–21; tenure of sees: Wilfrid's case, discussed below.

35. The king rejected Wilfrid's first papal judgment on grounds of bribery. Eddius xxxiii, *Doc.,* 171–72. There was a compromise six years or so later. Eddius xlii, *Doc.,* 171–72; Stenton 139; pace Deanesly 98. For the papal instruction on Wilfrid's second expulsion, see Eddius lii, *Doc.,* 262–63, and for the en-

suing compromise, Eddius lviii, *Doc.*, 264–66, Whitelock 695–97. Stenton 144 indicates that the papal judgment actually called for a compromise. Bertwald, in Whitelock's translation interpreted it that way. But it is hard to get that interpretation out of the text of the pope's letter or the events leading up to it, and Whitelock's is not the only possible way of translating Bertwald's Latin.

36. Barlow 141–46.

37. In the first of the above categories: Ethelbert (ca. 602) 1, Attenborough 4, Whitelock 357; Wihtred (695) 1, Attenborough 24, Whitelock 362. In the second category: Wihtred 6–7, Attenborough 26, Whitelock 362. In the third: Wihtred 3–5, Attenborough 24, Whitelock 362; Wihtred 12–13, Attenborough 26, Whitelock 363. In the fourth: Ine (688–94) 4, Attenborough 36, Whitelock 364; Ine 61, Attenborough 56, Whitelock 371. In the fifth: Wihtred 9–11, Attenborough 26, Whitelock 363; Ine 3, Attenborough 36, Whitelock 364.

38. It appears that Dunstan held some kind of a council in 969, but nothing much in the way of canonical legislation seems to have emerged from it. Barlow 261 n; Wilkins, i, 247. The early eleventh-century compilation, called the Northumbrian Priests' Law, Whitelock 434–39, seems to me to be a compendium of existing practice rather than a piece of current legislation.

39. Deanesly 306–9.

40. It is interesting here that the ecclesiastical ordinance known as I Athelstan purports to have been issued by Athelstan (925–ca. 939) with the advice of the bishops only.

41. The series of Clovesho synods discussed in Stenton 234–36 seem to be of ecclesiastical provenance. For a case of the King's taking a back seat, see *Doc.*, 360–76 (747).

42. Barlow 245–46.

43. Robertson 234–37, Johnson 21–22, Gee and Hardy, 57–58.

44. III Edgar 5, Robertson 26, Whitelock 397.

45. Stenton 294–97. The first reference in the laws to a court held by a royal official is in II Edward 8, Attenborough 120 (900–925).

46. Stenton 661, Whitelock 80, and Godfrey 427, seem to take this view, as does the *Report of the Archbishop's Commission on Ecclesiastical Courts* (London, 1954). It is the traditional Anglican view. It is set forth in its pristine form in "Courts," Burn, i, 409, with a number of authorities to support it. Johnson 20, though, is more cautious. He says that the bishops and prelates "had ever their distinct judicatures for merely spiritual matters," For a new and persuasive interpretation of William's ordinance, see Morris *E.H.R.*, 449 (1967). Morris argues that William's purpose was limited to taking the hundred out of the business of correcting morals.

47. C. 4, 6, Whitelock 435. Cf. Barlow 274 on an earl's conveyance of a piece of land to a bishop as a penalty for the offence of *oferhyrnes* in disobeying the bishop's summons. On the regular process of the shire and hundred courts, see Pollock and Maitland, ii, 591–92. Other laws that envisage a bishop hearing cases are Ine 13, Attenborough 40, Whitelock 366; Wihtred 6, Attenborough 26, Whitelock 362.

48. On accused clerics, see Q. III, *Doc.*, 404–5. It is not crystal clear that the proceedings in question are before the bishop, but there is no reason why Egbert should describe them so fully if they are in a lay court. On excluding laymen, see Q. VIII, *Doc.*, 406–7. On property claims, see Q. X, *Doc.*, 407–8.

49. The provision of Egbert's Dialogue on exclusion from the ministry is Q. IV, *Doc.* 405. On excommunication, see Wihtred 3–4, Attenborough 24, White-

lock 362; I Edmund 2, Robertson 6 (942–46). See also the 798 litigation reported in *Doc.*, 512, Whitelock 468, in which the threat of excommunication seems to have been among the considerations that led King Cynewulf of Wessex to restore certain charters to the church of Canterbury. As for secular penalties, Wihtred 5 follows up with financial penalties the excommunications provided in 3 and 4 for illicit cohabitation. Articles 9–15 of the same code, Attenborough 26, Whitelock 363, impose exclusively secular penalties—money payments for freemen, flogging for slaves—for offenses such as fast-breaking, idolatry, and Sunday work. See Barlow 145 for legislation following up with secular penalties the provision of I Edmund excommunicating people who refuse to pay church dues. The laws assimilating an excommunicate to a secular outlaw are VIII Ethelred 42, Robertson 128, Whitelock 413 (1014); II Cnut 66, Robertson 206, Whitelock 428 (1020–23). The terminology of these enactments raises a problem or two. Ethelred refers to "God's outlaw" (*Godes utlagan*), which it seems reasonable to take for an excommunicate. Cnut refers in one paragraph to "God's fugitive" (*Godes flyman*) and in the following paragraph to "an excommunicate or outlaw" (*amansodne* [= amansumodne] *man oððon utlagene*). Whitelock translates "God's fugitive" as "a fugitive from an ecclesiastical process." I gather from her footnote that she means not a formally ecclesiastical process but a process involving the status of the Church.

50. Ethelbert 1, 4, 9, *Doc.*, 42, Attenborough 4, Whitelock 357; Wihtred 2, 16, 18–21, Attenborough 24, Whitelock 362; Ine 45, Attenborough 50, Whitelock 369, all reflect different kinds of assimilation. Seebohm, *Tribal Custom in Anglo-Saxon Law* (London, 1902), 382–83, suggests clerical counterparts for the clerical wergilds in Egbert's Dialogue Q. XII, *Doc.*, 408–9. The early eleventh-century compilation on status, Whitelock 431–34, seems to reflect a complete assimilation by custom, independently of legislation. It is interesting, incidentally, that the multiple compensations arrived at in this way are contrary to Gregory's instructions. Bede, H.E. i, 27.

51. Q. VIII, *Doc.*, 406–7 as to the nuns; Q. XII, *Doc.*, 408–9 as to the wergilds.

52. Q. VIII, *Doc.*, 407 (my translation). For a different translation of the same passage, see Barlow 256.

53. The mainstream of canonical tradition would call for either a division of jurisdiction according to the nature of the offense or a complete exclusion of lay jurisdiction over the persons of the clergy. Torquebiau, "Compétence," *D.D.C.*, iii, 1190, 1204–7; 5 Thom. 497–530; Dumas, "Juridiction de l'église," *D.D.C.*, vi, 235, 243–47. On the tribal custom regarding offenses within the kindred, see Seebohm, *Tribal Custom in Anglo-Saxon Law* (London, 1902), 71, 242, 335–36, 497–98.

54. Laprat, "Bras séculier (livraison au)," *D.D.C.*, li, 981. As to Beowulf, see Seebohm 61. The provision in II Edmund 1, Robertson 8, Whitelock 391–92, discussed in Seebohm 356–57, may or may not have been an innovation in this regard.

55. Barlow 183–208.

56. Deanesly 196–210 has the fullest discussion I have seen in a single place of how the different monasteries were founded.

57. Thompson, "Double Monasteries and the Male Element in Nunneries," appended to *Report of Archbishops' Commission on the Ministry of Women* (1919).

58. It seems that monasteries were often founded for the express purpose of evangelizing the surrounding country. Stenton 148. The founding of monasteries

was also an essential part of the Anglo-Saxon missionary effort in Germany. Sullivan, "The Carolingian Missionary and the Pagan," *Speculum* xxviii (1953), 705.

59. *Doc.* 314, 320, Whitelock 735, 741. On the situation generally, see Stenton 160-63.

60. C. 5, Clovesho 747, *Doc.*, 364.

61. Bede, H.E., v, 4, 5,

62. Torquebiau, "Chanoines," *D.D.C.*, iii, 471, 475-76; see c. 4 of the English legatine synods of 787, *Doc.* 450. Thompson, "Notes on Colleges of Secular Canons in England," *Archaeol. Jour.* xxiv (1917), 139.

63. For the church at such and such place, see *Doc.*, 405, 512. For the episcopal see, see *Doc.*, 484. For the patron saint, see *Doc.*, 52.

64. The forms of tenure described in text can be borne out in Domesday Book. It should be noted, though, that in the days before the Danish invasions a whole monastery might belong to someone, as the one at Cookham belonged to the church of Canterbury until the archbishop gave it to its own abbess in exchange for 100 hides of land. *Doc.*, 512-13 (798). I have not found any evidence on whether the landed endowments of a house in such a case were held in the name of the owner or in that of the house.

65. Ine 4, 61, Attenborough 36, 56, Whitelock 365, 371.

66. Stenton 154-55. On the canonical obligation, see Thom., vi, 23-26; c. 17 of the legatine synods of 787, *Doc.*, 456-57. The first general imposition of a secular penalty on failure to pay tithe is in II Edgar 3, Robertson 20-21, Whitelock 394 (959-63). The treaty improperly attributed to Edward and Guthrum, Attenborough 104, may have been a little earlier, but not much. See the discussion in Attenborough 97. I Athelstan, Attenborough 122-25 (925-39), applies only to the king's own estates and those of his immediate tenants.

67. Barlow 178-79.

68. Whitelock 738.

69. Stenton 154 pays special attention to *Th. Pen.* II, XIV, 10, *Doc.*, 203: "Decimas non est legitimum dare nisi pauperibus et peregrinis sive laici suas ad ecclesias." There is early canonical material that stakes out a claim for the "baptismal churches." C. 55, C, 16, q. 1 fourth or fifth century); c, 45, C. XVI, q. 1 (ca. 850). Perhaps the tradition indicated by these authorities was influential on the actual course of events. No doubt it affected the legislation enacted by King Edgar on the subject. II Edgar 1, Robertson 20, Whitelock 395 (959-63). But there is no evidence that it was given the force of law in England before Edgar's time. Both the 787 canon, *Doc.*, 456-57, and King Athelstan's instructions to his reeves, supra note 66, are silent as to who is entitled to the tithe and give no indication that anyone besides God is wronged if it is not paid. This is in marked contrast to Athelstan's instructions in the same document concerning churchscot and soulscot, both of which are to be paid "at the places where they are legally due."

70. Deanesly 202-7.

71. Stenton, *Abingdon.*

72. For the Domesday entry, see *V.C.H.*, Berks., i. For the establishment of the prebend and the reference to "bishops of sonning," see *Bishop Osmund's Register*, i (R.S. lxxviii, 1883), 335.

73. *Doc.*, 512-13; Whitelock 468-80.

74. The Domesday entries on Cookham and Bray are in *V.C.H.*, Berks., i, 327, 330. The land was held under the name of one Regenbald the Priest.

Regenbald has sometimes been referred to as a pluralist, but there is evidence
that his lands were those of a collegiate church at Cihencester. Ross, "Introduction," *The Cartulary of Cihencester Abbey* (1964), i, p. xix.
   75. *V.C.H.*, Berks., ix, 200; Stenton, *Abingdon*, 51.
   76. There may have been a fifth site at Basildon. See Stenton, *Abingdon*,
10–13.
   77. Knowles, M.O., 31–36.
   78. *V.C.H.*, Cambs., ii, 199–200, indicates that this is what happened at Ely.
Cf. Stenton 427.
   79. For proponents of this explanation, see Hunt, *A History of the English
Church from its Foundation to the Norman Conquest* (1899), 191, 256–57,
371; Lingard, *The History and Antiquities of the Anglo-Saxon Church* (1845),
227–36.
   80. Deanesly 271–75; Torquebiau, "Chanoines," *D.D.C.*, iii, 471, 475–76.
   81. E.G., the two Hertfordshire churches of Caddington and Kensworth,
V.C.H., Herts., ii, 192, 233, held by the bishop though the secular estates belonged to the dean and chapter of St. Paul's, id., i, 316, and that of Hemington,
V.C.H., Northants., iii, 82–83, held by the incumbent subject to some intervention by the bishop.
   82. This is the view taken by Round in *V.C.H.*, Essex, i, 423–24. The important alternative view is that taken by Boehmer at 302–9. He argues that the
central authorities were not interested in churches so that these churches were
included or not in accordance with the idiosyncrasies of the local commissioners
who asked the questions and the exchequer clerks who compiled the answers.
His evidence is too narrow to support so broad an explanation. Also, the conclusions he draws from the fact that mention of churches seems to begin
abruptly at a certain folio of the Norfolk compilation are somewhat vitiated
by Darby's later finding that even after that folio all the churches were not
included. *The Domesday Geography of Eastern England* (1952), 190.
   83. Maitland, *Domesday Book and Beyond*, 129–35, 144, and passim.
Cambridgeshire, where only three churches are mentioned in Domesday Book,
is a county where the local holdings were very much broken up.
   84. The ensuing discussion, where not otherwise documented, is based on
the Domesday entries, *V.C.H.*, Berks., i, 321–69, and the topographical entires
in the subsequent volumes. My conclusions should be compared with Page,
"Some Remarks on the Churches of the Domesday Survey," *Archeologia*, lxvi
(1915), 61, and with Barlow 183–208. As to correlating the situation I describe
with the expansion of West Saxon administration, a beginning can be made by
listing the counties in parallel columns according to whether they were regarded
in later times as subject to West Saxon, Mercian, or Danish law (Stenton 498)
and then comparing them with the analysis in Page (supra). We find a definite
correlation. In the nine West Saxon counties, the situation seems to have been
about the same as that in Berkshire as I have described it. In the Mercian counties, Page finds the church served through minsters and manorial churches without the intervention of hundred churches. In the Danelaw, he finds again no
hundred churches, fewer minsters than in Mercia, and a number of churches in
the hands of their own clergy or of groups of small holders.
   85. *Hist. Mon. Abingd.* ii (Record Comm., 1858), 183; Bigelow, *Placita
Anglo-Normannica* (1879), 167. The grant on which this litigation is based goes
back to William II, so it should not be affected by the appropriation that was
supposed to have taken place in the reign of Henry I, *V.C.H.*, Berks., iv, 359.

In any event, the reign of Henry I is too early for anything like a canonical appropriation.

86. The hundreds I would propose to reconstruct are, first, Sparsholt Hundred, with a heavily endowed church at Sparsholt. It would include a detached portion of Wantage Hundred (Sparsholt 19 1/2 hides, Childrey 35), the intervening area of Eagle Hundred (Letcombe Regis 3, Letcombe Basset 10, Challow 7), 20 hides of Sparsholt entered under Hillslau Hundred (which, with 140 hides, can spare them), 2 1/2 hides, 1 virgate, of Sparsholt entered by mistake under Esliteford Hundred, and 3 hides, 1 virgate, appearing immediately after a Sparsholt entry but not clearly attributed. Total, 100 hides, 2 virgates. Second, Hanney Hundred, with a heavily endowed church at West Hanney. It would include the 47 hides of Marcham Hundred south of the River Ock (E. Hanney 10, Goosey 17, Ganford 10, Lyford 10—without these Marcham Hundred would have 99 hides), and neighboring part of Wantage Hundred (Denchworth 13, N. Denchworth 5, E. Hanney 12, W. Hanney 23). This would leave Wantage Hundred with 133 hides. It would leave Eagle Hundred rather depleted, but another tier of villages could be added on to the neighboring hundred of Lambourn to bring that up to 96 hides. At this point, the game becomes more difficult. But before abandoning it, I might point out that Reading Hundred has 153 hides in Domesday Book, the neighboring hundred of Bucklebury has 47, and that the three adjoining hundreds of Shrivenham, Wilfol, and Ganfield, add up to 400 hides.

87. Stenton, *Abingdon*, 7-8, 47-49. The account in A.S.C. an. 963 F, that has Saint Ethelwold extracting a grant from Edgar on the strength of a charter he found in the ruined walls of Medehamsted is a twelfth-century interpolation. On the other hand, from what we know of Ethelwold, he can hardly have been less zealous than the interpolator.

88. II Edgar 1-2, Robertson 20, Whitelock 395.

89. The practice may have been uncanonical, c. 29, X, III, 30 (Innocent III, 1210). Cf. note 69 supra. But Innocent III bears witness to its existence in the decretal, M.P.L., ccxiv, 672 (1200), that is generally taken as abolishing it. Boehmer 322 seems to suppose that the grantor makes grants of this kind as lord of the church previously entitled to receive the tithes in question rather than as lord of the titheable estate. The wording of the grants belies this interpretation. E.g., *Bishop Osmund's Register*, i (R.S. lxxviii, 1883), 215, 217; *Reg. Antiq.* no. 2, 319. Cf. *Domesday of St. Paul's*, ed. Hale (Camden Soc., 1857), 146, where the "fruits of the church" in a given place are treated as distinct from the tithes arising in that place.

90. In this I take issue with Stenton 155, who seems to suppose that the old minsters were a class of churches with recognized parochial rights in Edgar's time, and with Barlow 252, who equates them with the hundred churches. I do not think the hundred churches as a class were old minsters because many of them must have been neither old nor minsters in Edgar's time. I do not think the old minsters can have been a class of churches with a fully established role in the public ministry in Edgar's time because if they were it is hard to see why Edgar's law would not have been implemented. The accompanying provision requiring a thane to give one-third of his tithes to his own church seems to have taken effect without much difficulty. In Norman times, the lord still tended to reserve one-third of his tithes for his own church, bestowing only the other two-thirds of his tithes at will. Stenton 156. This fact is mentioned in the 1200 decretal. Meanwhile, churchscot, which Edgar's law gave to the old minsters

along with two-thirds of the tithes, was in as chaotic a state as tithe was. Stenton 152–54.

91. As to Marcham Hundred, see note 85 supra. We may suppose that the neighboring hundreds of Ganfield and Roeberg were in the same case. The abbey also came by the hundred church at Sutton Hundred, where it held no other land. That church, on the royal manor of Sutton Courtenay, was held of the abbey in Domesday Book by a priest named Alwi, with a hide of land that we know from other evidence was glebe. *V.C.H.*, Berks., i, 340, iv, 377.

92. Cf. note 86 supra. The church on the royal manor of Letcombe Regis in Eagle Hundred appears in Domesday Book in the hands of the Amesbury nuns, who also hold the church at Kintbury. It may have come to them along with Kintbury as a dependency of the latter. See *V.C.H.*, Wilts., iii, 243 n. Along similar lines, I wonder if the churches in the western part of Berkshire that appear in the hands of Geoffrey de Mandeville in places where Geoffrey has no other land may not at one point have been attached to the ecclesiastical complex at Cookham and Bray. One of them, Warfield, is probably a hundred church. If I am on the right track in these speculations, it would seem that the benefit of Edgar's enactment was claimed by secular minsters occupying sites of former monasteries as well as by the refounded monasteries.

93. See note 85 supra. It was evidently considered better estate management to entrust the temporal estate to different hands from the cure of souls with the purely spiritual revenues. *Domesday of St. Paul's*, ed. Hale, 146.

94. *Hist. Mon. Abingd.* ii, 120.

95. Ibid.

96. *V.C.H.*, Berks., iii, 259; *Hist. Mon. Abingd.* ii (Whistley), 18. Cf. the case of Sindlesham, also in Charlton Hundred, where all the altarage, stole fees, and offerings went to Sonning at the time of the 1220 visitation of the latter church. *Bishop Osmund's Register*, i, 275.

97. See *Reg. Antiq.* no. 317 (1129–38), where the bishop settles, after considerable fuss, the attempt of a certain local magnate to set up a church on his manor, and no. 319 (1135–47), where a layman grants half a hide of land to a neighboring church for the privilege of having a graveyard in his village. It is noteworthy not only that a hard bargain is driven in both cases, but in fact full parochial status is not achieved by the dependent church in either case. For the subsequent history of the church involved in no. 319, see *V.C.H.*, Bucks., ii, 326.

98. In addition to the text from Edgar's law, discussed below, see Whitelock 432 on the compilation on status that we have already considered in other contexts. One of the versions of this document includes a church among the things (such as five hides of land and a special duty in the king's hall) that a ceorl must come by in order to rise to the status of a thane.

99. A.S.C. an. 855 (858), Whitelock 174, *Doc.*, 636. For a group of charters of dubious authenticity that purports to be implementations of this benefaction, see *Doc.*, 638–45. For the one such charter that is considered genuine, see Whitelock 484.

100. II Edgar 2, Robertson 20, Whitelock 395. The translation is Whitelock's.

101. Addleshaw 11. The canonical rule in question is now found in c. 1162, para. 2 of the 1918 Code, with source notes going back to the late fifth century.

102. Fliche and Martin, *Histoire de l'église*, vii (1948), 286.

103. Boehmer 319–23.

104. Boehmer 317–20, 328. It should be noted that Boehmer's position on

this point is heavily dependent on his assumption that there was something accidental in the Domesday survey that determined whether churches were or were not included. As he believes that all churches paid services at the time of Domesday Book, he cannot regard payment or nonpayment of services as the standard for including them in the survey. My reasons for rejecting his assumption on this point are set forth in note 82 supra.

105. Perhaps it is the imposition of services on churches properly not subject to them that is envisaged in V Ethelred 10, Robertson 83, Whitelock 407 (1008); and VI Ethelred 15, Robertson 97, which forbid anyone to enslave (*þeowige*) a church. Robertson translates this term as "oppress," and Whitelock as "bring under subjection." But as *þeow* answers to the Latin *servus*, the imposition of a *servitium* might well be what is intended by the verb.

106. Boehmer 330-33. Boehmer's view that the local bishop had no control where the patron was another bishop (id., 300-303) rests on other, and stronger, evidence.

107. IV Edgar 1. 8, Robertson 33, Whitelock 399.

2: The Gregorian Reform

1. On the various currents that flowed together into the Gregorian program, see Tellenbach, *Church, State and Christian Society*, ed. and tr. Bennet (Oxford, 1959); Ryan, *The Canonical Sources of Peter Damian* (Toronto, 1956); Fliche, *La Réforme Grégorienne*, i (Louvain, 1924).

2. The fullest treatment of the historical development of this principle is still Lea, *An Historical Sketch of Sacredotal Celibacy in the Christian Church* (Philadelphia, 1867). By the end of the reform period, subdeacons were in the same case as priests and deacons. For their earlier treatment, see Lea 214 n.

3. The usual sanctions were the traditional ones—deprivation, penances, and the like. Sometimes, though, the reformers let their imaginations run away with them. C. 10, D. XXXII (Melfi, 1089), for instance, provides for the enslavement of the consorts of the clergy. Lea 198, 256; Damian, Opusc. XVIII, D. 2, cap. 7, *M.P.L.*, cxlv, 514, is to the same effect. There is no indication that this rule was ever enforced. See also c. 6, D. XXXII, providing that the faithful are not to attend the masses of incontinent priests. This naturally put the authorities to the necessity of painfully combating the heretical doctrine that such masses are invalid. Lea 203-4 n.

4. Fliche, i, 175-264. The Virgin Birth analogy is in Opusc. XVII, cap. 3, *M.P.L.*, cxlv, 384-85. Old Testament examples are in Opusc. XVIII, D. 1, cap. 4, *M.P.L.*, cxlv, 393. As to the moral superiority of the celibate, see Opusc. XVIII, D. 2, cap. 2, *M.P.L.*, cxlv, 400; Opusc. L, cap. 13, *M.P.L.*, cxlv, 747. For Damian's use of monastic analogies on this point, see Opusc. XVIII, D. 2, cap. 8, *M.P.L.*, cxlv, 413; id., D. 1, cap. 4, *M.P.L.*, cxlv, 393. He does not accept the view that the burden of celibacy must be voluntarily assumed. Opusc. XVI, cap. 5, *M.P.L.*, cxlv, 571-73. Nor does he address himself to the argument set forth by spokesmen for the married clergy (Fliche, iii, 1-12) that the monk has special vocation distinct from that of the priest. On family responsibilities interfering with attention to God, see Opusc. XVIII, D. 2, cap. 4, *M.P.L.*, cxlv, 404-5; id., cap. 8, *M.P.L.*, cxlv, 414. Damian takes I Cor. 7:5

4, *M.P.L.*, cxlv, 404-5; id., cap. 8, *M.P.L.*, cxlv, 414. Damian takes I Cor. 7:5 and I Cor. 7:32-33 to indicate that the layman devotes part of his time to his religious duties and part to his marital duties, whereas the priest must devote full time to religion. He argues to the same effect from duty of the Jewish priest to separate himself from his wife during his term of service at the altar (Lev. 8:33-35; Luke 1:23-24). This last is an old argument; Gratian's sources for it go as far back as Saint Jerome, c. 7, D. XXXI.

5. Opusc. XVIII, D. 2, cap. 7, *M.P.L.*, cxlv, 412. Gratian's material from before Alexander II falls into three categories: (a) requiring a vow of celibacy as a condition for ordination: cap. 1, D. XXVII; cap. 1, 3, 6, 7, D. XXVIII; (b) deposition of the married cleric: cap. 9, D. XXVII; (c) forbidding the clergy the use of marriage legitimately entered into: cap. 2, 10, 11, D. XXXI. Cap. 16-18, D. LXXXI, from Alexander II, speak only of fornication, but it is likely that they are meant to cover fornication under cover of marriage. The fact that two of them are addressed to the clergy of Milan who considered themselves validly married (Lea, 231 n) bears this out. Cap. 8, D. XXVII, from Callistus II, provides that if clergy marry they will be separated and put to penance, but it does not expressly say that their marriages are invalid. The language should be contrasted with that of the Second Lateran Council, c. 7, Mansi, xxi, 528: "Hujusmodi namque copulationem quam contra ecclesiasticum regulam constat esse contractam, matrimonium non esse censemus," or the modern "Invalide matrimonium attentant clerici in sacris ordines constituti." *C.J.C.*, c. 1072. On clerical marriage in England, see Moorman 63-66, Moorman has an example from 1276 of a rector ceremonially married in church. The 1233 questionnaire, art. 6, distinguishes between married and concubinary clergy. The legate Otto in 1237, c. 15, Powicke and Cheney, 252, Johnson 161-62, alludes to marriages by the higher clergy and seems to take an ambiguous attitude toward their validity. As to the illegitimacy of priests' sons, see *Lincs. Assize Rolls, 1202-9* (L.R.S., xxii, ed. D. M. Stenton, 1926), no. 404.

6. On the canonical rule, see Thom., iv, 77; Clercq, *Des sacrements* (Naz, ii), 245; Poitiers, c. 8, Mansi, xx, 498; Melfi, c. 14, Mansi, xx, 724 (both provisions make an exception for religious); c. 1-8, D. LVI; c. 21 Second Lateran 1139, Mansi, xxi, 531; c. 1, X, I, 17. On the rationale, see *S. Theol.*, IV, D. 25, q. 2, art. 2, as quoted in Capello, *De sacramentis*, iv, 344. The encapsulated rationale given in Capello's twentieth-century treatise, id. 345, probably represents a summary of medieval formulations. As for priests arranging careers for their sons, see Thom. iv, 77; Lea 150.

7. Thom., iv, 65-71; Vergier-Boimond, "Bigamie (l'irrégularité de)," *D.D.C.*, ii, 853. The Pauline texts are I Tim. 3:2; Titus 1:5. On the unfaithful husband, see c. 8, D. XXXIV (sixth century). As to the man who fails to repudiate an adulterous wife, see c. 11-12, D. XXXIV (fourth and seventh centuries). On the general subject of whether a man should retain an adulterous wife, see Esmein, *Le Mariage en droit canonique*, ii (2d ed., Paris, 1935), 108-9, and Gratian's dicta on c. 4, 14, C. XXXII, q. 1. On the remarriage of priests' widows, see Esmein, supra, i, 230-32 (2d ed., Paris, 1929). The Old Testament texts on priestly marriage are Lev. 21:7 and 21:13-15; Ezek. 44:22. What these authorities seem to be worried about is the mingling of priestly with common seed in the same womb if the priest's wife should not be a virgin. Lev. 21:15. Hence Ezek. 44:22 allows him to marry the widow of another priest. On the union between Christ and the church, see Damian, Opusc. XI, cap. 12, *M.P.L.*, cxlv,

240-41; c. 5, X, I, 21 (Innocent III), and the passage from Durant (1230-96), quoted by Vergier-Boimond, *D.D.C.*, ii, 853.

8. Thom., iv, 24, 44-49; cf. c. 40-41, D. L; c. 4, D. LI. For the penance imposed on William's soldiers, see *English Historical Documents*, ii, ed. Douglas (1968), 606, no. 81; Mansi, xx, 460-62.

9. Thom., iv, 24 (Innocent III). On the various rationales, see, as to passion, c. 2, 10, X, V, 12; as to mercy versus justice, Thom., iv, 1-68, passim; cf. Gratian, D. XLV, and his introductory statement to C. XXIII, q. 8; as to armies and weapons, c. 1-6, C. XXIII, q. 8. Note that Innocent III permits a cleric to report an offender to the lay authorities even though bloodshed will result, c. 21, X, V, 12, and Gratian finds it lawful for the clergy to exhort the laity to fight, although the clergy may not themselves do so. C. 7-9, C. XXIII, q. 8. Thomassin's point about the Heavenly Lamb is in Thom., iv, 49. The rhetorical flourish is his own, but it has a fair basis in c. 36, D. L sixth century); c. 14, London 1138, Mansi, xxi, 513.

10. Thus, in c. 8, London 1102, Mansi, xx, 1151, Johnson 20, the blood-judgment rule seems an appendage to the rule about secular offices, whereas in c. 3, London 1175, Mansi, xxii, 148, Johnson 60, the rule about secular offices seems to be an appendage to the blood-judgment rule. Compare c. 6-7, London 1268, Powicke and Cheney, 754-756, Wilkins, ii, 5, Johnson 220.

11. C. 18, Mansi, xxii, 1006-7, c. 9, X, III, 50. On the provenance of the surgery rule, see the source notes to *C.J.C.*, c. 139, para. 2. This rule is to be distinguished from the one dealing with a cleri̊c who causes death by practicing medicine without sufficient skill. His case is one of negligent homicide and is covered by much older rules.

12. See c. 3, Nemours 1096 (Urban III), Mansi, xx, 934-35, which seems to suggest that a monk can exercise the priestly ministry better than a secular priest can.

13. Thom., vii, 283-85. A. Palea, c. 11, D. 88, erroneously attributed to Chrysostom, seems to condemn the trader out of hand. Epiphanius, Lactantius, and Saint Leo I, whom Thomassin cites, admit at least a theoretical possibility of engaging in trade without sin. Canons of the reform period include c. 37, Westminster 1173, Mansi, xxii, 143; c. 10, London 1175, Mansi, xxii, 150; c. 16, Fourth Lateran 1215, Mansi, xxii, 1003, c. 15, X, III, 1. Examples of violations are the case of the curate of Wootton, Oxon., presented for being a common buyer and seller of cows and sheep, *Lincoln Visitations*, i (1519), 131, and the fifteenth-century case in Thompson 231. The chaplain presented for the secular offense of forestalling, *Some Sessions of the Peace of Lincolnshire, 1360-75*, ed. Sillen, L.R.S. xxx (1937), no. 427, p. 95, must have been guilty of the canonical offense also.

14. C. 11, D. 88; Thom., vii, 244-70, 277-82. For clergy working their own lands, see Moorman 61-62, 110-14.

15. Thom., vii, 308-43, collects a good many of them. On early precedent, see Brunini, *The Clerical Obligations of Canons 139 and 142* (Washington, 1937), 28; Thom., vii, 287, 219, 298-319. The blanket prohibition is c. 12, Third Lateran 1179, Mansi, xxii, 225, c. 4, X, III, 50. I can find no precedent for it earlier than c. 12, Avranches 1172, Mansi, xxii, 140. For the English developments, see Cheney 22-26. As to Peter of Blois, compare ep. XIV, *M.P.L.*, ccvii, 42, with ep. CL, id. 439. The 1215 canon is c. 18, Mansi, xxii, 1006-7, c. 9, X, III, 50, and the 1268 English one is c. 6, Powicke and Cheney, 754-55, Wilkins, ii 4, Johnson 219. Note that none of the canons purported to affect

the discharge by ecclesiastics of the secular functions that inhered in the tenure of their lands.

16. Cheney 23–25; Thom., vii, 343.

17. Cf. Cheney 21 on the criteria used by Alexander II and Innocent III in selecting bishops. Pantin 9–11, Thompson 15–16, 72, and Smith, *Tudor Prelates and Politics* (Princeton, 1953), 226–32, 259–62, take the situation through the mid-sixteenth century.

18. Thom., vii, 344–473. On specific condemnations re: Rioting and drunkenness: c. 17, Fourth Lateran 1215, Mansi, xxii, 1006, c. 9, X, III, 41. Hunting: Naz, "Chasse," *D.D.C.*, iii, 662; Thom., vii, 430–33, 435, 440–441, 447–50. The main objections to hunting were the pomp with which it was carried on in ancient and medieval times, the oppression of the peasantry through the assertion of hunting rights, and the waste of church funds on keeping up hawks and dogs. Shows and dances: Thom., vii, 431–32, 440–42, 451. The original basis for this prohibition was the immoral content of the shows in Roman times and their origin in pagan rituals. Gambling: Thom., vii, 435–36, 440–41, 444–46. This rule goes back to the "apostolic" canons (c. 41–42, c. 1, D. XXXV). Its original basis was evidently the desire for riches involved in gambling. Damian, though, must have had noneconomic considerations in mind, for he condemned chess too. Thom., vii, 444–46. I have found only one canon (c. 24, Beziers 1255, Mansi, xxiii, 882–83) that followed him in this. Taverns: Thom., vii, 443–44, 450–51.

19. C. 4, Third Lateran 1179, Mansi, xxii, 219, c. 6, X, III, 39. On keeping hawks and hounds, see Moorman, 177n, 187. On enforcement of hunting rights, see, e.g., *Reg. Greenfield*, iii, 180, 185; *Reg. Trillek*, 83, 86.

20. On sobriety of dress, see c. 8, D. XLI; Thom., ii, 30–40, 46–49, 54–57. On tonsure, see Thom., i, 541–46; Thom., ii, 1–22; Ganter, *Clerical Attire* (Washington, 1955), 5–10. The only indication of an external mark of distinction for the clergy in the centuries preceding the reform is presented by a local custom in ninth-century France of priests wearing their stoles for this purpose. Thom., ii, 54–55; c. 25, C. XVII, q. 4. Reform canons include c. 4, Second Lateran 1139, Mansi, xxi, 527, c. 16, Fourth Lateran 1215, Mansi, xxii, 1006, c. 15, X, III, 1.

21. C. 7, Gerona 1078, Mansi, xx, 519.

22. Ganter 10–12. There may have been a touch of nationalism lurking in these strictures in the early centuries. The Romans wore short hair and long tunics, whereas the barbarian invaders wore long hair and short tunics.

23. C. 5, Powicke and Cheney, 752, Wilkins, ii, 4, Johnson 217.

24. See *Lincolnshire Assize Rolls, 1202–9* (L.R.S. xxii, ed. D.M. Stenton, 1926), no. 602, p. 969; Moorman 156. For a later example, see *Some Sessions of the Peace in Lincolnshire, 1381–96* (L.R.S. xlix, ed. Kimball, 1955), no. 101, p. 26.

25. Fliche, i, 225–28; Chenu, *La Théologie au douzième siècle* (Paris, 1957), 228.

26. On the longstanding effort to impose a common life on the secular clergy, see Torquebiau, "Chanoines," *D.D.C.*, iii, 471–83. The orders of canons regular that developed in the reform period are attributable in part to a renewal of this effort. In the end, though, the canons regular were so far assimilated to monks as to be pushed out of the parish ministry along with them. Moorman 49–50; Thompson, "Book Review," *Antiquaries' Journal*, xi (1931), 300; Thompson, "Ecclesiastical Benefices and their Incumbents," *Leics. Arch. Soc. Tr.*, xxii (1941), 1.

27. See c. 30, Ottobuono 1268, Powicke and Cheney, 777, Wilkins, ii, 13, Johnson 243.

28. For the history of this rule, see Dumas, "Juridiction de l'église," *D.D.C.*, vi, 235, 243–47, 255–56. On the rationale, see the language attributed to Constantine, quoted in Bourque, *The Judicial Power of the Church* (Washington, D.C., 1955), 27; c. 51, C. XI, q. 1 (Saint Gregory I); Smith, *Innocent III* (Baton Rouge, 1951), 24, quoting *M.P.L.*, ccxv, 714–15; Knowles, *The Episcopal Colleagues of Thomas Becket* (Cambridge, 1951) 145–60 (Saint Thomas Becket); Pantin, "Grosseteste's Relation with the Papacy and the Crown," in *Robert Grosseteste*, ed. Callus (Oxford, 1955), 128, 197–98 (Grosseteste). The solution that Henry II attempted to impose at Claredon, whereby the guilty cleric would be degraded by the ecclesiastical court, then sentenced by the secular, was not inconsistent with the basic ideals of the reform, nor was it without canonical authority. Pollock and Maitland, i, 125; Maitland, *Canon Law in England,* (1898), chap. 4; Laprat, "Bras séculier (livraison au)," *D.D.C.*, ii, 981, 996–98, 1005–6.

29. See Naz, "Esclave", *D.D.C.*, iii, 448, 453–54; Thom., iv, 41. The medieval canon law continued to speak of *servi* (e.g., c. 5, X, I, 18). For the difference between the Roman slave and the English villein, see Pollock and Maitland, i, 412–32. On performance of villein services, see Pollock and Maitland, i, 498, Moorman 113; and for the earlier practice, c. 4, X, I, 18.

30. Pollock and Maitland, i, 242; Statute of Westminster II, 13 Edw. 1, c. 41 (1285); Fitzh. N.B., 481–82.

31. An express undertaking to perform such services would be punished as simony. C. 12, X, V, 3. Performing them without an express undertaking was regarded by moralists as also simoniacal, but no administrative implementation was attempted.

32. By statute, 13 Edw. 1, st. 1, c. 5 (1285), a patron was entitled to damages equal to two years' proceeds of the benefice if he lost his presentation through the wrongful interference of another.

33. *Reg. Pontissara*, 207–39; pp. xlii–xliii. *Cal. Pat. Rolls, 1348–50,* 106 (1348), shows a person who has acted as a receiver and is being sued for an accounting. Id., *1446–52,* 151–52 (1448), is one of a number of cases where parsons or chaplains act as feoffees to uses or straws in multiple real estate transactions.

34. Thom., iv, 464–73.

35. C. 17, Clermont 1095, Mansi, xx, 817; c. 8, Rouen 1096, Mansi, xx, 925. The Rouen council was generally a local promulgation of the Clermont canons. See Thom., iv, 466. The full text of the Clermont canon has not come down to us; it probably contained the language about adulterers and murderers that was reported from Rouen. It would have been odd for a group of prelates that included the formidable Odo of Bayeux to come up with such sentiments on their own.

36. C. 43, Mansi, xxii, 1028, c. 30, X, II, 24.

37. Cf. Cantor, *Church, Kingship and Lay Investiture in England, 1089–1135* (Princeton, 1958), 319.

38. On the history, see Weber, *History of Simony in the Christian Church* (Baltimore, 1909), passim; Fliche, i, 23–30. For statements of the moral and theological aspirations involved, see Thom., vi, 471–72; Fliche, i, 216; Ryder, *Simony* (Washington, 1931), 61; and especially Tellenbach 128.

39. Ryder 10–25; Tellenbach 101; Moorman 6. The fifteenth-century cases collected in Thompson 238–41 indicate that such violations as came up could

be routinely coped with. Smith, *Episcopal Appointments,* does not find any bribery in the maneuverings he describes.

40 Ferry, *Stole Fees* (Washington, 1930), 10–27; Naz, "Taxe," *D.D.C.,* vii, 1167. On attitudes and doctrine, see Weber 17–23. For some reason, simony has always been considered heretical as well as immoral. Tellenbach 128; cf. *C.J.C.,* c. 2371.

41. C. 66, Mansi, xxii, 1054, c. 42, X, V, 3. See also Richardson, *The Just Title in Canon 730* (Rome, 1936), 47, and Thom., vi, 477–79, 482.

42. See Richardson 50 on the circumspection that must be used even in our own time to avoid the appearance of evil in asking for the customary offerings.

43. C. 11, Amalfi 1909, Mansi, xx, 753; c. 5–7, Piacenza 1095, Mansi, xx, 805; c. 1, C. I, q. 5; c. 5–7, Rome 1099, Mansi, xx, 961; c. 7, Poitiers 1100, Mansi, xx, 1123; c. 14, London 1102, Mansi, xx, 1151; c. 30, Westminster 1173, Mansi, xxii, 144; c. 9, London 1175, Mansi, xxii, 149; c. 38, X, V, 3 (Innocent III); Moorman 6.

44. E.g., c. 4, Palencia 1129, Mansi, xxi, 387 (under the names of *prestimonium* and *villicatio,* which seem equivalent to the more familiar *firma*); c. 7, Avrances 1172, Mansi, xxii, 135; c. 11, Westminster 1173, Mansi, xxii, 141; c. 10, London 1175, Mansi, xxii, 150. C. 9, London 1127, Mansi, xxi, 357, seems to forbid clergy to *be* farmers—perhaps because it is a form of business. Cf. c. 10, London 1175, supra. Thompson, "Pluralism in the Medieval Church," *Asso. Arch. Soc. Rep.,* xxxiii (1915), 35, shows how a cleric could circumvent the canons against holding two benefices by acting as the farmer, instead of the incumbent, of one of them. Simony is mentioned in c. 20, Ottobuono 1268, Powicke and Cheney, 769, Wilkins, ii, 10, Johnson 234. As to psychological effect, see Hartridge 208. On risk, see Noonan, *The Scholastic Analysis of Usury* (Harvard, 1957), 90–95, 128–31.

45. C. 20, Powicke and Cheney, 769, Wilkins, ii, 10, Johnson 234.

46. Many of them are collected in F.G.A. under the title "Jurisdiction"; see no. 1, *Abbot of Osney* v. *Anon.,* Y.B. 1 H. VI, p. 5; no. 17, *Anon.* 12 R. 2, Ames Found. 63; no. 40, *Anon.,* Y.B. 7 H. IV, p. 35. See also *Abbot of Sawtry* v. *Netherstrete,* 13 R. II, Ames Found. (1389), 84, where the abbot seems to be suing the farmer for the agreed-on-rent.

47. Similarly, the reformers were not able to do much about wealthy parents who provided for their children by paying religious houses to let them join. Ryder 29–32, 46; Deshusses, "Chape (droit de)," *D.D.C.,* iii, 519. Reform canons forbidding the acceptance of such payments include c. 17, Rome 1099, Mansi, xx, 964; c. 8, London 1175, Mansi, xxii, 149; c. 10, Third Lateran 1179, Mansi, xxii, 224; c. 66, Fourth Lateran 1215, Mansi, xxii, 1054, c. 42, X, V, 3. Such payments had not only strong social forces behind them but also a certain amount of justification, as cutting the financial incentive to force your children into the religious life. Ryder 3. Modern canon law has relented on them somewhat on the theory that they are a contribution to the support of the new member, not a consideration for accepting him (or more usually her). Naz, "Dot des religieuses," *D.D.C.,* iv, 1431. Compare c. 34, X, V, 3, with *C.J.C.,* c. 1450, para 2. Other practices that seem to me to savor of simony passed entirely without comment throughout the Middle Ages. These were rendering masses and prayers as services for land and taking money to promote the marriages of heirs, Pollock and Maitland, ii, 318–29.

48. E.g., c. 6, Rheims 1148, Mansi, xxi, 715; c. 1, Westminster 1173. Mansi, xxii, 141; c. 9, Third Lateran 1179, Mansi, xxii, 222; c. 14, Third Lateran 1179, Mansi, xxii, 225, c. 4, X, III, 38.

49. E.g., c. 12, Lillebon 1080, Mansi, xx, 557; c. 18, First Lateran 1123, Mansi, xxi, 285; c. 9, Third Lateran 1179, Mansi, xx, 222; c. 3, X, V, 33; c. 61, Fourth Lateran 1215, Mansi, xx, 1047, c. 31, X, III, 5.

50. On the patron's filling the office himself, see c. 15, X, III, 38 (Alexander III); c. 5-7, Piacenza 1095, Mansi, xx, 805. Nor can the patron, even if an entirely suitable cleric, be received into a benefice on his own presentation. C. 26, X, III, 38 (Innocent III). This last rule was held in *Walsh* v. *Bishop of Lincoln, L.R.* 10 C.P. 518 (1875), never to have been in force in England. The practice of self-presentation seems to have been quite prevalent in the nineteenth century with consequences that amply vindicate the wisdom of Innocent III in forbidding it. On collegiate cures, see c. 21, London 1102, Mansi, xx, 1149; c. 6, Rheims 1157, Mansi, xxi, 845; c. 9, Third Lateran 1179, Mansi, xxii, 222; Thompson, "Ecclesiastical Benefices and Their Incumbents," *Leics, Arch. Soc. Tr.*, xxii, (1941), 1; Hartridge 38-39. On hired priests, see c. 9, Rheims 1131, Mansi, xxi, 460; c. 5, Tours 1163, Mansi, xxi, 1178.

51. As to lay patrons, see c. 10, Second Lateran 1139, Mansi, xxi, 528, and other canons excluding the laity in general from the possession of tithes. See also c. 1, London 1151, Mansi, xxi, 750-51. C. 6, Rheims 1148, Mansi, xxi, 715, seems to allow the patron to take an anciently established due. This we must presume to apply to religious houses and the like. As to installation, see c. 9, Lillebon 1090, Mansi, xx, 557; c. 6, Rheims 1157, Mansi, xxi, 845, c. 10, 13, 20, X, III, 38 (Alexander III).

52. E.g ., c. 7, Nemours 1086, Mansi, xx, 935; c. 16, Second Lateran 1139, Mansi, xxi, 530, c. 7, C. VIII, q. 1.

53. E.g., c. 7, 18, First Lateran 1123, Mansi, xxi, 283-85; c. 1, Westminster 1173, Mansi, xxii, 141.

54. Bernard, "Bâtard," *D.D.C.*, ii, 252, 256-57. Bernard confines the prohibition to illegitimate children, but the texts are not all so confined. See, for instance, c. 31, Fourth Lateran 1215, Mansi, xxii, 1018-19, c. 16, X, I, 17: "ne canonici fillii, *maxime spurii*, canonici fiant in saecularibus ecclesiis in quibus instituti sunt patres eorum" (emphasis supplied). For other sources in which the prohibition is clearly applied to legitimate sons, see Burn, i, 131-32.

55. Thom., vi, 23-26. The reformers do not make as much of the Old Testament precedent as we might have expected. The only canon that seems to look to an Old Testament source is c. 13, London 1175, Mansi, xxii, 150, which begins: "Omnes decimae terrae, sive de frugibus, sive de fructibus, Domini sunt et illi sanctificantur." The canons mentioned in text are c. 6, Rome 1078, Mansi, xx, 510; c. 1, C. XVI, q. 7, repeated in c. 10, Second Lateran 1139, Mansi, xxi, 528. Those embodying the one-third rule include c. 3 (3d list), Rouen 1074, Mansi, xx, 399; c. 4, Lillebon 1080, Mansi, xx, 556; c. 5, Rouen 1095, Mansi, xx, 928; c. 16, Palencia 1129, Mansi, xxi, 387. Occasional payments were another kind of ecclesiastical revenue that required some legislation in the early stages of the reform to keep it out of the hands of laymen. E.g., c. 13, Gerona 1078, Mansi, xx, 520; c. 4, Lillebon 1080, Mansi, xx, 556; c. 5, Rouen 1095, Mansi, xx, 928; c. 14, First Lateran 1123, Mansi, xxi, 285; c. 4, Toulouse 1119, Mansi, xxi, 227. After the early twelfth century, the state of the legislation would indicate that this ceased to be a problem.

56. *Reg. Pontissara*, 774-75: "cum ea ad personem laicalem nequeant pertinere."

57. See c. 10, London 1127, Mansi, xxi, 375; c. 13, London 1175, Mansi, xxii, 145. The Spanish canon on Jews' land is c. 10, Gerona 1078, Mansi, xx,

519. To the same effect is c. 16, X, III, 30 (Alexander III). But cf. c. 2, Palencia 1129, Mansi, xxi, 386, which is not altogether clear but seems to be saying that the tithes of excommunicates are not to be received. On deducting rents and wages, see c. 54, Fourth Lateran 1215, Mansi, xxii, 1042; c. 33, X, III, 30; c. 7, X, III, 30 (Alexander III); c. 22, id. (Celestine III). As tithes of produce become a charge on land, there developed a distinction between real and personal tithes—the latter continuing to constitute an obligation of the tithepayer rather than a right in the land. Personal tithes, having no basis in the land-centered economic and juridical structure of the time, tended to die out, although they persisted to some extent throughout the Middle Ages. Little, "Personal Tithes," *E.H.R.*, lx (1945), 67. The present discussion is concerned only with real tithes.

58. C. 54, Mansi, xxii, 1042, c. 33, X, III, 30.

59. The respective positions can be traced as to tithes of wood in para. 199 of the clergy's petition, *Rot. Parl.*, ii (1376), 357b, para. 59 of the Commons' petition, *Rot. Parl.*, iii (1400-1401), 470a, and the statute 45 Edw. 3, c. 3 (1366). The medieval material assembled by Coke in *The Case De Modo Decimandi*, 13 Co. Rep. 36, 77 Eng. Rep. 1448, is also worth examining.

60. See *Cal. Pat. Rolls, 1348-50* (1348), 162, *Rot. Parl.*, iii, 648b (1411).

61. E.g., *Reg. Trillek*, 33-34, a mandate to pronounce a sentence of excommunication against those who chop down trees in the bishop's woods. They are characterized as "certain sons of iniquity, unmindful of their salvation, moved by diabolical suasion." Their conduct is called "a great harm to us and our church, a manifest undermining of ecclesiastical liberty, a danger to their souls and a dangerous example to many."

62. Bloch 410-12. On wergilds and compensation, see id., 125-30; on the peace, see Pollock, "The King's Peace," *L.Q. Rev.*, i (1885), 37.

63. The ecclesiastical authorities made some efforts to mitigate the violence of lay society by norms of general applicability such as those against tournaments, e.g., c. 14, Second Lateran 1139, Mansi, xxi, 530, and against setting fire to the lands and buildings of enemies e.g., c. 18, Second Lateran 1139, Mansi, xxi, 531, c. 32, C. 23, q. 8. These efforts seem to have been almost completely abortive. Note also the prohibition in c. 29, Second Lateran 1139, Mansi, xxi, 533, against using on Christians the latest technical developments in the art of warfare, as represented by "Artem illam mortiferam et Deo odibilem ballistrariorum et sagittariorum." In the Fourth Lateran Council of 1215, the fathers content themselves with imposing such a prohibition on the clergy. C. 18, Mansi, xxii, 1006-7.

64. Cox 6-8; see, e.g., Wihtred, c. 2, Attenborough, 25 (695); I Canute, c. 2, para. 1-2. Robertson 155 (1020-34). Compare c. 2, Rouen 1096, Mansi, xx, 923: "De rebus & personis quae perpetua in pace debent esse," including "omnes ecclesiae & atria earum" in an enumeration.

65. Pollock, "The King's Peace," *L.Q. Rev.*, (1885), 40. Pollock and Maitland, ii, 454.

66. C. 9, C. XVII, q. 4, is a source from Charlemagne's empire. For the same rule among the Anglo-Saxons, see Ine 5, Attenborough 39 (688-94).

67. This is to prescind from the utility the institutions continued to have in the case of political refugees; Cox refers to a number of cases.

68. See the complaints about Westminister Abbey in this regard in 1379, *Rot. Parl.* iii, 51a. This sanctuary was one of those that boasted a royal charter from Saxon times, giving it more scope than the common run of churches had. Cox 50ff.

69. Messerey, "Asile en occident," *D.D.C.,* i, 1090, 1098–1101. The English procedures were peculiar and not wholly satisfactory to the church. They called for the felon to come out within forty days and submit either to trial or to exile; failing this, he was to be starved out. Pollock and Maitland, ii, 590–91, contains succinct exposition of this process.

70. For different forms of rhetoric, see *Rot. Parl.,* iii, 51 a (1379); c. 6, X, III, 49; Thom., v, 494; Masserey, supra, note 69, 1093–94; bk. III, tit. 36, of the *Summa Decretalium* of Bernard of Pavia, ed. Lespeyres, pp. 126–29; c. 12, Ottobuono 1268, Wilkins, ii, 8, Johnson 228.

71. This discussion is based largely on McGrath, *The Privilege of the Canon* (Washington, 1946), 4, 9, 14, 18–19.

72. C. 12, 21, 27, C XVII, q. 4.

73. Mansi, xxi, 529–30. The material in the Decretals interpreting "si quis . . ." is in bk. V, tit. 39.

74. *Articuli Cleri,* 9 Edw. 2, c. 3 (1315). A money commutation of a corporal penance seems, however, to have been permitted.

75. For general discussions of this subject, see Bloch 412–20; Fliche, *La Réforme Grégorienne et la reconquête chrétienne,* eds. Fliche and Martin, viii (1946), 283. Thom., v., 426–66. A fair sample of the legislation on the peace is presented by c. 2, Rouen 1096, Mansi, xx, 923; c. 11, Second Lateran 1139, Mansi, xxi, 539; c. 22, Third Lateran 1179, Mansi, xxii, 229–30, c. 1, X, I, 34. The truce is sometimes lumped together with the peace in a single canon, e.g., c. 1, Clermont 1095, Mansi, xx, 816. More often, it is the subject of a separate enactment. Each of the above canons on the peace is immediately preceded or followed by one on the truce. The late twelfth-century decretist Bernard of Pavia tells us that the truce is kept on Thursday in honor of our Lord's Ascension, on Friday in honor of his Passion, on Saturday because of the Sabbath rest, and on Sunday in honor of the Resurrection. *Summa Decretalium,* bk. 1, tit. 24, ed. Laspeyres, 20. For instances of the integration of the law of sanctuary into that of the ecclesiastical peace, see Masserey, "Asile en occident," *D.D.C.,* i, 1090, 1091. On secular analogues, see Pollock, "The King's Peace," *L.Q. Rev.,* i (1885), 40, 42.

76. Bloch 413, 415.

77. See Dumas, "Juridiction ecclésiastique," *D.D.C.,* vi, 235, 255–59; Pollock and Maitland, i, 125–30; c. 3, X, II, 1. Thom., v, 551. Cf. c. 16, X, II, 2, and the introductory language to c. 3, X, II, 1. This is, of course, the church's counterpart to the king's "crown and dignity," which are invaded when his jurisdiction is trespassed upon.

78. On offenses, see Pollock and Maitland, i, 454–56. The authors question whether Becket's opposition had any firm base in canon law, but the principle that there could not be two judgments seems, from the authorities they cite, to have been more firmly rooted than was Becket's application of it. As to legitimacy, see Pantin, "Grosseteste's Relation with the Papacy and the Crown," in *Robert Grosseteste,* ed. Callus, 178, 197; Pollock and Maitland, ii, 377–79 and 364–99 passim; and the elaborate argument of Innocent III in c. 13, X, IV, 17.

79. Bourque, *The Judicial Power of the Church,* 41–57, lists all the claims made by Innocent IV to jurisdiction over temporal matters. There are eleven all told, of which three relate to the temporal affairs of the church. The others are all reducible in some way to a defect of secular justice and seem to be traceable no further back than Innocent III. Bourque's reference to Alexander III

on p. 51 is evidently an oversight; actually it was Innocent III who was involved. Innocent III's most important innovations were the evangelical denunciation based on Matthew 18:15-17 and developed in c. 13, X, II, 1, to assert an ecclesiastical jurisdiction over all forms of sin, and the jurisdiction in hard and doubtful matters, based on Deut. 17:8-12 and applied in c. 13, X, IV, 17. The claim to jurisdiction over the causes of the poor and unbefriended is in one sense an old one, but it was Innocent III again who institutionalized it. In his hands it, too, was only operative in case of default of the secular authorities. C. 11, X, II, 2. Honorius III seems to have gone a step further, c. 15, X, II, 2, as does Innocent IV. It seems that in later times the French clergy went still further and regarded as a usurpation the intervention of lay courts in these causes. Thom., v, 553. C. 20, Second Lateran 1139, Mansi, xxi, 531, c. 32, C. 23, q. 8, which preserves lay jurisdiction in cases of incendiarism but seems to regard such jurisdiction as a concession on the part of the ecclesiastical authorities, is not in the mainstream of canonical thought on the subject.
    80. C. 3, X, II, 1; Cheney 108-18.
    81. 20-21 Vic. c. 71, 85 (1857).
    82. Pollock and Maitland, i, 128-29. Id., ii, 198-202. On the distinction between perjury and *fidei laesio*, or breach of faith, see id., 189-92. In the early fourteenth century, an additional device was developed for bringing contract cases into the ecclesiastical courts. The party obligating himself would attach a penalty clause reciting that the penalty was to be contributed to the funds being collected for the Holy Land. This is alluded to in the letter of the Commons to the pope, *Rot. Parl.*, i, 207a, and in the petitions against William Testa, id., 219a. The Commons were complaining of the *fidei laesio* jurisdiction as late as 1409-10. *Rot. Parl.*, iii, 645b.
    83. During the crucial period of institutional fluidity, it does not appear that either system possessed the conceptual equipment to see the question of how to draw the line between the two jurisdictions as constituting a jurisdictional question in its own right. See *Adam* v. *Parson of C.*, 21-22 Edw. 1, R.S., xxia, 588 (1294), for example of the way in which the lay courts habitually made the question of jurisdiction over a case depend on their own determination of the merits. As for the canonists, I find nothing up to and including the Decretals that deals expressly with "jurisdiction to determine jurisdiction." C. 2, X, II, 1, taken from an 1148 synod at Rheims (c. 5, Mansi, xxi, 715), orders ecclesiastical judges not to give over exercising the judicial power of the church by virtue of prohibitions from the lay authorities but leaves in the air the question whether it is in fact the judicial power of the church that is being exercised. C. 13, X, IV, 7 (Innocent III), claims hard and doubtful cases for the church courts but not jurisdictional cases as such (pace Bourque, *The Judicial Power of the Church*, 42; Carlyle, *Medieval Political Theory*, ii, 232-35). Note also that it is collected under its substantive subject rather than in the title *De foro competenti*. Grosseteste, bishop of Lincoln, 1235-53, does expressly claim jurisdictional questions for the church on account of its moral and legal superiority to the state. *Roberti Grosseteste epistolae*, ed. Luard (R.S., xxv, 1861), 220-21. But his doctrine does not seem to have made its way into the canons. It was set forth in opposition to the lay courts issuing writs of prohibition— a lost cause.
    84. Petition of Commons no. 72, *Rot. Parl.*, iii, 645b (1410).
    85. Woodcock 88-92, 107-8.
    86. For two cases in which jurisdiction seems to be commuted for a money

payment, see *Reg. Antiq.* no. 325 and no. 388. See also *Prior of Great Malverne v. Bishop of Worcester, Rot. Parl.*, i, 62a (1290), where the prior seems to have bought off the bishop's visitation rights with the grant of a secular manor.

87. Pantin 93–94. See *Chronicle of Jocelin of Brakelond*, ed. Butler (1949), 82–85. There is a dramatic incident, id., 52–53, where Abbot Samson, confronting his adversary before the tomb of Saint Edmund, calls on the saint to defend one of the franchises of Bury. Comparable is the role of Saint Cuthbert's body is securing the palatine franchises of the bishop of Durham. *Rot. Parl.*, iii, 177a (1384).

88. Thurston, "Celibacy," *Cath. Ency.*, iii (1908), 481; Jombart,"Célibat des clercs," *D.D.C.*, iii, 132, 138. Damian's argument, supra, note 4, and Innocent III's, c. 5, X, III, 3, are somewhat similar but seem to conceive of family responsibilities as distracting from prayer rather than from pastoral activity.

89. Milman, *History of Latin Christianity*, iii, (New York, 1889), 375.

90. This argument takes us into rather deep waters. Dopsch, *The Economic and Social Foundations of European Civilization*, 283–302, and Bloch 163–75, 190–210, will serve as an introduction to the problem. See also Maitland, *Domesday Book and Beyond* (1897), 171.

91. Lea 690; Moorman 63; Cheney 14–15. Compare Damian's famous testimony to the good character of the married clergy of one diocese. Opusc. XVIII, D. 2, praef., *M.P.L.*, cxlv, 398, quoted Lea 212n.

92. Lea 17–20, 234–37. Curiously enough, though, Lea concedes that Damian was innocent of any such motive (p. 213).

93. C. 19, Third Lateran 1179, Mansi, xxi, 228.

94. C. 25, London 1102, Mansi, xx, 1152; c. 10, 14, Rheims 1148, Mansi, xxi, 719.

95. C. 5, Tours 1163, Mansi, xxi, 1178.

96. C. 4, Rome 1078, Mansi, xx, 509.

97. Giraldus Cambrensis in *Gemma Ecclesiastica*, D. 2, cap. 6, ed. Brewer, ii, (R.S., xxib, 1862), 187–91, has an instructive passage on the point. I do not agree with Moorman 66 in reading Giraldus as saying that the requirement of celibacy should not be enforced.

98. E.g., c. 9, Nemours 1096, Mansi, xx, 936.

99. Saint Thomas Aquinas argues to the same effect in defending the rule against the ordination of *bigami*. The whole subject is developed at some length in Gilson, *Abelard and Heloise* (Chicago, 1954).

100. *Church, State, and Christian Society*, ed. and tr. Bennet (Oxford, 1959).

101. Ullman, *Principles of Government and Politics in the Middle Ages* (New York, 1961), 67–69, indicates that medieval papal theorists used the term *utilitas publica* in connection with certain of their doctrines. Their *utilitas* does not seem to be "utility" in the sense I am using the term because its major articulation is in terms of a priori structural principles. Id., 63–66. Thus Ullmann's analysis tends in this particular respect to support Tellenbach's, albeit with certain terminological variances.

102. This analysis relates to an interpretation with certain utilitarian overtones, that of Previté-Orton, *Shorter Cambridge Medieval History*, i (Cambridge, 1960), 473, 501, who points out how well calculated the asceticism of the early reformers was to capture the imaginations of the warriors who were their patrons. The reformers were no doubt aware of this, but I suspect they would have stated it in terms of witness rather than in terms of conversion. And as a

matter of fact, the nobles, however their imaginations were captured, did not turn to the ascetic life in such numbers as to have a profound influence on society. Still less did they find in their spiritual advisers the models they needed for leading their lives as Christian laymen.

103. Cf. Maitland, *Canon Law in England* (1898), 74 n (*E.H.R.*, xi, 656 n).

104. Ullman, *Principles of Government and Politics in the Middle Ages*, chap. 2–3, compares the French and English monarchies in this regard.

105. See Grosseteste, Ep. LXXII, *Roberti Grosseteste epistolae*, ed. Luard (R.S., xxv, 1861), 205, 214;"In libro quoque Machabaeorum decretum est, ut *Jerusalem sit sancta et libera cum finibus suis. Et quae est Jerusalem nisi collectio virorum ecclesiasticorum per contemplationem et segregationem a tumultu seculari in visione pacis existentium?*"

3: The Canon Law

1. See Munier, *Les Sources patristiques du droit de l'église* (Mulhouse, 1957), for a careful and instructive analysis of one form of theological input into the system.

2. Claeys-Bouuaert, "Évêques," *D.D.C.*, v, 569, 575; Lepointe, "Dime," *D.D.C.*, iv, 1231–32.

3. C. 8, Fourth Lateran 1215, Mansi, xxii, 994, c. 34, X, V, 1.

4. Lefebvre, "Evangelique (denonciation)," *D.D.C.*, v, 557.

5. For the use of particular texts in the canonical collections, see deClercq, "Corpus Juris Civilis " *D.D.C.*, iv, 644, 661–80. Esmein, *Le Mariage en droit canonique,* i (2d ed., 1929), 101–19, shows an interesting example of a dialectic between a theological deduction and a rule of the Roman law in the development of a canonical rule. The Roman Law, which quite clearly provided that the essential for the marriage relation was consent (*Nuptias consensus non concubitus facit*), ran counter to the deduction the theologians made from the scriptural analogy of the physical union of Christ and the church. As a result, the medieval canon law vacillated a great deal between consent and marital intercourse as the effective conclusion of the marriage. For a general discussion of the place of Roman Law in the canon law of marriage, see Jolowicz, *Roman Foundations of Modern Law* (Oxford, 1957), 141–60.

6. Gaudemet, *La Formation du droit seculier et du droit de l'église* (Paris, 1957), 163–76: Jolowicz, *Roman Foundations of Modern Law,* passim.

7. Ullman, *Principles of Government and Politics in the Middle Ages* (New York, 1961), 32–37. It was also Roman law that formed the theory of the manner of the pope's succession to the prerogatives of Peter. Id., 37–39.

8. The personal character of the pastorate may, incidentally, offer some clue to the reason for the rule that visitation involves a complete supersession of the authority of the person visited by that of the visitor. The rule has nothing practical in its favor, and I have found no rationale offered for it. It is tempting also to attribute to the ethos of the personal pastorate the phenomenon noted by Professor Jacob of the failure of Archbishop Chichele's register to note in which of his several capacities—diocesan, metropolitan, papal legate—the archbishop does his various acts. *Reg. Chichele*, i, pp. lix–lxi.

9. *Th. Code* 7:20:7.

10. Id., 7:18:14.

11. Id., 7:18:17.

12. Sohm, *Institutes*, sec. 26, trans. Leslie (Oxford, 1907), 139; Lefebvre, "Natural Equity and Canonical Equity," *Natural Law Forum* viii (1963), 122, 130. Naz, "Préscription," *D.D.C.*, vii, 194; 5, X, II, 26 (Alexander III); c. 41, Fourth Lateran 1215, Mansi, xxii, 1027, c. 20, X, II, 26.

13. Gaius in *Digest*, bk. 41, tit. 3, law 1.

14. For a good example of the ambivalent attitude of the canonists toward appeals, see c. 6, Third Lateran 1179, Mansi, xxii, 220–21; c. 26, X, II, 28. For the difficulties encountered in their attempts to control appeals in the light of this ambivalent attitude, see Amanieu, "Appelatione remota," *D.D.C.*, i, 827.

15. It is well established theologically that the power of the bishop to govern his diocese is of divine law. The relation between this principle and the equally well-established principle of the primacy of the pope has given rise to some fine-spun controversies in its time. For a description of one of them, see Claeys-Bouuaerst "Evéques," *D.D.C.*, v, 569, 571–73. There continues to be no really satisfactory way of structuring the theological relation juridically. The *plentitudo potestatis* of the pope is, as I say, an oversimplification. Maitland's analogy of a federal system (*Canon Law in England*, c. 1) will not do because there is no allocation of powers and functions between central and local authority. I suspect that the analogy actually used was that of the relation between the Roman people and the other peoples of the empire.

16. See c. 4, 8, C. II, q. 6, especially c. 8 (attributed by Gratian to Pope Zephyrinus [199–217]): "To the Roman church everyone—but especially those who are oppressed—may appeal, may run as to a mother, to be nourished at her breasts, to be defended by her authority, to be relieved of his oppression, for a mother neither can nor should forget her son."

17. Barraclough, *Papal Provisions* (Oxford, 1935), c. 12.

18. C. 5, Amalfi 1089, Mansi, xx, 723; c. 15, Rome 1099, Mansi, xx, 963.

19. A by-product of the same High Church approach was a tendency to divert the pastoral ministry itself to institutional objects, i.e., preaching and ecclesiastical censures used for the purpose of collecting ecclesiastical revenues and maintaining clerical immunity rather than on disseminating the Gospel message.

20. The concept is discussed at length in Hannan, *The Canonical Concept of Congrua Sustenatio for the Secular Clergy* (Washington, 1950).

21. Moorman 39; Thompson 110. See c. 21 (15), Oxford 1222, Powicke and Cheney, 112, Mansi, xxii, 1156.

22. See Ottobuono's canon on appropriation quoted on p. 82 of text; cf. Thom., vii, 385–429.

23. C. 32, Fourth Lateran 1215, Mansi, xxii, 1019, c. 5, X, III, 5, seems to recognize that the lack of a *congrua sustentatio* may produce an illiterate ministry. But to recognize this is not to recognize that there may be a scale of literary attainments available in proportion to the amount we are willing to pay and that it is our business to strike a balance at some particular point on the scale. The existence of such a scale was so far recognized that a number of the medieval commentators taught that higher pay was to be given for higher attainment (i.e., that a *congrua sustentatio* for a better man might be higher than for a worse)

Hannan, supra, note 20 at 54. But they did not draw from this fact the logical deduction that higher pay would elicit a more highly qualified man for a given post.

24. Knowles, R.O., ii, 291.

25. On the first category, see the views collected in Davitt, *The Nature of Law* (St. Louis, 1951). Holmes, "The Path of the Law," *Harv. L. Rev.,* x (1897), 457, is generally regarded as the cornerstone of the second category. For the third, see Hart, "Definition and Theory in Jurisprudence," *L. Q. Rev.,* lxx (1954), 37. Kelsen's "pure theory of law" seems to amount to rather the same thing.

26. For the basic recognition that the methods and purposes of canon law differ inherently from those of secular law, I am indebted to Kemp, *An Introduction to Canon Law in the Church of England* (London, 1957). See also Mortimer, *Western Canon Law* (Berkeley, 1953), 75–90.

27. The fullest treatment of this important topic is Thompson, "Pluralism in the Medieval Church," *Assoc. Architectural Soc. Rep. and Papers,* xxxiii (1915), 35. For more accessible material, see Thompson 11–12; Pantin 36–38. For the continuity of the problem in England after the Reformation, see Sykes, *Church and State in England in the XVIIIth Century* (Cambridge, 1934), 147–49, 215–20.

28. C. 29, Fourth Lateran 1215, Mansi, xxii, 1015, c. 28, X, III, 5.

29. C. 13, Third Lateran 1179, Mansi, xxii, 225, c. 3, X, III, 4.

30. C. 12, Third Lateran 1179, Mansi, xxii, 225, c. 4, X, III, 50. See also c. 7 of the same council, Mansi, 221–22: "Should anyone presume to violate this, let him know that he shall have his lot with Giezi, whose deed he imitates by his wicked exaction."

31. C. 19, Ottobuono 1268, Mansi, xxiii, 1234. The subject is the acceptance of procurations by a visitor when he has not visited.

32. C. 5, Rheims 1157, Mansi, xxi, 844.

33. 21 Henry VIII, c. 13 (1529). This, to be sure, is relatively late, as the secular authorities did not address themselves to the subject of pluralism before Henry VIII's time. The rhetorical style, however, does not differ from that of earlier English statutes.

34. Sometimes the references to social evils are inextricably intertwined with moral vituperations. See the introduction to c. 29 (30), London 1268, Powicke and Cheney, 774, Mansi, xxiii, 1241.

35. The 1179 canon, cited supra, note 29, provides that benefices are to be committed to such persons as will reside and serve the cures in person. The sanction referred to in the 1215 paraphrase applies to violators of this clause and not to violators of the prohibition against pluralism as the paraphrase would indicate. It should be noted in this regard that when the Decretals were compiled the 1215 canon was inserted in the title *De prebendis* to serve as the canon on pluralism, whereas the 1179 one was inserted in the title *De clericis non residentibus* to serve as the canon against nonresidence, although in fact it dealt with both topics.

36. *Rot. Hugh of Wells,* i, 26. A mystery comparable to that discussed in text is presented by Hugh's treatment of a presentee who kept a concubine but had been presented before the promulgation of the council. Id., i, 87.

37. Under the 1179 canon, instituting a man into a second benefice would make him *de jure* as well as *de facto* a pluralist—which he is not allowed to be—

whereas under the 1215 canon institution into the second benefice would automatically deprive him of the first so that he would not be in violation of any
law unless he attempted to hold onto the first as well. Note also that the 1179
canon would seem to call for refusing institution to a man who does not plan
to reside. See note 35 supra. It is so interpreted by Alexander III in c. 4, X, III,
4. As a man who already has another benefice would seem more likely to be
not planning to reside on this one, this principle might support refusing institution to the pluralist.

38. Otto had contented himself with a reference to the 1215 canon and those
who presumed to imperil their salvation by violating it, saying that it seemed
to him to be more a matter of enforcing what had been laid down than of setting
forth new sanctions. C. 13, London 1237, Powicke and Cheney, 251, Mansi,
xxiii, 454.

39. Supra, note 34.

40. C. 4 (1), Reading 1279, Powicke and Cheney, 837, Mansi, xxiv, 257.

41. A literal reading of the two canons in question would seem not to yield
this result. The deprivation of the first benefice under the 1215 canon appears
to depend upon a *de jure* institution into the second benefice, which the 1268
canon would prevent from taking place if the requisite inquiries are not made.
If, on the other hand, the requisite inquiries are made but fail to disclose the
existence of the first benefice, the 1268 canon appears not to invalidate the institution into the second. Rather, the first is lost by force of the 1215 canon,
and the second is legitimately held. In fact, however, no analysis of this kind
seems to have been applied to these canons. This fact provides some additional
evidence that their provisions as to sanctions were not to be literally carried out.

42. C. 25, Lambeth 1281, Powicke and Cheney, 916, Mansi, xxiv, 419.

43. "Ut eorum status patitur ecclesiis sic fraudatis." The provision as to satisfaction for past violations seems to be an innovation.

44. See Van Hove, "Coutume," *D.D.C.*, iv, 731, for a discussion of the circumstances under which canonists, medieval and modern, will allow a custom
to have the force of law in their system.

45. See, e.g., c. 3 (5), Reading 1279, Powicke and Cheney, 837, Mansi, xxiv,
263-64.

46. On this process as regards the dissemination in England of the canons of
the Fourth Lateran Council of 1215, see Gibbs and Lang, *Bishops and Reform,
1215-1272* (Oxford, 1934).

47. The indult says: "To be sure, it may seem superfluous to seek a special
concession concerning that which is conceded by the common law. Since, however, it is customary to stand more in awe of that which is conceded by special
indulgences than of that which is disposed of by general law . . ." This is an indult of Innocent IV to the dean and chapter of Lincoln, dated 1247, authorizing them when their churches are visited to furnish no procuration for the
visitor's retainers beyond the number allowed by the canon issued on the subject
in the Third Lateran Council of 1179. *Reg. Antiq.* no. 260.

48. It should be noted also that the provision for automatic effect did not
prevent the papacy itself from making use of other sanctions on occasion. Note
in this regard the retention in the Decretals of a decision of Alexander III (c. 7,
X, III, 5) allowing the pluralist to choose which of his benefices he will keep.
See also *Cal. Papal. Reg.*, i, 247, containing a papal mandate to the bishop of
Bath and Wells to compel certain pluralists to resign their excess benefices. The
case of Richard Tittesbury, cited infra, note 52, suggests that resignation and

automatic deprivation were not considered mutually exclusive, as we would consider them. Richard was required to resign his preferment, but the papal mandate disposing of it thereafter treats it as long vacant rather than vacant by the resignation. The same treatment is found in the case of the pluralist John ap Rys, *Cal. Papal Reg.*, v, 170 (1398). What I suspect is that the distinction between *de jure* and *de facto* tenure was not fully worked out at the time so that resignation could be treated as a relinquishment of either one.

49. In 1460 the suffragans of Canterbury Province complained to the archbishop that a great part of the population of England was excommunicated *lata sententia*—i.e., by dispositions of automatic effect—a fact which occasioned dissensions and other evils. Mansi, xxxv, 135. See also the discussion of irregularity below, especially the remarks of St. Germain cited infra, note, 79. In both cases, we may suspect special pleading. Even so, a device that can give rise to this kind of criticism has serious drawbacks.

50. Presumably, as the system of plural benefices for members of the bureaucracy was brought more thoroughly under the central direction of the papacy, the pluralist who lacked the necessary papal dispensation would be more apt to be a stranger to the bureaucratic elite represented by the authorities charged with bringing him to book.

51. If the cleric presented to a benefice were to appear in person to respond to an inquiry of this kind, he would have to give some account of how he had been supported in the past. Such an account might have given a chance of turning up any other benefices he held, albeit not a foolproof chance, as he might have some other source of income to show. Furthermore, a practice evidently grew up of allowing a cleric to be instituted into a benefice through his proctor without showing up in person. This was denounced at a 1460 council in Canterbury, Mansi, xxxv, 136. Another way in which the ordinary course of administration might have turned up a pluralist was through discovering on a routine visitation of one of his churches that he did not reside there. This was not very satisfactory either, as there might be a number of reasons, legitimate or illegitimate, besides pluralism for not residing. As the nonresident would have on his own person any documents relevant to his reasons for not residing, it would be necessary to find him before passing on them—a task of considerable difficulty in the case of a nonresident. See Capes, "Introduction," *Reg. T. Cantilupe,* pp. xxxv–xxxvii. Then, the nonresident when found might exhibit a valid reason—such as the royal service—for not residing on any of his benefices. This, of course, would tell us nothing about how many benefices he held.

52. Oesterle, "Irrégularitiés," *D.D.C.,* vi, 42, 54–55. See the case of Richard Tittesbury, *Cal. Papal Reg.,* 88–89 (1398). Richard sought and received absolution from irregularities incurred on ten different grounds, including bloodshed, simony, and saying mass in unconsecrated places. According to Emden, *A Biographical Register of the University of Oxford to 1500,* iii (Oxford, 1969), 1880, he was ordained in 1395, so he must have been a young priest with a foot just planted on the ladder of preferment when he made a clean breast of all this. It may have been increased maturity that led him to do so, or he may have been afraid for his career if he should be found out later on. All ended happily for him. After resigning his preferment, he was restored to it by papal provision. *Cal. Papal Reg.* v, 174. The provision recited that the benefices involved had long been vacant—presumably Richard's irregularity had made his institution into them nugatory.

53. Supra, note 40.

54. C. 8, Third Lateran 1179, Mansi, xxii, 222, c. 2, X, III, 8; Thom., iii, 528–29.

55. The automatic deprivation would seem at first blush to be of interest to the patron, who could put a new man into the benefice, the ordinary, who could do so after six months (see *Reg. Sudbury, London,* i, 24), and the parishioners, who could show that the person claiming their tithes was not entitled to them. In fact, though, none of these interests contributed significantly to enforcing the laws against pluralism.

56. C un. title III in Extravag. Joan. XXII. After a sufficiently long vacancy, the right to collate to a benefice would have devolved upon the pope under the earlier legislation. C. 3, X, I, 10. While in theory this devolution did not take place unless the ordinary had known of the vacancy for the stipulated period (ibid., Mollat, "Bénéfices ecclésiastiques en occident," *D.D.C.,* ii, 406, 414–15), it seems likely that the popes provided to such benefices on petitions reciting that they had been vacant for the required period without knowing whether or not the ordinary had been aware of the vacancy. Richard Tittesbury's case, supra, note 52, is evidently an example of this; so, perhaps, is the case at *Cal. Papal Reg.,* x, 400–401 (1448). It appears incidentally, that persons seeking preferment through royal rather than papal bounty also made use of *Execrabilis* to establish a vacancy of the benefices they sought. Maitland, "Execrabilis in the Court of Common Pleas," in *Roman Canon Law in England* (1898), c. 5.

57. Jombart, "Erreur commune," *D.D.C.,* v, 441.

58. C. 22 (23), Powicke and Cheney, 770, Mansi, xxiii, 1237-38. The translation quoted in text is from Johnson 236, except for the word "manifestly," which I have added.

59. For examples of papal confirmations of appropriations already approved by local ordinaries and where no ground of invalidity is apparent, see *Cal. Papal Reg.,* i, 240 (1248); v, 157 (1398); v, 176 (1398). See also id., iii, 305 (1348), for a papal faculty to a bishop to make appropriations.

60. See validations of collations to benefices at id., iii, 282 (1348); v, 165 (1398); an election of a prior at id., v, 151 (1398); an ordination of a vicarage at id., v, 189 (1398); a foundation of chantry at id., iii, 300 (1348).

61. O'Neill, *Papal Rescripts of Favor* (Washington, 1930), 117–34; Naz, "Rescrit," *D.D.C.,* vii, 607, 618–24. The doctrine set forth in text is greatly ramified by such matters as the distinction between rescripts *motu proprio* and other rescripts or that between "subreption" (concealment of a material fact) and "obreption" (setting forth as true something that is false).

62. C. 14, I, 6 in VI° (emphasis added). The automatic deprivation provided in this canon seems to have been caught up into the system of papal provisions in much the same way as that provided in *Execrabilis.* See cases in *Cal. Papal Reg.,* v, 103, 104 (1398). Here, however, as the vacated benefice was not reserved to the pope, the patron had a space of time to fill the benefice. See id., v, 166 (1398), for a case of a priest who came by his benefice in this way but received a papal collation to the same benefice because he was unsure of his title.

63. C. 6 (7), London 1268, Powicke and Cheney, 754-55, Mansi, xxiii, 1223.

64. The following discussion is based mainly on Naz, "Dispense," *D.D.C.,* iv, 1283; Mortimer, "Dispensation in the Western Church," in *Dispensation*

Report, 1; Alivisatos, " 'Economy' from the Orthodox Point of View," in *Dispensation Report,* 27. The practice of dispensation applies only to those rules that can be assigned a human, rather than a divine, origin.

65. Lefebvre, "Natural Equity and Canonical Equity," *Nat. Law Forum,* viii (1963), 122, 123-38.

66. *Th. Code* 1:2:2.

67. C. 1-9, 16, C, XXV, q. 1. See especially c. 7, taken from a letter of Pope Zosimus in 410. "Nor, indeed, can the authority of this see change what is laid down by the holy Fathers or concede anything against it. For with us there lives a firmly rooted antiquity, which the decrees of the Fathers have guarded in due reverence [cui decreta Patrum sanxere reverentiam]." See also c. 16 from Pope Leo IV in the mid-ninth century: "By the divine permission we are so far made shepherds of men that we ought by no means to go outside what our Fathers have established, whether in the holy canons or in worldly laws, and we do indeed act against their most salutary dispositions if we do not conserve inviolate what they, by divine counsels, have laid down."

68. Dictum to C. XXV, q. 1.

69. Naz, "Dispense," *D.D.C.,* iv, 1290-91. Thomassin disagrees, holding that extra compensation for noble or learned clerics was for the common good of the church. Thom., v, 108.

70. In addition to the temporizing, already referred to, on the part of Archbishop Pecham, see Capes, "Introduction," *Reg. T. Cantilupe,* pp. xxxv-xxxvii; Thom., iv, 621. It would seem also that the constitution *Ordinarii Locorum* of the Council of Lyons (1274), c. 3, I, 16 in VI°, was responsive to a certain tolerance of pluralists on the part of local bishops. See Waugh, "Archbishop Pecham and Pluralities," *E.H.R.* xxviii (1913), 625.

71. See Lefebvre, "Privilège," *D.D.C.,* vii, 225, 228. See c. 1, 2, I, II in VI°, for examples of limitations on the effect of common forms; see *Cal. Papal Reg.,* v, 87-88 (1398), for an example of a dispensation from such limitations.

72. Pantin 40. The broad reference to the sacred canons in this case seems to reinforce the conception advanced in text that they are basically conceived of as formulations of moral principles.

73. I say this despite the fact that internal analysis in the modern sense seems to have been an important part of the work of the late medieval canonists.

74. Gibbs and Lang, *Bishops and Reform, 1215-72,* is devoted, especially in the latter part, to an examination of the manner in which the decrees of the Fourth Lateran Council of 1215 were disseminated in England. Of particular interest is the concluding discussion, which deals with attitudes moving the decision of the local bishops as to which of the canons of the general council were the most important.

75. "The Path of the Law," *Harv. L. Rev.,* x (1897), 457.

76. See Pantin 39, where Bishop Walter Cantilupe refers to "young men, ferocious and strenuous," who "would face the greatest dangers, sooner than let themselves be deprived of their benefices and reduced to a single benefice."

77. See Thompson 234-35, 237, for cases where excommunication is disregarded. It appears that a man who regarded himself as innocent in the matter on which his excommunication was founded would be apt to regard him-

self as not bound by the excommunication. Hill, "Theory and Practice of Excommunication in Medieval England," *Hist. N.S.*, xlii (1957), 1, 5–6.

78. Hill, "Public Penance," 216; Woodcock 95–97.

79. St. Germain, *The Addicions of Salem and Byzance* (London, 1534), fol. 5, suggests a further source of ineffectiveness in that the grounds of automatic irregularity are so numerous that no priest can hope to avoid them all. This seems an exaggeration.

80. It should be noted also that the forms of misbehavior to which irregularity was attached were not ones that a reasonably sober-minded cleric in middle life would find it particularly difficult to renounce. See note 52, supra.

81. Thompson 235–36.

82. Thompson 237 has a case of a man who has been absent five years. Cf., *Reg. Trillek,* 468 (two years).

83. Generally, there was supposed to be a monition before a person was excommunicated. C. 47, Fourth Lateran 1215, c. 48, X, V, 39. So also in many cases there was supposed to be a monition before he was deprived of a benefice. Mollat, "Bénéfices ecclésiastique en occident," *D.D.C.,* ii, 406, 433. On nonresidence, see, in addition to the case quoted above, *Reg. Trillek,* 110; *Reg. Sudbury, London,* i 223; *Reg. Chichele,* iii, 381. There is, however, a case in Thompson 231 of a man put to penance for not residing. In this case, the accompanying monition threatened excommunication rather than deprivation if the monition were not obeyed. On forbidden employments, see c. 16, X, III, 1; on concubinage, c. 3, X, III, 2.

84. E.g., Thompson, 206–19 (violence); 221 (sorcery); *Reg. Trillek,* 98 (adultery). See also the cases referred to, Hill, "Public Penance," 217–19.

85. C. 12, 13, D. 81, both taken from the Apostolic Canons, seem to be inconsistent on this point.

86. Hill, "Public Penance."

87. Thompson 206–46.

88. Hill, "Public Penance," 216. The examples that follow are all taken from id., 217–24.

89. See also "Kent Visitations," xxxii, 164, where a knight is let off for a series of sexual offenses with a twenty-mark donation to the poor "quia non decet militem facere publicam penitenciam."

90. Hill, "Public Penance," 223.

91. Id., 219.

92. To be sure, the medieval man was more concerned with appearances than we are. John Wathe, a forger of papal documents, after performing his penance of riding in a procession with the documents hung from his neck and a high paper cap on his head with "Falsarius Litterarum Apostolicarum" in large letters for all to read, is said to have remarked that he would rather have been put to death. And even the papal penitentiary called it a "penitentiam publicam et horribilem." *Reg. Chichele,* iii, 92–93, 100–101, iv, 287.

93. *Reg. Chichele,* iii, 76–78.

94. See Perry, "Introduction," *Reg. Trillek,* pp. iii–v; Hale, *Precedents and Proceedings in Criminal Causes, 1475-1640* (London, 1847).

95. C. 3, V, 9 in VI°, Gratian's material is c. 7–11, D. 81. See also c. 6, X, V, 37. Innocent III in c. 35, X, V, 39, seems to envisage imprisonment for incorrigible clerics who cannot be safely kept in a monastery, although he is not perfectly clear on the point. The lay statute 1 Hen. 7, c. 4 (1485),

authorizing ordinaries to impose a term of imprisonment on clerics for incontinence, is worded as if they had not previously had that power. Perhaps the *locus penitentiae*, as a form of penance, had to be voluntarily submitted to. Refusal so to submit, however, would be grounds for excommunication, whereby the offender could be put in the secular prison until absolved. I can find no canonical basis for the three entries *Cal. Papal Reg.*, i, 249 (1247), 303 (1253), 424 (1266), which seem to envisage the imprisonment of forgers of papal documents as a distinct punishment. Nor do I find later examples of this treatment.

96. Gabel, 92–115; Pollock and Maitland, i, 439–57. I gather that the imprisonment in these cases was regarded canonically as a form of custody pending final disposition of the case. The final disposition would require a canonical purgation, which the lay courts prevented from taking place.

97. See Archbishop Islip's constitution on this, Mansi, xxvi, 295 (1351). See also the case of *Shirbourne* v. *Jenycoght de Gales, Rot. Parl.*, v, 106b (1444), involving a cleric who had himself committed to the bishop's prison on a trumped-up felony charge in order to escape confinement in a lay prison for debt.

98. On the pledge of faith, see Pollock and Maitland, i, 128–29; ii, 197–98. As to restitution, see Hill, "Public Penance," 217.

99. Woodcock 87–92, 107–08.

100. See Ottobuono's language in c. 19 (20), London 1268, Powicke and Cheney, 768–69, Mansi, xxiii, 1235–36. As to corporal penances being taken more seriously than money payments, note the request of the clergy to the bishops that corporal penances be imposed—presumably instead of pecuniary—in cases of notorious and repeated adultery. Art. 8, London 1399, Mansi, xxvi, 924. In 1413 the Commons complained to Henry V about money penances for adultery or lechery: "so that your lieges of your kingdom are impoverished, and such sins are the more used and sustained, whereas by the law of God they should chastize such sinners by corporal penance to the end that such sin be the sooner put down among the people." *Rot. Parl.*, iv, 9a. Deriving personal gain from money penances is denounced by Alexander III in c. 3, X, V, 37, and in an English synod of 1295, *Reg. Pontissara*, 207–39. The approved practice was to have the money payment go to the poor, as was done in "Kent Visitations," xxxii, 164.

101. The prevalence of money commutation was a constant ground of Puritan denunciation of the entire medieval penitential apparatus as carried over into post-Reformation Anglicanism.

102. Naz, "Séquestre," *D.D.C.*, vii, 973.

103. C. 16, X, III, 4.

104. Churchill, i, 118; cf., id., 325, where it is used to compel a man to come into court.

105. C. 28, X, II, 28, seems to treat this as a means of providing for the cure *pendente lite;* so does c. 2168 of the 1918 Code. Title IV of book III of the Decretals, dealing with nonresidence, has only one canon, c. 11, that expressly addresses itself to the eventuality that the incumbent cannot be found. That canon provides not for sequestration but for deprivation six months after a citation is made public for the third time. Cf. *Reg. Trillek*, 46–48. This is to be followed by personal sanctions and excommunication if the ousted cleric does not return to the obedience of his ordinary. Canon 2381 of the 1918 Code provides for depriving a nonresident of the fruits of

his benefice, but so far from using the benefice as a means of reaching the incumbent, it uses the incumbent as a means of reaching the benefice, calling upon him to forward his receipts to the ordinary. Thus, neither medieval nor modern Catholic canon law arrived at a general use of sequestration to coerce the nonresident in the manner of the nineteenth-century Anglican practice initiated with 43 Geo. 3, c. 84 (1803).

106. C. 17 (18) London 1268, Powicke and Cheney, 766–67, Mansi, xxiii, 1233–34. For examples of sequestrations for dilapidation, see *Reg. Trillek,* 109; *Reg. Lacy,* i, 181.

107. In the Decretals, see c. 4, X, III, 48 (*cogi debeant*). C. 1 of the same title calls for the assistance of the beneficed clergy in the repair of their church but sets up no sanction. Gratian's material is c. 10, C. X, q. 1; c. 3, D, 1 *de cons.*

108. "Sequestration," Burn, iii, 316–19. For examples of the royal writ involved, see *Reg. Trillek,* 256–57. It appears that the kings used this process to reach clerics for other purposes as well as the collection of debts. Id., 326. The 1918 Code (c. 1673) provides for a comparable process, but the compilers give no source for their enactment in the previous law. A more general use of *in rem* sanctions by ecclesiastical authorities on their own is suggested by a letter in *Reg. T. Cantilupe,* 149 (bishop of Hereford, 1275–82), ordering his deans to warn the beneficed clergy not to store tithes elsewhere than on glebe land—as some have done to avoid ecclesiastical distraint—on pain of immediate sequestration. I can find no indication of the nature or use of the ecclesiastical distraint to which Cantilupe refers. But cf. *Reg. Lacy,* i, 79 (sequestration of goods).

109. Ullman, supra, note 7 at 74. "The pope's jurisdiction and law were concerned with the conduct and actions of Christians, not with their (dead) possessions."

110. Some of the cases of sequestration in the English materials seem to involve penalties of this kind. That is, they are imposed after appropriate proceedings and constitute partial deprivations of ecclesiastical income. E.g., *Reg. T. Corbridge,* i, 95. This may also be what is envisaged by c. 39, Exeter 1287. Powicke and Cheney, 1033–34, Mansi, xxiv, 821. See also c. 67 (37) Worcester 1240, Powicke and Cheney, 313, Mansi, xxiii, 538. The distinction between this use of sequestration and that previously discussed depends on whether the sequestration is imposed only after a canonical proceeding directed at the incumbent personally.

111. Mollat, supra, note 83. It appears that this principle was departed from in order to reward the zeal of informers in search of papal provisions. See *Cal. Papal Reg.,* v, 98 173 (1398), for mandates ordering the trial of a beneficed cleric for an offense, the accused to be deprived if found guilty and the informer put into his benefice.

112. See in this connection c. 11, X, I, 2, an interpretation by Innocent III of a statute of the University of Paris providing for the dismissal of a member who violates the statutes after three monitions. Innocent says that unless the statute expressly provides otherwise, the person so dismissed is to be reinstated upon his repentance and promise to reform.

113. Hill, "Public Penance," 218. C. 1, C. XXI, q. 2, seems more severe.

114. On physical disability, see c. 3, 5, 6, X, III, 6. C. 4 of the same title seems at first blush to envisage his removal on a pension "ab administrationis debet officio removeri," but in the light of the other canons, I would not so interpret it. On inability to speak the language, see c. 10, X, I, 9.

115. C. 1, X, III, 6. The provisions of c. 2147 of the 1918 Code, allowing the ordinary to remove a man from his benefice in the interest of an effective ministry rather than by way of punishment, are modern in origin. Naz "Offices ecclésiastiques," *D.D.C.*, vi, 1074, 1100. The circumstances authorizing such a procedure seem to be drawn from the traditional grounds for appointing a coadjutor (which procedure is preserved in c. 475 and is to be used instead of privation unless it appears that the good of souls cannot be served that way) and the grounds listed by Innocent III, c. 10, X, I, 9, as warranting the resignation of a benefice.

116. Compare the foregoing analysis with Le Bras, "Prolégomènes," *Histoire du droit et des institutiones de l'église en occident,* i (Paris, 1960), 23–29.

4: Provincial and Diocesan Authorities

1. It may have been this process of decentralization that evoked the prohibition in c. 1, Tours 1163, Mansi, xxi, 1176, c. 8, X, III, 5. The process did in fact run its course by the end of the twelfth century, though there are later examples. See *Cal. Pat. Rolls, 1396-99,* 377 (1398). On the philosophical and legal conceptions that protected the decentralized endowments and functions, see Barraclough, 76–89; Gierke, *Political Theories of the Middle Ages,* ed. and tr. Maitland (1900), 7–8.

2. On exemptions from episcopal jurisdiction as referred to in text, see Pantin 93–94; Knowles, M.O., 575–91; Cheney, *Episcopal Visitation,* 36–53, Lunt, i, c. 2. For royal claims to fill diocesan offices, see *Reg. T. Cantilupe,* 1; *R. v. Archbishop of York,* 17 Edw. 2, R.S. xxxim, 524. For an exercise of papal power, see *Reg. Chichele,* i, 234–37, discussed in id., lxi–lxiii.

3. On capitular endowments and prebends, see Edwards, 5–6, 33–34, 98. *Bishop Osmund's Register,* i (R.S., lxxviii a), 335, sets forth the foundation document of Salisbury Cathedral. On cathedral peculiars, see Edwards 126–28; on the scope and limits of the bishop's rights over his chapter, see id., 113–35; Thompson 73–75; Knowles, R.O., i, 254–62. It is interesting that even after most of the disputes were settled, bishops tended to keep away from their see cities as much as possible in order to avoid becoming embroiled with their chapters. Edwards 100, 104–5; Thompson 74.

4. On advising the bishop, see Edwards 100-101. On *sede vacante* administration, see Churchill, i, 161–240, 551–70. On episcopal elections, see c.6, I, A. As to residence and employment of secular canons, see Edwards 33–96. On bestowal of canonries, see id., 84–88, 121–22. The administrative advantages of secular over monastic chapters led late in the twelfth century to two abortive attempts to supplant the monastic chapter at Canterbury and a temporarily successful one to do the same at Coventry. Knowles, M.O., 318–27.

5. On the frequency and scope of exemptions, see Knowles, M.O., 586, 600–606, 633; Knowles, R.O., i, 98. In addition to gaining exemption from the bishops, Bury bought off most of the king's rights in 1448 for a fixed a annual payment. *Cal. Pat. Rolls, 1446-52,* 233. In the same year, the bishop of Norwich got a papal indult to override the exemptions of the houses in his diocese, *Cal. Papal Reg.,* x, 37, but I find no indication that he made it good against Bury.

6. Denton, *English Royal Free Chapels* (Manchester, 1970); Thompson 75

on Richmond, see id., 60; Thompson, "Introduction," *Reg. Greenfield,* i, pp. xiii–xiv.

7. The following discussion of the archdeacon is based on Thompson 56–64, and Amanieu, "Archidiacre," *D.D.C.,* i, 948. See also Thompson, "Diocesan Organization in the Middle Ages: Archdeacons and Rural Deans," *British Academy Prcdgs.,* xxix (1943), 153. On the archdeaconry as a benefice, see Edwards 252. *Reg. Antiq.* no 346 (1151–55), is an example of a document creating such a benefice. As to the archdeacon's duties, see art. 3–5, 1233 questionnaire (supervising clergy); *Reg. Grandisson,* xli (same); Sheehan 199–200 (probate business); Woodcock 68–71 (correction of morals).

8. As to financial exactions, c. 4, Third Lateran 1179, Mansi, xxii, 219, forbids archdeacons to levy taxes. The late thirteenth-century synodal statutes collected in Powicke and Cheney, 700, 721, *Reg. Pontissara,* 207–39, limit a payment called the Archdeacon's pig. Excessive procurations were evidently the subject of an automatic censure: see the absolution in *Cal. Papal Reg.,* i, 579 (1298). Commuting visitations is denounced in various places, including c. 19, Ottobuono 1268, Powicke and Cheney, 768, Johnson 233. Among canonical denunciations of the acceptance of pecuniary fines in lieu of corporal penances, special reference to archdeacons is made in c. 20, London 1237, Powicke and Cheney, 254, Mansi, xxiii, 457, in the synodal statutes referred to above, and in *Reg. Grandisson,* 807, para. 7.

9. The discussion of these two offices is based on Thompson 46–56. On the bishop's right to sit in his consistory court or reserve particular matters to himself, see the historical discussion in *Davey* v. *Hinde,* [1901] P. 95 (Chichester Consistory, 1900), prohibition denied sub nom. *R.* v. *Tristram,* [1901] 2 K.B. 141, reversed and prohibition granted [1902] 1 K.B. 816 (C.A.). The facilities for hearing reserved cases often developed into additional courts. Churchill, i, 470–99. On the crystallization of functions after the Reformation, see *Anonymous,* 11 Mod. 46, 88 Eng. Rep. 874 (1705).

10. This discussion of the rural dean is based on Thompson 63–69. See also Jacob, "Introduction," *Reg. Chichele,* i, p. lxvii. For the situation on the continent, see Amanieu, "Archiprêtre," *D.D.C.,* i, 1004, and for the post-Reformation situation in England, Marchant, *The Church under the Law* (Cambridge, 1969), 127 and passim. Examples of the functions referred to in text are: *Reg. Trillek,* 30–31, 291 (serving citations); id., 99, and *Reg. Lacy,* i, 143 (promulgating excommunications); *Reg. Chichele,* iii, 381 (admonishing to reside); cf. *Reg. Lacy,* i, 6, 48 (making chaplains serve cures); *Reg. Chichele,* iv, 116, 118, 119 (reporting on public penances); *Reg. Trillek,* 109 (checking dilapidations).

11. For examples of ad hoc commissions developing into offices, see Churchill, i, 446–50, 483–86, 486–88. For cases of duplicative commissions, see *Reg. Trillek,* 118, 119, 129, 141, and 234, 243; *Reg. Lacy,* i, 16. On the royal attitude toward nonroutine handling of cases, see Holdsworth, i, 276–84; *Rot. Parl.,* i, 290a (1314–15).

12. Though he could remove it any time before judgment. Churchill, i, 469; *Reg. Trillek,* 234.

13. This section is largely based on Cantor, *Church, Kingship, and Lay Investiture* (temp. William II and Henry I); Knowles, *The Episcopal Colleagues of Thomas Becket* (Cambridge, 1951) (temp. Henry II); Cheney 19–41 (1170–1213); Gibbs and Lang (1215–1272); Moorman 158–209 (thirteenth century); Smith, *Episcopal Appointments* (temp. Edward II); Edwards, "The Political Importance

of the English Bishops in the Time of Edward II," *E.H.R.*, lix (1944), 311; Highfield, "The English Hierarchy in the Reign of Edward II," *T.R.H.S.*, 5th ser., vi, 115 (1956); Pantin 9-26 (fourteenth century); Thompson 1-46 (mostly fifteenth century); Scofield, *The Life and Reign of Edward IV* (1923) i, 79, 86, 87, 134; Smith, *Tudor Prelates and Politics* (Princeton, 1953) (temp. Henry VIII and Edward VI).

14. Churchill, passim. On specific functions, see: c. 13, Third Lateran 1179, Mansi, xxii, 225, c. 3, X, III, 4 (filling benefices); *Reg. Trillek*, 168-69, 234 (intervening in lawsuits); c. 5, X, III, 6 and *Cal. Papal Reg.*, i, 250 (1248) (appointing coadjutors); Kemp, 1-61 (provincial synods); Amanieu, "Appel," *D.D.C.*, i, 763, 794-97 (hearing appeals).

15. Kemp, passim. The canonical basis for Convocation taxing the clergy seems to be c. 19, Third Lateran 1179, Mansi, xxii, 228, c. 4, X, III, 49. Examples of grievances appear in *Rot. Parl.*, ii, 129a-130b (1341), 244a-245b (1351-52), iii, 25a-27b (1377), 494a (1402); *Reg. Chichele*, iii, 76-78 (1421). For a draft of another set, evidently toned down before it was presented, see Powicke and Cheney, 1338ff, *Reg. Pontissara*, 771ff.

16. On York, see Brentano 67-82; Richie, *The Ecclesiastical Courts of York*, 11-14 (1956); Kemp 118; Johnson 513 (wholesale adoption of Canterbury legislation by York in 1462).

17. Churchill, ii, 207-10 (the "Black Book of the Arches").

18. On the advantages of litigating at Canterbury, see Jacob, "Introduction," *Reg. Chichele*, i, p. clxv-clxxi. For examples of the archiepiscopal boasting referred to in text, see Churchill, i, 431, 435 n. Compare the language used by the popes in praising their jurisdiction, e.g., c. 8, C. II, q. 6. There is a complaint about diocesan judges in art. 11, London 1399, Mansi, xxvi, 924. For an attempt to improve a diocesan court system, see *Reg. Grandisson*, 807-9 (1335-36).

19. On the failure of suffragans to render justice, see *Reg. Trillek*, 168-69, 234. For the abuse referred to in text, see Churchill, i, 441 n. The canon of the Fourth Lateran on *provocacio* is c. 35, Mansi, xxii, 1022, c. 59, X, II, 27. Examples of the procedure in *Reg. Trillek*, 155 and 170, comply with that canon's requirement that a reasonable cause be shown but not with the further requirement that the cause be passed on in the first instance by the lower court. The Statute of Citations is 23 Hen. 8, c. 9 (1532). The practice of issuing letters of request is discussed in *Jones* v. *Jones*, Hobart, 185, 80 Eng. Rep., 332 (K.B., c. 1615); *Sheppard* v. *Bennet*, L.R. 2 A. & E. 335 (Arches, 1869) reversed 6 Moore N.S. 59, 16 Eng. Rep. 649 (P.C.).

20. Churchill, i, 460-65. *Acta Langton* no. 143 seems to be the same procedure in an early inchoate form. *Reg. T. Cantilupe*, 197, has a tuitorial appeal from papal judges-delegate, a procedure forbidden by Archbishop Stratford in 1342. *Cal. Papal Reg.*, v. 159 (1399), may be an example of papal resistance to encroachment on its jurisdiction by Canterbury. Churchill's lone example of a tuitorial appeal from York Province was part of the convoluted York-Durham litigation and cannot be taken too seriously. Brentano 39-40.

21. Graham, "Introduction," *Reg. Winchelsea*, i, pp. xx-xxv; Gibbs and Lang, 171-73.

22. Papal taxation of the clergy is discussed at greater length in chap. 6, royal taxation in vol. 2. The primary example of a royal concession in exchange for a subsidy is the Statute for the Clergy, 25 Edw. 3, st. 3 (1350). For ex-

amples of royal resistance to papal subsidies, see the letters: Mansi, xxv, 517 (1312); *Cal. Close Rolls, 1346-49*, 270; *Reg. Trillek*, 299-300 (1347); *Rot. Parl.*, iii, 405a; *Cal. Close Rolls, 1389-92*, 27 (1389). Edward I's response to *Clericis laicos* was to seize all the temporalities of the church and exact a fine for their return. *Cal. Close Rolls, 1296-1302*, 14; *Lincs. Assize Rolls, 1298*, ed. Thompson (L.R.S., xxxvi, 1944), 181. On papal legates, see Lunt, "William Testa," *E.H.R.*, lxi (1946), 332. *Lincs. Assize Rolls, 1298*, supra, no. 400, refers to a "procession" against the cardinals who came to collect subsidies in 1296 and 1297. A royal subbailiff was presented for taking sixpence to let certain villagers out of attending. It is difficult to know what the procession was: it would be pleasant, but probably anachronistic, to think of it as the counterpart of a modern political demonstration. Treatment of papal legates became more decorous but no less firm by the fifteenth century. *Rot. Parl.*, iii, 616 (1407); *Reg. Chichele*, i, pp. xlvii-xlix.

23. Capes, "Introduction," *Reg. T. Cantilupe*, p. xxxiii.

24. Bennett, "Medieval Ordination Lists in the English Episcopal Registers," in *Essays Presented to Sir Hilary Jenkinson*, ed. Davies (1957), 20.

25. Churchill, i, 104-5. But see *Reg. Grandisson*, 331, and *Reg. Lacy*, i, 3, where the whole burden of inquiry is placed on the ordaining bishop.

26. Bennett, supra, note 24; Naz, "Titre," *D.D.C.*, vii, 1275; Bowker 61-64; Heath 17.

27. *Romanus Pontifex*, 14 October 1568, *Codicis Juris Cononici, Fontes*, no. 129, ed. Gasparri (Rome, 1947).

28. Naz, "Séminaire," *D.D.C.*, vi, 929, 931; Moorman 198-99, 231-32; Heath 17; Bowker 42-61; Rashdell, *Medieval Universities* (2d ed., 1936) iii, 451-52.

29. Thom., iii, 311-12; Hill, "Public Penance," 218.

30. Carr, *Vocation to the Priesthood* (Washington, 1950); Thom., iii, 312.

31. On changing dioceses, see c. 1, Oxford 1322, Johnson 333-34. I do not read this as requiring all priests from outside the diocese to be licensed by the bishop but only those who lack the customary letters of orders to establish their status. Cf. *Reg. Lacy*, i, 190; Jombart, "Celebret," *D.D.C.*, iii, 126, 128. The twelfth-century canons requiring household chaplains to be licensed (London 1138, Mansi, xxi, 517; cf. c. 10, Rheims 1148, Mansi, xxi, 719) seem not to have been enforced in later centuries. The 1233 questionnaire, art. 13, asks if the parish priest is adequately paid by the incumbent, and one diocesan statute, c. 28, Exeter 1287, Powicke and Cheney, 1025-26, Mansi, xxiv, 815, fixes his compensation at 40/ (60/ according to some manuscripts). The only mention of tenure is c. 25, loc. incert. 1236, Johnson 141, which admonishes rectors not to remove annual chaplains without reasonable cause but says nothing about enforcement. On making chaplains serve cures, see Wilkins, iii (1350); *Reg. Lacy*, i, 6, 9, 48.

32. *Reg. Chichele*, i, pp. lxxii, 178-229; *Reg. Lacy*, iii, 47. Cf. *Reg. Trillek*, 39, 41; *Rot. Hugh of Wells*, i, 18, 27, 37, 40; iii, 108.

33. Strawley, "Grosseteste's Administration of the Diocese of Lincoln," in *Robert Grosseteste*, ed. Callus (Oxford, 1955), 146, 158-60; *Rot. Hugh of Wells*, i, pp. xiii-xiv, 19, 67, 136; Thompson 243 n. It was not easy to get a sound canonical basis for such a practice. Hugh put unqualified presentees into benefices by less than canonical institution (cf. *Rot. Hugh of Wells*, i, 97; *Rot. Grosseteste*, 41; *Reg. T. Cantilupe*, 24), a device that looked a good deal like

the forbidden *commendam.* Thompson, "Pluralism," Leprat, "Commende," *D.D.C.,* iii, 1029, 1035–38; *Reg. T. Cantilupe,* 1 n. Bekynton made the presentee promise, and sometimes post bond, to resign if he failed to bring himself up to standard within a specified time. See *Reg. Bekynton,* xxi, and cases cited there.

34. Art. 12, London 1399, Mansi, xxvi, 924; id., xxxv, 136 (1460).

35. Thompson 238–41 has a set of routine simony cases. The oath is set up in c. 23, Oxford 1222, Powicke and Cheney, 113, On superannuation, see Churchill, i, 118; Moorman 201–2; *Rot. Grosseteste,* p. iv; *Reg. Chichele,* i, 159–60, iv, 289–90; *Reg. Lacy,* i, 147–48, 160–61.

36. The devices in question are enumerated in Archbishop Courtney's 1392 constitution, Johnson 447–52, and discussed in Thompson 107–9. On exchanges and chop-churches, see also Mollat, "Bénéfices ecclésiastiques en occident," *D.D.C.,* ii, 406, 435–36; Heath 44–47; Bowker 73–74. Lambarde's reference to a chop-church is cited in *O.E.D.* The first use of the word shown in *O.E.D.* is in Courtney's constitution; the last is in a work of 1695. The 1869 case referred to in text is *Lee* v. *Merest,* 39 L.J. Ecc. 53 (Arches, 1869). After the Reformation, it became possible for a cleric to buy the patronage rights and present himself; thus, the chop-church could operate like a real estate broker.

37. *Rot. Parl.,* iii, 301a (1392–93); iv, 81b (1415); Art. 28, Mansi, xxvi, 927 (1399); Jacob, "Introduction," *Reg. Chichele,* i, pp. clii–clix; id., iii, 41–44 (1417); 72–75 (1421). Compare Paul, *The Deployment and Payment of the Clergy* (Westminster, 1964), 107–9.

38. Art. 3–5, 9, 17, 18, 28, 46, 50, 1233 Questionnaire; "Kent Visitations"; "Hereford Visitations"; *Lincoln Visitations,* passim; Bowker 106–8, 116–29; Heath 104–12. For the attribution of the 1233 Questionnaire to Grosseteste, see Frere, "Introduction," *Visitation Articles and Injunctions* (Alcuin Club Coll. xiv, 1910), 98; cf. Powicke and Cheney, 262 n.

39. "Kent Visitations," passim; "Hereford Visitations," *E.H.R.,* xliv, 282, xlv, 99; *Reg. Chichele,* i, pp. cxlvii–cl; *Reg. Trillek,* 107; Thompson 132–60.

40. Pollock and Maitland, i, 441; *Reg. Pontissara,* 226, 773–74; *Reg. Trillek,* 291, 339; *Reg. Lacy,* i, 119–120.

41. The canon *Si quis* is c. 15, Second Lateran 1139, Mansi, xxi, 530, c.29, C. XVII, q. 4. On dissemination, see *Reg. Chichele,* i, pp. cxxvii–cxxix; on treatment of offenders, c. 11, X, V, 39 (Alexander III); *Reg. Sutton,* iii, p. xlvii; Thompson 206–19; Woodcock 81. On abuse of lay process, see *Reg. Chichele,* iii, 76–78 (1421); *Reg. Trillek,* 323–24 (1349); Woodcock 88–89. Henry VI's pardon is 27 Hen. 6, c. 6 (1448).

42. On armed occupation of churches, see Hill, "Public Penance," passim; *Reg. Sutton,* passim (28 cases); *Reg. Trillek,* 99. The case of the sheriff's brother is *Acta Langton,* no. 6 (1213). As to protection money, see c. 1, London 1151, Mansi, xxi, 750–51 (*tenseria*); cf. Wood, *English Monasteries and their Patrons in the Thirteenth Century* (Oxford, 1955). Examples of the confrontations referred to in text are *Acta Langton* no. 109–10, and *Reg. T. Cantilupe,* pp. xxvii–xxix, 153, involving secular estates; *Hereford* v. *Appleby, Rot. Parl.,* ii, 32a (1330), involving a benefice; *Reg. Trillek,* 181, and *Cal. Pat. Rolls, 1348–50,* 245 (1348), involving jurisdictional disputes. On the more minor invasions, see *Reg. Chichele,* iv, 104–5 (1414) (tolls); *Reg. Trillek,* 36 (the bishop's fair), 33–34 (trees), 83, 86 (hunting), 109 (swans).

43. In addition to the regular common-law remedies, commissions of oyer and terminer were sometimes issued, *Sutton's Petition, Rot. Parl,* i, 401a (1321-22); *Cal. Pat. Rolls, 1348-50,* 245 (1348), and the commissioners of the peace sometimes dealt with offenses against church property. *Some Sessions of the Peace in Lincolnshire, 1381-96,* ed. Kimball (L.R.S., lxix, 1955), xxxiii. Ironically, in a number of these cases, the offender escaped through benefit of clergy. Id., 26; *Rot. Parl.,* v, 632b (1467-68). On the royal attitude toward the use of ecclesiastical censures, see *R.* v. *Bishop of Worcester,* S.S., lviii, 1 (K.B., 1294); *Archbishop of York* v. *Burgesses of Kingston on Hull, Rot. Parl.,* i, 431a (1325).

44. E.g., *Reg. T. Cantilupe,* 97; *Reg. Grandisson,* pp. xvii, xix, 427-28. The peasant was exhibited by Prof. F. R. H. du Boulay in a lecture at Lambeth Palace, 2 Nov., 1960.

45. C. 9, Westminster 1200, Johnson 89. This of course is what Chaucer's Parson was ful loth to do. Moorman 125. Synodal statutes such as c. 44, Exeter 1287, Powicke and Cheney, 1041-42, extend this right of the parish priest to other payments.

46. See para. 25 of the clerical grievances of 1399, Wilkins, iii, 241 (harvest festivals); c. 47, Canterbury 1213-14, Powicke and Cheney, 33 (harvesters' wages). On commutations, see *Tenants of Lyskerede* v. *Vicar, Rot. Parl.,* i, 313 (1314-15), where a village was farmed at £18/0/18, and the rector and vicar got only 14/8 between them.

47. Churchill, i, 376, 543-46; Heath, i, 45-46. C. 4, Third Lateran 1179, c. 6, X, III, 39, seems to allow the bishop to exact similar subsidies from his diocesan clergy. I do not find that the right was exercised, but certain customary payments may have been based on it. Moorman 120.

48. On the collection process generally, see Kemp 120-34. On papal collectors, see Lunt, i, c. 12, and on the collection of subsidies for the archbishop, Churchill, i, 545-46.

49. On excommunication, see *Petition of Collectors, Rot. Parl.,* iii, 128b (1381-82). The collectors say they are afraid to follow up on the excommunications by further measures: "Nepurquant les ditz Coillours n'osent mye lur pursute per Brief de Significavit n'autrement, pur paour du mort." For a writ of assistance in aid of the collection process, see *Cal. Pat. Rolls, 1396-99,* 350 (1398).

50. Moorman, 308-11; Knowles, R.O., i, 95-96, 100, 103-5; *Reg. Greenfield,* 219-20; *Reg. Pontissara,* xxvi; *Reg. T. Cantilupe,* 144.

51. Knowles, R.O., ii, 320. Art. 4 of Pecham's articles for rectors and vicars, Powicke and Cheney, 1079, Mansi, xxiv, 781-82 (1287), forbids making contracts to the prejudice of one's successors. As to the specific ways of dipping into capital described in text, see *Reg. Greenfield,* xxvii, and Pecham, supra, art. 8, on long-term loans; Thompson, "A Corrody from Leicester Abbey, 1393-94, with some notes on Corrodies," *Leics. Archaeol. Soc. Trans.,* xiv (1925), 113, and Thompson, 174-75, on corrodies; Mansi, xxi, 769-70 (York, 1153); c. 9, London 1328, Johnson 353, and *Lincoln Visitations,* i, 129-30, on misuse of dilapidation payments (cf. 14 Eliz. 1, c. 11 (1573) for a post-Reformation attack on the same problem); on alienations, Thompson 174 n (land); Moorman 306 n (trees); "so-called statutes of John Pecham," Powicke and Cheney, 1123, Johnson 267-68 (trees); "Hereford Visitations," *E.H.R.,* xlv, 456 (movable goods).

52. On lay farmers, see Hartridge 208. The pluralist accomplished his purpose by having the second benefice conferred on another then farmed to himself at a nominal rent. Thompson, "Pluralism"; c. 9, London 1237, Powicke and Cheney, 249, Johnson, 156. 1233 questionnaire, art. 14, asks about lay farmers, and art. 10 asks about unlicensed farms. The requirement of a license appears in *Reg. Greenfield,* p. xxvii, and Mansi, xxiii, 908 (Salisbury diocese, 1298). Examples of such licenses appear in *Reg. T. Cantilupe,* 239; *Reg. Trillek,* 49, 116. In some reports of farms in the "Hereford Visitations," the lack of a license is mentioned. In some cases, a sequestration is then ordered.

53. Woodcock 86; Moorman 143–44; Drew, passim; *Lincoln Visitations,* passim; "Hereford Visitations," *E.H.R.,* xliv, 286, xlv, 95, 97, 98, 457; art. 15, 1233 questionnaire.

54. On licenses to collect alms, see c. 47, Exeter 1287, Powicke and Cheney, 1043, Mansi, xxiv, 828; *Reg. Sutton,* iii, 1, 61–62. As to restricting the use of papal indulgences, see *Reg. Chichele,* iii, 93 (1424); Lunt, ii, 473–620 passim. On the complaints of the parish clergy, see Moorman 390–93; Knowles, R. O., ii, 103.

55. Art. 49, 1233 Questionnaire; c. 16, Ottobuono 1268, Powicke and Cheney, 766, Johnson 231; Winchester Synodal Statutes; *Reg. Greenfield,* p. xxvi; "On Stipendiary Priests," Powicke and Cheney, 1382–85, Johnson 322–324. For licenses, see *Reg. Trillek,* 98 and passim; *Cal. papal Reg.,* v, 261 (1398). For complaints and disputes, see *Reg. Sutton,* iii, pp. 1–1i; *Reg. Lacy,* i, 144–47 (1425); *Lincoln Visitations,* 129. Some of these are macabre. See "Hereford Visitations," *E.H.R.,* xliv, 287, where a chaplain is complained of for having "despoiled the rector of three bodies"; *Reg. Trillek* 105, 120, where the bishop has corpses dug up and buried on unconsecrated ground because the deceased have incurred excommunication by being buried in the wrong place; and id., 195, where an inadvertent invasion of the incumbent's burial rights is remedied by setting up a catafalque where he can say mass and take up a collection.

56. Thompson 123–26. *Reg. Antiq.* no. 317 (1128–29), seems to mark a point at which resistance to new parishes had pretty well crystallized. On chapelries, see *Reg. Antiq.* no. 376; *Rot. Hugh of Wells,* ii, 202; *Reg. Lacy,* i, 4 (1420), 175–76 (1426); *Lincoln Visitations,* 132. On uniting parishes, *Reg. Trillek,* 174 (1352); *Reg. Chichele,* iii, 372–79 (1416).

57. On the general canon law, see Chassagnade-Belmin, "Églises," *D.D.C.,* v, 171, 205–6; c. 4, X, III, 48; *Cal. Papal Reg.,* x, 290 (1448). On the responsibility of the parishioners, see Drew 8–9; on sequestration, c. 18, London 1268 (Ottobuono), Powicke and Cheney, 767, Mansi, xxiii, 1233–34; *Reg. Trillek,* 109; "Hereford Visitations," *E.H.R.,* xliv, 285; *Reg. Lacy,* i, 181 (1426). On collecting from predecessors, see *Reg. Lacy,* i, 79 (1421); *Cal. Close Rolls, 1346–49,* 463 (1348) (claim superior to debt due king); *Cal. Papal Reg.,* x, 41 (1448) (exemption granted). Every new archbishop of Canterbury was entitled by custom to 700 marks from his predecessor's estate in commutation of this right. *Reg. Chichele,* i, p. xxxiii.

58. On pollution, see *Reg. Trillek,* 115, and the historical discussion in *Reconciliation of St. Paul's,* Tristram 164 (Con. London, 1891). On sanctuary for civil defendants, see *Whytegift's Petition, Rot. Parl.,* i, 476b (uncert. date, temp. Edw. I or II); *Reg. Sudbury, London,* i, 56–58. On goods left for safekeeping, see *Reg. Pontissara,* 775.

59. Moorman 146–48; c. 34, London 1268, Powicke and Cheney, 780, Johnson 246–47; c. 1, York 1363, Johnson 431; *Cal. Papal Reg.*, v, 89 (1398). Despite the legislation, the Wakefield Manor Court was held in church, evidently as a matter of course. *Wakefield Rolls*, i, 148 (1275). On pasturing sheep or cattle in the churchyard, *Lincoln Visitations* has twenty-one cases in the Oxford archdeaconry alone. The case of the tombstones made into a watering trough is id., i, 134 (Kencott). For inquiries on visitation, see art. 25–26, 1233 questionnaire. Compare the 1869 visitation papers, Bodl. Ms. Oxf. Dioc. Papers, c. 283.

60. C. 4, 5, Oxford 1362, Johnson 336–38; Moorman 244–45. "On Church Ornaments," Powicke and Cheney, 1385–86, Johnson 317–18, has an exhaustive list of the required equipment. Other matters looked into were secular use of chrism, art. 34, 1233 Questionnaire; handling of sacred vessels by laymen or married clergy, *Reg. Pontissara*, 207–39 (1295); adequate staff of subordinate personnel, art. 24, 1233 Questionnaire, "Hereford Visitations," *E.H.R.*, xliv, 447.

61. Moorman 69, 73; Bowker 110–28; art. 16, 27, 29, 47, "Hereford Visitations," *E.H.R.*, xlv, 447; *Lincoln Visitations*, i, 122, 131, 132, 138.

62. Manning, c. 9; "Hereford Visitations," *E.H.R.*, xlv, 100, 454; *Reg. Lacy*, i, 143; Woodcock 80–81. The blackmail case is *Warwickshire and Coventry Sessions of the Peace, 1377–97*, ed. Kimball (1939), no. 8, p. 97.

63. Moorman 88; Bowker 113; art. 33, 1233 Questionnaire; *Reg. Pontissara*, 209.

64. Moorman 81–83; Heath 93ff.; c. 9–11, Lambeth 1281, Powicke and Cheney, 900–908, Johnson 282–89. Oxford 1408, Johnson 457–75, imposes the requirement that outside preachers be licensed. I have found only one complaint about lack of preaching: *Lincoln Visitations* i, 132. Id., 130, is the case of the priest complained of for refusing to instruct children.

65. The constitutions erroneously supposed to have been enacted by Saint Edmund Rich in 1236, Johnson 130–46, are an exception. They contrast vividly both with the stock unctuousness of Ottobuono and with the matter-of-fact tone of most English canons. On their provenance, see Cheney, "Legislation of the Medieval English Church," *E.H.R.*, 1 (1935), 400–402.

66. Woodcock 87–89. The manor courts evidently heard more defamation cases than the king's courts did. *Wakefield Rolls*, passim.

67. *Reg. Sutton*, iv. 149, iii, p. xlvii.

68. Powicke and Cheney, 1192–96, Johnson 308–11 (Winchelsea, 1298); c. 1, London 1343, Johnson 380–81; *Reg. Trillek*, 179; *Reg. Chichele*, iii, *Statutes at Large*, i, 33 (1254) (Magna Carta); *Rot. Parl.*, ii, 64b–65a (1331), iii, 252a–b (1387–88), iv, 421a (1433), vi, 158b (1472–75). Cf. id., i, 224b (1254) (general excommunication withdrawn on king's orders).

69. On the Statute of Laborers, see *Reg. Trillek*, 321 (1349). On chaplain's wages, see Putnam, "Maximum Wage Laws for Priests after the Black Death," *Am. Hist. Rev.*, xxi (1915), 12; c. 1, York 1347, Johnson, 404–6; c. 1–2, Canterbury Province 1362, Johnson 421–25; *Reg. Trillek*, 157–59 (1350). The Commons were very interested in having this legislation enacted. *Rot. Parl.*, ii, 271b (1362), iv. 51a (1414), 21a (1419). Other cases where the prelates followed a lead from the lay authorities include *Reg. Trillek*, 224 (1354), concerning drinking clubs, Chichele's constitution against the auncel weight, Johnson 489–92 (1430), and perhaps *Reg. Lacy*, i, 118 (1425), offering an indulgence for contributing to the building of a bridge.

70. See *Reg. Trillek*, 77, and *Reg. Lacy*, i, 38–42, for indulgences; *Reg. Trillek*, 350, for a thanksgiving service.

71. On prostitution, see *Reg. Sutton*, iii, 112; *Reg. Pontissara*, 207–39. On tournaments, see *Acta Langton* no. 46; Powicke, *Henry III and the Lord Edward* (1947), 20–23. This prohibition was done away with in 1316. C. un. title 9 in Extravag. Joan. XXII. On care of children, see c. 36, Canterbury 1213–14, Powicke and Cheney, 32; c. 2, York 1347, Johnson 406. I find no authority for ecclesiastical licensing of physicians and surgeons before 3 Hen. 8, c. 11 (1511), and none for licensing of midwives before *Reg. Parker*, 470–72 (1567), but I do not suppose the Tudors would have put these functions on the church without some medieval precedent for doing so. I suspect that ecclesiastical jurisdiction over the medical profession related to the need for learning and jurisdiction over midwives to the need for seeing that the newborn were baptized. As fur usury, the English canons have only c. 50, Canterbury 1213–14, Powicke and Cheney, 83, a nugatory condemnation of a primitive form of mortgage (Pollock and Maitland, ii, 119), repeated occasionally, and passing references in general compendia like c. 9, Lambeth 1281, Powicke and Cheney, 900, 903, Johnson 282, 285. "Hereford Visitations" has two cases, *E.H.R.*, xliv, 285 and 453. Woodcock 87 finds only a few cases. There was no general secular remedy until 1495, 11 Hen. 7, c. 8, except perhaps when the usurer was dead. *Rot. Parl.*, iii, 451a (1403–4); cf. *Clernans* v. *Appleby*, id., i, 46b (1290). The city of London had an ordinance, evidently not sufficiently enforced, id., ii, 350b (1372). The Wakefield Manor Court dealt with some usury cases. *Wakefield Rolls*, iv. 156, 159 (1316).

72. C. 10, Rouen 1074, Mansi, xx, 399; Naz, "Mariage en droit occidental," *D.D.C.*, vi, 740, 775. For a spectacular case, see *Cal. Papal Reg.*, x, 36 (1448).

73. "Hereford Visitations," *E.H.R.*, xlv, 445 and passim. The reconciliation cases are in "Kent Visitations." Cf. the reference to "ecclesiastical coercion" in 13 Edw. 1, c. 34.

74. *Reg. Pontissara*, 773, 775, 776; *Reg. Trillek*, 79, 95, 179; c. 4, London 1328, Johnson 349. Cf. "Hereford Visitations," *E.H.R.*, xlv, 92 (spurious will), 453 (lord administers goods of intestate villein without authority).

75. On the traditional doctrine, see Thom., vii, 344–85. On the sufficiency of the available funds, Tierney 96–97 seems more persuasive than Moorman 138–39. On hospitality and its enforcement, see Tierney 97–109, 120–24. For complaints on the subject, see "Hereford Visitations," *E.H.R.*, xliv, 93, *Lincoln Visitations*, passim ten cases in Oxford archdeaconry). The parliamentary complaints on the same subject, *Rot. Parl.*, i, 207a (1306), ii, 172b–173a (1347), iv, 290b (1425), should probably be taken with a grain of salt. On churchwardens' funds, see Thompson 130; Webb, *English Poor Law History*, i (1927), 6–16.

76. On solicitation, see Woodcock 81 (punishment); Churchill, i, 130; c. 47, Exeter 1287, Powicke and Cheney, 1043, Mansi, xxiv, 828 (licensing). On sturdy beggars, see Tierney 128–30; *Reg. Trillek*, 321.

77. Gibbs and Lang; Cheney, "The Legislation of the Medieval English Church," *E.H.R.*, l, 193 (1935).

78. C. 1–7 (1), Oxford 1222, Powicke and Cheney, 106–7, Johnson 101–2; c. 11 (3), Reading 1279, Powicke and Cheney, 848, Johnson 257; c. 1, London 1343, Johnson 380; Johnson 349 (1434). C. 7, Westminster 1200,

Johnson 88, and c. 49, Canterbury 1213-14, Powicke and Cheney, 33, were earlier and less elaborate versions. Lyndwood uses the 1222 version. The truncation of the list by parish priests is complained of by St. Germain in *A Treatise Concernynge the Division Betwene the Spiritualtie and the Temporaltie* (London, 1532—published anonymously, for date and authorship see *D.N.B.*, St. Germain).

79. See, respectively, *Reg. Trillek*, 84; id., 95; *Reg. Lacy*, iii, 56-58.

80. The ceremony is given in Myrc, *Instructions for Parish Priests*, lines 750-80, Early English Text Society, xxxi, 23-24. Its use is ordered in *Reg. Trillek*, 33-34 and 179, but not in id., 86 and 95. On forcible prevention, see *Reg. Chichele*, iii, 223.

81. The canon on celibacy to be read to the clergy is c. 3 (5), Reading 1279, Powicke and Cheney, 837, Mansi, xxiv, 263-65. The 1287 injunctions appear in Mansi, xxiv, 781-82. The order to cite lay offenders is *Reg. Chichele*, iv, 104-5 (1414).

82. The first modern licensing scheme was evidently that adopted for alehouses under Henry VII. Holdsworth, iv, 515, x, 183.

83. For use of licenses to control the incidence of nonresidence and the behavior of nonresidents, see Bowker 93-95; *Reg. T. Cantilupe*, 7-8; *Reg. Grandisson*, 337-38; *Reg. Lacy*, i, 10.

84. On confirmation of elections, see Churchill, i, 121-23, 241-54. Examples of local confirmation of papal documents include *Acta Langton* no. 84; *Reg. Grandisson*, 331; *Reg. Lacy*, i, 162-65. The idea was evidently to fortify the unfamiliar papal seal with a familiar local one. *Reg. Chichele*, iii, 93 (1424).

85. C. 15, I, 3, in VI°. On the royal writs of quo warranto, see Cam, "Manerium cum hundredo," *E.H.R.*, xlvii, 353 (1932).

86. C. 3, I, 16 in VI° (Lyons, 1274); Churchill, i, 116; Thompson 104. As to proofs of ordination, see Moorman 223; *Reg. Trillek*, 20-21. Other matters inquired into in the same way included appropriations, pensions, and dispensations for nonage and lack of orders. Churchill, i, 136-39. See also c. 81 (48), Worcester 1240, Powicke and Cheney, 316, Mansi, xxiii, 541 (rights to tithes).

87. Examples of authoritative exhortations include *Reg. Trillek*, 196 (master of hospital is to correct brethren, "ne sanguis confratrum suorum predictorum de nostris vel suis manibus ut propheta clamat, requiratue"); *Reg. Chichele*, iii, 516-21 (letter to Abbot of Abingdon on results of metropolitan visitation). Monitions are dealt with in chapter 3. Additional examples include *Reg. Trillek*, 86, 107; *Reg. Sudbury, London*, i, 223; *Reg. Lacy*, i, 6, 9; *Reg. Chichele*, iii, 381. On abjuration of sexual offenses, see *Reg. Sudbury, London*, i, 223; "Kent Visitations," xxxiii, 164; "Hereford Visitations," passim; *Reg. Pontissara*, 207-39 (provision for abjuration by prostitutes). Most of these oaths have a pecuniary penalty attached. Violation is also sometimes punished as perjury. E.g., "Hereford Visitations," *E.H.R.*, xlv, 447. I can find no evidence of how the money penalty was collected. Presumably the lay courts would have prohibited an ecclesiastical proceeding for the purpose.

88. Baccrabère, "Visite canonique de l'évêque," *D.D.C.*, vii, 1512.

89. The following discussion of monastic visitation is based on Cheney, *Episcopal Visitation*, 54-103; Thompson, "Introduction," *Visitations of*

Lincolnshire Religious Houses, p. i. On the difficulties of deposing a superior, see the case of Evesham, Knowles, M.O., c. 19; Cheney, *Episcopal Visitation*, 90-91, and that of Bardney, *V.C.H.*, Lincs., ii, 100-101. The latter case raised further complications concerning the possession of the abbey by the king's escheators pending an appeal by the deposed abbot. *Rot. Parl.*, i, 323a, 328b, 478a. It also burdened the house with a loan of 1,000 marks taken out by the abbot to pay his expenses in the Roman tribunals. *Cal. Papal Reg.*, ii, 25 (1307). In addition to litigious complications of this kind, the deposition of superiors was inhibited by the financial burden on the house of providing for their support. Knowles, R.O., i, 112. But a superior who was not deposed could make life miserable for the members of the community who reported shortcomings. *Visitations of Lincolnshire Religious Houses*, iii, 119-27 (Gracedieu Priory, 1441). For other comments on the effectiveness and frustrations of the system, see Knowles, R.O., i, 110, ii, 212-13, 334-64; Thompson 179-81. *Reg. Trillek*, 240, has a follow-up commission, evidently a rare example. The monastic authorities resented the bishop's bringing his secular staff with him (Cheney, *Episcopal Visitation*, 66-71) and would no doubt have resented still more his sending them after he left.

90. Thompson, "Introduction," *Lincoln Visitations;* Moorman 191-96. *Reg. Trillek*, 30-31; *Reg. Chichele*, iii, 494-95. The 1233 questionnaire is typical of the articles used on these occasions. Moorman says they were sent ahead of the visitor rather than put to the parishioners at the time of visitation.

91. Drew; Moorman 143-44. The office of parish constable was developing in the same way in connection with the sessions of the peace. Sillem, "Introduction," *Some Sessions of the Peace in Lincolnshire, 1360-75*, L.R.S., xxx (1937), p. xxxvi; Pollock and Maitland, i, 567. Despite both Drew and Maitland, I am inclined to believe that the parish was not as a general matter distinct from the vill in Middle Ages. I have Toulmin Smith, *The Parish* (London, 1854), on my side in this, and I believe also the Webbs, *English Local Government*, vi (London, 1904), and Round, "The Domesday Survey," *V.C.H.*, Essex, i, 330, 400-45.

92. Moorman 192 seems to be relying on the words "Inventum est" and "Inventa sunt" in *Reg. W. Giffard*, 332-33. The invariable formula "parochiani dicunt" in the "Hereford Visitations" would argue the other way. C. 29 (25) Oxford 1222, Powicke and Cheney, 115, Johnson 110, seems clearly to require physical inspection. C. 16 (11) of the same council, Powicke and Cheney, 110, Johnson 107, and c. 6, Oxford 1322, Johnson 339, are less definite. Lending equipment is forbidden by the 1295 synodal statutes in *Reg. Pontissara*, 207-39.

93. "Hereford Visitations," passim; *Reg. Greenfield*, xxiii; *Reg. Trillek*, 31, 108. For cases of the bishop acting on the spot, see id., 177, 215. In other cases, the bishop would hear matters after the visitation was over, id., 62, or the regular church courts would do so, Woodcock 30, or the parish clergy would follow up, "Hereford Visitations," *E.H.R.*, xliv, 449, 450. On nonresidence licenses, see *Lincoln Visitations*, i, 119, where "licenciatus" is interlineated after a report of nonresidence. On the fabric, see *Reg. Grandisson*, 605-11, for a special visitation evidently limited to that subject.

94. It is not clear whether the general law required these visitations to be

made in person. Churchill, i, 131, says it was "a moot point." The frequency of papal indults to visit by deputy suggests a general duty to visit in person. C. 3, III, 20 in VI°, indicates that a visitor can send a deputy but cannot receive cash procurations if he does. *Reg. Grandisson*, liv (1342), shows an archdeacon about to starve for lack of procurations because he is too old to make visitations in person. But cf. Woodcock 68–69.

95. This discussion of metropolitan visitation is based mainly on Churchill, i, 288–347. The limitation on parish visiting is established in c. 1, III, 20 in VI°. Evidently, the morals of the laity were not to be inquired into nor those of the clergy under oath. As to displacement of local authority, see also Baccrabère, "Visite canonique de l'évêque," *D.D.C.*, vii, 1512, 1517. What particularly annoyed the suffragan was that benefices in his gift could be filled by the metropolitan. Unless there was a special indult (e.g., *Reg. Grandisson*, xxiii–xxxv), the only canonical objection to a metropolitan visitation was that the metropolitan had not yet visited his own diocese, if that was the case. Most actual objections went to the scope, not the fact, of visitation. Brentano 115–47 shows a magnificent and largely successful resistance on virtually no grounds at all. On concessions, see also *Reg. Chichele*, i, pp. cx–cxiv.

96. On reticence, I find Cheney, *Episcopal Visitation*, more persuasive than Knowles, R.O., i, 84.

97. I have found only one case of direct resistance: "Kent Visitations," xxxiii, 81.

98. The following discussion of procurations is based on Moorman 121–23; Cheney, *Episcopal Visitations*, 104–18; Churchill, i, 288–347; Naz, "Procuration," *D.D.C.*, vii, 314. The 1179 canon on retainers is c. 4, Third Lateran 1179, Mansi, xxii, 219, c. 6, X, III, 39. The canon law forbade cash procurations entirely until 1298, when they were permitted with the consent of the person paying. C. 3, III, 20 in VI°. The visitor had to collect them in person and could take only one procuration a day, even if he visited more than one place. Benedict XIII in 1336 laid down a schedule of what sum was a day's procuration for each type of visitor in each part of Europe. C. un., III, 10 in Extrav. Commun. But he expressly preserved the right to render procurations in kind instead of paying these sums. Churchill, i, 309 n shows the only clear case I have found of a visitor with papal authority to take cash against the wishes of those visited. On procurations without visiting, see Thompson, 61–62. The canons forbidding the practice are c. 33, Fourth Lateran 1215, Mansi, xxii, 1021, c. 23, X, III, 39; c. 18, Ottobuono 1268, Johnson 232.

99. This discussion is based on Woodcock 48–49; Bowker 32–33; Amanieu, "Appariteur," *D.D.C.*, i, 757. The "gestapo" characterization is Woodcock's. English canons on the subject include c. 27, Lambeth 1261, Powicke and Cheney, 683, Wilkins, i, 754–55; c. 9, London 1342, Wilkins, ii, 700. The final form of the post-Reformation rule on citations is c. 138 of the Canons of 1604.

100. The following discussion is based in large part on Gabel. See also, Heath 119–33. On the status of the secular conviction as a canonical accusation, see *Reg. Chichele*, iv. 245, where the offense is stated in the common form of the secular indictment: *felonice furatus fuisset, cepisset et asportasset*. The orders concerning purgation in *Reg. Trillek*, 81 and 231, mention

a secular conviction; that in *Reg. Pontissara,* 461–62, does not. The purgation process is discussed further in section H, infra. See also *R. v. Walton, Rot. Parl.,* i, 100a (1293), a secular proceeding against a group of men procured by the father and brothers of a certain vicar to beat up one who came forward to oppose the vicar's purgation. The 1261 constitution referred to in text is c. 29 (21), Lambeth 1261, Powicke and Cheney, 684, Johnson 207–8. The practice of imprisonment may have developed a little earlier. A 1351 constitution of Archbishop Simon, Mansi, xxv, 295, attempts to see that imprisoned clerical offenders are not too comfortable. It recites that it was enacted under some prodding from the king. See also *Rot. Parl.,* iii, 494b (1402).

101. *Reg. Trillek,* 174.

102. On correcting moral abuses, see *Reg. Sudbury, London,* i, 206; on protecting royal rights, id., 326; on searching records, id., 257–59, 283; *Cal. Pat. Rolls, 1292-1301,* 370; id., *1348-50,* 205, 218; *Cal. Close Rolls, 1296-1302,* 204; on aliens, *Reg. Trillek,* 284.

103. Bowker 29–30. *Reg. Trillek,* 131, is an ad hoc commission to hear a case pending in the consistory. Id., 118, 119, 129, 141, is a case that vacillates between routine and nonroutine handling, ending with the latter. The case in *Reg. Chichele,* iv, 116, 118, 119, indicates that the offender is being cited before the archbishop because he did not respond when cited before the official.

104. Respectively, *Reg. Trillek,* 115, 107, 109, 98 (the adulterer involved in this case, Fulk Glas, was evidently a Fitz-Warin and lord of Alburbury), and 110.

105. This paragraph is based on Woodcock 68–71.

106. The most important piece of provincial legislation is c. 6, London 1342, Johnson 366. Woodcock 73 indicates that the regular courts in Canterbury were still following this in the early sixteenth century. For complaints see Sheehan 2, 199, 246; Woodcock 22–23; *Rot. Parl.,* ii, 171a (1347), iv, 84b (1415); *Warwickshire and Coventry Sessions of the Peace, 1377-97,* ed. Kimball (Dugdale Soc., xvi, 1939), no. 190, 192, pp. 49–50.

107. Woodcock 87–92. Usury, assault on the clergy, abuse of process, and the like made up the remainder.

108. Examples of supervised settlements include *Reg. Antiq.* no. 353 (judges-delegate, 1253) (pension); *Rot. Grosseteste,* 85–86 (tithe case submitted to bishop and settled with party collecting the tithes paying a pension to the other party); *Reg. Trillek,* 195 (1353) (burial rights); *Reg. Sudbury, London,* i, 222 (criminal proceeding by parishioners against vicar); *Reg. Chichele,* iii, 383–88 (Norwich sede vacante, 1416) (augmentation of vicarage); *Reg. Lacy,* iii, 215–35 (1437–38) (criminal process against abbot).

109. On the effectiveness of citations, see Woodcock 101; Bowker 95–96. On default judgments, Woodcock 54; *Reg. Trillek,* 67. On taking possession of property or income, Churchill, i, 325; *Reg. Lacy,* i, 79; *Reg. Grandisson,* 372, 398; Naz, "Séquestre," *D.D.C.,* vii, 973. Women involved in matrimonial suits were also "sequestered" on occasion—i.e., placed in custody. Woodcock 83.

110. Dumas, "Serment judiciaire," *D.D.C.,* vii, 580; Pollock and Maitland, ii, 600; "Purgation," Burn, iii, 258; c. 15, X, V, 34; Woodcock 57–58.

111. Woodcock 55–57; Holdsworth, ix, 185–86. Jolowicz, *Historical Intro-*

duction to the Study of Roman Law (1939), 188, 462, describes the comparable Roman procedure.

112. Amanieu, "Appel," *D.D.C.*, i, 764, 800-801.

113. Haskins, *Norman Institutions* (Cambridge, Mass., 1925), 196-238; Pollock and Maitland, i, 138-44.

114. Torquebiau, "Enquête," *D.D.C.*, vii, 344.

115. See the description of the inquest *de jure patronatus* in Burn, i, 22-24. This institution, largely moribund in Burn's time, seems to be an authentic survival from the inquest we are considering. On the secular counterpart, see Pollock and Maitland, ii, 622-29; Holdsworth, i, 333-35. On the difference between an inquest and a group of witnesses, see *Reg. Lacy*, iii, 6 (1448), where the witnesses are ordered to be examined "secrete et singillatim." The entries from *Reg. Chichele* indicating that evidence was taken are i, 178-80 (1420), and iii, 383-88 (1426).

116. See, as to purgation, Gabel 95-98; *Reg. Trillek*, 81, 231; as to dilapidations, c. 9, London 1328, Johnson 353; *Reg. Trillek*, 109; as to presentments, *Reg. Sudbury, London,* i, 40-42; *Reg. Chichele*, i, lxxiii, 178-80, 186, 229; as to uniting parishes, *Reg. Chichele,* iii, 383-88; as to ecclesiastical dues, *Reg. Trillek,* 177. The Clarendon provision referred to in text is art. 6, Johnson 52.

117. Pollock and Maitland, ii, 600-601.

118. Moorman 212.

119. Hill, "Introduction," *Reg. Sutton,* iii, p. xvii. See *Reg. T. Cantilupe,* 101, where the bishop, instead of depriving an incumbent as he deserves, appoints a curator for the benefice with instructions to pay the incumbent six marks a year lest he starve or beg "in obprobrium ordinis clericalis."

120. Churchill, i, 309 n, is instructive in this regard in showing the record that had to be made up so the bishop and monks of Ely could invite the archbishop's commissaries to eat with them: "non cum eis tanquam commissarii visitantes sed tanquam amici comederent quia dominus Archiepiscopus vellet habere procuracionem per bullam sibi concessam."

121. Note by contrast the way c. 2147-2156 of the 1918 code sort out these different levels of concern in their provision for the removal of an ineffective parish priest, or the modern Anglican practice described in Crockford Preface for 1933, *The Editor Looks Back* (Oxford, 1947), 135-36, and criticized in Paul, *The Deployment and Payment of the Clergy* (Westminster, 1964), 107-9, 171-74.

5: The Parish Ministry

1. The early canons on the subject are ambivalent. C. 6, Poitiers 1078, Mansi, xx, 498; c. 1, Nemours 1096, id., 933; c. 18, First Lateran 1123, Mansi, xxi, 285, all seem concerned with preserving episcopal control by having someone in the parish to answer to the bishop. But a decree of Pope Pascal II (1098-1118), taken up by Gratian as c. 19, C. XVI, q. 7, uses a mystical justification based on not rending the seamless robe of Christ. The Decretals use c. 17, Third Lateran 1179, Mansi, xxii, 227, collected as c. 3, X, III, 38, which seems to come half-way between the two lines.

2. On each church having its own priest, see c. 18, First Lateran 1123, Mansi, xxi, 285; c. 9, Rheims 1131, id., 460 (repeated as part of c. 10, Second Lateran 1139, id., 528, collected in c. 5, C. XXI, q. 2). As to personal presence, c. 13, Third Lateran 1179, Mansi, xxii, 225, collected as c. 3, X, III, 4, appears to be the first provision expressly requiring residence. There is nothing earlier in the source notes to c. 465, para. 1, of the 1918 Code. But the requirement that a priest be juridically attached to a particular church and participate occasionally in its liturgy goes back to Roman times. Naz, "Residence," *D.D.C.*, vii, 656–57. Cf. also c. 2, Rouen 1128, Mansi, xxi, 375. On pluralism, see c. 12, Clermont 1095, Mansi, xx, 817; c. 2, Rouen 1128, Mansi, xxi, 375. As to not moving, see c. 13, Clermont 1095, Mansi, xx, 817; c. 9, Nemours 1096, id., 936. See Thom. vii, 142–43, for the relation between this rule and those on pluralism and nonresidence. On tenure, see c. 9, London 1123, Mansi, xxi, 332; c. 10, Rheims 1148, id., 716; and on fixed sources of income, c. 10, Rheims 1148, Mansi, xxi, 716; c. 32, Fourth Lateran 1215, Mansi, xxii, 1019, c. 30, X, III, 5. The examples on which the following description is based, where not otherwise documented, were introduced in chap. 1.

3. The only evidence I have found of a clash is in *Cartulary of St. Mary Clerkenwell* (Camden 3d. ser., lxxi, London, 1949), no. 157–59 (ca. 1190), where the parson of Broadway succeeded, at least for his own incumbency, in keeping the patron from giving the nuns of Clerkenwell a pension out of his church.

4. The case in *Rot. Grosseteste*, 268–69 (pension for patron's brother, a cleric), invites a raised eyebrow, but there may be some other explanation. Id., iv.

5. On the documentary style, see Major, "Introduction," *Acta Langton*, xxv–xxvii, and the colloquy in *Abbot of Newenham* v. *Dean and Chapter of York*, F.G.A., "Quare Impedit," no. 19 (1334). The assize of darrein presentment, applicable only to advowsons, seems to have existed as early as John's time. *Yorks. Assize Rolls* (Yorks Archaeol. Soc., xliv, ed. Clay, 1911), 21, whereas a church was subjected to an ordinary land litigation as late as the reign of Henry I. *Hist. Mon. Abingd.* (R.S., ii [b] 1858), 188. So the change must have come in during the last half of the twelfth century.

6. C. 15–16, London 1102, Johnson 27, Mansi, xx, 1151; c. 12, London 1138, Mansi, xxi, 513, Johnson 44, seem to require no more than the bishop's permission. But the bishop would not act unless the mother church was bought off.

7. *Reg. Antiq.* no. 317 (1129–38); id., no. 319 (1135–37).

8. See Knowles, M.O., 596–600. For additional examples, see Hambleton, *V.C.H.*, Rutl., iii, 66ff., and Sutton Courtenay, Berks., where the incumbent seems to be a feudal tenant of the house Knowles, M.O., 598. The late twelfth-century rule referred to in text is found in Knowles, M.O., 596–97.

9. C. 13, X, III, 38 (Alexander III). I interpret the evidence assembled in Hartridge, chap. 2 (Hartridge himself interprets it rather differently), as indicating a growing adherence to this rule by seeking the permission it requires. C. 3, Rouen 1128, Mansi, xxi, 376, may mark an intermediate stage in this development. The rule is probably the basis of Hugh of Wells's campaign against pensions that could not be shown to be "debita et antiqua." *Rot. Hugh of Wells*, i, pp. xx–xxi and passim.

10. E.g., c. 1, Nemours 1096 (c. 6, c. 16, q. 2), Mansi, xx, 933; c. 6, Rheims 1157, Mansi, xxi, 845; cf. c. 21, London 1102, Mansi, xx, 1152; c. 9, London 1123, Mansi, xxi, 332.

11. The rule against stipendiary priests appears in c. 9, Rheims 1131, Mansi, xxi, 460, c. 5, c. 21, q. 2; the rule that requires a priest to have sufficient revenue to maintain himself appears in c. 12, Lillebon 1080, Mansi, xx, 557; c. 21, London 1102, Mansi, xx, 1152 (see Hartridge, chap. 1). The two were put together to provide the language of c. 10, Rheims 1148, Mansi, xxi, 716. The Fourth Lateran's canon requiring fixed sources of revenue is c. 32, Mansi, xxii, 1019, c. 30, X, III, 5. Hartridge 20-35.

12. See *O.E.D.* for the origin of the term *parson*. In its first canonical appearance, c. 31, Clermont 1095, Mansi, xx, 818-19, c. 4, C. I, q. 3, it seems to designate a person put into a church by a religious community (pace Thom., vi, 403). I do not find it used for the presentee of a lay patron before c. 1, Westminster 1173, Mansi, xxii, 141. For its use in the later Middle Ages, see Thompson, 101-5. On a community as parson, see e.g., *Reg. T. Cantilupe*, 49-51, where the bishop "imparsons" a religious house. The purpose of treating the house as corporate parson may have been to prevent the bishop taking the revenues during vacancies. See Hartridge 28. On pensions established to settle disputes, see Gibbs and Lang, 168-69. *Reg. Antiq.* no. 217, 388, 609, 816, and 825, appear to be examples. For pensions "debita et antiqua," see *Rot. Hugh of Wells*, i, pp. xx-xxi and passim.

13. Moorman 48-49; Hartridge 25; Knowles, M.O., 595; Knowles, R.O., ii, 288-89, 292-93; Thompson 119-21. For legislation on monks serving cures, see c. 17, First Lateran 1123, Mansi, xxi, 277, c. 10, C. 16, q. 1. As to canons regular, compare c. 10 and 11, Poitiers 1100, Mansi, xx, 1123-24. See Hartridge 165.

14. This seems to be the most important of the cases envisaged by c. 32, Fourth Lateran 1215, Mansi, xxii, 1019, c. 30, X, III, 5. See *Reg. Antiq.* no. 86; *V.C.H.*, Hunts, ii, 16; *Reg. Gravesend*, 185, for the history of the church of Brampton, Hunts., which was given to a bishop in the mid-twelfth century, made a prebendal church later in the same century, and furnished with a vicarage late in the thirteenth, all without a canonical appropriation having taken place.

15. Moorman 18-22. For additional examples, see Wothorpe, Northants, *Reg. Antiq.* no. 347, and Owston, Dugdale, vi, 424.

16. E.g., Cirencester, Dugdale, vi, 176-77.

17. E.g., *Reg. Antiq.* no. 52 (Peterborough); *V.C.H.*, Berks., ii, 15 (St. Nicholas, Abingdon). But see *V.C.H.*, Hunts., iii, 212 (Sawtry Judith). Where a monastery enjoyed papal exemption, that exemption might apply to its extern church as well. Knowles, M.O., 573.

18. Moorman 19 (Salisbury); *Visitations and Memorials of Southwell Minster*, (Camden Soc., n.s., lxviii, 1891), lv, 198.

19. Thompson 86-87; Addleshaw, *Rectors, Vicars, and Patrons* (London, 1956), 11. King: *Reg. Antiq.* no. 88, 98; cf. no. 41. Secular magnate: id., no. 812. Monastery: Knowles, M.O., 598.

20. E.g., *Reg. Antiq.* no. 45, 158, 327.

21. *Reg. Antiq.* no. 35 (Henry I).

22. E.g., *Reg. Antiq.* no. 332, 805, 816.

23. Knowles, M.O., 597-600.

24. E.g., Sonning, *V.C.H.*, Berks., ii, 4.

25. E.g., *Reg. Antiq.* no. 358-66, all imposed by Hugh of Wells, an especially vigorous pension fighter. Bishops also appropriated their churches in the same way others did. Moorman 41-42.

26. See the list in *Rot. Hugh of Wells*, i, 238ff., where many appropriations are characterized as *ab antiquo*, whereas one (p. 240) was by someone's authority with a blank to fill in his name. When a church had always been in corporate ecclesiastical hands, the endowment fixed on for the priest who served it must have been somewhat arbitrary, as must the determination of whether to call him a parson or a vicar. Compare the enumeration of the patron's rights in *Reg. Antiq.* no. 378 (Nettleham, Lincs.) with the 1219 charter of Bishop Foliot in *Reg. T. Cantilupe*, 49–51, expressing doubt as to whether the incumbent of Great Cowarne, Gloucs., should be called a parson or a vicar. If the incumbent was called a vicar, the later authorities would treat the case as one of an appropriation *ab antiquo*. In my opinion, the treatments of the origins of appropriation in Hartridge, chap. 1, and Knowles, M.O., 599–600, do not take sufficient account of churches of this kind.

27. On Dorchester, see *V.C.H.*, Oxon., ii, 87–88. The church of Sawtry Judith, referred to, supra, note 37, is another example.

28. Denton, *English Royal Free Chapels, 1100–1300* (Manchester, 1970); Thompson 81–85; cf. "Donative," Burn, ii, 192. On Wolverhampton, see *V.C.H.*, Staffs, iii, 321ff.

29. Thompson 123–28. For further examples, see *Reg. Antiq.* no. 317, 376.

30. See, e.g., c. 44, Wells diocese 1258 (?), Powicke and Cheney, 610; c. 19, Exeter diocese 1287, id., 1016 (quoted in Thom., iv, 146). On the other hand, there are examples of express dispensations for nonresidence in this situation, e.g., *Cal. Papal Reg.*, v, 111 (1398). The case envisaged by c. 32, Fourth Lateran 1215, c. 30, X, III, 5, where a prebendary resides in his cathedral or collegiate instead of his prebendal church and is technically distinct from nonresidence through pluralism, as the prebend and its church are canonically a single benefice.

31. Bowker 95 suggests that the bishop exercised some discretion in determining which of his benefices the pluralist should serve in person. Cf. Winchester Synodal Statutes, c. 55.

32. Moorman 32–33; Laprat, "Commende," *D.D.C.*, iii, 1029–38; Thompson, "Pluralism." Examples of use for a probationary incumbency include *Rot. Hugh of Wells*, i. 19 (lack of learning); id., iii, 108 (doubt as to right of patron to present). For legislation, see, e.g., Ottobuono, c. 16, London 1268, Johnson 243 (commends to be tolerated only for good of commended church), and c. 14, Lyons 1274, c. 15, I, 6, in VI°, establishing the six-month rule. For examples of commends that seem to be limited in compliance with that rule, see *Reg. T. Cantilupe*, 1, 158–59.

33. C. 34, I, 6, in VI°. Boyle "The Constitution *Cum exo eo* of Boniface VIII," *Medieval Studies*, xxiv (1962), 263; Capes, "Introduction," *Reg. T. Cantilupe*, pp. xxxv–xxxvii; Thompson, "Introduction," *Reg. Gravesend*, pp. xxvii–xxix.

34. *Cal. Papal Rep.*, v, 97 (1398), has an indult to the earl of Northumberland to keep seven clerics nonresident while in his service. Id., 111, has two examples of dispensations issued to the cleric himself. As to the king's rights, see *Reg. T. Cantilupe*, 126, 169; Art. Cler., 9 Edw. 2, St. 1, c. 8 (1315). On the London clergy, see Jacob, "Introduction," *Reg. Chichele*, i, pp. lxxv–lxxvii.

35. Papal service: Pantin 41; c. 14, X, III, 4. Personal affairs: *Cal. Papal*

Reg., v, 111 (1398); *Reg. Sudbury, London*, i, 221. Service of Local church: c. 13, X, III, 4.

36. C. 15, I, 3 in VI°. As I read this decretal, it leaves intact dispensations for a specified length of time. It is explicit in saving dispensations granted to specific churches or offices rather than to individuals.

37. Capes, "Introduction," *Reg. T. Cantilupe*, pp. xxxv–xxxvii; Bowker 95–96; Heath 57–62. See *Lincoln Visitations*, i, 119 (Easington), where "rector non residet" is reported by the parishioners, and "licentiatus" is interlineated.

38. E.g., Pantin, chap. 3.

39. Moorman 210–12; Bowker 89–93; Heath 56–57; Thompson 102–3. Tierney 94 seems overly sanguine. In the "Hereford Visitations," I found in 281 parishes only three complaints of nonresidence plus two more of prolonged absence not amounting technically to nonresidence. As to nonresidence of vicars, see Hartridge 122–23; Moorman 47; Thompson 121–22. Observe the language of the institutions in *Rot. Hugh of Wells*, i, 148, and *Reg. Chichele*, i, 129, and of the citation in id., iii, 381.

40. It seems that the bishop could recall a nonresident if his curate was bad enough. Bowker 95. As to the duty to endow a vicar, see *Acta Langton*, passim; "Kent Visitations," passim; *Reg. T. Cantilupe*, 7–8; *Cal. Papal Reg.*, i, 242 (1248).

41. Capes, "Introduction," *Reg. T. Cantilupe*, pp. xix–xx.

42. Bowker 106–9.

43. See *Cal. Pat. Rolls, 1350–54*, 122 (1351); *Reg. Trillek*, 243 (1354), for a case in which a lay patron benefited from the practice by arranging with Llanthony Abbey to exchange a secular manor for his advowson and then appropriate the advowson.

44. Knowles, R.O., ii, 291. Thompson 115 and Moorman 42 are higher.

45. While most of these transactions were probably quite straightforward, there are a few thirteenth-century cases in which the bishop appears to have been given a pension for licensing the appropriation. *Reg. Antiq.* no. 388, 391–92, 404. On overcommitment and need, see Moorman 39–42, 294–313; Thompson 109–16, 173–75.

46. See, for example, the document appropriating the rectory of St. Mary's to Oriel College, Oxford. *Oriel College Records* (Oxf. Hist. Soc., lxxv, ed. Shadwell and Salter, 1926), 82–85. On the motives for founding chantries and the like, see Thompson 141. For a substantial list of people to be prayed for, see *Cal. Papal Reg.*, iii, 300 (1348).

47. 7 Edw. 1, St. 2 (1279). For examples of high payments for royal licenses, see *Cal. Pat. Rolls, 1348–50*, 8 (1348) (100 pounds); id., *1396–99*, 447 (1398) (100 marks).

48. Gibbs and Lang, 168; Hartridge, chap. 3–4, and appendix B. These authorities do not distinguish between vicarages ordained simultaneously with the license to appropriate and those ordained afterward. For indications that the custom came to be simultaneous ordination, see Capes, "Introduction," *Reg. Swinfield*, pp. xxii–xxiii; *Reg. Trillek*, 243; *Reg. Antiq.* no. 392; *Cal. Papal Reg. Pet. 126* (1348). 15 Ric. 2, c. 6 (1391), provided that the necessary royal licenses for appropriation could not be issued unless a vicarage was provided. The process of picking up the stragglers went on throughout the Middle Ages; the papacy sometimes helped it along by providing informers to new vicarages. See *Cal. Papal Reg.*, v, 106 (1398).

49. In the entries for the year 1398 in *Cal. Papal Reg.*, v, I find thirteen licenses to appropriate without vicars or to serve without vicars churches previously appropriated as compared with twelve licenses to appropriate in the usual way. Examples of such licenses are on pp. 86-87, 155-56. I do not find examples of this practice in the papal registers for 1348, so I cannot say when it started. Perhaps the withdrawal of royal permission, *Rot. Parl.*, iii, 499b (1402), put an end to it, as I find no examples in 1403 or 1404 or in 1448.

50. C. 21 (15), Oxford 1222, Powicke and Cheney, 112, Johnson 108 (5 marks); *Reg. Chichele*, iii, 286-87, Johnson 498-99 (1439) (12 marks). See Jacob, "Introduction," *Reg. Chichele*, i, pp. cl-cli. On the vicar's share of tithes and offerings, see Hartridge, chap. 3 and appendix B; Tierney 69-74. As to offerings, see also Moorman 127-28. As to land, see Richardson, "The Parish Clergy of the Thirteenth and Fourteenth Centuries," *T.R.H.S.*, 3d ser., vi (1912), 88, 106. See e.g., *Reg. Trillek*, 252-53; Hartridge 46. As to living with the monks, see Moorman 96.

51. *Cal. Papal Reg.*, 258 (1398).

52. The evidence on this point, although negative, is persuasive. In no case does the financial condition of the appropriator figure among the inquiries in an augmentation suit—although in fact (according to Jacob, *Reg. Chichele*, i, pp. cl-cli), it was a major obstacle to adequate augmentations.

53. Hartridge 193-94. See art. 4-5 of those submitted by the clergy in 1399, Mansi, xxvi, 923. The oath would be illegal because the exaction of it was a form of simony and because the cleric had no power to waive his right to a *congrua sustentatio*. But the vicars in Hartridge's examples were worried enough about their oaths to seek express relaxations from the papacy. Also, the oath was sometimes accompanied with a penalty bond whereby the vicar would forfeit a large sum (20 pounds or 30 pounds in one of Hartridge's cases) if he sought augmentation. This would be enforceable in the lay courts and perhaps even the church courts. Cf. *Dean of Windsor* v. *Vicar of Saltash*, Y.B., 2 Hen. 4, 9, F.G.A., "Consultacion," no. 3 (1401).

54. Hartridge 54 gives an example (albeit an early one—1254) of an augmentation quashed by a papal delegate "probably on strictly legal grounds."

55. Johnson 498-99; Jacob, "Introduction," *Reg. Chichele*, i, pp. cl-cli.

56. E.g., "Kent Visitations," xxxii, 143, 152-58; *Reg. Trillek*, 252-53; cf. 1233 Questionnaire, item 13. Hartridge is not as clear on this point as one might wish, but some of his examples, e.g., 86, 134, seem to arise in this way.

57. *Reg. Trillek*, 92, 168-69, 234.

58. Tierney 91-96; Cutts, *Parish Priests and their People* (London, 1914), 406-7; Hartridge 42-43; Homans, *English Villagers of the Thirteenth Century* (Cambridge, Mass., 1960), 388.

59. The estimates in Moorman 137 and 45 and the statistics in Bowker 139-45 indicate that most rectors made somewhat more, but not a lot more, than most vicars. The few rich vicarages tended to become nonresident in the same way as the rich rectories did. Thompson 121-22.

60. Thompson 174-75.

61. Hartridge 161. The statute 15 Ric. 2, c. 6 (1391), required the appropriator to feed back into the parish a sum expressly allocated to poor relief. Hartridge 160 seems to find a good deal of compliance.

62. Homans, supra, note 58.

63. Thompson 132–60 passim. See *Reg. Chichele*, iii, 485, where the patron of a chantry is moved by the poverty (*exilitas*) of the local vicar to present him to the chantry.
64. Pantin 41, 45–46; Thompson 141; c. 5, X, V, 5 (Honorius III, 1216–27); cf. Pantin 64–65.
65. Manning, chap. 2.
66. Pantin, chap. 9.
67. Thompson 102-3; see also Edwards 81–82.
68. This and the following paragraph are based largely on Manning, *People's Faith in the Time of Wyclif* (Cambridge, 1919).
69. It is perhaps not fair to expect the *Canterbury Tales* to hang together like a single, unified literary work. Nonetheless, it is worth remarking that the moral treatise embodied in the Parson's Tale seems to a modern reader terribly inappropriate for the occasion and yet seems to be about what the other pilgrims expected of so good a parson.
70. Innocent III in c. 32, Fourth Lateran 1215, c. 30, X, III, 5, says, to be sure, that it is because those serving cures are not given sufficient of the revenues to sustain themselves properly that the parish priests are almost all illiterate or nearly so. This seems at least a recognition that an illiterate man can be hired cheaper than a literate, but that is as far as the recognition goes. It does not recognize that a mediocre literate man can be hired cheaper than a first-rate literate man, or that a really good man can ask—and get—more than simply enough to sustain himself properly.

6: The Papacy

1. See Sayers, *Papal Judges Delegate in the Province of Canterbury, 1198–1254* (Oxford, 1971), 56–58, 68–69, for the limited opportunities an adverse party had to head off the papal process at the source.
2. Grimaldi, *Les Congrégations romains* (Siena, 1890), 452–53 and passim. Note that where the pope feels that a favor has been too freely granted, he blames the importunity of his petitioners, not the laxity of his advisors. E.g., c. 15, I, 3 in VI°.
3. Brentano, 148–64; Pantin 67; *Reg. T. Cantilupe*, pp. xxii–xxiv; Lunt, i, 516–21. Naz, "Rescrit," *D.D.C.*, vii, 607, 611–13, gives a succinct account of the steps from the handing in of a petition to the issuance of a rescript. It is interesting that very little of the elaborate structuring of the process seems to relate to the subject-matter of the petition dealt with.
4. See *Reg. T. Cantilupe*, 274, for the bishop's instructions as to whom to pay to expedite a certain matter. Brentano 150 does not hesitate to characterize these payments as bribes. Lunt, i, 179–86, suggests caution in such a characterization. The ethics of medieval administration evidently distinguished between hearing a matter out of its proper order through favor to a party and actually deciding it on the basis of favor. The incorruptible Thomas More made such a distinction. Campbell, *Lives of the Lord Chancellors*, ii (4th ed., 1856), 33-34.
5. See, generally, Gibbs and Lang, 53–93; and Smith, *Episcopal Appoint-*

ments, 11–49 and passim; Claeys-Bouuaert, "Évêques," *D.D.C.*, v, 569; Pantin 54–59.

6. C. 41–44, X, I, 6.

7. C. 42, X, I, 6. The formulation seems to be an ancient one; it is adumbrated in the provisions of the Rule of Saint Benedict for electing an abbot. C. 8, Lyons 1274, c. 9, I, 6 in VI°, cut off this ground of appeal if the winner had a two-thirds majority after two elections.

8. On Innocent's policies, see Smith, *Innocent III: Church Defender* (Baton Rouge, 1951), 63–64. *Selected Letters of Innocent III*, 16, 21, 115–16, 166–67, 210–11. On elections at Rome, see Wilkins, i, 515–29 (election of Langton to Canterbury, 1207); *Cal. Papal Reg.*, i, 583 (1298); cf. *Cal. Close Rolls, 1346–49*, 558 (1348), prohibiting such a procedure.

9. E.g., *Cal. Papal Reg.*, i, 574 (1298); id., iii, 279 (1348).

10. E.g., id., i, 582–84 (1298).

11. This was done in six of the ten rejections found by Miss Gibbs in the period 1215–72. Cf. the 1348 cases in *Cal. Papal Reg.*, iii, 290, involving an Irish bishopric, and *Cal. Pat. Rolls, 1348–50*, 142, involving an abbey.

12. Guillemain, *La Politique bénéficiale du Pape Benoît XII* (Paris, 1952), 21–23; Barraclough, 9. See c. 4, I, 3, in Extrav. Comm., for a list drawn up by John XXII (1316–34). *Licet Ecclesiarum* is c. 2, III, 4, in VI°. On Theodore of Tarsus, see Bede, H.E., iii, 29, iv, 1.

13. Cf. *Cal. Papal Reg.*, i, 580 (1299).

14. According to Pantin, the form of election was still gone through, even though it was invariably displaced with a provision. Cf. *Petition of Elect of St. Asaph, Rot. Parl.*, iii, 247b (1389). Election remained the common law of the church until the 1918 Code. Claeys-Bouuaert, "Évêques," *D.D.C.*, v, 569, 575. On Trillek, see Pantin 55. On Martin V's policy, see Jacob, "Introduction," *Reg. Chichele*, i, pp. lxxxviii–xciv; cf. *Rot. Parl.*, iv, 71b (1415).

15. Guillemain, *La Politique Bénéficiale du Pape Benoît XII*, 23–24 (my translation). It might be added that increasing careerism made for more cases in which sees were filled by translating bishops from less important sees: this only the pope could do.

16. Pantin 83. For complaints by the Commons, with less than enthusiastic endorsement by the king, see *Rot. Parl.*, ii, 337a–340a (1376); iii, 138a (1382).

17. Smith, *Episcopal Appointments*, 49.

18. The major confrontations were those brought on by Pecham's canons on jurisdiction, Winchelsea's attacks on nonresidence, and his attempt to enforce *Clericis laicos*. See respectively Maitland, *Canon Law in England*, 61–62 (1898), and Graham, "Introduction," *Reg. Winchelsea*, i, pp. x–xii. For a couple of less important cases, see *Reg. Antiq.* no. 242 (1241); *Cal. Pat. Rolls, 1247–58*, 65, 68; *Cal. Papal Reg.*, i, 265, 270 (1250–51). Cf. c. 5, V, 7 in VI°, on the exemption of kings and their families from local ecclesiastical jurisdiction. On negotiating over subsidies, see c. 46, Fourth Lateran 1215, Mansi, xxii, 1030; *Acta Langton* no. 85–86. As to provisions, see Pantin 84–93; Jacob, "Introduction," *Reg. Chichele*, i, pp. xxxix–xlvii, lxxxviii–xciv; Lunt, ii, 420–21.

19. For an example of nimble footwork, see *Rot. Parl.*, iii, 304a (1392–93).

20. France: *Cal. Papal Reg.*, i, 2 (1198); id., 98–100 (1224); id., 589 (1300), as well as the famous c. 13, X, II, 1; *Selected Letters of Innocent III*, 56–68. Scotland: *Cal. Papal Reg.*, i, 584–85 (1299). Domestic affairs: *Selected Letters of Innocent III*, 212–19 (1215); *Cal. Papal Reg.*, i, 224–26 (1246).

21. Suffragan v. metropolitan: Brentano, passim: *Cal. Papal Reg., i,* 576 (Winchester, 1298); *Reg. Grandisson,* i, pp. xxvii (Exeter, 1327); Bishop v. chapter: *Cal. Papal Reg.,* i, 1–6 (Canterbury, 1198); id., 2 (Coventry, 1198); id., 603 (Durham, 1303); id., x, 31–34 (Lincoln, 1448). Ordinary v. ordinary; *Reg. T. Cantilupe,* 197. Abbey v. cell: *Reg. Trillek,* 153–55; *Cal. Pat. Rolls, 1446-52,* 154, 279. On canonization, see c. 1-2, X, III, 45; Kemp, *Canonization and Authority in the Western Church* (London, 1948).

22. Both kinds of recitals are found among the indults issued to Peter des Roches on his consecration to Winchester in 1205. *Cal. Papal Reg.,* i, 22–23; *Selected Letters of Innocent III,* 79–82. The fact that different kinds of recitals are used on the same occasion suggests that they may be common forms, having little to do with the actual reasons for the grants.

23. E.g., *Cal. Papal Reg.,* i, 121–22 (1209) (mandatories); *Selected Letters of Innocent III,* 35–36 (1202) (enforcing c. 4, X, III, 5, by making bishop support man he has ordained without title).

24. For Innocent's views, see *Selected Letters of Innocent III,* 45. Gibbs and Lang, 174, remark that his whole program in the Fourth Lateran Council was dependent on the cooperation of the local ordinaries, which he was unable to find effective measures to elicit.

25. E.g., *Reg. Trillek,* 153–55; *Cal. Papal Ltrs.* v, 89 (1398).

26. Brentano 151 quotes the maxim *si prius appelles tunc bene tutus eris.* Maitland, *Canon Law in England* (1898), 113–15, suggests as the reasons for litigating in Rome in the first instance the likelihood that the case will be appealed there anyhow, the nationwide reach of papal process, and the opportunity for the plaintiff to choose his judges. As to the last point, see below under Institutional Resources.

27. Examples: grant by pope after denial by ordinary: *Cal. Papal Reg.* i, 575 (1298); confirmation by pope of favorable action by ordinary: id., v, 167 (1398); id., x, 390–91 (1448); grant by ordinary set aside: id., x, 400–401 (1448).

28. The following examples, all taken from *Cal. Papal Reg.,* v (1398), are typical enough: pp. 88–89, the absolution of Richard Tittesbury from his various irregularities, as to which, see chap. 3, note 52; p. 91, the protection of the right of the duchess of Norfolk to dispose of her goods by will; p. 93; a tithe case between a rector and a prior, where the rector recites that he fears the local power of the priory; p. 95, a case between a priory and a rector over burial rights—a specific burial was involved, but the case was no doubt intended to settle the right for good; p. 151, a confirmation sought by a prior who was elected by his brethren and confirmed by the bishop but was still not sure of his title; p. 157, a confirmation of the action of the local ordinary appropriating a church to a priory; p. 173, permission for the inhabitants of a village situated a mile from their parish church to have certain services in their village chapel.

29. *Cal. Papal Reg.,* v, 98–99 (1398). I am guessing that the person to be collated is an informer, but the guess seems a safe one. It is hard to see how else a case of so little intrinsic significance would come to the pope's attention. As to other informer cases, I have noted in 1398 clear examples at *Cal. Papal Reg.,* v, 106, 169, and 194, probable ones at pp. 103, 104, 106, 173. Interestingly enough, the cases at pp. 169 and 173 involve the same informer. For 1448 (*Cal. Papal Reg.,* x), I have noted two clear cases, pp. 290–93. The practice is evidently that complained of by the Commons in *Rot. Parl.,* iii, 614b (1407).

30. E.g., *Cal. Papal Reg.*, x, 290 (1448). To be sure, if the incumbent had already been absolved in a local proceeding, the informer could probably not deprive him under the papal mandate.

31. Barraclough 162–65 argues persuasively that it was not.

32. The other important ones were for nonage, failure to take orders, and illegitimacy. The first two were probably sought for family rather than bureaucratic reasons—one could hardly be a successful bureaucrat without growing up and getting enough education to have no trouble being ordained. I can find no evidence of what kind of people benefited from the dispensations for illegitimacy, but there is no reason to suppose that bureaucrats did so more than other clergy.

33. *Quum ex eo* is c. 34, I, 6 in VI° (Boniface VIII, 1299). The time is seven years, and the purpose study. In the decretal, *Quia per ambitiosam*, of Boniface VIII, c. 15, I, 3 in VI°, it was recited that there were many papal licenses for indefinite nonresidence outstanding. After this decretal, I found no general indefinite licenses but a number that were not limited in time, e.g. *Cal. Papal Reg.*, v, 555–56 (1402). See also id., iii, 261 (1347), and v, 97 (1398), both licenses to lay magnates to keep a specified number of clergy nonresident while in their service, and id., v, iii (1398), a license to the cleric himself for nonresidence, while in the service of a named magnate.

34. The 1347 case and one of the 1398 ones include permission to let benefices to farm. I counted six such permissions in 1448, plus faculties to prelates to grant such permission to eight clerics. On receiving revenues reserved for residents, see *Cal. Papal Reg. Pet.* 142 (1348). Note also the cases in which an archdeacon is allowed to visit by deputy and receive procurations in cash—tantamount to a license for nonresidence. E.g., *Cal. Papal Reg.*, v, 97 (1398). I found five of these in 1448.

35. This and the following paragraph (except for the statistics, which I compiled from *Cal. Papal Reg.*) are based on Barraclough, passim.

36. On licensing exceptions, see Lunt, ii, 418–28. The use of such licenses where benefices have already been filled on presentation of the proper patron is complained of by the Commons in 1407, *Rot. Parl.*, iii, 621a, and again in 1415, id., iv, 80a. For the plight of the universities, see Jacob, "Introduction," *Reg. Chichele*, i, pp. clii–clix; *Rot. Parl.*, iv, 816. For a royal servant who picked up a provision in Rome, see *Cal. Pat. Rolls*, x, 175 (1448).

37. I counted thirty one in 1448 as compared with twenty-three in 1398, sixteen in 1348, twenty-five in 1248.

38. See the complaints quoted in Pantin 70–71. See *Cal. Papal Reg.*, iii, 284 (1348), where the bishop of Exeter is given permission to provide canonries to five clerics and to fill three benefices in his own gift ahead of papal provisors. Cf. Barraclough 144–52. The case of the abbot's nephew is *Cal. Papal Reg.*, iii, 299 (1348).

39. Deely, "Papal Provisions and Royal Rights of Patronage in the Early Fourteenth Century," *E.H.R.*, xlii (1928), 497. The percentage estimate is my own.

40. Dispensation to have an archdeacon visit by deputy: *Cal. Papal Reg.*, x, 25 (1448). Pluralities: *Cal. Papal Reg.*, iii, 282, 304 (1348); x, 29 (1448). Provisions: Pantin 49, 64; *Cal. Papal Reg.*, v, 101 (1398); *Rot. Parl.*, i, 274b (1308–9).

41. Thompson, "Pluralism," 59–60.

42. Pantin 58-63, 95.
43. Pantin 66. For examples, see *Rot. Parl.*, ii, 219a (1337), and the nostalgic id., 336b, 337a-340a (1376).
44. Smith, *Medieval Marriage Laws* (Baton Rouge, 1940), 5-53, 187-97. Examples of matrimonial dispositions illustrating the various points made in text include *Reg. Trillek*, 56-58 (1345); e.g., *Cal. Papal Reg. Pet.* 133-34, 144 (1348); *Cal. Papal Reg.*, iii, 268 (1348); id., v, 169, 261 (1398); id., x, 16 (1448). The grounds for dispensation should be compared with the modern list of "canonical causes" in Bouscaren and Ellis, *Canon Law* (Milwaukee, 1947), 437 n. Three of the five dispensations I found in 1398 and six of the eight I found in 1448 were after the event. In one of the other two 1448 cases, the parties had committed fornication together. Note that laws with automatic effect tended to unsettle marriages just as they did other matters. Smith gives a number of cases where marriages were contacted without knowledge of impediments. Sometimes the parties even had a dispensation but were worried about its validity.
45. Three of the seven provisions and eight of the thirty-one licenses for pluralism that I found in 1448 mention noble birth or kinship to a specified person as a ground for the favor. On placing underage clerics, see *Cal. Papal Reg.*, x, 26 (1448). On entering religious houses, see id., v, 91, 117 (1398). Cf. id., iii, 303 (1348), giving the newly created archbishop of Canterbury permission to impose monks on all the monasteries of his diocese. For a vignette that seems to me especially illustrative of the relation between the papacy, the religious houses, and the English middle class, see the petition of the two nuns who left their house for another "on account of the penury of victuals" and now want the pope to restore them "each to her old room over the parlor." Id., v, 162 (1398).
46. *Cal. Papal Reg.*, iii, 300 (1348); id., v, 271, 285 (1400), are confirmations of chantries; *Cal. Papal Reg. Pet.*, 144, is a petition (granted) by a Scottish earl to set up a Dominican house in his castle.
47. For examples of these favors in varying combinations, see *Cal. Papal Reg.*, iii, 249, 272, 301 (1348); *Cal. Papal Reg. Pet.*, 133 (1348); *Cal. Papal Reg.*, v, 73 (1397); id., 149 (1398); id., x, 16, 24, 26 (1448).
48. E.g., *Cal. Papal Reg. Pet.*, 135 (1348).
49. I found twenty-seven cases of indulgences granted for repair of churches in 1398. See Lunt, ii, 484-506, on the growth of these favors and comparable favors issued to members of guilds.
50. I have not been able to find the exact scope of these privileges, but they were sufficient to make the king order that no papal chaplain be elected abbot of St. Mary's, York. *Ca. Pat. Rolls, 1396-99*, 282 (1398). During the Great Schism, when this status was rather freely granted, it furnished a pretext for religious to depart from their profession and obedience. Knowles, R.O., ii, 171-72. Knowles indicates that the status carried *de jure* exemption from religious authority, but popes occasionally treated disobedience as an abuse warranting cancellation. *Cal. Papal Reg.*, 153, 546 (1398).
51. Knowles, R.O., ii, 172-73; *Cal. Papal Reg.*, v, 164 (1398), 354-55 (1401), 552 (1403). While the permissions to take secular benefices were mostly for the benefit of the individual religious, some were evidently sought for the benefit of the house, which was thereby freed from the obligation of supporting the cleric in question. See *Cal. Papal Reg.*, v, 552 (1403); cf., id.,

x, 39 (1448). Steps were taken to bring permissions of this kind under secular penalties. *Rot. Parl.,* ii, 486b (1400-1401).
52. Respectively, id., iii, 283 (1348), and i, 242 (1248). On relaxations without permission, see Knowles, R.O., i, 281–83.
53. These favors seem to run in fashions. I found, for instance, two appropriations in 1298, three in 1348, none in 1448, but twelve in 1398, and in addition thirteen permissions to houses to serve cures with their own inmates—cures in some cases not previously appropriated at all. In 1448, I found six licenses to farm benefices, plus a permission to a local prelate to license eight more. In 1398, I found two such licenses and permission to an earl to have eight clerics in his service similarly licensed. On the farms, see Knowles, R.O., ii, 173.
54. E.g., *Cal. Papal Reg.,* v, 173 (1398) (New College, Oxford); id., 489 (1402) (a hospital at York); id., x, 185 (1448) (King's College, Cambridge).
55. Id., i, 569 (1297). Cf. *Reg. Grandisson,* pp. xxxiii (indult against metropolitan visitation); *Cal. Papal Reg.,* v, 283 (1348) (against excommunication by metropolitan); id., 302 (1348) (abbot of Chester not to be excommunicated, suspended, interdicted, or deprived by ordinary—comparable privilege for his successors evidently refused: *Cal. Papal Reg. Pet.,* 134–35); *Cal. Papal Reg.,* iii, 412 (1401) (archdeacon exempted from all superior jurisdiction).
56. *Cal. Papal Reg.,* x, 416 (1448); Knowles, R.O., ii, 173.
57. *Cal. Papal Reg.,* x, 19–20; *Cal. Pat. Rolls, 1446-52,* 154 (1448); *Cal. Pat. Rolls,* 279 (1448). The second case is more complex and is involved with the laws concerning alien priories. See *V.C.H.,* London, i, 581. For an earlier case, see *Cal. Papal Reg.,* v, 506 (1398).
58. Respectively, *Cal. Papal Reg.,* v, 293 (1398); id., iii, 409 (1401); id., 173 (1398); and id., 282 (1400).
59. Examples of indults referred to in text include id., i, 246, 247 (1248), 546 (1291), x, 37, 188, 190 (1448). Indults against provisions had evidently become so common by 1399 that a counteracting clause had become a common form in papal provisions. Id., v, 190 (1399).
60. Moorman 213-19 gives examples.
61. Lunt, i, 542–70; ii, 621–92. Legates did do some administrative work on ad hoc delegations, however. E.g., *Cal. Papal Reg.,* i, 561 (1295). What I say about papal legates does not, of course, apply to the archbishop of Canterbury in his capacity of *legatus natus.* He had this status not to do the pope's business but to have more power in doing his own. On collectors, see Lunt, i, 571–88; ii, 693–713; *Rot. Parl.,* i, 207a (1306). The remarks in Lunt, i, 571–73, on the efficiency of the papal collectors bear out my view that other aspects of the pope's business would have fared better if they had been done by a full-time staff.
62. This account is based primarily on Brentano, 148–64, and Maitland, *Roman Canon Law in England* (1898), 100-31. See also Sayers, *Papal Judges Delegate in the Province of Canterbury, 1198-1254* (Oxford, 1971). As to appeals, see Amanieu, "Appel," *D.D.C.,* i, 762; Amanieu, "Appellatione remota," *D.D.C.,* i, 827; McClunn, *Administrative Recourse* (Washington, 1946).
63. For an example, see *Reg. T. Cantilupe,* 197.
64. Sayers 14-19. For examples of mandates to persons characterized as "papal chaplain and auditor," see *Cal. Papal Reg.,* v, 337, 312 (1400). For

examples of mandates directed to persons characterized as "dwelling in the Roman Court," see id., 153 (1398), 312 (1400). This volume of the papal registers is full of such mandates, but I find none in the volumes covering the period before 1350.

65. For an example, from the late thirteenth century, see *Reg. Pontissara*, pp. lx–lxii, 586–73.

66. For examples, see *Cal. Papal Reg.*, iii, 259 (1348); v, 165 (1397). The latter is an especially involved case that went through five sets of judges-delegate, the winner prevailing not by a favorable decision but by surviving three rivals.

67. *Cal. Papal Reg.*, i, 121.

68. *Reg. Antiq.* no. 385.

69. *Cal. Papal Reg.*, v, 93 (1398); id., 271 (1400).

70. Brentano suggests that the inconclusive character of the papal proceedings in the York-Durham dispute provided the basis for royal intervention to effect a settlement. Note also that Canterbury jurisdiction was not always withdrawn when the papal delegates reached an end of their proceedings. See *Cal. Papal Reg.*, ii, 553 (1341). Nor was it always exercised in due subordination to ongoing papal proceedings. See id., x, 18 (1448).

71. *Oseney Cartulary*, vi (Oxf. Hist. Soc., ci, 1936), 338–44. In my sampling of the papal registers, incidentally, I found reference to seven suits before judges-delegate in 1198, none in 1248.

72. O'Neill, *Papal Rescripts of Favor* (Washington, 1930), 156–76; Naz, "Rescrit," *D.D.C.*, vii, 607, 628–30. The rescript entrusted to an executor was called "in forma commissoria," that with no executor, "in forma gratiosa."

73. *Cal. Papal Reg.*, i, 247 (1248), is an example of an indult to override non-residence licenses. Id., 244, 249 (1248); v, 190 (1398), contain *non obstante* clauses. *Cal. Papal Reg.*, i, 246 (1248), has examples of indults overriding such clauses.

74. C. 15, I, 3 in VI°, annulled licenses for nonresidences. I have not found any of the general annulments of appropriations, but I have found references to them in *Cal. Papal Reg.*, v, 16 (1397), 601 (1404); x, 21, 418 (1448). The annulment of the Hospitallers' exemptions is id., 190. We might add to this list the cancellation or restriction, on the relation of Richard II and others, of the privileges of Dominican papal chaplains. This is referred to id., v, 9 (1397), where one Walter Somminton is exempted from complying with it.

75. See *Cal. Papal Reg. Pet.* 138, *Cal. Papal Reg.*, iii, 291 (1348), for a man receiving a provision to make up for a previous one he lost to a holder of an earlier provision to the same benefice.

76. This was the claim of one of the parties in *Cal. Papal Reg.*, v, 194–95 (1398); cf. the case cited infra, note 78.

77. C. 3, 9, 23 X, I, 3; Naz, "Rescrit," *D.D.C.*, vii, 607, 627–28.

78. *Cal. Papal Reg.*, X, 400–401 (1448), and id., v, 188 (1398).

79. In c. 9, X, V, 20, the question of authenticity was raised in the course of a proceeding. In *Cal. Papal Reg.*, v, 540–42 (1403), it was raised in a collateral proceeding. For the wholesale examination of a cartulary, see *Cal. Papal Reg.*, i, 102 (1255). Cf. ibid., calling on ordinaries to examine all papal rescripts issued during past five years, as a forger has been caught at Rome. See also id., 384 (1262), ordering nuncio to make wholesale examination. The question of authenticity is raised by a local official in *Cal. Papal Reg.*, ii, 246 (1325). C. 2, X, V, 20, and c. 11, X, I, 3, decretals of Pope Lucius III (1181–85), commend this

course. These cases call for sending the documents to Rome. In *Cal. Papal Reg.*, v, 540–42 (1403), and id., 549–50 (1402), the "tenor" was examined there, presumably by means of copies. Examination was committed to judges-delegate in id., ii, 101 (1312); id., 246 (1325). On grounds for questioning, see c. 11, X, I, 3 (bad Latin); c. 6, X, V, 20 (style); *Cal. Papal Reg.*, v, 540–42 (1403) (style). As to presence in the registers, in the case in *Cal. Papal Reg.*, v, 540–42 (1403), the document is definitely in the registers; it is suggested that it was put in "perhaps in haste" (*per occupacionem*). See, however, id., ii, 564 (1337), in which the pope suggests to the king of France that it is always possible to tell true papal documents from false ones by checking in his registers. Cf., id., x, 45 (1448), where the pope appears to be committing to a judge-delegate the question of the existence *vel non* of a judgment of one of his predecessors rather than looking in the registers for it. Examples were sent for comparison in id., ii, 246 (1325); id., 255 (1326). A copy was examined in Rome in id., i, 349 (1257). See also the cases cited above where the pope says that he has had the tenor of the documents examined. Perhaps the determination whether to use this procedure or that of sending authentic documents to be compared depended on whether the ground for suspicion was given by the style of the document, or by the seals, or by the hand.

80. C. 9, X, V, 20 (Innocent III in a case involving an English benefice).

81. C. 8, X, V, 20 (Innocent III). The facts are not included in the traditional form of the Decretals but will be found in a modern edition that collates the documents with other sources.

82. *Selected Letters of Innocent III*, 33 n; Naz, "Rescrit," *D.D.C.*, vii, 607, 630. It appears that the executor might also refuse execution if he found the recipient to be so far unworthy as to cause scandal. As to when errors of fact can be raised, see *Cal. Papal Reg.*, 157–58 (1398), where a party excommunicated for disobeying a sentence raises this objection against the rescript on which the proceeding was passed; id., x, 20 (1448), where the bishop of Dunkeld, in full possession of his see, seeks a confirmation of his title because the letters on which he was provided to the see characterize him as a doctor of canon law rather than a licentiate; id., v, 334 (1400), contains an indult that St. Albans abbey and its cells shall not have to show documents in support of their appropriation of parish churches if they have been in peaceful possession for forty years or more. Except for the rule of continuous good faith, I can see no reason why there should not have been adequate prescriptive rights in these cases without the need for an indult. Naz, "Prescription," *D.D.C.*, vii, 178, 192–93. On the effect of a favorable determination, see Naz, "Chose jugée," *D.D.C.*, iii, 695. Where the rescript initiated a full-fledged litigation, there would presumably be no power to reopen a definitive sentence resulting from the litigation, unless, indeed, it could be argued that the invalidity of the originating rescript made the proceeding *coram non judice*. Be that as it may, where the executor was to act *ex parte*, whatever determination of fact he made to comply with the terms of his mandate would not be binding on an adverse party who was not before him at the time.

83. This contention was evidently made in all seriousness in the litigation between Henry Chichele and Nicholas Bubwith over the archdeaconery of Dorset, *Cal. Papal Reg.*, v, 205–6 (1399). Actually the facts seem not to bear out the contention, id., 82–83 (1397). But its sufficiency in law is indicated by the entry, id., 297–98 (1400).

84. The case of the religious superior is *Cal. Papal Reg.*, x, 158 (1448). For a double annulment, see the case of the appropriation of the rectory of Kemsing, Kent, by Bermondsey Priory. Id, v, 13, 506-7 (1397-1402). A priest named Adam Usk, alleging that divine worship had been greatly diminished since the appropriation, got a rescript annulling the appropriation and, evidently, providing him to the rectory. Subsequently, the priory, alleging that Adam's charges were false, procured a revocation of the annulment. Still more complicated is the case between the parishioners of Liskret and the prior and convent of Launceston over the suppression of a vicarage (1398-1402): *Cal. Papal Reg.*, v, 156, 357, 391, 591; *Rot. Parl.*, 505a. Note that Adam's rescript in the Kemsing case, like that granted to the religious superior in the 1448 case, did not call for an investigation of the facts, whereas the priory's did. Similarly, in a case referred to in *Cal. Papal Reg.*, v, 495-96 (1401), mandatories were directed to annul letters permitting baptisms and marriages in a certain chapel if they found that the parishioners had misstated the difficulty of getting to the mother church. Procedurally, the priory in the Kemsing case seems to have initiated the annulment of Adam's rescript by ignoring it and proceeding against Adam as an intruder. A similar course was followed in the Irish litigation in *Cal. Papal Reg.*, v, 179-80, 307-8 (1400).

85. On common forms, see Barraclough, c. 9; Naz, "Clausules apostoliques," *D.D.C.*, iii, 820. On the scope of clerical dispensations, see c. 1, 2, I, ii in VI°. See also the case of Robert de Dalton of the diocese of York, who went through many difficulties on account of insufficient dispensations before he got the broad one in *Cal. Papal Reg.*, v, 479 (1401). Not only did he try to change benefice did he try to change benefices under a dispensation good for only one, he also failed, when he sought a dispensation as the son of an unmarried man and an unmarried woman, to add that they were related in the double fourth degrees of affinity (as would be the case, for instance, if the mother had successively married two third cousins of the father) and had lived together in concubinage. See *Cal. Papal Reg.*,v, 542 (1403), where a dispensation, for assurance of validity, recites that the recipient is "the son of a priest and an unmarried woman related five-fold in the double second and third degrees of affinity." Other cases involving the rule against changing benefices under a common form dispensation include *Cal. Papal Reg.*, iii, 133 (1348), and id., v, 475, where a simple one-church dispensation is suitably expanded. As to matrimonial dispensations, see id., v, 578 (1403), permitting Henry Hoghton and Joan Radeclyf to marry "notwithstanding that they are distant from a common stock on one side in the second and on the other in the third degree of kindred, that Henry has committed incest more than once with Joan, and that he has committed fornication with a woman related to Joan in the third degree of kindred." In such a case as this, the question of scope merges with that of misstatement of facts. If all these matters had not been put in the petition, the ensuing dispensation would have been invalid on account of "subreption" (concealment of material facts). Of course, the materiality of these particular facts depends on the custom of the curia as to the scope of its dispensations. C. 1052 of the 1918 Code provides a much broader scope. Bouscaren and Ellis, *Canon Law* (Milwaukee, 1947), 450.

86. *Cal. Papal Reg.*, v, 92 (1398).

87. *Cal. Papal Reg.*, v, 157 (1398) (procedure for rehabilitating apostate religious).

88. Putting a man in ahead of a provisor: *Cal. Papal Reg.*, i, 580 (1299); Barraclough 146–47. Continuing a case after inhibition: *Cal. Papal Reg.*, x, 18 (1448); cf. id., ii, 553 (1341). Force: *Cal. Papal Reg.*, i, 243 (1248); cf. *Reg. Grandisson*, xxiv–xxv, and the Irish case, *Cal. Papal Reg.*, v, 254 (1398). See Barraclough 146–47.

89. E.g., *Cal. Papal Reg.*, x, 18 (1448).

90. The following account of these writs is taken from Fitzh., N.B., 124–26 *(vi laica amovenda)* and 144–52 *(excommunicato capiendo)*.

91. *Rot. Parl.*, i, 178b (1305); id., 207a (1306); id., 219a (1306); id., 374b (1320); id., ii, 7–11 (1326–27); id., 141b (1343); id., 153a–154a (1344); 25 Edw. 3 St. 5, c. 22 (1350); 25 Edw. 3 St. 6 (1350); 38 Edw. 3 St. 2 (1363); 13 Ric. 2 St. 1, c. 15 (1389); 13 Ric. 2 St. 2, c. 2–3 (1389), 16 Ric. 2, c. 5 (1392); 2 Hen. 4, c. 3–4 (1400); 9 Hen. 4, c. 8, 9, 10 (1407); Waugh, "The Great Statute of Praemunire," *E.H.R.*, xxxvii (1922), 173; Ellis, *Anti-Papal Legislation in Medieval England* (Washington, 1930), 80–125 passim; Pantin 82–96. See also the case, antedating all the Parliamentary material, that runs in *Cal. Close Rolls, 1296-1302,* 223, 292, 300, 301, 309 (1298–99).

92. *Reg. Trillek,* 326; *Cal. Pat. Rolls, 1348-50,* 66, 70, 152–54 (1348); *Rot. Parl.*, iii, 288b (1391); *Cal. Close Rolls, 1396-99,* 278, 359 (1398). See also the saga of Nicholas Hethe, as developed in *Reg. Trillek,* 326, 354, 356; *Cal. Pat. Rolls, 1348-50,* 310, 313; id., *1350-54,* 178, 189, 198, 206–7, 224, 277–78, 418; id., *1354-58,* 513, 635. All of these cases seem to have involved benefices except that from the Parliament Rolls, which involved a knight named William Brian who obtained papal process to find out and excommunicate the unknown persons who broke into his house. As the intervention of the spiritual jurisdiction was evidently necessary to make the wrongdoers come forward, it is difficult to see why the process was regarded as prejudicial to the king.

93. *Cal. Papal Reg.*, v, 98 (1398). Note that Nicholas Hethe also prevailed in the end, although he had to pay a fine of 200 marks. For a complaint of Commons about the resourcefulness of papal provisors, see *Rot. Parl.*, ii, 267b (1376–77). A provisor might, incidentally, try to have the best of both worlds by using royal writs to counter a rival's papal process and, at the same time, enforcing papal process of his own. See *Cal. Papal Reg.*, v, 194–95 (1398).

94. 2 Hen. 4, c. 3–4 (1400; 7 Hen. 4, c. 6 (1405). What was forbidden was papal exemption from regular or ordinary obedience or from payment of tithe.

95. For instance, a writ *de excommunicato capiendo* was regularly suspended if it appeared that the excommunicate had appealed to Rome. Fitzh. N.B., 148–49. Fitzherbert says that the pope's bulls should not be mentioned in the *supersedeas* awarded on this showing but should be referred to as "certain public instruments." But an earlier period was not so coy. See *Cal. Close Rolls, 1396-99,* 279, 288, 291, 323 (1398). See also the cases referred to in Waugh, supra, note 91. It should be noted also that Henry IV specifically refused to deal with papal appropriations and pluralities as he did with provisions. *Rot. Parl,* iii, 468a (1400-1401).

96. F.G.A., "Premunire Facias," no. 1 (1425). Waugh, supra, note 91, Pantin 86–87, and the Patent Roll entries cited supra, note 92, all indicate that the main concern of the royal authorities was with the jurisdiction of their courts.

97. In addition to the case of William Brian, supra, note 92, see *Ludgate's Case, Rot. Parl.,* i, 49b (1290)(bastardy case); id., iii, 405a (1389) (collection of money from clergy); *Cal. Pat. Rolls, 1292–1301,* 340 (1298) (dispensation to hold royal donative in plurality); *Petition of the Bishop of Byblos, Rot. Parl.,* i, 178b (1305) (order giving priory over to support of bishop ousted from see by Saracens); *Archbishop of Canterbury's Petition, Rot. Parl.,* iii, 529b (1403–4) (attempting to have pope establish new prebends in cathedral); *Cal. Pat. Rolls, 1446–52,* 279 (1449) (bulls exempting alien priory from jurisdiction of motherhouse—rights of motherhouse being in king's hands): id., 260 (process sued out by abbey against cell made independent by pope with king's permission); *Abbot of Waltham's Case,* F.G.A., "Premunire Facias," no. 8 (1373) (abbot-elect accepts provision in lieu of confirmation).

98. *Succession of William of Monte Canis, Rot. Parl.,* i, 16b, 38b, 84a (1290) (bastardy case; permission to use denied); *Petition of Bishop of Byblos,* supra, note 97; *Petition of Fitz-Thomas, Rot. Parl.,* iii, 327a (1393–94) (man sought confirmation in benefices held beyond scope of dispensation and was reprovided to them instead of confirmed in them); *Petition of Elect of St. Asaph,* id., 274b (1389) (permission sought to present election to pope for confirmation and accept provision as consolation if pope has provided see to another); id., 317a (1393–94) (acceptance by bishop-elect of provision issued by pope to same see instead of confirmation of election); id., 407b (1397% (same); *Cal. Pat. Rolls, 1446–52,* 154 (1448) (license to make priory into abbey); id., 251 (1449) (permission for religious to accept secular benefice).

99. The partial figures given in Lunt, ii, 717, show collections between £317/7/11¼ and £348/1/5½ with a total of £129/0/0 paid over to the papal collectors.

100. The "tenths" of which these subsidies often consisted evidently furnished the pretext for the royal exaction of a tenth of the value of every living over 50 pounds value, as established in 26 Hen. 8, c. 3 (1534) in connection with the overthrow of papal authority. In fact, of course, the papacy had seldom succeeded in collecting such tenths, while the king collected them regularly.

101. This revenue evidently furnished the pretext for the royal levy of the first fruits of every benefice in England, as established in 26 Hen. 8, c. 3 (1534), along with the tenths discussed supra, note 100. In fact, however, the pope did not collect on any but the benefices he provided to. Both revenues continued to swell the royal coffers till the time of Queen Anne, when they were turned over to commissioners for the augmentation of small livings under the name of Queen Anne's Bounty. Most of them were finally done away with by the First Fruits and Tenths Measure, 1926, 16–17 Geo. 5 no. 2.

102. The diversion of Holy Land collections was complained of *Rot. Parl.,* i, 207a (1306). It was said that the uses to which the papacy put the money were not profitable to the donors, indicating evidently that the good work involved in contributing the money was taken more seriously than the indulgence attached to doing so. On diversion of funds, see *Cal. Papal Reg.,* v, 214 (1398), where sums left for the relief of the poor are diverted by papal mandate to the repair of the Castle of St. Angelo.

103. *Cal. Papal Reg. Pet.*, 127 (1348). *Cal. Papal Reg.*, i, 574, 583–84 (1298); Thompson 24. *Reg. T. Cantilupe*, 186. Cf. *Cal. Papal Reg.*, x, 422 (1448), where a man who won a benefice case gave his rival a pension to cover expenses.

104. *Cal. Pat. Rolls, 1396–99*, 406 (1398).

105. *Cal. Papal Reg.*, i, 574 (1298); Compare *Cal. Pat. Rolls, 1348–50*, 143 (1348), with *Cal. Papal Reg.*, iii, 278 (1348); *Rot. Parl.*, ii, 317a (1392–93). See the description of the abortive concordat of 1398 in Pantin 92–93. Cf. *Cal. Papal Reg.*, v, 112 (1398), which gives the pope's nuncio a general power to rehabilitate and provide, in return for cash payments, those put into benefices in opposition to papal provisors.

106. *Cal. Papal Reg.*, i, 581–83 (1298).

107. See Huizinga, *The Waning of the Middle Ages* (Garden City, 1962), chap. 3 ("The Hierarchic Conception of Society").

108. So Bishop Jewel, of the first generation of Anglican apologists, argues that the claims of the papacy are like the claims of the Jews of Jeremiah's time to possess the Temple of the Lord or like the claim of the Pharisees to be the children of Abraham. *An Apology of the Church of England (Works*, iii, Cambridge, 1848), 77–79.

109. The language is Yeats's, but the vision of late medieval thought is Huizinga's.

Index

Record-keeping, 80–81, 193
Rectories
   maintenance of, 126
   women living in, 120
Rectors. *See* Parish priests
Reformation, ix, 199, 200
Regularis Concordia, 12
Religious houses. *See* Monasteries and
   religious houses
Rescripts, papal, 83, 86, 172, 181,
   187, 188–97
   authenticity of, 192–93
   cost of, 200
   enforcement of, 191, 195–97
   exemption from, 191
   false statements in procuring, 193–
      94
   priorities among, 192, 194
   revocation or annulment of, 192,
      194
   scope of, 194–95
Residence of beneficed clergy. *See*
   Nonresidence
Resignation bonds, 118–19
Rich, St. Edmund, archbishop of Canterbury (1234–40), constitutions attributed to (1236),
   248
Richard II, king (1377–99), 106
Richmond, archdeaconry of, 102
Rochester, diocese of, 11
Roman curia
   advantages of proceeding in, 179
   business with, as excuse for non-
      residence, 161
   death or resignation of incumbent
      at, 175
   dilatoriness of, 184
   expenses of business in, 113, 173,
      200,202
   organization and functioning of,
      113, 172–73, 187, 189, 195,
      202
   style of, 193
   use of common forms by, 86, 195
   See also Pope
Roman Empire, church organization
   in, 6–10
Roman law, 65–66, 68–70, 85, 99,
   133

Royal free chapels, 102, 158–59, 183

Salisbury, cathedral at, 23
Sanctions, in canon law, 17, 79, 87,
   89–98, 146–48, 161
Sanctuary, xi, 53–55, 127
Scotland, English claim to suzerainty
   over, 177
Secular offices. *See* Clergy, bureau-
   cratic involvement of
Seebohm, Frederic, 18
Sequestration, 95–96, 120, 126, 132
   147, 196
Services, church
   attendance at, 127
   maintenance of, 127, 168
   papal privileges concerning, 185
Servitium (payment by church to
   landholder), 28–29, 153
Sexual offenses
   abjuration of, 135
   by clergy. *See* Clergy, celibacy of
   correction of, 128, 140
Shaffer, Thomas L., xiv
Si quis suadente diabolo, 54–55, 121
Sick, visitation of, 127, 168
Simony, 45–49, 118, 124, 153
Slaves, ordination of, 43
Smith, W. E. L., 175, 177
Sonning, Berks., church at, 23, 25, 27
Spiritualities, 51
Split rectories, 156
Stenton, F. M., on old ministers, 218–
   19
Status among Anglo-Saxons, 4–5, 18–
   19
Stephen, king (1135–54), 106
Stigand, archbishop of Canterbury
   (1060–72), 14
Sturdy beggars, 131
Subreption, 268
Subsidies from clergy, 123–24, 177,
   198
Suffragan bishops, 104
Sunday, observance of, 126, 127
Supplicatio, 188, 190
Surgeons, 130
   clerics as. *See* Clergy